Economic Growth
of Nations

Economic Growth
of Nations

Total Output and
Production Structure

Simon Kuznets

The Belknap Press of
Harvard University Press
Cambridge, Massachusetts
1971

Preface

This volume is the product of a plan initially much wider in scope. The plan related to the ten papers with the general title, Quantitative Aspects of the Economic Growth of Nations, that were published between October 1956 and January 1967 as parts of, or supplements to, various issues of *Economic Development and Cultural Change*. The intention was to edit the papers, eliminate the obvious errors, bring up-to-date at least the earlier papers, and put all ten between two covers for greater usefulness as a reference source.

As work progressed, however, it proved difficult to limit revisions to editing and up-dating. It was impossible to neglect major additions to data, as well as the analytical connections which the complete set of ten papers suggested and which were not (and perhaps could not be) clearly seen when the first papers were written. As a result, over three years have been devoted to the revision of findings on the aspects of growth that were covered in the first three papers published — those relating to aggregate growth and to shares of production sectors in product and labor force (Papers I, II, and III, appearing in October 1956, July 1957, and July 1958). Since the time required for realization of the complete plan thus promised to extend far beyond our expectations, and its eventual completion was subject to doubt, it seemed best to publish the revisions that have been completed. They should be of interest and value in themselves, whether or not followed by similar revisions of the other papers.

While the volume includes much that is probably familiar by now, which cannot be avoided if an adequately complete review is to be presented, I trust that it contains enough that is new to warrant its addition to the literature in the field. Some of the general discussion in the last chapter was presented in two Marshall lectures delivered at the University of Cambridge in May 1969.

Much of the discussion in the original papers, and in the present volume, is based on estimates and analysis in studies initiated, or assisted, by the Committee on Economic Growth of the Social Science Research Council.

I am greatly indebted to Lillian E. Weksler for her skillful assistance in preparing the tables, checking the results of analysis, and editing the manuscript. I am also grateful to Professor Gustav Ranis of Yale University for helpful comments on Chapters V and VI. And I retain warm memories of the late Thomas J. Wilson, Director of the Harvard University Press at the time, who urged upon me the decision and effort that resulted in this volume.

SIMON KUZNETS

Contents

Tables

Economic Growth
of Nations

I
Level and Variability of Rates of Growth

This book summarizes results of a study of quantitative characteristics of the economic growth of nations in modern times, largely
by means of long-term estimates of national product and its components. Such comprehensive estimates, in which significantly different components are distinguished and measured, are indispensable for observation and analysis of the essentially quantitative
process of economic growth — if only to avoid the common pitfalls
of many historical and theoretical studies, in which uncertainly
weighted details are woven into a merely plausible narrative or
broad categories are combined into untestable general statements.
Moreover, a variety of countries and periods should be covered
in the observation of economic growth if we wish to find some
general characteristics and test the limits within which they hold.
The stock of uncoordinated and partial data makes it difficult to
assemble a comprehensive and articulated set of measures even for
a single country; and these difficulties become almost insurmount-
able in any attempt at comparative study. The estimates of national
product and its components, which in fact are summaries of a mass
of primary but partial data fitted into a common framework, provide at present the only way out of the dilemma caused by the need
for comprehensive measures for a number of countries, on the one
hand, and the near impossibility of securing, on a systematic basis,
fully particularized data, on the other.

Only a few long-term series of national product and its components are available, and these are subject to uncertain margins of

1

error. The scarcity, particularly for aspects of the changing economic structure that may be crucial for the understanding of the economic growth process, may introduce a bias in presentation and analysis. The latter, while primarily reflecting the available data, may indirectly reflect established, possibly obsolete, views on what had been in the past deemed important aspects of economic growth, views that generated demand for data and accumulation of the relevant statistics. This is a danger that always confronts a social analyst committed to the use of testable evidence and hence dependent upon data accumulated by society and reflecting past views as to what is important. But the danger must be faced, and the available data used with full awareness of their limitations and the hope that some aspects will be found to link them to a relevant analytical framework.

In regard to the errors in the long-term estimates of national product, one can only say that these estimates are for most countries, particularly the developed, the result of laborious and sustained compilation and estimation, geared to a common set of clearly defined economic concepts, and summarizing a vast amount of basic statistical data. Given the difficulties in attaining both accuracy and comprehensiveness, and the amount of judgment involved, errors of estimation are inevitable — yet their magnitude cannot be measured simply. I have tried to use all the available estimates, indicating divergence between variants when necessary — for even rough orders of magnitude or of limits within which the basic estimate may lie are preferable to ignorance or partial and hence potentially misleading indexes. Errors should be judged in relation to the uses to which the estimates are put, and for some uses, the permissible margins of error may be wide. To illustrate: the long-term estimates for Egypt and Ghana rest upon much more slender foundations than those, say, for the United States and Sweden. But the series for Egypt indicates decline or stagnation in per capita product since the late nineteenth century, and the one for Ghana reveals a substantial rise; these findings are significant and can be treated at least as provisional indications of the diversity of growth experience among the underdeveloped countries.

In short, with all the measurement difficulties, the long-term records of national product and its components are indispensable in the search for the general and variant characteristics of the modern economic growth of nations. Moreover, the available estimates can be subjected to far more revealing comparative analysis than has been attempted thus far. Provided that the assumptions and the difficulties are recognized, much can be learned.

The problems of an acceptable definition of national product, discussed at length by generations of scholars in the field, can be grouped under three heads: (a) delimitation of scope, involving the distinction between economic activity and social life; (b) basis of valuation, involving the common denominator to which economic activities are to be reduced; and (c) determination of netness and grossness, involving the distinction between costs and net returns of economic activity. Adequate discussion of these three complexes is impossible here. I can only indicate the major effects of their treatment on long-term estimates of national product. This should help to avoid two extreme impressions: that the conceptual difficulties are so great that useful estimates are unattainable; and that the conceptual compromises are so negligible that the estimates represent an unequivocal record.

(a) In general, only activities whose results are channeled through the marketplace or through some other social institution extraneous to the family (government, for example) are easily recognized as economic and are likely to be fully reflected in measurement. Economic activities within the household tend to be mixed with others, and one cannot tell whether housework is a truly economic activity or part of life in general. Even when such activities are recognized as economic and are measured in terms of persons engaged, hours spent, or products turned out, their evaluation is far from easy. Economic growth is often accompanied by a shift in economic activities from the household into the marketplace; or by a more rapid rise in the volume of market- or society-bound activities than in the volume of those within the household. It follows that long-term product estimates tend to have an upward bias (that is, they exaggerate the rate of growth): the omission of activities producing goods (whether consumer or capital goods) for internal consumption is likely to be relatively more important for the early part of any long period than for the later. This is particularly true if, for the country and period under observation, economic growth has been substantial: other conditions being equal, the greater the growth, the greater the shift from the household into markets (private or public), and the greater the possible upward bias arising from differential underestimation of nonmarket production.

While we cannot measure this bias for the developed countries whose growth records are studied below, some idea of the order of magnitude can be gleaned from data for the United States. Robert E. Gallman's estimates for 1839 (or 1834–1843) and for 1889 (or 1884–1893) indicate that, in the earlier year, the value of improvements to farm land (made with farm construction materials, variant I) and the value added by home manufacturing (to materials that would have been processed in factories had the structure of the economy been the same as in 1889) amounted to 17.5 percent (in current prices) of gross national product excluding these two items; in the later year the proportion was only 1.5 percent.[1] If it is assumed that the proportions were the same in constant prices, the rate of growth over the half century in gross national product, excluding these items, was 51.0 percent per decade; including them, it was 46.7 percent, almost a tenth lower. However, this not insubstantial bias is for a period when urbanization and the shift from the household to the market were quite rapid.

(b) The activities subsumed under national product, whether in terms of services of factors or in terms of the products which they yield, are weighted by prices, the only socially determined system of weights. However, even this system of weights is not a true reflection of socially set priorities, since it may be affected by government intervention and by monopoly elements in the distribution of income and wealth and in the supply of goods. Where such intervention and distortion are extensive, as in the Communist countries, the use of internal prices as weights may bar effective comparability with estimates for other countries not subject to such distortion. In this and similar cases the price weights should be checked and adjusted; but since this cannot be done easily, we are often forced to omit the deviant countries and narrow the universe of comparison. Even for this narrower range of comparisons the price weights, although meaningful, may still be defective; but there is no better alternative. The use of unweighted partial indexes may seem to avoid the problem, but the meaningfulness of any partial index depends upon its implicit and not easily defensible link to the whole in whose magnitude and growth we are interested. Price weights provide the link.

With respect to the use of price weights in long-term records of

1. See his "Gross National Product in the United States, 1834–1909," in Dorothy S. Brady, ed., *Output, Employment, and Productivity in the United States After 1800*, vol. 30 of *Studies in Income and Wealth* (New York: Columbia University Press for the National Bureau of Economic Research, 1966), tables A-4, A-5, A-1, pp. 35, 26.

national product, two specific points should be noted. First, systems of price weights selected from different parts of a long period may yield different rates of growth in national product in constant prices. The use of price relations for the early part of a period may yield a higher rate of growth, since goods that are highly priced in the early years are likely to grow more than other products, in response to these higher price levels, and their relative price position may be lower at the end of the period. Conversely, use of a more recent system of price relations is likely to yield a lower rate of growth in national product. Such difficulties cannot be resolved by mixing the price weights, which only obscures the meaning of the resulting measures; or by using chain indexes, in which the shifts in weights become fractionalized in short links — only to be reassembled when the entire period is brought into focus.

The term "bias" is misleading in connection with the use of "early" and "late" price weights: these are not biases but reflections of different vantage points from which economic growth is seen. In the former case it is viewed with the eyes of the contemporaries of the early period, say the 1860's; in the latter case with the eyes of contemporaries of the recent period, say the 1960's. One may argue that in general economic growth should always be examined from the vantage point of the present, if only because this is a more comprehensive view than that from the past looking forward. Whatever the argument, the usual practice is to employ recent-year weights, which means that the indexes must be revised continually and history partially rewritten.

The other peculiarity of price series is a distinct defect: they lack sensitivity to changes in quality. Such changes are not reflected in prices unless they are expressed through some overt product-differentiation, and even then not too well. Two consequences follow. First, for the components of total product that are based on physical output indexes weighted by prices, the failure of prices to reflect quality changes will result in an underestimate of the difference between growth rates yielded by initial and those yielded by terminal price weights; and indeed the growth rates presumed to reflect initial price weights will be quite short of the true. Second, and more important, for the components of total product based on current values "deflated" by price indexes (for example, most service components and many highly fabricated commodity components), the failure of the price indexes (whether based on initial or terminal year quantities) to reflect changes in quality will result in an underestimate of the growth rate of product, since it can be assumed that over the long run quality improvements far outweigh quality deterioration.

No thorough testing of the price weight effects and of the sensitivity to quality of price series is feasible here. But we can, again with the data for the United States, compare the rate of growth of national product, a price-weighted total, with those shown by major physical volume indexes. National product of the United States, like most of the long-term series, is weighted largely by terminal prices, although there are some changes in the price base over long subperiods. The physical volume indexes cited are independent of prices and are limited to single commodities or factor components. Since the illustration is for one country and one period it can be only suggestive, but similar detailed comparisons are feasible for several developed countries.

The gross national product of the United States rose by a factor of about 17.8 between 1869–1878 and 1960–1964. For a similar period (1870 to 1962) the multiplication factor was 15.2 for public school attendance (average daily attendance multiplied by number of days in the school year); 120.6 for the number of high school graduates; and 54.9 for the number of graduates of institutions of higher learning. This rise in the volume of formal education was accompanied by a growth factor of 38.8 in the horsepower of all prime movers (excluding the automotive). Thus the education of the labor force and the sheer power at its command were growing more rapidly than national product.[2] To be sure, the growth rates of such agricultural products as wheat (factor of 4.3), cotton (factor of 3.4), and milk equivalents of dairy products (factor of 6.2) were far below that of gross national product; on the other hand, the growth rates of refined sugar (factor of 14.9), cigars and cigarettes (weighted 10 and 1 respectively; factor of 50.9), and steel ingots and castings (factor of 1,277.0) were close to or well above that of national product. The point, which could be elaborated, is that the growth rate of national product, although dependent upon price

2. All the rates except that for national product were calculated from the United States Bureau of the Census, *Historical Statistics of the United States, Colonial Times to 1957* (Washington, D.C., 1961), and *Historical Statistics of the United States, Colonial Times to 1957, Continuation to 1962 and Revisions* (Washington, D.C., 1965), series H 229, H 230, H 232, H 237, K 233, K 270, K 302, P 188, P 195–197, P 203, S 3. The rate for GNP is from sources used for Table 1.

weights, falls within a range set by the growth rates of major physical quantities of output (or of productive factors). It is therefore most useful, and justified, to view the growth rate of national product as a central tendency in the distribution of growth rates of physical volumes, none of which is dependent upon price weights. Although these weights may affect the precise location of the central tendency, it must fall within relatively narrow limits imposed partly by the range of the physical volume rates and partly by the weights of the various products when measured in physical inputs of a single major factor (such as labor).[3]

(c) The distinction between costs and net returns of economic activity, or between intermediate (used in production) and final (for ultimate users) goods, turns essentially on what we recognize as the basic purposes of economic activity; and these may differ from one social order to another. But if we agree that in the economic societies of the last two centuries the basic purpose is satisfaction of wants of ultimate consumers, present and future, we can draw the main line of distinction and narrow the problem to institutional changes that shift that line perceptibly. Viewed in this fashion, the long-term records of national product suffer from a bias that reflects the increasing complexity of society in the process of economic growth and the increasing use of resources that are on the borderline between business costs and ultimate consumption. In the private sector there are the increasing outlays on professional training; on union, association, banking, and other fees; and so on — the whole array of expenses undertaken in good part for the sake of effective performance as an income earner in a complex urban civilization. In the public sector much of the increased governmental expenditure is not on services to ultimate consumers but on intermediate goods, whether services to business or for the maintenance of the fabric of society at large. Yet the customary estimates of national income include these outlays as final products, suspect

---

3. From the sources cited in note 2 indexes (price- or value-weighted) for farm output (series K 190) and manufacturing output (series P 11–13) can be derived; these show growth factors for 1870–1962 of 5.5 and 42.9 respectively. Weighting these by the shares in gainful workers in 1870 (series D 57), about 3 and 1 respectively, we derive a growth factor of 14.9, not much lower than that for GNP; and if the weights were adjusted to allow for the higher educational level of the labor force in manufacturing, the growth factor would be even closer to that of GNP. To be sure, the farm and manufacturing output indexes are internally price-weighted; but even employment weights would yield growth rates for total product not much different from those based on price weights.

though they are of being at least in part costs of production. The resulting upward bias in the long-term series of national product is relative to a set of measures geared to stricter concepts of ultimate consumption and capital formation.

In addition to these economic costs there may be noneconomic costs not subject to the usual calculus — as in cases where, in order to augment the economic product, political and intellectual freedom is curbed. National product measurement cannot take account of such noneconomic costs. Meaningful comparisons must therefore assume either that economic product is of interest regardless of its noneconomic costs, or that the latter are not radically different among the countries being compared and the gross product totals can be taken as representative of the net. The assumption bars inclusion, in the comparative study, of countries with different political and social structures, however difficult it is to decide when the differences are sufficiently large to become decisive.

The complex problems in the definition and measurement of national product arise from the use by observers of one yardstick over long stretches of space and time, whereas different standards are in fact used in the real world. In the real world, institutional changes shift the line of distinction between what is currently recognized as economic activity and as human activity at large; the relative scales of valuation in different markets differ and change; increasing complexity of life produces confusion between economic costs and net returns. The raw facts would, therefore, be no help. In essence, the very concept of "economic," let alone of economic growth, is an abstraction; and it is a distortion of the observable flow of life, since it exaggerates elements which are obscured and beset by numerous changes and deviations.

Yet, to abandon the attempt to study economic growth, to refuse to introduce some comparability and continuity into changing historical reality, would be even a greater distortion. It would imply that no similarity of purpose and organization exists between the societies of today and yesterday, between the United States in 1960 and in 1850, or for that matter between the United States and India in 1960. Such an implication is belied by numerous elements of historical continuity within the development of any one society and by numerous links that bind various societies in the world to a common heritage. Even in individuals, whose life spans are so much shorter than those of societies, memory, motivation, and decisions cover long periods and involve comparison of the present with the past — denying that these are two different and separate worlds without continuity. This chain over time is all the more apparent in the ties that bind successive generations. One is compelled to distill a common set of purposes, a common set of criteria that will provide the basis for comparability over time and space — a basis that should be acceptable, in one of several variants, so long as there is no major break in historical continuity or in the concert of societies with a common heritage.

Although the relevance of and the need for these common bases that transcend institutional shifts or differences over time and space is generally accepted, there may be disagreement as to precisely where to draw the lines in specific measurement for given countries and periods, and it may be desirable to present variant expressions or formulations of one set of common purposes and criteria, which would be most illuminating in their quantitative differences. It is possible and would be useful, in estimating national product for a country over a long period, to attempt to approximate at least the order of magnitude of biases. An adequate attempt in this direction would, however, involve detailed monographic studies, since it is only through careful scrutiny of the changing institutional structure of a country that useful estimates of such biases can be secured. Such attempts would be welcome, and it is to be hoped that they will be made in years to come. Meanwhile we must operate with the available long-term records, crude and subject to biases though they are, and, treating them as approximations, study them for the findings they may yield.

A rough approximation of the order of magnitude of biases connected with the possible inclusion of intermediate products and misclassification of capital investment as consumption, again on the basis of data largely for the United States, is attempted in the next chapter. It follows the review of the findings on the growth rates of aggregate product and productivity (output per unit of input), both measured in what might be called conventional national economic accounting.

But the conclusion of this attempt, and those suggested by the illustrations above, can be foreseen. The rates of modern economic growth revealed in the available series are high and the differences among them overshadow these conceptual biases, at least when the latter are approximated roughly. Furthermore, the biases partially offset each other: some tend to raise rates of growth, others to lower them. In short, the similarities and differences reflected in the conventional measures of national product are real and generally accepted by students of economic events and of the differences in economic fortune among nations. The differences in ability to satisfy wants expressed through disparities in rates of economic growth or in per capita income are not statistical illusions. They find their embodiment in the flow of goods to consumers, in the stock of real capital at the people's command, and in the protection of the members of society from material insecurity. Although our measures are subject to conceptual biases, they depend on basic criteria that are indispensable if quantifiable results are to be secured; and the consequent conceptual biases are qualifications, not negation, of the significance of the measures.

Average Rates of Growth: Summary of Evidence

Table 1 presents the average rates of growth of total product, population, and per capita product, for all non-Communist developed countries for which we have long-term records — no shorter than five decades. In identifying developed countries, the main criterion is a per capita product in recent years high enough to indicate a relatively successful attempt to exploit the economic potential of modern material and social technology. And, indeed, no country in Table 1 had a per capita GNP of less than $800 in 1965 (see Table 2). But per capita product is only one criterion. Several countries (many of them small), with a large natural resource (large relative to the size of the country and its population) enjoy a financial return that produces a high per capita product despite a backward economic and social structure (for example, Brunei, Kuwait, the Netherlands Antilles, and even Venezuela). On the other hand, a country like Japan, with a per capita product that is relatively low by standards of developed countries, belongs to the group because of its advanced production structure and despite its poor endowment with natural resources. The definition is based on the attainments of the economic and social system, not on natural endowments.

Because the social structure and the institutional means by which economic growth is secured in Communist countries are so different from those of the non-Communist countries, the record for the

Table 1. Rates of growth, total product, population, and product per capita, developed countries, long periods.

	Duration of period (years) (1)	Rates of growth per decade (%)			Coefficients of multiplication in a century		
		Total product (2)	Population (3)	Product per capita (4)	Total product (5)	Population (6)	Product per capita (7)

Great Britain–United Kingdom

England and Wales, total output index, 1800 prices

1. 1695/1715 to 1765/85	70	5.0	3.0	1.9	1.6	1.3	1.2
2. 1765/85 to 1785/1805	20	16.1	9.3	6.2	4.4	2.4	1.8

Great Britain, gross national income, 1865 and 1885 prices

3. 1801/11 to 1851/61/71	55	28.4	13.9	12.7	12.2	3.7	3.3

Great Britain, national income, 1913–14 prices

4. 1855–64 to 1920–24	62.5	23.0	10.7	11.1	7.9	2.8	2.9

United Kingdom, national income, 1913 prices and GNP, 1958 prices

5. 1920–24 to 1963–67	43	22.5	4.8	16.9	7.6	1.6	4.8

Summary

6. 1855–64 to 1963–67 (lines 4–5)	105.5	22.8	8.2	13.4	7.8	2.2	3.5
7. 1765/85 to 1963–67 (lines 2–5)	180.5	23.7	10.1	12.4	8.4	2.6	3.2

France

Net national product, 1901–10 prices

8. 1831–40 to 1861–70	30	26.3	3.9	21.6	10.3	1.5	7.1
9. 1861–70 to 1891–1900	30	15.7	1.9	13.5	4.3	1.2	3.6

GDP index, 1929 = 100, 1959 prices

10. 1896 to 1963–66	68.5	22.7	3.5	18.6	7.7	1.4	5.5

Table 1 — continued

	(1)	(2)	(3)	(4)	(5)	(6)	(7)
Summary							
11. 1861–70 to 1963–66 (lines 9–10)	98.5	20.5	3.0	17.0	6.5	1.3	4.8
12. 1831–40 to 1963–66 (lines 8–10)	128.5	21.8	3.2	18.1	7.2	1.4	5.3
Belgium							
Gross commodity product index, 1953 = 100, and GNP, 1963 prices							
13. 1900–04 to 1963–67	63	20.3	5.3	14.3	6.3	1.7	3.8
Netherlands							
National income index, 1900 = 100							
14. 1860/70 to 1900/10	40	22.2	12.3	8.8	7.4	3.2	2.3
National income, 1949 prices, and GNP, 1963 prices							
15. 1900–09 to 1963–67	60.5	31.5	14.2	15.1	15.5	3.8	4.1
Summary							
16. 1860/70 to 1963–67 (lines 14–15)	100.5	27.7	13.4	12.6	11.5	3.5	3.3
Germany							
NNP, 1913 prices, prewar boundaries							
17. 1850–59 to 1910–13	57	29.2	11.1	16.3	12.9	2.9	4.5
NNP, 1913 prices, interwar boundaries							
18. 1910–13 to 1934–38	24.5	18.0	5.9	11.5	a	a	a
NNP, 1913 prices, and GNP, 1954 prices, Federal Republic							
19. 1936 to 1963–67	29	47.3	14.5	28.7	a	a	a
Summary							
20. 1910–13 to 1963–67 (lines 18–19)	53.5	33.1	10.4	20.5	17.4	2.7	6.5
21. 1850–59 to 1963–67 (lines 17–19)	110.5	31.0	10.8	18.3	14.9	2.8	5.4

Table 1 — continued

	(1)	(2)	(3)	(4)	(5)	(6)	(7)
Switzerland							
NNP, 1938 prices, and GNP, 1958 prices							
22. 1910 to							
1963–67	55	26.3	8.8	16.1	10.4	2.3	4.5
Denmark							
GDP, 1929 and 1955 prices							
23. 1865–69 to							
1963–67	98	32.5	10.2	20.2	16.6	2.6	6.3
Norway							
GDP, 1910, 1938, 1955, and 1958 prices							
24. 1865–69 to							
1963–67	98	31.4	8.3	21.3	15.3	2.2	6.9
Sweden							
GDP, 1913 and 1959 prices							
25. 1861–69 to							
1963–67	100	37.4	6.6	28.9	23.9	1.9	12.6
Italy							
GNP, 1938 and 1963 prices							
26. 1861–69 to							
1895–99	32	8.1	6.8	1.2	2.2	1.9	1.1
27. 1895–99 to							
1963–67	68	31.4	6.9	22.9	15.3	2.0	7.8
Japan							
GDP, 1934–36 prices, and GNP, 1960 prices							
28. 1874–79 to							
1963–67	88.5	48.3	12.1	32.3	51.4	3.1	16.4
United States							
GDP, 1840 prices							
29. 1800 to 1840	40	52.3	34.1	13.5	67.0	18.8	3.6
GNP, 1860 prices							
30. 1834–43 to							
1859	20.5	60.2	35.4	18.3	111.5	20.8	5.4
31. 1859 to							
1879–88	24.5	47.4	25.9	17.0	48.3	10.0	4.8

Table 1 — continued

	(1)	(2)	(3)	(4)	(5)	(6)	(7)
GNP, 1929 prices							
32. 1880–89 to							
1910–14	27.5	40.1	21.2	15.6	29.2	6.8	4.3
GNP, 1954, 1958, and 1963 prices							
33. 1910–14 to							
1963–67	53	35.1	14.2	18.4	20.3	3.8	5.4
Summary							
34. 1859 to							
1963–67							
(lines 31–33)	105	39.2	18.7	17.3	27.3	5.5	4.9
35. 1834–43 to							
1963–67							
(lines 30–33)	125.5	42.4	21.2	17.5	34.4	6.9	5.0
Canada							
GNP, 1935–39 prices							
36. 1870–74 to							
1920–24	50	38.7	18.7	16.9	26.4	5.5	4.8
GNP, 1949 and 1957 prices							
37. 1920–24 to							
1963–67	43	44.4	19.4	20.9	39.4	5.9	6.7
Summary							
38. 1870–74 to							
1963–67							
(lines 36–37)	93	41.3	19.0	18.7	31.8	5.7	5.6
Australia							
GDP, 1911 prices							
39. 1861–69 to							
1900–04 (F)	37.5	39.8	32.5	5.5	28.5	16.6	1.7
GDP, 1910/11 prices, GNP, 1938/39 prices, and GDP, 1959 prices							
40. 1900–04 (F) to							
1963–67 (F)	63	34.4	18.8	13.1	19.2	5.6	3.4
Summary							
41. 1861–69 to							
1963–67 (F)							
(lines 39–40)	100.5	36.4	23.7	10.2	22.3	8.4	2.7

(F): fiscal years beginning July 1.
ᵃ Period too short to be used.
The product concepts, when two or more are indicated, are given chronologically in the stubs.

When years in stubs are connected by a slash (/), data are for the single years indicated; when connected by a dash (–), they are for all years in the interval.

All rates are geometric per decade for the periods indicated in the stubs, the duration of the period being calculated from the midpoints of the terminal dates. When the terminal dates cover several single years or a decade or thereabout, the basic value of product is the geometric mean of the single values or of the arithmetic means for quinquennia. The basic population estimate is generally for the midpoint of the terminal periods. Unless otherwise indicated, rates for per capita product were derived from those for total product and population.

The rates for the most recent period indicated in the stubs for each country are based on the historical series described later and the official United Nations data, generally for 1950–54 to 1963–67; but when the historical series or the United Nations data do not cover the entire 1950–54 quinquennium, the dates for the overlapping period are given in the country notes. The United Nations figures on product for 1950–54 are unpublished data and those for 1963–67 are from the United Nations, *Yearbook of National Accounts Statistics, 1968*, vol. I. *Individual Country Data* (New York, 1969); those for population are from the United Nations, *Demographic Yearbook, 1965* (New York, 1966), and *1967* (New York, 1968), table 4.

United Kingdom

Lines 1–2: Total and per capita product are derived from Phyllis Deane and W. A. Cole, *British Economic Growth, 1688–1959*, 2nd. ed. (Cambridge: Cambridge University Press, 1967), table 20, p. 80.

Line 3: Total product is from *ibid.*, table 72, p. 282. Population is from *ibid.*, table 3, p. 8.

Line 4: Per capita national income is given for the United Kingdom, including Ireland, in *ibid.*, table 90, pp. 329–331, and adjusted for 1855–64 to exclude Ireland on the assumption that per capita income in Ireland was half that in Great Britain. For 1920–24 I took the arithmetic mean of the per capitas as given in table 90 for 1921–24 and adjusted for 1920 on the assumption that per capita income was the same in Great Britain and the United Kingdom (including Northern Ireland). Population is derived from B. R. Mitchell, *Abstract of British Historical Statistics* (Cambridge: Cambridge University Press, 1962), pp. 8-10, with a minor adjustment for military personnel in 1920.

Line 5: For 1920–24 to 1950–54 total income and population are derived from Deane and Cole, table 90, with one adjustment — the use of the per capita income for 1920–24 as calculated for line 4.

France

Lines 8–9: Per capita income is from François Perroux, "Prise de vues sur la croissance de l'économie française, 1780–1950," in Simon Kuznets, ed., *Income and Wealth, Series V* (London: Bowes and Bowes, 1955), table V, p. 69. Population is by logarithmic interpolation of the series for a constant territory, given in Robert R. Kuczynski, *Measurement of Population Growth* (London: Sidgwick and Jackson, 1935), table I, pp. 230–231.

Line 10: Estimates for 1896 to 1950–54 are based on annual rates of change in total and per capita product for 1896 to 1929, 1929 to 1963, and 1949 to 1963, given in E. Malinvaud and others, "Croissance Française," a mimeographed preliminary report for the Social Science Research Council study of Postwar Economic Growth in Historical Perspective (Paris, July 1968), table 2, p. 12; and on the annual production index in *ibid.*, table 3, p. 15, which was used for interpolation between 1949 and 1963 to derive total product for 1950–54. Per capita product in 1950–54 was then calculated on the basis of population for 1949, 1952, and 1963, given in the *Demographic Yearbook, 1965* and *1967*, table 4. The terminal period is 1950–54 to 1963–66 because the United Nations series on GDP ends in 1966.

Development," in Lawrence Klein and Kazushi Ohkawa, eds., *Economic Growth: The Japanese Experience since the Meiji Era* (Homewood, Ill.: Richard Irwin, 1968), table 3A-3, pp. 104–105. I extrapolated the Hitotsubashi estimates of product in 1879–83 for the A and M (manufacturing) sectors and assumed that the ratio of output in the S sector to the sum of those in the A and M sectors was the same in 1874–78 as in 1879–83. I then added the estimated product for 1874–78 to the Hitotsubashi estimate for 1879 to derive the average for 1874–79. Population for the midpoint of 1874–79 was extrapolated from the 1882 Hitotsubashi series by the series given in Bank of Japan, *Hundred-Year Statistics of the Japanese Economy* (Tokyo, 1966), series 1, pp. 12–13. For 1935–38 (comparable with early years) both product and population are based on the Hitotsubashi series. Product for 1935–38 (comparable with later years) is from *Hundred-Year Statistics*, series 11, p. 51, given in 1934–36 prices and shifted to the 1960 base by means of the implicit price indexes to the two bases, also given on p. 51. Product for 1952–54 is from the *Supplement to Hundred-Year Statistics*, which contains revised estimates. Population for 1935–38 is from *Hundred-Year Statistics*, series 1, pp. 12–13, and for 1952–54 from the *Demographic Yearbook, 1965*, table 4.

United States

Line 29: Product is variant I of the index given in Paul David, "The Growth of Real Product in the United States Before 1840: New Evidence, Controlled Conjectures," *Journal of Economic History*, vol. XXVII, no. 2 (June 1967), table 8, p. 184. Population is based on the Bureau of the Census, *Historical Statistics of the United States, Colonial Times to 1957* (Washington, D.C., 1961), series A 2, p. 7.

Lines 30–31: Product is from Robert E. Gallman, "Gross National Product in the United States, 1834–1909," in Dorothy S. Brady, ed., *Output, Employment, and Productivity in the United States after 1800*, vol. 30 of *Studies in Income and Wealth* (New York: Columbia University Press for the National Bureau of Economic Research, 1966), table A-1, p. 26. Population again is from *Historical Statistics*, series A 2.

Line 32: Product is based on Simon Kuznets, *Capital in the American Economy: Its Formation and Financing* (Princeton: Princeton University Press for the National Bureau of Economic Research, 1961), tables R-25, R-26, pp. 561–564. The estimates for 1880–89 were revised on the basis of Gallman's adjustment coefficients (see Gallman, table A-6, p. 40), which were apportioned by quinquennia and applied to the Kuznets estimates of GNP (excluding net change in inventories) in current prices. The original implicit price indexes were then applied to derive adjusted totals in 1929 prices. Population is from Kuznets, table R-37, pp. 624–627.

Line 33: For 1910–14 to 1930–34 product is from United States Office of Business Economics, *U.S. Income and Output* (Washington, D.C., 1958), table I-16, pp. 138–139, and table I-2, p. 119. Population, given for 1930–34 in the United States Office of Business Economics, *National Income, 1954 Edition* (Washington, D.C., 1954), table on pp. 24–25, was extrapolated to 1910–14 with the estimates used for line 32 as index. For 1930–34 to 1950–54 the *Economic Report of the President* (Washington, D.C., January 1967), table B-2, p. 214, gives product, and table B-16, p. 232, gives population.

Canada

Line 36: Product and population are from O. J. Firestone, *Canada's Economic Development, 1867–1953* (London: Bowes and Bowes, 1958), table 88, p. 280.

Line 37: For 1920–24 to 1950–54 official estimates of product, beginning in 1926 and given in M. C. Urquhart and K. A. H. Buckley, eds., *Historical Statistics of Canada* (Cambridge: Cambridge University Press, 1965), series E 45, p. 132, were carried back to 1920 by earlier official estimates of national income, given in Firestone, table 97, p. 341. The 1950–54 estimates were adjusted to exclude Newfoundland on the basis of personal income estimates given in *Historical Statistics*, series E 71 and E 79, p. 134. Population is given in *ibid.*, series A 1, p. 14, and adjusted for 1950–54 to exclude Newfoundland on the basis of the 1961 census figures.

Australia

Line 39: Product is from N. G. Butlin, *Australian Domestic Product, Investment and Foreign Borrowing, 1861–1938/39* (Cambridge: Cambridge University Press, 1962), table 269, pp. 460–461. Population, given for 1871–75 in Kuczynski, table I, pp. 230–231, was carried back to 1861 by the series on changes in population, given for 1861–90 in N. G. Butlin, "Colonial Socialism in Australia, 1860–1900," in Hugh G. J. Aitken, ed., *The State and Economic Growth* (New York: Social Science Research Council, 1959), table 2, p. 33, and interpolated logarithmically for 1900–04.

Line 40: For product in 1900–04 and 1920–24 and for population in 1900–04 see the notes to line 39. Population for 1920–24 is from the *Demographic Yearbook, 1960*, table 4. For 1920–24 to 1953–54 (fiscal years) product is an unpublished revision and extension of the Butlin estimates by Bryan D. Haig, Research School of Social Science, Australian National University. Population is from the *Demographic Yearbook, 1960* and *1965*, table 4.

U.S.S.R., the major country that would be in the developed group, does not lend itself to easy comparison with those in Table 1. As already indicated, increases in aggregate output of commodities and services are comparable only when the weights, reflecting prevailing social and institutional practices, are roughly the same; they are not comparable if the means to secure such increases used by one country are not acceptable in another. In this case comparability between the U.S.S.R. and other developed countries would require elaborate recalculations and shifts in weights — a task beyond practical scope here.

The group also excludes very small countries with a population of less than 2 million (Luxembourg, for example), because the economic growth of such small units is hardly independent. To be sure, there is an element of interdependence among all countries; and even the largest cannot be viewed as completely independent, in the sense that its growth would be the same if it were completely isolated. But there are degrees of dependence, and the satellitic position of a tiny nation in the modern economic world makes the comparison of its growth record with those of other, much larger, and much less dependent units analytically improper.

Within the limitations set, the fourteen countries in Table 1 almost exhaust the list. New Zealand is omitted because tested estimates are available only for the post-World War II years. The Union of South Africa is omitted because its low overall per capita product (as distinct from the very high per capita income of its white residents) indicates that the economic growth that took place (and it was notable) was not substantial enough to raise the per worker and per capita product for *all* the population to levels comparable with those of the presently developed countries.

Subperiods were distinguished in Table 1 only for two types of discontinuity. First, when the record included a preindustrialization, a premodern development, phase of the country's economic history — as for England and Wales and the United Kingdom, Italy, and the United States — the earlier period was distinguished from the later one, which presumably represented the country's experience in modern economic growth. A similar division of the long period was made in the case of major territorial or political breaks, as for Germany before and after World War II. Second, when different periods were covered by estimates that differed significantly in their foundation or in the continuity of their coverage, averages were derived for the shorter period covered by the more reliable and continuous series and also for the longer more inclusive period. This was done for France, the Netherlands, the United States, Canada, and Australia. The averages were taken for the full period, including wars and their aftermaths, to avoid at this juncture the difficult decisions as to when the immediate consequences of a war are ended; and whether wars are an integral part of modern economic growth, the omission of which would yield an unrealistic account. Further evidence is provided in Table 4, in which long subperiods, some covering major wars and others not, are distinguished.

Finally, I have used long-term records largely for gross product (domestic or national, at factor cost or market prices), since they are more easily available than the net product series, which is, on logical grounds, more suitable. But, for the long periods covered here, and for the high growth rates observed, the differences between gross and net concepts (or between factor cost and market prices) in the growth rates would be negligible. As will be shown, the growth of total gross product at the typical rate of 3.0 percent per year or 34.4 percent per decade would mean, with the usual change in the proportion of fixed capital consumption (the difference between gross and net), a growth rate in total net product of 2.9 percent per year or 33.1 percent per decade. The differences between growth rates derived from factor cost and market price bases, when used for constant base valuation of product, would also be negligibly small for long periods. We therefore disregard the differences here; and view the growth rates in Table 1 as representative of all the common variants of aggregate product.

In summarizing the evidence in Table 1, I concentrate on the averages for the long periods, assumed to cover each country's modern economic growth since its beginning (lines 7, 12, 13, 16, 21, 22, 23, 24, 25, 27, 28, 35, 38, 41). This assumption is fairly realistic for countries for which the record is long and extends to the beginning of modern economic growth (Great Britain, France, Germany, Norway, Sweden, the United States, Canada, and Australia). For Canada and Australia there is some question as to when modern economic growth began, but the full period is included because there is no evidence of an early time span within the record with a distinctly low growth rate in per capita product followed by a rise to higher rates. This assumption is also valid for countries with records that do not extend back far enough, but miss only brief periods of modern economic growth (as is presumably true of Japan, and probably also of Denmark). However, records for Belgium and Switzerland extend back only to the beginning of the twentieth century and do not cover a substantial portion of their modern growth period; this may also be true of the Netherlands, with its longer record. Yet periods of five to seven decades are long enough to reveal characteristics of growth, and the addition of the earlier missing decades could not modify the parameters substantially. At any rate, it seemed better to include them than to ignore the evidence completely.[4]

4. The significant acceleration of economic growth that indicates the entry of a country into the modern growth process is presumably accompanied by an accelerated rise in the share of urban in total population; and the available series on the urban proportions may help date the beginnings of economic modernization and thus judge the coverage of our series. The urban population proportions cited below are, with one exception, from the classical monograph by Adna F. Weber, *The Growth of Cities in the Nineteenth Century*, Columbia University Studies in History, Economics, and Public Law, vol. XI (New York: Macmillan, 1899), pp. 47, 71, 82, 84, 110, 111, 113, 115, 116, 117.

For the Scandinavian countries the initial dates seem to fall well in the second half of the nineteenth century. Thus, for Denmark, urban population, which was 20.9 percent of the total in 1801 and only 23.7 percent in 1860, rose to 34.0 percent in 1890 (the share of the Copenhagen population alone moved from 10.9 to 10.4 and then to 17.3 percent). In Norway, the share of urban population was 10.7 percent in 1801 and 13.6 percent in 1855, and rose to 23.7 percent in 1891. In Sweden, urban population accounted for 9.6 percent of the total in 1805, 11.3 percent in 1860, and

(a) The rate of growth of per capita product ranges from 10 to 12 percent per decade for Australia, the Netherlands, and Great Britain–United Kingdom to 29 to 32 percent for Sweden and Japan. The rates for the remaining nine countries cluster between 14 and 23 percent per decade.

(b) Compared with this relatively narrow range for the long-term growth rate in per capita product, that for the rate of population growth is rather wide. Here the contrast is clear and expected between the overseas offshoots of Europe (the United States, Canada, and Australia), with population growth rates of 19 to 24 percent per decade, and Japan and the older countries of Europe (Belgium, France, Sweden, and Italy), in some of which the growth rates were 7 percent or less per decade. Even for the European area the range from 3 percent for France to over 13 percent for the Netherlands is relatively wide.

(c) There is no simple association, within the sample of developed countries, between the rates of growth of per capita product and population, at least for the long periods in Table 1 (excluding

---

rose to 18.8 percent in 1890. This evidence is confirmed in Dorothy S. Thomas, *Social and Economic Aspects of Swedish Population Movements, 1750–1933* (New York: Macmillan, 1941), tables 7, 8, pp. 42–43, which show that the proportion of population in cities of over 2,000 was 7.3 percent in 1800, 10.8 percent in 1865, and 19.6 percent in 1895. The record for Switzerland does not extend that far back, but here again the proportion of population in cities of 5,000 or more was 6.5 percent in 1822 and 12.7 percent in 1850, and rose to 24.7 percent in 1888.

Belgium appears to have shown some acceleration of the urban proportion at an earlier date: the share in cities of 10,000 or more was 13.5 percent in 1802–1815, rose to 20.8 percent (including suburbs) in 1846, and to 34.8 percent (again including suburbs) in 1890. And in the Netherlands, the urban proportion, which was already high in the early nineteenth century, rose substantially in the second half of the century: the proportion in cities of 10,000 or more was 29.5 percent in 1795, 29.0 percent in 1849, and 43.0 percent in 1889. One may assume that in these two countries city growth and economic growth accelerated after the mid-century.

For countries with records of total product that are adequately long, the series on the urban population proportion confirm the findings. Thus, for England and Wales, the proportion for all cities of 20,000 or more, already high at 16.9 percent in 1801, rose to 35.0 percent in 1851, and 53.6 percent in 1891 — showing continuous growth since at least the beginning of the century. In France, the proportion in towns of 2,000 or more was 20.5 percent in 1801, and only 22.2 percent in 1836, but rose to 25.5 percent in 1851 and 37.4 percent in 1891. In Germany, population in the twenty-five great cities of 1890 was 4.7 percent of the total in 1819, still only 6 percent in 1855, and rose to 12.1 percent in 1890; while in Prussia, the largest constituent member, urban population, 25.5 percent in 1816, was still only 27.7 percent in 1855, but rose to 40.7 percent in 1895. It is pointless to cite the proportions for the overseas offshoots of Europe — the United States, Canada, and Australia — since for them our economic records extend back far enough.

the preindustrialization subperiods). Countries with low rates of population growth do not necessarily show high rates of growth of per capita product (negative association), nor do countries with high rates of population growth show high rates of growth of per capita product (positive association). France, with the lowest rate of population growth, and the overseas offshoots of Europe, with their high rates of population growth, show rates of growth in per capita product that are average or slightly above average.[5]

(d) Despite the absence of positive association between the growth rates of population and per capita product, the range of the growth rate of total product is somewhat wider than that for per capita product. Some countries with rapidly growing population also had fairly high rates of growth of per capita product (the United States and Canada, for example), and some countries with fairly low rates of population growth also showed below-average rates of growth of per capita product (for example, Belgium). The rate of growth of total product ranged from about 20 percent per decade for Belgium to over 48 percent for Japan — a spread of 28 percentage points, compared with about 22 percentage points in the growth rate of per capita product. As will be noted later, such differences in growth rates have some bearing on the rapidity of shifts in economic magnitude among the developed countries.

(e) Even the lowest rates of growth of per capita product in the developed countries are much higher than the rates in the premodern subperiods covered; much higher than direct evidence for the few less developed countries suggests, and indirect evidence confirms; and much higher than they could have been over the many past centuries. With few exceptions, such as France, this is true also of population growth, for which our past records are far more ample. These records reveal the much higher rate of population growth in the developed countries during the last century and a half to two centuries than in the long-term past. With such historically high rates of growth of both per capita product and population, those in total product must be high. In fact, the rates at which the economies of developed nations grew are little short of

5. The Spearman coefficient of rank correlation between growth rates of population and per capita product is —0.05 for Japan and the ten developed countries in Europe; and —0.27 for all fourteen developed countries. Neither coefficient is statistically significant.

astounding. Even in the older European countries they suggest a growth factor of 6 to 24 in a century; in the overseas offshoots of Europe the coefficient of multiplication over a century ranges from 22 to 34, and in Japan it is over 50. Since in the preceding centuries population in Europe was growing at a rate that cumu-

Table 2. Approximate product per capita at the beginning of modern growth, developed countries.

| | GNP per capita, 1965 (US $) (1) | Extrapolation to initial date | | |
		Date[a] (2)	Reduction factor (growth) (3)	GNP per capita, initial date, 1965 $ (col. 1 : col. 3) (4)
1. United Kingdom– Great Britain	1,870	1765–85	8.23	227
2. France	2,047	1831–40	8.46	242
3. Belgium	1,835	(1865)	3.80	483
		(1831–40)	5.63	326
4. Netherlands	1,609	(1865)	3.27	492
		(1831–40)	4.64	347
5. Germany[b]	1,939	1850–59	6.41	302
6. Switzerland	2,354	(1865)	4.45	529
7. Denmark	2,238	1865–69	6.05	370
8. Norway	1,912	1865–69	6.65	287
9. Sweden	2,713	1861–69	12.64	215
10. Italy	1,100	1895–99	4.06	271
		1861–69	4.22	261
11. Japan	876	1874–79	11.88	74
12. United States	3,580	1834–43	7.56	474
13. Canada	2,507	1870–74	4.94	508
14. Australia	2,023	1900–04	2.18	930
		1861–69	2.66	760

[a] Dates in parentheses are conjectural.

[b] In 1936 per capita income in the Federal Republic and pre-World War II territory differed by only 2 percent.

Column 1: Per capita GNP for 1966 in U.S. dollars, given in the *Yearbook of National Accounts Statistics, 1968*, vol. II. *International Tables*, table 2C, was shifted to the 1965 base by the price index implicit in GNP in the United States, given in the *Economic Report of the President* (Washington, D.C., February 1968), table B-3, p. 212. These estimates were then extrapolated to 1965 by per capita product in constant dollars derived from GNP, given in the *Yearbook of National Accounts Statistics, 1968*, vol. I. *Individual Country Data*, and population, given in *Demographic Yearbook, 1967*, table 4. For France, Sweden, and Australia the per capita product is based on GDP.

Column 3: Derived from Table 1.

lated to about 17 percent per century,[6] and per capita economic product must have been growing quite slowly, the growth factor per century must have ranged from 1.25 to 1.50, or from less than a fourth to a twentieth of that in modern times.

The relatively high rate of increase of total, and particularly, of per capita product in modern economic growth can be confirmed by extrapolation of the current per capita product of the developed countries back to the time when they entered the modern growth process. These initial levels of per capita product in the presently developed countries will indicate whether the high rates of increase of per capita product shown in Table 1 could have occurred in the premodern past; and also whether it is these high growth rates in the modern decades that largely account for the strikingly wide differences in per capita product among the developed and the less developed countries today.

The results of the extrapolation are summarized in Table 2. Where the record extended back to the date of the country's entry into modern economic growth, and this date was known, if roughly, the extrapolation was carried back to that date (the end of the eighteenth century in Great Britain; the 1830's in France and the United States, and so on). This was also done when it could reasonably be assumed that the available record covers the modern growth period fully (as for Germany, the Scandinavian countries, Canada, and Australia). Finally, when the record was short (as for Belgium and Switzerland) or possibly failed to reach back to the desired beginnings by a substantial margin, I carried the extrapolation back a century (for Switzerland) or to the 1830's (for Belgium and the Netherlands). The results are crude, partly because of uncertainties in dating the initiation of modern economic growth, partly because of the statistical and conceptual qualifications of our long-term records. But the estimates can be viewed as based on terminal price weights, and, while crude, suffice as rough orders of magnitude in support of the conclusion and inferences that follow.[7]

6. Between 1000 and 1750 the population of Europe grew 1.6 percent per decade (see Simon Kuznets, *Modern Economic Growth: Rate, Structure, and Spread* [New Haven: Yale University Press, 1966], table 2.1, p. 35).

7. Comparison of the extrapolations with the Mulhall estimates of earnings per capita for the middle 1890's may seem unwarranted, but it has an element of value if we grant, as we must, that Mulhall's judgments of the relative economic magnitude of European nations and their offshoots overseas were quite good. For the comparison, I extrapolated the estimates of GNP per capita in 1965 U.S. dollars to 1895, applied

The conclusion is that, with the single exception of Japan, the initial levels of per capita product in the developed countries, on the eve of their entry into modern economic growth, were fairly high, ranging from $215 and $227 (in 1965 prices) for Sweden and Great Britain to $474 to $760 for the European offshoots overseas. Each currently developed country, except Japan, began its modern growth with a per capita product of more than $200 (in 1965 prices). Japan is unique in that its initial per capita product was low enough to fall within the range of current per capita product levels of many of the populous underdeveloped countries in Asia and Africa.

Two inferences follow. The first, relevant directly to the older European countries, is that, if modern economic growth is characterized by multiplication factors for per capita product over a century that range about 5, and if most of the older developed countries in Europe began with a per capita product of between $200 and $250, the preindustrial past could not have witnessed

---

the price index implicit in our records of total product for the United States to convert them to 1895 prices, and finally converted to pounds sterling at the official exchange rate of almost $5 per pound sterling. The results are (in pounds sterling per capita, at 1895 prices):

	Mulhall Earnings	Extra-polated GNP		Mulhall Earnings	Extra-polated GNP
1. Great			8. Norway	18	17.0
Britain	38.8	42.0	9. Sweden	22	34.2
2. France	31.2	27.8	10. Italy	14	11.8
3. Belgium	28.3	31.4	11. United		
4. Netherlands	25.8	26.2	States	44	47.0
5. Germany	24.7	25.6	12. Canada	36	36.8
6. Switzerland	23.3	36.2	13. Australia	49	39.4
7. Denmark	27.3	27.4			

The Mulhall data are from Michael G. Mulhall, *Industries and Wealth of Nations* (London: Longmans, Green, 1896): Great Britain, pp. 58, 96; France, Belgium, Netherlands, Germany, Switzerland, Denmark, Italy, the United States, and Canada, p. 391; Norway and Sweden, p. 229; Australia, p. 347. Extrapolations are based on the records cited in Table 1, with conversion to 1895 prices by the price index for the United States (used for aggregate product), which in 1965 was 458 to 1895 as 100.

In eight of the thirteen countries, the difference between the extrapolation and the Mulhall estimate was less than 10 percent of the larger total. The major discrepancies are for Switzerland and Sweden, for both of which the Mulhall estimates are almost a third lower than the extrapolated values; and for Australia, for which the Mulhall estimate is about a quarter higher than the extrapolated value. It is intriguing, and mildly reassuring, to find that for so many countries, particularly the larger ones, the agreement is so close.

such high growth rates. If minimum per capita product in European countries is set at $50 (GNP in 1965 prices), a rather low figure considering that this is the current per capita product of Ethiopia and several other African countries at an exceedingly low state of economic development, the assumption of the multiplication factor of 5 to a per capita product of even $250 would allow for just one century of preindustrial development; and would mean stagnation all the way back to the early Middle Ages — a picture at variance with historical records. In fact, Table 1 shows that the growth rate in the first three-quarters of the eighteenth century in England yielded a multiplication coefficient over a century of 1.2; and that in Italy the rise in per capita product between the 1860's and the 1890's was about 1 percent. We also know that from the beginning per capita product tended to be even higher in the European offshoots overseas than in the mother country — if we omit the stage when the offshoot may have been primarily a penal colony. In short, the record of growth of per capita product for the developed countries shown in Table 1 represents a striking acceleration of the growth rate in premodern times, for Western Europe possibly by a factor of 10.[8]

The second inference is that, while the high rate of increase in per capita product during the modern century to century and a half in the presently developed countries must have contributed substantially to the currently wide international differences in per capita product, the difference in *initial* levels, in favor of the developed countries (again with the exception of Japan), must also have contributed substantially. Table 2 shows that for the developed European countries GNP per capita in 1965 varied from about $1,100 to $2,700, with a typical middle range of about $1,900. The per capita GNP for East and Southeast Asia (excluding Japan) was $114 in 1966; and that for SubSaharan Africa, excluding South Africa and Southern Rhodesia, was about $98;[9] and population for these two groups of countries was about 1.2 billion in that year. The range is thus about 19 to 1. If we assume a multiplication

8. If we assume that the trough of per capita product in Western Europe can be dated at about year 900, and that the approximate date at which modern economic growth began in Western Europe is the middle of the nineteenth century, a rise from $50 to $250 over a span of some 950 years means a quintupling of the product in about 10 centuries instead of one.

9. These figures and others in this paragraph are from United Nations, *Yearbook of National Accounts Statistics, 1968,* vol. II. *International Tables* (New York, 1969), table 2C.

factor of 5 for per capita product of the European developed group in the recent century (which is probably too high), and no growth in the per capita product of the less developed group (which ignores any growth that did occur, and thus results in an underestimate of the difference in initial levels), the implied difference in initial levels a century ago is almost 4 to 1. And for the overseas offshoots of Europe with per capita GNP ranging in 1965 from $2,000 to $3,600, and a representative middle level of say $3,000, the current ratio to per capita GNP of the Asian-African less developed countries is 30 to 1; and on the same assumptions regarding growth over the last century for the developed countries, the difference in per capita product a century ago would have been about 6 to 1. The importance of such differences in initial levels for present international differences can be demonstrated by assuming that the initial differences were in favor of the presently less developed countries. If the initial per capita product of developed countries were, say, one-quarter less than that of the less developed, given the same extreme differences in growth rates during the ensuing century, current international differences in per capita product would be in a range of 3.75 to 1, instead of 19 or 30 to 1.

The implications of this rather obvious arithmetic are wide-reaching. One is the possible dependence of modern economic growth of the presently developed countries on high initial levels of per capita product, and the related question as to how successful modernization and growth was achieved in Japan. The second is the relevance of modern economic growth experience, as observed so far, to the growth mechanisms and prospects of the less developed countries. Current per capita product for this group ranges widely, from over $700 in 1966 for some parts of Europe and Latin America to as low as $70 in parts of Africa. Obviously, the relevance of past and observable growth experience is quite different for the several distinctive levels of initial per capita product characterizing the less developed countries today, since income levels presumably reflect levels of related economic and social institutional structures and practices.

It follows that the failure to reach the per capita product (and related structure) that would put a country in the developed class, may have resulted from too low an initial per capita product despite a high growth rate over a sufficiently long period or from too low a growth rate despite a fairly adequate initial level of per capita product — and this rate may have been too low *continuously* through the long period, or may have accelerated only relatively recently. High and low and length of period in the present context are all relative to the parameters observed for the developed countries in Tables 1 and 2.

The summary of growth rates and initial levels in Table 3 for seven less developed countries for which long-term records are at hand illustrate these three different reasons for failure to reach adequate levels of per capita product. The underlying estimates are far less reliable than those for the developed countries. A striking example is found in the case of Mexico, for which two sets of estimates for the decades from the 1920's to the early 1950's yield substantially different growth rates (and therefore different derived earlier levels of per capita product). But the evidence is adequate for purposes of realistic illustration.

In the case of Argentina, the initial per capita product ($443 in 1900–1904) was far below that for Australia in the same quinquennium, and probably lower than those for the United States and Canada. It was nevertheless high enough so that a growth rate of the same order of magnitude as that in most of developed Europe or in North America, say 19 percent per decade, would have meant a per capita product in 1965 of over $1,300 and put the country into the developed group. The major source of failure was a low rate of growth of per capita product, not only in the period after the 1920's but even before.

Jamaica and Egypt (the latter less striking) are examples of countries with low growth rates that amounted to stagnation or decline in per capita product over a long period, followed by a significant recent acceleration. If the estimates can be trusted, per capita product in Jamaica in the first half of the nineteenth century was not much lower than that in some presently developed countries of Europe, but it did not rise until after World War II. In Egypt the initial level of per capita product (at the end of the nineteenth century) was not as high; but again there was no significant acceleration until well after World War II.

The Philippines are still another case of a fairly adequate initial per capita product but rather low growth rate over the period of observation — low because of World War II. While the period covered in Table 3 is too short to have permitted a sufficient shift in the status of the Philippines to that of a developed country,

Table 3. Rates of growth, total product, population, and product per capita, and estimated product per capita at initial date of period, selected less developed countries.

	Duration of period (years) (1)	Rates of growth per decade (%)			Derived GNP per capita, 1965 $, at initial date of period (5)
		Total product (2)	Popu- lation (3)	Product per capita (4)	
Argentina					
GDP ($811)					
1. 1900–04 to 1925–29	25	57.0	40.2	12.0	443
2. 1925–29 to 1963–67	38	31.8	21.1	8.9	587
3. Lines 1–2	63	41.3	28.3	10.1	
Mexico					
GNP, GDP ($461)					
4. 1895–99 to 1925–29	30	20.7	6.5	13.3	148 (92)
5. 1925–29 to 1963–67	38	59.0 (80.1)	30.0	22.3 (38.5)	215 (134)
6. Lines 4–5	68	40.8 (51.0)	19.1	18.2 (26.8)	
Jamaica					
GDP, national income, and GDP ($504)					
7. 1832 to 1930	98	10.9	10.9	0	193
8. 1929–31 to 1950/52	21	27.6	17.2	8.9	194
9. 1950–52 to 1963–66	13.5	110.5	18.5	77.7	232
Ghana					
GDP ($312)					
10. 1891 to 1911	20	32.1	10.1	20.0	107
11. 1911 to 1950–54	41	45.2	27.5	13.9	154
12. 1950–54 to 1963–67	13	49.1	30.6	14.2	263
13. Lines 10–12	74	42.2	23.0	15.6	
Philippines					
Gross value added and GNP ($255)					
14. 1902 to 1938	36	34.2	22.5	9.6	138
15. 1938 to 1950–54	14	19.8	24.7	−3.9	192
16. 1950–54 to 1963–67	13	77.8	36.7	30.0	181
17. Lines 14–16	63	38.7	25.8	10.3	

Table 3 — continued

	(1)	(2)	(3)	(4)	(5)
United Arab Republic (Egypt)					
GDP, GNP, NDP ($185)					
18. 1895–99 to 1945–49	50	11.9	14.4	−2.2	131
19. 1945–49 to 1963–66	17.5	65.4	27.4	29.8	117
India					
NDP ($86)					
20. 1861–69 to 1881–89	20	19.1	5.3	13.1	47
21. 1881–89 to 1901–09	20	1.4	4.6	−3.1	60
22. 1901–09 to 1952–58	50	16.8	9.9	6.3	57
23. 1952–58 (F) to 1963–67 (F)	10	41.4	26.1	12.2	77
24. Lines 20–23	100	16.2	9.4	6.2	

(F): fiscal year beginning April 1.

The general notes to Table 1 are applicable here unless otherwise indicated in the country notes below.

The dollar entries in parentheses in the stubs are GNP per capita for 1965 in 1965 dollars, calculated by the procedure described in the notes to Table 2, column 1, unless otherwise indicated in the notes.

Column 5 is derived from the data underlying column 4.

Argentina

Line 1: Product is from Alexander Ganz, "Problems and Uses of National Wealth Estimates in Latin America," in Raymond Goldsmith and Christopher Saunders, eds., *Income and Wealth, Series VIII* (London: Bowes and Bowes, 1959), table XVI, p. 245. Population for the midyear of 1925–29 is from the *Demographic Yearbook, 1960*, table 4, and for the midyear of 1900–04 was extrapolated by the series in United Nations, Economic Commission for Latin America, *Economic Survey of Latin America, 1949* (New York, 1950), table 1, pp. 90–91.

Line 2: For 1925–29 to 1950–54 product is from the source given for line 1; population for 1952 is extrapolated from 1947, given in the *Economic Survey* cited in the notes to line 1, by the series in the *Demographic Yearbook, 1965*, table 4.

Mexico

The 1965 per capita GNP was extrapolated from 1966 by the change in per capita GDP.

Line 4: GNP is based on Enrique Perez Lopez, "El Producto Nacional," in Fondo de Cultura Económica, *Mexico: 50 Años de Revolución, I: Económica* (Mexico City: Fondo de Cultura, 1960), tables 2–4, pp. 587–589. Population for 1897 is by logarithmic interpolation between census figures given in the *Demographic Yearbook, 1952*, table 2; for 1927 from *ibid., 1960*, table 4.

Line 5: For 1925–29 to 1950–54 GNP and population are from the sources cited in the notes to line 4. GDP (for the entries in parentheses) is from Ganz, table II, p. 225. For 1950–54 to 1963–67 product is GDP.

Jamaica

Line 7: Total and per capita GDP are from Gisela Eisner, *Jamaica, 1830–1930: A Study in Economic Growth* (Manchester: Manchester University Press, 1961), table LVI, p. 289.

Line 8: For 1929–31 to 1938 national income in current prices is given in Phyllis Deane, *The Measurement of Colonial National Incomes*, National Institute of Economic and Social Research, Occasional Paper XII (Cambridge: Cambridge University Press, 1948), table 100, p. 137. It was adjusted for price changes by the weighted average of the general price index (weight of 4) and the index of the value of exports (weight of 1), both given in *ibid.*, table 104, p. 141. Population is from the *Demographic Yearbook, 1960*, table 4. For 1938 to 1950/52 GDP is from Alfred P. Thorne, "Size, Structure and Growth of the Economy of Jamaica," *Social Economic Studies*, supplement to vol. 4, no. 4 (December 1955), table 12, p. 88, and population is from *ibid.*, p. 92.

Line 9: The terminal period ends with 1966, since that is the last year for which U.N. data are available.

Ghana

Line 10: GDP and population are from R. Szereszewski, *Structural Changes in the Economy of Ghana, 1891–1911* (London: Weidenfeld and Nicolson, 1965), table C-6, p. 149, and table B-5, p. 126.

Line 11: Product and population for 1911 and 1960 are from *ibid.*, p. 92. The estimates for 1950–54 are extrapolated from 1960 by the indexes given in Organisation for Economic Co-operation and Development, *National Accounts of Less Developed Countries, 1950–1966* (Paris, July 1968), tables C, D.

Line 12: Product, given in the *Yearbook of National Accounts Statistics, 1968*, for 1960–67, and population, given in the *Demographic Yearbook, 1965* and *1967*, table 4 for 1960 and 1965, were both extrapolated to 1950–54 by the indexes given in OECD, *National Accounts . . .* , tables C, D.

Philippines

Line 14: Product is gross value added in agriculture (crops and livestock), forestry, mining, manufacturing, electric light and power, railroads, other land transport and communications, interisland and overseas shipping, and commerce. Total and per capita product are from Richard W. Hooley, "Long Term Economic Growth in the Philippines," in International Rice Research Institute, Growth of Output in the Philippines, mimeographed papers presented at a Conference, December 9–10, 1966, tables 1, 2, pp. 4–10, 4-14.

Line 15: GNP, derived for 1950–54 in line 16 by the procedure described in the general notes to Table 1, was extrapolated to 1938 by the national income index in the United Nations, *Statistical Papers, Series H*, no. 2 (August 1952), table 3, p. 19, linked at 1950. Population was taken from the *Demographic Yearbook, 1960* and *1965*, table 4.

United Arab Republic (Egypt)

The 1965 per capita GNP was extrapolated from 1966 by the index of product per capita given in OECD, *National Accounts . . .* , table E, pp. 27–30.

Line 18: The index of GDP was derived on the basis of indexes of agricultural output, their relation to the labor force engaged in agriculture, and the ratio of product per worker in the non-A sector to that in the A sector. The index of agricultural output for 1935–39 and 1945–49, prepared by the National Bank of Egypt and given in Donald Mead, *Growth and Structural Change in the Egyptian Economy* (Homewood, Ill.: Richard Irwin, 1967), table III-A-1, p. 318, was extrapolated to 1915–19 by the index of ten basic crops, given in *ibid.*, table III-A-3, p. 320, and to 1895–99 by an index of four crops (cotton, wheat, maize, and rice), derived from Patrick O'Brien, *The Revolution in Egypt's*

Economic System (London: Oxford University Press, 1966), table 1, p. 5. The outputs of these four crops, given in physical units, were combined by weighting each by its 1925–29 price, given in Mead, table III-B-1, p. 323 (the unit for rice having been shifted from ardeb to dariba on the basis of information in the footnote to Mead, table III-A-4, p. 323).

The number employed in the A and non-A sectors, given for 1907, 1927, 1937, and 1947, in Mead, table II-B-1, p. 304, shows a relatively constant ratio of agricultural to total employment before 1947, and I used the 1907 estimate for 1895–99.

By means of the agricultural output index and labor force in the A sector, gross output per worker in agriculture was calculated. On the basis of gross output per worker in the A and non-A sectors in 1937 (in current prices) and 1947 (in constant prices), derived from Mead, tables I-A-1, I-A-10, II-B-1, pp. 270–271, 291, 304, I calculated the ratio of output per worker in the non-A sector to that in the A sector.

By means of the per worker output and labor force proportions for the A and non-A sectors I calculated an index of gross product per worker and multiplied it by the total employment index (given for 1907 and later years in Mead, table II-B-1, p. 304, and extrapolated to 1897 by the movement of total population, given in *ibid.*, table II-A-1, pp. 294–295), to obtain the index of gross domestic product.

Line 19: For 1945–49 to 1950–54 GNP is from Mead, table I-A-6, p. 286. Population is from the *Demographic Yearbook, 1965,* table 4. For 1950–54 to 1963–66 I used the index for NDP given in the OECD, *National Accounts* . . . , table C; population is from the *Demographic Yearbook, 1965* and *1967,* table 4.

India

The 1966 per capita GNP was extrapolated to 1965 by the change in per capita GDP.

Lines 20–22: Per capita income (implicitly NDP) is from M. Mukherjee, *National Income of India: Trends and Structure* (Calcutta: Statistical Publishing Society, 1969), table 2.5, p. 61. Population beginning in late 1940's is given in the *Demographic Yearbook, 1965,* table 4; and was extrapolated back (with an overlap in 1947–51) by the series on population of the Indian Union in Mukherjee, table A2.14, p. 99.

Line 23: NDP, for fiscal years starting April 1, is from the U.N. unpublished data for 1950–54, and from the *Yearbook of National Accounts Statistics, 1968* for 1963–67 (the series on a 1948 price base linked in 1965 to the one on a 1960 price base). Population is from the *Demographic Yearbook, 1965* and *1967,* table 4.

even with a high growth rate in per capita product, it could have come close to it if only at the high rates that prevailed in Japan and Sweden.

The case of India is particularly distinctive, with moderate rises in two of the early periods distinguished and a decline in the third (lines 20–22).[10] The effect of a very low initial level is more striking. Even if over the long period of a century, covered in lines 20–22, per capita product were multiplied by a factor of 10 (rather than 5, found for most developed countries), it would still have fallen short of the developed group threshold. To a lesser extent this is also true of Ghana and Mexico.

10. For a similar finding, with even lower growth rates for the period between the beginning of this century and the 1920's or 1930's, see Krishan G. Saini, "The Growth of the Indian Economy: 1860–1960," *The Review of Income and Wealth,* no. 3 of *Income and Wealth, Series 15* (September 1969), pp. 247–263.

Selected Aspects of Aggregate Growth Rates

Several aspects of the aggregate growth rates are of some analytical interest but have not been mentioned so far. Here three aspects discussed suggest related questions: (a) international implications of the differences in growth rates, even among the developed countries; (b) long-term trends, if any, in the growth rates, and developments in the post-World War II period; (c) long swings in the aggregate growth rates. The comments will necessarily be brief, despite the fact that each aspect and the analytical question that it suggests deserve detailed study.

*International implications of
differences in growth rates*

In discussing Tables 1, 2, and 3 we noted that a major source of the wide differences in per capita product in the world today, particularly between the developed and the less developed countries, is the difference between their growth rates of per capita product. In general, over the last century to century and a half per capita product grew much more rapidly in the presently developed countries; and since they, with the single exception of Japan, entered on modern growth with per capita product already well above that of the less developed countries today, these international differences must have widened. And the rapidity with which they widened was largely a function of the unusually high growth rates in the developed countries.

But, until the very recent decades, population also tended to grow more rapidly in the developed countries (except for France) than in the less developed. This meant that both per capita and total product grew at much higher rates in the developed countries — and relative economic magnitudes shifted rapidly, in favor of that group.

All this is familiar, but the interesting aspect is that the same rapid shifts in economic magnitude, caused by wide differences in the growth rates of per capita product, population, and total product, are found *within* the group of developed countries. Despite the fairly high rates of growth of per capita product over long periods in all developed countries, usually well above 10 percent per decade, and despite the impressive rates of population growth in most of these countries, these rates and those for total product differed widely among the countries themselves. Consequently, over the long periods, there were drastic shifts in relative economic magnitude.

It is not difficult to cite conspicuous examples of such shifts. In the period from 1834 through 1843, when the United States was just entering its modern industrialization, it had a population of 16.7 million and a total product of some $7.9 billion (in 1965 dollars). About the same time (1831–1840), France had a population of 33.9 million and a total product of some $8.2 billion (in the same prices). Thus the ratio for population in France to that in the United States was about 2.0; for total economic product it was slightly over 1.0. By 1965 the population of the United States was 195 million and its total product close to $700 billion, compared with a population of about 49 million and an economic product of about $100 billion for France, with ratios of France to the United States of about one-quarter for population and about one-seventh for total economic product. The comparison of the United States with the United Kingdom for the two dates reveals a similar shift. And such illustrations could be repeated (for example, between the late 1870's and the late 1960's for Japan, in comparison with either France or the United Kingdom).

The important point is that the overall high rates of growth tend to yield large absolute differences in growth rates; and such large absolute differences in growth rates tend to produce rapid shifts in magnitude. This can be shown, in a general form, by simple algebra.

Assume A_1 and A_2, two initial magnitudes (for population, total product, or per capita product); define the initial relative as $D = A_1/A_2$ (the percentage difference being $[D - 1] \times 100$); designate the percentage rates of growth per decade for the two initial magnitudes r_1 and r_2 respectively; and then define the terminal relative, after a period of growth over time t, as F (the percentage difference being $[F - 1] \times 100$).

Then:

$$F = A_1(1 + r_1)^t/A_2(1 + r_2)^t = D(1 + r_1)^t/(1 + r_2)^t$$

or in logarithms:

$$\log F = \log D + t[\log (1 + r_1) - \log (1 + r_2)].$$

The terminal relative disparity will be the greater, the greater the initial disparity, the longer the period of time involved, and the greater the difference between rates of growth of the initial quantities — provided all the disparities are in the same direction.

The aspect of this relationship most significant here is the *absolute* difference between the rates of growth. Consider the following illustrative application:

r_1 (%)	r_2 (%)	Spread between r_1 and r_2 (%)	F, terminal relative t = 5	t = 10	t = 20
2	1	1	1.051	1.104	1.218
10	5	5	1.262	1.592	2.535
20	10	10	1.545	2.387	5.699
40	20	20	2.161	4.672	21.830

On the assumption that $A_1 = A_2$, or that $D = 1$, what is the relation between the terminal quantities with varying spreads between r_1 and r_2 and varying numbers of decades in t?

In every line of the illustrative tabulation r_2 is half of r_1. But if the decade rates of increase are low, so that the spread between them is small absolutely, even after twenty decades the disparity is barely above 20 percent. If, however, the percentage rates are high, and the absolute spread between them is large, as in the fourth line, in less than five decades the second item, originally equal to the first, will be more than twice the size of the first.[11]

The relevance of this simple algebra becomes clear if it is argued that, under conditions in which absolutely large rates of growth can occur, large *absolute* differences among them are also more likely than in a situation in which, in general, rates of growth are low. If technical and other conditions are such that growth of population and of per capita product vary around 5 to 10 percent per decade, absolute spreads among percentage rates — especially long-term average rates — cannot be expected to run large either, cer-

---

11. Many illustrations can be found in Table 1. For example, let us take Norway and Sweden (lines 24, 25). The population growth rate of Norway, 8.3 percent per decade, was almost a third above that for Sweden, 6.6 percent; yet over the century, the two rates cumulated to growth factors of 2.2 and 1.9 (column 6), not an impressive difference. The growth rate of per capita product for Sweden, 28.9 percent per decade, was only about a third above that for Norway, 21.3 percent, but over the century the growth factors were 12.6 and 6.9 respectively, the former almost double the latter. Obviously, the *absolute difference* between the growth rates determined the difference in growth factors — and the former was over 7 percentage points for per capita product, and less than 2 percentage points for population.

tainly not as large as when the rates of growth are 20 percent per decade.[12]

The significance of this association between high average growth rates, the wide absolute differences that can then be generated, and rapid shifts in economic magnitude among nations lies in the possible connection between the shifts and strain-producing attempts to modify political relations to correspond to the changed relations in economic magnitude, and hence possibly in economic and military power. The acceleration in the aggregate growth rates that produces acceleration of shifts in relative magnitude among nations may therefore cause acceleration in political adjustments and strains, and, under some conditions, in the frequency of conflicts in response to recognized but disputed shifts in economic power.

Long-term trends in growth rates

The discussion of Table 1 stressed growth rates over very long periods. It should also be of interest to examine the movement of the growth rates over successive subperiods, to search for any indications of acceleration or deceleration with the passage of time, or of some other features that might be common to all or most developed countries.

Table 4 presents such a summary of growth rates for successive subperiods for most of the developed countries, omissions resulting only from the lack of continuous long series (as in the case of Switzerland). The periods distinguished are sufficiently long to be relatively free of the effects of long swings — a pattern of fluctuation over periods of eighteen to twenty-five years (discussed later); and I have tried to delimit the subperiods to include a war within a somewhat long interval, so that its effects could be averaged out with the prewar and postwar years. The only exception introduced was to distinguish a period following World War II, from 1950–1954 to 1963–1967, to check on the impression of a marked acceleration of growth in these postwar years.

Four or five subperiods can be distinguished for ten of the

12. The important exception to this generalization occurs when the rate of change dips below the zero line, that is, when the change is a decline. Since the average rates are algebraic averages, low positive levels may then mean large deviations. The assumption of a positive association between high average rates of growth and large absolute differences among them should, therefore, be confined to countries and periods in which long-term declines are absent. This is certainly true of modern times, but not of some earlier periods of history.

Table 4. Rates of growth, total product, population, and product per capita, developed countries, successive long periods.

	Duration of period (years) (1)	Rates of growth per decade (%)		
		Total product (2)	Popu-lation (3)	Product per capita (4)
Great Britain				
1. 1801/11 to 1831/41	30	32.1	15.4	14.5
2. 1831/41 to 1861/71	30	23.8	12.2	10.3
3. 1861/71 to 1891/1901	30	38.6	12.4	23.3
United Kingdom (excluding Ireland through line 6)				
4. 1855–64 to 1885–94	30	35.4	12.5	20.4
5. 1885–94 to 1905–14	20	23.8	11.1	11.4
6. 1885–94 to 1925–29	37.5	14.0	8.4	5.2
7. 1925–29 to 1963–67	38	22.3	4.9	16.6
8. 1925–29 to 1950–54	25	16.3	4.5	11.3
9. 1950–54 to 1963–67	13	34.9	5.6	27.8
France				
10. 1831–40 to 1861–70	30	26.3	3.9	21.6
11. 1861–70 to 1891–1900	30	15.7	1.9	13.5
12. 1896 to 1929	33	18.4	2.0	16.1
13. 1929 to 1963–66	35.5	26.9	4.9	21.0
14. 1929 to 1950–54	23	11.5	1.3	10.0
15. 1950–54 to 1963–66	12.5	61.0	11.7	44.1
Belgium				
16. 1900–04 to 1925–29	25	19.6	6.0	12.8
17. 1925–29 to 1963–67	38	20.8	4.8	15.2
18. 1925–29 to 1950–54	25	10.5	4.0	6.3
19. 1950–54 to 1963–67	13	43.1	6.4	34.6
Netherlands				
20. 1860/70 to 1890/1900	30	20.3	11.7	7.6
21. 1890/1900 to 1925–29	32	33.0	15.1	15.5
22. 1925–29 to 1963–67	38	29.8	13.6	14.3
23. 1925–29 to 1950–54	25	17.1	13.4	3.3
24. 1950–54 to 1963–67	13	58.2	13.9	38.9
Germany — West Germany				
25. 1850–59 to 1880–89	30	26.7	8.9	16.4
26. 1880–89 to 1905–13	24.5	32.9	13.5	17.0

Table 4 — continued

	(1)	(2)	(3)	(4)
27. 1895–1904 to 1925–29	27.5	17.7	9.7	7.3
28. 1925–29 to 1963–67	38	43.6	12.4	27.8
29. 1925–29 to 1950–54	25	26.5	12.5	12.5
30. 1950–54 to 1963–67	13	83.2	12.2	63.3
Denmark				
31. 1865–69 to 1885–94	22.5	31.4	10.2	19.3
32. 1885–94 to 1905–14	20	41.0	12.1	25.8
33. 1905–14 to 1925–29	17.5	24.4	11.8	11.3
34. 1925–29 to 1963–67	38	32.5	8.6	22.0
35. 1925–29 to 1950–54	25	24.5	9.2	14.1
36. 1950–54 to 1963–67	13	49.3	7.4	39.0
Norway				
37. 1865–69 to 1885–94	22.5	18.8	7.2	10.8
38. 1885–94 to 1905–14	20	24.9	9.2	14.3
39. 1905–14 to 1925–29	17.5	32.5	9.2	21.4
40. 1925–29 to 1963–67	38	42.6	8.0	32.1
41. 1925–29 to 1950–54	25	38.8	7.5	29.1
42. 1950–54 to 1963–67	13	50.4	9.0	38.0
Sweden				
43. 1861–69 to 1885–94	24.5	28.5	6.5	20.7
44. 1885–94 to 1905–14	20	38.8	7.1	29.6
45. 1905–14 to 1925–29	17.5	28.6	6.2	21.1
46. 1925–29 to 1963–67	38	47.0	6.5	38.0
47. 1925–29 to 1950–54	25	45.5	6.5	36.6
48. 1950–54 to 1963–67	13	49.9	6.5	40.8
Italy				
49. 1895–99 to 1925–29	30	24.6	6.5	16.9
50. 1925–29 to 1963–67	38	37.0	7.2	27.8
51. 1925–29 to 1951–54	25.5	22.7	7.4	14.3
52. 1951–54 to 1963–67	12.5	71.5	6.9	60.4
Japan				
53. 1874–79 to 1895–1904	23	39.2	9.3	27.3
54. 1885–94 to 1905–14	20	39.8	11.4	25.5
55. 1905–14 to 1925–29	17.5	50.7	13.5	32.8
56. 1925–29 to 1963–67	38	56.7	13.2	38.4
57. 1925–29 to 1952–54	26	25.6	14.3	9.9
58. 1952–54 to 1963–67	12	152.8	10.7	128.4

Table 4 — continued

	(1)	(2)	(3)	(4)
United States				
59. 1800 to 1840	40	52.3	34.1	13.5
60. 1839 to 1859	20	59.1	35.7	17.3
61. 1834–43 to 1869–78	35	49.7	31.5	13.9
62. 1869–78 to 1889–98	20	50.0	24.7	20.3
63. 1885–94 to 1905–14	20	44.7	20.5	20.1
64. 1900–09 to 1925–29	22.5	36.7	17.4	16.5
65. 1925–29 to 1963–67	38	36.2	13.7	19.8
66. 1925–29 to 1950–54	25	33.2	11.8	19.2
67. 1950–54 to 1963–67	13	42.1	17.6	20.8
Canada				
68. 1870–74 to 1890–99	22.5	41.8	13.2	25.2
69. 1880–89 to 1900–09	20	35.2	15.3	17.2
70. 1900–09 to 1925–29	22.5	34.3	23.7	8.6
71. 1925–29 to 1963–67	38	44.1	19.6	20.5
72. 1925–29 to 1950–54	25	39.9	16.3	20.2
73. 1950–54 to 1963–67	13	52.7	26.1	21.1
Australia				
74. 1861–69 to 1890–99	29.5	45.1	36.9	6.0
75. 1885–94 to 1905–13 (F)	20	27.8	20.2	6.2
76. 1900–09 (F) to 1925–29 (F)	22.5	26.9	21.5	4.4
77. 1925–29 (F) to 1963–67 (F)	38	37.1	17.3	16.8
78. 1925–29 (F) to 1950–54 (F)	25	29.6	14.3	13.3
79. 1950–54 (F) to 1963–67 (F)	13	52.8	23.3	23.9

(F): fiscal year beginning July 1.
For sources of the underlying data and the procedures used, see the notes to Table 1.
When years in the stubs are connected by a slash (/), data are for the single years indicated; when connected by a dash (–), they are for all the years in the interval.

thirteen developed countries covered in the table. This supply of measured growth rates is adequate to indicate any trends toward acceleration or deceleration. But the general impression is that there is no common pattern of trends over time, although there is a suggestion that long subperiods of higher or lower than average growth tend to occur at about the same time in a number of countries.

In several countries (Great Britain–United Kingdom, Denmark, and particularly the United States and Australia), the growth rate of population declines; but even this feature is far from general. In several countries (Belgium, the Netherlands, Norway, Germany since the 1880's, Sweden, and Italy), the population growth rate has been constant, at fairly low levels. In others it showed some tendency to rise: in France in the recent period; in Japan, until the post-World War II decline; in Canada, after migration to the United States had dropped off. Thus, despite the long-term movements of birth and death rates in the developed countries which for a while tended to produce a common trend, the rate of population growth shows no general trend, reflecting migration flows, which differ over time and among countries, and also some reversals in birth rates.

For per capita product, no significant acceleration or deceleration is found, particularly for the periods after modern economic growth began. In Great Britain the growth rate shows an upward movement from the early nineteenth century to about the third quarter, then a decline, particularly conspicuous for the period spanning World War I, that is followed by a return to the average in the period since the 1920's. Indeed, the only countries that show a distinct systematic trend pattern, one of acceleration, are Japan, possibly Sweden, and Norway: in the last per capita product growth rates rise systematically from about 10 to over 30 percent per decade. The only fairly general feature of the time pattern of the per capita product growth rates is that the period including World War I, extending usually from the 1890's or the first decade of the twentieth century to the second half of the 1920's, shows lower than average growth rates (in the United Kingdom, Germany, Denmark, Sweden, Canada, Australia, and possibly Belgium, Italy, and the United States).

Despite the relatively full coverage of developed countries, the data are not adequate for testing hypotheses concerning the time patterns of the growth rates. But they do not provide support for W. W. Rostow's "take-off" theory which suggests that an initial rapid acceleration in the rate of growth of per capita product is followed by sustained growth at a constant high rate achieved at the end of the take-off period of some two to three decades.[13] Neither the slow climb of the growth rates in the United Kingdom to a peak in the third quarter of the nineteenth century (from a take-off presumably in the eighteenth century) nor the upward movement in Norway and Japan conforms to the pattern expected from the hypothesis. Nor do the data support the Gerschenkron hypothesis which suggests that the later the entry of a country into the modern growth process, the higher the growth rates are likely to be, at least in the early phases — as is implied by the strains and advantages of greater "backwardness." [14] Italy, a relative latecomer, is not distinguished by high growth rates, and yet Japan is. Sweden, no latecomer compared with Italy, has distinctly higher rates, approximating those of Japan. Indeed, the variety of experience — reflecting in part variety in size, location, historical antecedents, and historical conditions at the time of entry, and different datings of the growth phases — is such that, given the relatively small number of countries and the large number of qualifying variables, an empirically common set of features (other than those like the minimum level of the growth rates, which in fact constitutes development, and related features characterizing changing structure) is unlikely to emerge.

The high rates of growth attained after World War II are shown in the breakdown of the long period since the late 1920's, which distinguishes the span from 1950–1954 to 1963–1967. The 1950–1954 quinquennium was chosen to exclude the immediate postwar recovery; and the rates are based on quinquennial averages to minimize short-term effects. The results are striking and intriguing.

For eleven of the countries, the growth rate in per capita product (and often that in population) is much higher than the average suggested by the long subperiods stretching back into the nineteenth century. The two exceptions are the United States and Canada, where the post-World War II rates are about the same as the long-term average.

In six of the countries with high growth rates in this recent period, the high rates follow a long period since the late 1920's in

---

13. For a formulation and extensive discussion of this hypothesis see W. W. Rostow, ed., *The Economics of Take-Off into Sustained Growth* (London: Macmillan, 1963).

14. See Alexander Gerschenkron, *Economic Backwardness in Historical Perspective* (Cambridge, Mass.: Harvard University Press, 1962), essay I, pp. 5–30.

which the rates of growth were unusually low, perhaps because of the effects of World War I. These are the United Kingdom, France, Belgium, the Netherlands, perhaps Denmark, and Japan. And in five of them (all but Japan) the addition of the high growth rate after World War II to the lower-than-average growth rate back to the late 1920's yields a rate for the full period, 1925–1929 to 1963–1967, that is close to the average for the long-term record. In these cases one could argue that the unusually high growth rate after World War II was a response to the constraints on growth that existed over the preceding period, and to the destruction that occurred during the war.

This leaves us with a group — Germany, Norway, Sweden, Italy, Japan, and Australia — in which the growth rate from the late 1920's to the early 1950's was not markedly low, or in which the post-World War II acceleration was so large that it produced a very high average for the long period from the late 1920's to the middle 1960's. Interestingly, the group includes not only countries that were shatteringly affected by World War II (Germany, Italy, and Japan), but also countries that were affected relatively little (Australia, Sweden, and perhaps even Norway, at least not as physically damaged and socially restructured as the major losers in World War II).

We cannot say that the acceleration of economic growth that occurred in this post-World War II period is a lasting one. But the contrast between it and the relatively constant rates in the United States and Canada, and the different combinations of postwar acceleration and preceding slowdowns that characterize the older developed countries, pose intriguing questions. These questions are beyond the scope of this book.

Long swings in growth rates

In addition to the long-term trend in one direction, acceleration or retardation, just discussed, there may be oscillations in the growth rates, up and down movements extending over a longer period than the four-to-nine-year spans of business or economic cycles but short enough to be observed with some recurrence within the full periods covered by our series. Long swings — covering some eighteen to twenty-five years — in growth rates of product, population, and a number of economic components have been found in several countries.[15]

An adequate analysis of these long swings requires data on a variety of components in addition to continuous series on the aggregates; it would take us too far afield to attempt such an analysis and discuss the mechanism connecting them. All I can do here is illustrate the character of these long swings, and suggest the apparently systematic interrelations among them for several countries. This illustration is limited to the period before World War I, since the effects of World War I and the world depression of the 1930's created a swing in the interwar period that was common to many countries but was largely due to the impact of the war and its aftermath. And the period since World War II may be too short for the purpose at hand. The period before World War I, and back to the middle nineteenth century, free as it was of major wars of world dimensions, seemed to permit a better test. I chose the United Kingdom (excluding Ireland, by assuming that its per capita product was half of that in the United Kingdom), Germany, Sweden, and Australia — the four countries for which we have a continuous record since the 1860's, and which belong to the developed group throughout the period (although there is some question about Sweden in the early years). The United States was added beginning with the 1870's; the 1860's were omitted because of the Civil War. For the period from the mid-nineteenth century to 1913 or 1914, the growth rates of per capita product, population, and total product were subjected to an analysis designed to reveal long swings, unaffected either by shorter business cycles or by long-term underlying trends (Table 5).

The technique, described in detail in the notes to the table, was to deal with decennial averages, of which two sets were formed: one for years ending with 0 through those ending with 9; the other for years ending with 5 through those ending with 4. Growth rates were calculated for decennial intervals within each of the two sets separately, and arrayed in a single series in chronological order (by the midyear of each interval); a straight line was fitted to the logs of these successive decennial growth rates by semi-averages, and

15. For a recent discussion of these movements see Moses Abramovitz, "The Nature and Significance of Kuznets Cycles," *Economic Development and Cultural Change*, vol. IX, no. 3 (April 1961), pp. 225–248; and "The Passing of the Kuznets Cycle," *Economica*, vol. XXXV, no. 4 (November 1968), pp. 349–367.

Table 5. Long swings in rates of growth, the United Kingdom, Germany, Sweden, Australia, and the United States, mid-nineteenth century to World War I.

	United Kingdom excluding Ireland, 1860–1914 (1)	Germany, 1850–1913 (2)	Sweden, 1861–1914 (3)	Australia, 1860–1914 (4)	United States, 1870–1914 (5)
A. Per capita product					
Trend relative in growth per decade					
1. First four, five, or three intervals, over-lapping decades	1.200	1.165	1.200	1.141	1.149
2. Second group of intervals	1.136	1.166	1.280	1.029	1.228
3. Full period	1.168	1.166	1.240	1.083	1.188
Deviation from straight-line trend in rate of growth (%)					
4. 1860–69 to 1865–74 (1867)	+1.7	+4.5	+10.8	−5.0	—
5. 1860–69 to 1870–79 (1869–70)	+1.1	+3.8	+12.3	+0.4	—
6. 1865–74 to 1875–84 (1874–75)	−2.8	−3.9	+2.4	+4.9	+21.6 (1877)
7. 1870–79 to 1880–89 (1879–80)	−2.3	−7.6	−7.6	+1.5	+11.7
8. 1875–84 to 1885–94 (1884–85)	+4.2	+0.1	−5.8	−6.4	−4.0
9. 1880–89 to 1890–99 (1889–90)	+7.5	+5.8	−0.8	−17.7	−6.8
10. 1885–94 to 1895–1904 (1894–95)	+3.6	+2.5	+1.8	−14.7	+1.1
11. 1890–99 to 1900–09 (1899–1900)	−4.5	−3.7	0	+9.6	+4.6
12. 1895–1904 to 1905–14 (1904–05)	−6.0	−4.3	−0.9	+29.9	−5.4
13. 1900–09 to 1905–14 (1907)	−3.9	−2.3	−0.5	+32.4	−13.4
B. Population					
Trend relative in growth per decade					
14. First group of intervals	1.128	1.090	1.067	1.389	1.240

Table 5 — continued

	(1)	(2)	(3)	(4)	(5)
15. Second group of intervals	1.113	1.130	1.068	1.224	1.202
16. Full period	1.121	1.110	1.067	1.304	1.221

Deviation from straight-line trend in rate of growth (%)

	(1)	(2)	(3)	(4)	(5)
17. 1860–69 to 1865–74 (1867)	−0.7	+0.2 (1864–65)	0	−2.5	—
18. 1860–69 to 1870–79 (1869–70)	−0.2	−0.6	0	−4.0	—
19. 1865–74 to 1875–84 (1874–75)	+0.5	+0.1	+0.8	−3.0	−1.1 (1877)
20. 1870–79 to 1880–89 (1879–80)	+0.1	−0.5	+0.4	+2.1	−0.3
21. 1875–84 to 1885–94 (1884–85)	−0.5	−1.5	−1.2	+5.2	+0.5
22. 1880–89 to 1890–99 (1889–90)	−0.2	−0.9	−1.5	+2.5	−0.1
23. 1885–94 to 1895–1904 (1894–95)	+0.4	+0.6	0	−1.9	−1.2
24. 1890–99 to 1900–09 (1899–1900)	+0.3	+1.3	+0.9	−2.5	−0.5
25. 1895–1904 to 1905–14 (1904–05)	−0.4	+0.5	+0.6	+2.0	+1.7
26. 1900–09 to 1905–14 (1907)	−0.9	−0.4	+0.6	+5.8	+1.8

C. Total product

Trend relative in growth per decade

	(1)	(2)	(3)	(4)	(5)
27. First group of intervals	1.353	1.270	1.280	1.585	1.424
28. Second group of intervals	1.266	1.318	1.367	1.260	1.476
29. Full period	1.309	1.294	1.323	1.413	1.450

Deviation from straight-line trend in rate of growth (%)

	(1)	(2)	(3)	(4)	(5)
30. 1860–69 to 1865–74 (1867)	+0.9	+4.7 (1864–65)	+10.8	−7.5	—
31. 1860–69 to 1870–79 (1869–70)	+0.9	+3.2	+12.3	−3.6	—

Table 5 — continued

	(1)	(2)	(3)	(4)	(5)
32. 1865–74 to 1875–84 (1874–75)	−2.3	−3.8	+3.2	+1.9	+20.5 (1877)
33. 1870–79 to 1880–89 (1879–80)	−2.2	−8.1	−7.2	+3.6	+11.4
34. 1875–84 to 1885–94 (1884–85)	+3.7	−1.4	−7.0	−1.2	−3.5
35. 1880–89 to 1890–99 (1889–90)	+7.3	+4.9	−2.3	−15.2	−6.9
36. 1885–94 to 1895–1904 (1894–95)	+4.0	+3.1	+1.8	−16.6	−0.1
37. 1890–99 to 1900–09 (1899–1900)	−4.2	−2.4	+0.9	+7.1	+4.1
38. 1895–1904 to 1905–14 (1904–05)	−6.4	−3.8	−0.3	+31.9	−3.7
39. 1900–09 to 1905–14 (1907)	−4.8	−2.7	+0.1	+38.2	−11.6

—: information not available.

Dates in parentheses in the stubs, and the few in the columns are for the midyears of the intervals.

For sources of the underlying data see the notes to Table 1. In a few cases the data are for a period varying slightly from a decade, but the growth rate in every case is for a decade.

For Germany, the three series extended back to 1850, and six decade averages (for years ending with 0 through those ending with 9), and six decade averages (for years ending with 5 through those ending with 4) were calculated — each set yielding changes in growth rates for five decennial intervals. For the United Kingdom, Australia, and Sweden, the period started in 1860 or 1861, and yielded two sets of five decennial averages, and from these I derived two sets of changes in growth rates for four decennial intervals. For the United States, the series extended from 1870 to 1914, yielded two sets of decennial averages of four decades each, and two sets each of three decennial changes in growth rates. The trend in growth rates was calculated from arithmetic means of logarithms of decennial growth rates (10, 8, or 6), arranged in chronological order, and interpolated along a straight line to yield successive ordinates. The deviations are the absolute differences between the logarithms of specific decennial growth rates and the corresponding ordinates of the trend. At the ends of the series (lines 4, 13, 17, 26, 30, 39), we computed the growth rate between *overlapping* decades, which meant growth over a quinquennium only. The logarithms of these growth rates were doubled; and the deviations taken from corresponding ordinates of the straight-line trend in decennial growth rates.

The absolute differences between the logarithms for the specific intervals and the logarithms of the straight-line trend were converted to antilogarithms; these, expressed as plus or minus percentages, are entered in lines 4–13, 17–26, 30–39. The deviations were calculated directly for population and per capita product. The average trend relatives and the percentage deviations for total product were then derived from those for population and per capita product.

the straight-line trend ordinates were calculated; and, finally, the absolute deviations of logs of specific decennial growth rates from the corresponding trend line ordinates were taken — the antilogs of which are shown in the form of percentages in lines 4–13, 17–26, and 30–39. The series were extended at both ends by decennial movements based on quinquennial changes in order to piece out the record. But it may be claimed that, since the underlying units are decennial intervals between decennial averages, little trace of the shorter business cycle (whose duration did not exceed nine years) remains; and that the movements of the percentage deviations are secular in character.

Table 5 reveals a substantial amplitude in the fluctuations in growth rates around the long-term linear trend; the succession of plus and minus signs in the deviations suggests considerable oscillation; and, most important, the similarity or diversity in timing of these fluctuations among the several countries hints strongly at some causal interrelations.

The amplitude of the fluctuations is fully revealed if we recognize that the entries in lines 4–13, 17–26, and 30–39, are in percentages of the trend relative, not in growth rates per decade. If we eliminate the trends revealed in lines 1–2, 14–15, and 27–28, we can use the *average* growth rate (in lines 3, 16, 29) as a base. Thus, for the United Kingdom, a peak percentage of +7.5 in line 9, means a decennial growth rate for that interval of $[(1.168 \times 1.075) - 1]$, or 25.6 percent, compared with an average of 16.8 percent, or almost half again as high; whereas a trough percentage of −6.0 in line 12, means a decennial growth rate of 9.8 percent, or almost a half lower. For per capita and total product the amplitudes of the fluctuations in the decennial growth rates are wide, the peaks of the long swings showing growth rates that are from two to three times as high as those at the troughs. For population the amplitudes are much narrower, as we would expect — although even here they are substantial for countries with large volumes of immigration, like Australia and the United States, and not insignificant for a small country like Sweden (at the peak, in the 1890–1899 to 1900–1909 interval, the growth rate of population was 7.7 percent per decade; and at the trough, in the 1880–1889 to 1890–1899 interval, it was only 5.1 percent).

The sequence of signs of deviations is important. If such deviations were merely a matter of the poor fit of the straight-line trend compared with a more complex, noncyclical curve, the sequence of signs would be a grouping of minuses and pluses in two complete clusters (although one might be centered at the middle, and the other divided between the two ends of the period). However, Table 5 suggests four clusters of signs, which for a period of some fifty to sixty years and long swings of about twenty to twenty-five years in duration is what we would expect. Unless significant elements of shorter business cycles somehow survived this procedure, the results can be credited only to long oscillations in decennial growth rates.

It is the timing of these fluctuations that is most significant, and analytically intriguing. For per capita product the fluctuations for the United Kingdom and Germany show marked similarity, with the positive deviations in the periods centered on the late 1860's and the middle and late 1880's (lines 4–5, 8–9), and the negative deviations in the periods centered on the middle and late 1870's (lines 6–7) and the next trough in the span from 1895–1904 to 1905–1914 (line 12). Australia, on the other hand, shows a swing inverted to those of the United Kingdom and Germany: in the former, the first peak, in the period centered on 1874–1875 (line 6), corresponds to the first trough in the United Kingdom; the next trough, in the period centered on 1889–1890 (line 9), corresponds to the major peak in the United Kingdom; and finally the growth rate from the 1890's to the eve of World War I is at its highest in Australia (although the trend line may exaggerate the magnitude of the deviations), while the growth rate in the United Kingdom is at its lowest. The other two countries, Sweden and the United States, do not fit as neatly into this pattern. The fluctuations in Sweden seem similar to those in the United Kingdom and Germany, particularly those of the latter. Those in the United States are at first, like the Australian pattern, inverted to the fluctuations in Europe (at least through the 1890's); but this inverted association is not found in the last two intervals (lines 12–13). The mechanism yielding these associations, which may operate through trade and particularly capital exports from the older European to the oversea countries, is discussed in the literature cited in note 15.

The deviations for population growth rates fall into a somewhat similar grouping. By and large, the similarity is quite close among the three older European countries, the United Kingdom, Germany, and Sweden, marred only by the failure of agreement in the last two intervals (lines 25–26). The swings in the United Kingdom are inverted to those in Australia and the United States, as are the swings in Germany and Sweden through the 1890's. The systematic interrelation among these fluctuations is impressive, and the mechanism was presumably international migration which, when accelerated, reduces the population growth rates of the older countries and increases those of the younger immigrant-receiving countries.[16]

Since the amplitude of the fluctuations is much wider for per capita product than population, the patterns of the fluctuations in total product are rather like those in per capita product. Consequently, the same similarity is found between the United Kingdom and Germany, and to a lesser extent, Sweden; and an inversion of the pattern is found in Australia, and to a lesser extent in the United States.

This discussion could be extended to consider the suggestive interrelations between fluctuations in growth rates of per capita product and population — for example, that a higher rate for the former, signifying a more accelerated growth of product per capita, might, with some lag, induce more migration to the overseas countries but reduce migration from the older, European countries. Hence inversion of long swings in per capita product between older European and younger overseas countries would be analytically connected with inversion of long swings in population growth (insofar as the latter result from international migration; or higher growth rates in per capita product might cause a higher natural growth rate of population, perhaps by higher birth rates). But consideration of such interactions of long swings in population and product is far removed from the central theme of this book.

The whole question of long swings was brought up primarily to show that the data testify to their existence. It should be clear that they were of substantial magnitude; that the mechanisms underlying them are of great analytical interest; and that whether such swings are prevalent or likely to be prevalent even in the post-World War II period, when shorter business cycles have had a much narrower amplitude than in the past, is still a significant question. It is of particular bearing on the interpretation of the high post-World War II growth rates shown in Table 4.

16. For an interesting analysis of this process and its influence on swings in the growth rates of economic product and of some of its major components, for several developed countries, see Brinley Thomas, *Migration and Economic Growth: A Study of Great Britain and the Atlantic Community* (Cambridge: Cambridge University Press, 1954).

II

Growth of Productivity and Nonconventional Costs

Does the high rate of increase of per capita product, characteristic of modern economic growth, result from a high rate of increase in per capita input of productive factors (labor and capital), or from a high rate of increase in productivity?

Growth of Productivity

Before dealing with the subject of productivity, I must stress that inputs, like output, are identified here in accordance with the accepted rules of national economic accounting. This means that labor input is limited to the contribution of those members of the working community who participate in the production of the output included under national product; those engaged in home care and similar activities are excluded. More important, the labor included may differ in quality, and, although its hours may be weighted differently to allow for quality differentials, such weighting cannot allow for quality differences attributable to investments not recognized as such in conventional economic accounting. Thus, the increasingly accepted view that formal education, at least in part, is investment and should be reflected in measures of input of labor is inconsistent with present national economic accounting concepts and practices, in which outlays on education, by individuals or by government, are treated as final consumption. Consistency could be attained by recasting the national accounting concepts and system. An illustrative discussion of this possibility is presented in the next section, but such recasting cannot be effectively applied on a wide, comparative scale, at least here; and we must retain the conventional definitions of labor and capital. The latter is limited to material, tangible goods, including both reproducible structures, equipment, and inventories and nonreproducible assets such as land, but excludes consumer durable commodities; for national units it is adjusted, when required, by the balance of international indebtedness.

In addition to growth of output the measure of growth of productivity requires estimates of the rates of increase of labor input, of capital input, and of the weights by which the rate of increase of combined inputs can be secured. Then a comparison of the growth rate of combined inputs with that of output yields a growth rate of productivity. Our discussion deals first with the evidence relating to the rate of increase of labor input; second, with that on growth of capital input; third, with the weights by which the inputs of labor and capital are combined; and, finally, with the comparison of combined inputs and output, and the resulting growth rate of productivity. Since major concern is with the contribution of the growth of productivity to the high rate of growth of per capita (rather than total) product, the measures of increase in labor and capital inputs on a per capita basis are stressed.

Labor input

Successive population censuses and supplementary sources for the developed countries provide abundant evidence on the relation of the labor force (or gainfully occupied) to the total population (Table 6). To be sure, the labor force concept and the practices followed in identifying its members differ among countries and vary over time — particularly with respect to the inclusion of unpaid family labor, of the very young and the very old, and of casual and seasonal workers. Although Table 6 is based largely on a compilation in which an effort has been made to assure comparability, undoubtedly some biases still remain in the ratios, with the later censuses using a higher minimum age of coverage and geared to a more precise definition of labor force. But the biases are not large, and the distinction of female workers and their reduction to some rough equivalence to full-time male workers strengthen the reliability of the long-term trends in the ratio of labor force to total population, that is, the supply of workers per capita.

Table 6. Long-term changes in the ratio of labor force to total population, developed countries.

	Proportion to total population (%)				
	Total labor force (1)	Females in A sector (2)	Females in non-A sector (3)	Males (4)	Total labor force, male equivalents (5)
Great Britain					
1. 1851	45.0	1.1	12.5	31.4	39.1
2. 1911	44.9	0.3	12.9	31.7	39.5
3. 1961	46.9	0.2	15.0	31.7	40.7
France					
4. 1856	39.1	6.0	6.2	26.9	31.8
5. 1906	53.3	8.6	11.2	33.5	41.9
6. 1962	42.4	2.7	11.5	28.2	35.6
Belgium					
7. 1846	46.3	7.9	9.1	29.3	36.3
8. 1910	46.6	2.9	11.5	32.2	39.7
9. 1961	38.2	0.5	9.7	28.0	33.9
Netherlands					
10. 1849	41.1	5.4	6.8	28.9	34.1
11. 1909	38.6	1.9	7.3	29.4	34.2
12. 1960	36.4	0.4	7.7	28.3	33.0
Germany Interwar boundaries					
13. 1882	38.3	5.5	3.8	29.0	32.4
14. 1925	51.3	8.0	10.4	32.9	40.7
Federal Republic					
15. 1939	51.7	7.1	11.3	33.3	41.5
16. 1964	46.3	2.8	14.1	29.4	38.4
Switzerland					
17. 1880	46.3	5.2	9.7	31.4	38.3
18. 1960	46.3	0.4	13.5	32.4	40.6
Denmark					
19. 1901	46.6	6.1	8.8	31.7	38.2
20. 1960	45.7	0.8	13.3	31.6	39.7
Norway					
21. 1875	45.0	0.9	15.2	28.9	38.2
22. 1910	39.6	2.2	9.7	27.7	34.0
23. 1960	39.2	0.4	8.6	30.2	35.4

Table 6 — continued

	(1)	(2)	(3)	(4)	(5)
Sweden					
24. 1870	39.8	7.4	5.3	27.1	31.8
25. 1910	39.8	4.7	6.4	28.7	33.5
26. 1960	43.3	0.5	12.8	30.0	37.8
Italy					
27. 1881	58.8	10.9	12.1	35.8	45.2
28. 1901	50.7	9.9	6.6	34.2	40.1
29. 1961	39.7	3.0	7.0	29.7	34.5
Japan					
30. 1920	48.7	11.4	6.9	30.4	36.8
31. 1964	49.3	7.2	12.7	29.4	38.5
United States					
32. 1870	32.5	1.1	3.7	27.7	30.1
33. 1910	40.6	1.3	6.8	32.5	36.8
34. 1960	39.0	0.3	12.2	26.5	33.9
Canada					
35. 1911	37.8	0.2	4.9	32.7	35.7
36. 1961	35.7	0.4	9.4	25.9	31.6
Australia					
37. 1901	43.8	1.0	8.5	34.3	39.6
38. 1961	40.2	0.4	9.7	30.1	36.0
New Zealand					
39. 1901	44.0	0.5	8.0	35.5	40.4
40. 1961	37.1	0.4	8.9	27.8	33.2

Unless otherwise indicated, underlying data are from P. Bairoch and others, *International Historical Statistics*, vol. I. *The Working Population and Its Structure* (Brussels: Institut de Sociologie de l'Université Libre de Bruxelles, 1963).

Column 1: Given in table A-1 except for Great Britain in 1961 and the Netherlands in 1849 and 1909. For Great Britain in 1961 the ratio was derived from the total labor force, given in table A-2, and total population according to the 1961 census, given in the United Nations, *Demographic Yearbook, 1965* (New York, 1966), table 2. For the Netherlands in 1849 and 1909 the underlying data for all the columns are from the Bos memoranda cited in the notes to Table 1.

Columns 2–3: The ratio of females to population was calculated by applying the ratio of the female labor force to the total labor force, also given in Bairoch, table A-1, to column 1, again except for Great Britain in 1961 and the Netherlands in 1849 and 1909. For Great Britain the ratio of the female labor force to total labor force was derived from Bairoch, table A-2. This ratio was then allocated to the A and non-A sectors on the basis of *ibid.*

Column 4: Column 1 minus columns 2 and 3.

Column 5: Weighted totals of columns 2–4, the weights being 0.2, 0.6, and 1.0 respectively.

The proportion for total labor force (column 1) is affected by the treatment of women, in that both levels and trends differ markedly among countries. Only some of these differences are genuine. The very high ratios for the early dates in Italy and for recent dates in Japan (lines 27–28, 30–31) result in large part from the inclusion of unpaid family labor, mostly female, in agriculture and handicrafts, and possibly in part from the employment of women in the textiles and clothing industries (in Italy in the nineteenth century). The marked declines in the proportion of total labor force to population in Belgium, the Netherlands, and Italy appear to be largely the result of the diminishing importance of women in agriculture and industry.

The proportion of male labor force in total population shows much greater similarity in level and stability over time (column 4). Here the range is from 26 to 36 percent, but most of the ratios cluster between about 27.5 and 32.5 percent. Some trends are marked, especially those in the overseas offshoots of Europe, where the decline in the twentieth century of some 4 to 7 percentage points (lines 33–40) can perhaps be explained by the greatly diminished immigration, which added so much to the male labor force of these countries before World War I. In the older countries in Europe (except Italy) and in Japan the trends are quite moderate, with changes over the long periods of fifty years to over a century of only 1 to 3 percentage points.

Such long-term stability of the male labor force–total population ratios could have been expected, particularly in countries not much affected by international migration flows. In these countries the proportion of working-age males to the total population changes slowly, and its trend over the period under review was upward, since the decline in the birth rates and the prolongation of life meant an increasing share within the population of males above the minimum age of entry into the labor force. However, the rise in the male labor force–total population ratio was checked by a continuous rise in the age of entry into the labor market, which in great part reflected longer periods of education and greater training requirements. A second retarding factor was the decline in the age of retirement. This was connected partly with the shift toward industries which, unlike agriculture, had more limited opportunities for workers of advanced age, and partly with the shift within the labor force from self-employed or independent to employee status, also unfavorable to continued employment into advanced age. The balance of the demographic trends favoring higher proportions of the male labor force to the total population, and those reducing labor force participation rates for the young and the old, may have differed somewhat from country to country and period to period, but in general it was relatively narrow. Needless to say, the forces that made for the stability of the long-term proportion of male labor force to total population were deep-seated, basic demographic and institutional aspects of the modernization of societies of which economic growth was only one if an important facet.

The female labor force is on the average about half the size of the male labor force, and its proportion to total population varies from 5 to over 20 percent. The proportion is affected by the same demographic variables as that of the male labor force — declining birth rates, extension of the life span, and the rise in the share of working age groups in total population. But the decline in the birth rates is more important here, since it releases women from their responsibilities of bearing and rearing children. Thus, the forces that make for a rise in the proportion of female workers to total population are greater than those raising the proportion for male workers. And these demographic forces are supplemented by urbanization and changes in mores that facilitate gainful employment for female workers, married or unmarried. On the other hand, some major institutional changes inhibit unpaid family labor, which in the past was the dominant form of participation of women in productive activity; and the decline in the relative importance of the small-scale family unit in manufacturing and other fields has reduced opportunities for women even in paid employment. The combination of these two opposing factors produced divergent trends. In half the countries the proportion of women workers to total population rose: in Great Britain from over 13 to over 15 percent; in France from over 12 to over 14 percent; in Germany from about 9 to about 17 percent; in the United States from about 5 to over 12 percent; in Canada from about 5 to almost 10 percent; and in Australia and New Zealand by a couple of percentage points. Thus, in all these countries the decline in the proportion of women in agriculture to the total population was more than offset by the rise in the proportion of women in nonagricultural pursuits. But in Switzerland, Denmark, Sweden, and Japan the proportion of women workers to the total population was roughly stable, at levels from about 12 to over 18 percent; and in Belgium, the Netherlands, Norway, and Italy it declined markedly.

An attempt to adjust for the other biases in the data and to weigh more explicitly the various factors that account for the changing and different engagement of women in economic activity would carry us too far afield. But, to secure some approximate trends in the total supply of workers per capita, these movements in the proportion of female workers in the total population can be combined with those for the male labor force.

The weighting by which this combination is achieved in column 5 rests upon two assumptions. First, we assume that women workers in agriculture are mostly unpaid family labor, at least for countries where, and periods when, this group is relatively large. (When its share is small, any assumption has little effect.) This assumption is partly supported by evidence for 1960, which shows that in France, the Netherlands, Canada, and particularly Japan, unpaid family labor accounts for some 70 to 80 percent of all female workers in agriculture and related industries.[1] Second, the relative weights of female and male workers in nonagricultural pursuits, which can be approximated for recent years on the basis of average earnings for the same age groups, can be applied over the long period. If these weights are accepted, their use over the past means that women workers are assigned a greater relative weight than they probably carried; and any adjustment for that bias would reduce even more the contribution of the female worker component to the trends suggested by the male workers alone.

The weight used for women workers outside of agriculture is 0.6 compared with 1.0 for males — based on earnings comparisons for men and women in the twenty-to-sixty-four age brackets for several developed countries.[2] Since unpaid family labor in agriculture would carry a much lower weight, because of shorter hours and lower-paid skills required, it was set, somewhat arbitrarily, at 0.2. While the weights are approximate, any reasonable changes that one might make — raising the weight of 0.2 for women in agriculture and lowering the weight of 0.6 for women elsewhere — would only tend to reinforce the major conclusions: that the addition of females to the male labor force qualifies only moderately the trends

1. See United Nations, *Demographic Yearbook, 1964* (New York, 1965), table 12.
2. See Edward F. Denison, *Why Growth Rates Differ: Postwar Experience in Nine Western Countries* (Washington, D.C.: The Brookings Institution, 1967), tables 7-3, 7-4, pp. 72–73.

in the proportion of the latter to total population; and that this weighted proportion of total labor force to total population, while showing some movement in one or two countries, strongly suggests stability over the long periods.

This last conclusion is confirmed by the entries in column 5. If we agree to consider changes of 3 or fewer percentage points too small to represent significant trends, the proportion of total labor force to total population was constant over the long periods in Great Britain, Belgium, the Netherlands, Switzerland, Denmark, Norway, and Japan — seven of the fifteen countries. In three of the remaining eight countries, overseas offshoots of Europe (the United States, Canada, and New Zealand), the proportion has declined since the early twentieth century (although in the United States it has risen since 1870). The proportion also declined in Italy and Australia, but this movement may have resulted from incomparabilities in the statistical record; and it rose in France, Germany, and Sweden. One might therefore state that by and large the supply of workers per capita, reduced to some equivalence, showed no definite trend, and that this factor as measured could not have contributed much to the rise in product per capita.[3]

While the number of workers per capita, adjusted for sex differentials and with some allowance for the unpaid family labor status of women in agriculture, failed to increase significantly, hours of work per member of labor force so defined declined. Supporting evidence of such a decline in hours in organized industry — manufacturing, transportation and public utilities, and the like — is abundant. However, we need to know the magnitude of this decline and, particularly, the levels and trends of hours in the other

3. While the analysis in Table 6 reveals some interesting components of change in the labor force proportion, the main conclusion could have been argued on the basis of column 1 alone. If a change of less than 5 percentage points is evidence of stability in these higher ratios, the proportions in Great Britain, France, the Netherlands, Switzerland, Denmark, Sweden, Japan, Canada, and Australia — nine of the fifteen countries — are stable. In Germany and the United States (over the full period) the proportion rises; and in Belgium, Norway, Italy, and New Zealand it declines. But, except for Italy, the rises and declines are fractions of a percent per decade even for these countries.

This conclusion does not mean that in some countries, particularly those like the U.S.S.R., where participation in the labor force is affected by forceful intervention by the government, major shifts in the relation of labor force to total population cannot occur. The very high labor force participation rates for women in the U.S.S.R. and the resulting high ratios of total labor force to population, are clearly a result of government policy (see Warren W. Eason, "Labor Force," in Abram Bergson and Simon Kuznets, eds., *Economic Trends in the Soviet Union* [Cambridge, Mass.: Harvard University Press, 1963], tables II.3, II.4, pp. 54, 57.

sectors, especially in agriculture and services. The only data readily available are for the United States, the one country for which long-term estimates of hours of work have been elaborated (as distinct from notional estimates that are intended to reflect broad impressions, but have no foundation in detailed statistics).

Table 7 suggests that average hours declined in the industry and service sectors of the private economy — throughout the period and at an accelerated rate in the twentieth century. But the number of hours in agriculture showed practically no change until after World War I. Even more interesting, until recently the average hours per worker in agriculture were distinctly below those in the rest of the private economy, while those in the private service sector were among the highest. The average number of hours in the private economy, which dominated the national economy, was thus sustained by the decline of the share of the labor force in the A sector and by the rise of the share of the S sector. And it was the reduction in disparity in sectoral hours from the average, which occurred by the end of the first period in Table 7, that facilitated the acceleration of the decline in average hours in the second period.

Of course the findings for the United States, particularly with respect to the differences in number of hours per worker among sectors of the economy, may not be representative of other developed countries. For Canada, the only other country for which data on hours per worker are readily available for agriculture and nonagriculture separately, but only for a shorter recent period, the evidence indicates a much longer work week in agriculture.[4] For other countries the rates of decline in average hours are similar to that for 1929 to 1957 for the United States. In France, average hours declined from 1896 to 1963 by 3.9 percent per decade; in Germany, estimates based mainly on records for large cities for the pre-World War I decades show a decline from 1870–1879 to 1950 of 3.7 percent per decade.[5]

4. In N. H. Lithwick, *Economic Growth of Canada* (Toronto: University of Toronto Press, 1967), table A-8, p. 74, average weekly hours in agriculture in 1926 are set at 64; and those for nonagriculture at 49.8. The Kendrick estimates of weekly hours in 1929 are 49.8 for farm and 49.2 for nonfarm (see John W. Kendrick, *Productivity Trends in the United States* [Princeton: Princeton University Press for the National Bureau of Economic Research, 1961], table A-IX, p. 310). Lithwick also shows a decline in average hours from 1926 to 1956 of 7.6 percent per decade, while for a roughly similar period, 1929–1957, Kendrick shows a decline of 6.9 percent per decade.

5. The results for France are calculated from E. Malinvaud and others, "Croissance Française," a mimeographed preliminary report for the Social Science Research Council study of Postwar Economic Growth in Historical Perspective (Paris, July

Table 7. Long-term changes in persons engaged and in average hours of work per year, by major sector, civilian economy, United States, 1869, 1909, and 1957.

	1869 (1)	1909 (2)	1957 (3)
A. Persons engaged			
1. Total (millions)	11.86	34.65	64.94
Shares in total (%)			
2. Farm, agricultural services, forestry, fishing (A sector)	48.5	30.5	9.5
3. Mining, construction, manufacturing, transportation, communication and public utilities (I sector)	29.0	39.1	40.9
4. Trade, finance, insurance, and real estate, private services (S sector)	19.4	26.0	38.6
5. Private economy (lines 2–4)	96.9	95.6	89.0
6. General government and government enterprises (excluding military service)	3.1	4.4	11.0
7. Total civilian (line 5 plus line 6)	100.0	100.0	100.0
B. Average hours of work per year			
8. A sector	2,387	2,380	2,140
9. I sector	2,940	2,687	2,044
10. S sector	3,757	3,222	2,168
11. Private economy	2,826	2,735	2,108
12. Government	1,883	2,088	1,779
13. Civilian economy	2,797	2,706	2,072

C. Rate of change per decade in average hours per year (%)

	1869 to 1909 (1)	1909 to 1957 (2)	1869 to 1957 (3)
14. A sector	−0.1	−2.2	−1.2
15. I sector	−2.2	−5.5	−4.0
16. S sector	−3.8	−7.9	−6.1
17. Private economy	−0.8	−5.3	−3.3
18. Government	2.6	−3.3	−0.6
19. Civilian economy	−0.8	−5.4	−3.4

Underlying data are from John W. Kendrick, *Productivity Trends in the United States* (Princeton: Princeton University Press for the National Bureau of Economic Research, 1961).

Lines 1–7: Based on table A-VII, p. 308. The discontinuity in the series before and after 1953 is slight, and has only a negligible effect on the rates of change.

Lines 8–13: Totals given in table A-XI, p. 314, divided by the absolutes underlying lines 1–7.

Despite the lack of detailed evidence and differences in the relative length of the work year (or week) shown for the agricultural and nonagricultural sectors in the United States and Canada, some acceptable suggestions can be made concerning the magnitude and pattern of the long-term decline in hours of work. First, hours probably declined over the long period in the economy as a whole, and in all its major branches, except possibly the general government sector. Second, the rate of decline in countrywide average hours seems to have been appreciably greater in the twentieth century, especially after World War I, than in the earlier decades. Third, the long-term rate of decline in hours over, say, the past century can reasonably be set between 3 and 4 percent per decade, and has perhaps been as high as 4 to 5 percent per decade after World War I.

Since the number of workers per capita barely rose, perhaps less than 1 percent per year, the total input of manhours per capita of total population must have declined over the long period under consideration by between 2 and 3 percent per decade. Output per manhour must therefore have increased over the long run at a higher rate than per capita product; but the important point here is that the rise in manhours could not have contributed to the high rate of growth of per capita product.

Capital input

The growth rate of capital input can be derived from a series on capital stock, reproducible and nonreproducible, net of accumulated depreciation of the former. As will be explained, hours of utilization are not relevant.

Continuous series on capital stock, at constant prices, are available for only a few countries, and some of these will be used later. But we do have many more estimates of net capital formation, usually in current and often also in constant prices. By combining these with estimates of total product, we can derive current capital formation proportions. On the basis of the common level and trends in these proportions in the developed countries, and some realistic assumptions concerning initial capital–product ratios, we can de-

1968), chapter 3, table 7, p. 21. The estimate for Germany is from Paul Jostock, "The Long-Term Growth of National Income in Germany," in Simon Kuznets, ed., *Income and Wealth, Series V* (London: Bowes and Bowes, 1955), table V, p. 99.

Table 8. Relation between growth of capital stock and total product, assuming realistic levels and trends for the capital formation proportion and plausible levels for the initial average capital-product ratio.

Assumptions:

1. Period for which growth is cumulated: a century
2. Changes in the capital formation proportion, in capital stock, and in total product: simple geometric progressions

Definitions:

C, K, Y: stock of reproducible capital and of total capital, and total product (all net domestic)

G_c, G_k, G_y: multiplication factors, over the century, in the stock of reproducible capital and of total capital, and in total product

r_y, r_{dc}, $r_{dc/y}$: growth rates per year in total product, in capital formation, and in the capital formation *proportion*

m_c, m_k: ratios of initial stock of capital, reproducible and total, to initial volume of capital formation

Then:

$$1 + r_{dc} = (1 + r_y) \cdot (1 + r_{dc/y}) \tag{1}$$

$$G_c = \frac{\dfrac{(1 + r_{dc})^n - 1}{(1 + r_{dc}) - 1} + m_c}{1 + m_c} \tag{2}$$

$$G_k = \frac{\dfrac{(1 + r_{dc})^n - 1}{(1 + r_{dc}) - 1} + m_k}{1 + m_k} \tag{3}$$

Base I: Capital formation proportion is 10 percent of product throughout the century

    II: Capital formation proportion rises from 7.5 to 15 percent
  III: "   "   "   "   " 5 to 15 percent
  IV: "   "   "   "   " 2.5 to 15 percent

	G_c			G_k		
	(1)	(2)	(3)	(4)	(5)	(6)
1. C/Y or K/Y	2	3	4	5	6	7
			$r_y = 0.02$; $G_y = 7.244$			
2. Base I	15.8	11.0	8.59	7.10	6.10	5.38
3. Base II	19.0	13.1	10.1	8.34	7.13	6.27
4. Base III	17.1	11.8	9.17	7.55	6.47	5.69
5. Base IV	14.6	10.1	7.86	6.50	5.58	4.93

Table 8 — continued

	(1)	(2)	(3)	(4)	(5)	(6)
			$r_y = 0.03; G_y = 19.23$			
6. Base I	29.9	20.6	15.8	12.9	10.9	9.54
7. Base II	37.4	25.5	19.5	15.9	13.4	11.7
8. Base III	34.4	23.4	17.9	14.5	12.3	10.7
9. Base IV	29.9	20.3	15.5	12.6	10.7	9.32
			$r_y = 0.04; G_y = 50.47$			
10. Base I	59.8	40.9	31.1	25.2	21.3	18.4
11. Base II	77.5	52.6	40.0	32.3	27.1	23.4
12. Base III	72.2	48.9	37.0	29.9	25.1	21.7
13. Base IV	64.4	43.4	32.9	26.5	22.3	19.3

rive rates of growth in total or reproducible capital stock for comparison with rates of growth of total output. The comparison of rates of growth of capital stock per capita (of total population) and total product per capita will be a crucial datum in determining the contribution of the growth of capital stock to the high rates of growth in per capita product observed in Table 1.

The simple assumption underlying the derivation of the growth rates (cumulated over a century) of capital stock for assumed initial ratios of capital stock (total or reproducible) to output, and for some realistic levels and movements of capital formation proportions and of growth rates of total product — all given in the algebraic introduction to Table 8 — is that the growth rates of both product and capital stock lie along a straight line on a log scale, the underlying magnitudes constituting geometric progressions. By means of the formula for the sum of a geometric progression, current net capital formation can be cumulated over a century; and when combined with the assumed initial capital–output ratio will yield the growth rate of total capital stock. The model must be geared to *net* capital formation since cumulation of gross capital formation over a long period would yield an inflated gross total of dubious relevance as a source of increase of output.

Since we have estimates of long-term growth of total product for the developed countries (see Table 1), derivation of the cumulative growth of capital stock will require in addition only the capital formation proportion (level and trends) and the initial capital–

output ratio. If the typical growth rate of product is about 3 percent per year, if the net capital formation proportion rises from 5 to 15 percent, and if the total capital–output ratio at the beginning of the century is at least 6 to 1, the resulting growth rate of total capital stock, net of depreciation, would fall short of the growth rate of total product (see Table 8, line 7, column 5). But what evidence is there on: levels and trends in the net capital formation proportions; and levels of the initial capital–output ratios, for total and reproducible capital?

The United Nations collection of national accounts data provides measures of net and gross capital formation proportions for fifteen developed countries. For a recent quinquennium, 1963–1967, the net capital formation proportion is 15–16 percent or less in Belgium, Denmark, Italy, Sweden (inferred from its gross domestic capital formation proportion of 25 percent), the United Kingdom, Canada, and the United States. In seven other countries, France, Germany, the Netherlands, Norway, Switzerland, Australia, and New Zealand, it ranges from about 17 to about 21.5 percent; and for Japan it is at the exceptionally high level of 26.4 percent. The gross capital formation proportion displays a much narrower relative range. In the seven countries with moderate net capital formation proportions, ranging from 9.0 to 15.6 percent, the gross proportions range from 18 to 25 percent; and, excluding Japan, in the other countries it lies between 25 and 29 percent, not much higher. There is some suspicion that the *net* capital formation proportion is exaggerated because the allowance for capital consumption (generally based on original cost) does not take full account of the rise in prices of fixed capital goods.

For this reason and because of the rather exceptional character of the post-World War II period in the light of long-term growth before World War II, it seems best to assume, as a general observation, 15 percent as the characteristic terminal level to which the net capital formation proportion could rise during the century (or more) for which Table 8 illustrates various possible combinations.

Having set a terminal value for the net capital formation proportion, we must consider its trend over time. The most conspicuous cases of rise in the net domestic capital formation proportion imply a movement from about 5 or 6 percent at the beginning of the modern growth process. We need not concern ourselves here with the initial national proportion, which could be much lower, since the analysis of productivity in terms of domestic capital stock is preferable — in order to avoid mixing the ratios of domestically located resources to domestically originating output with the quite different ratios of foreign capital to the part of domestic output that represents returns on such capital. An initial net domestic capital formation proportion of about 5 to 6 percent can be observed in the Scandinavian countries, Italy, Japan, and, if we go back to the eighteenth century, Great Britain. But in other countries, particularly the United States, the initial level was appreciably higher; and the tripling of the net capital formation proportion — the assumption for Base III in Table 8 — did not occur. There is an unavoidable ambiguity about the *net* capital formation proportion in preindustrial periods, for reasons to be discussed later in connection with the initial capital–output ratio; and while a difference between a 5 and a 3 percent net capital formation proportion is only 2 percentage points, it has a marked effect on the long-term growth rate of capital stock. But we must use the general level that the evidence suggests.[6]

The capital formation proportion relates to additions to reproducible capital alone — although they may be embodied in some natural resources that are not reproducible (such as land or mines). But they do not, and are not intended to, cover additions to nonreproducible resources that do not result from investing part of the current product or parts of the labor and reproducible capital currently available.

Three sources of increase in the value (in constant prices) of nonreproducible capital stock may be envisaged. The first, representing inputs of labor and capital in improving the resources (converting land from prairie into cultivated acreage, for example), is included under current capital formation, and raises no conceptual problems. The second, resulting from the movement of population and changing availability of natural resources because of changing proximity, represents an expansion of the natural base of a country's economy because of better distribution of population, a larger population, or both; and, although it is a possible source of in-

6. For details see Simon Kuznets, "Quantitative Aspects of the Economic Growth of Nations: VI. Long-Term Trends in Capital Formation Proportions," *Economic Development and Cultural Change*, vol. IX, no. 4, part II (July 1961), appendix tables; and a somewhat later summary in Simon Kuznets, *Modern Economic Growth: Rate, Structure, and Spread* (New Haven: Yale University Press, 1966), table 5.3, pp. 236–239, for gross domestic and national capital formation proportions; and table 5.5, pp. 248–250, column 5, for net domestic capital formation proportions.

creased productivity, it represents no extra outlay of resources, no inputs. The third source, scientific discovery and development in which the direct inputs are minute, is associated with the factor most often cited as the source of growth of productivity — scientific progress and technological change. The measures here are intended to record the growth rate of capital stock as a source of capital input into additional product, input in this case meaning absorption of current product or consumption of existing capital stock. Increases in capital stock as a source of such additional inputs can originate only from net capital formation as usually defined, even if the latter is added to total (and not only reproducible) initial capital stock — productivity thus being measured under the condition of a *fixed* supply of nonreproducible resources, with nonearned additions to the latter treated as part of the productivity gain.[7]

The initial capital–product ratio — of total capital stock, net of depreciation, to net domestic product — should relate to the date of entry into modern economic growth, about a century ago for most countries, but back to the late 1830's for the United States and France, and to the late eighteenth century for Great Britain. But it suffices for our purposes to approximate this ratio in some early phase of modern economic growth.

The broad conclusion from scattered evidence is that the early total capital–product ratios were well above 5, and probably between 6 and 7. For Great Britain, the reproducible capital–national income ratio in 1885 was as high as 6.7; and with an allowance of 18 percent for land, the ratio for total wealth rises to over 8; while this is a peak figure, the earliest level that can be approximated, for 1865, would probably be about 7.[8] A recent compilation on national wealth sets the ratio of net wealth to product for Belgium in 1846 and 1896, the United States in the late 1890's, and Australia in 1903

7. An alternative procedure, which would include unearned additions to non-reproducible resources would only strengthen my conclusion that under realistic assumptions concerning the capital formation proportion and initial capital–product ratio, the rate of growth of total capital stock is likely to fall short of the rate of growth of total product. The inclusion would raise the average net capital formation proportion moderately, but it would reduce significantly any upward trend over time in this proportion, since the relative contribution of such gains in natural resources to total additions to capital has dropped markedly with the increase in reproducible capital formation.

8. See Phyllis Deane and W. A. Cole, *British Economic Growth, 1688–1959*, 2nd. ed. (Cambridge: Cambridge University Press, 1967), table 71, p. 274, for the reproducible capital–product ratio; and table 70, p. 271, for the composition of national wealth, including land.

between 6 and 9; and shows a general tendency for these ratios to decline over time to between 4 and 5.[9] Given this trend, and total capital–product ratios for the developed countries in the early 1950's ranging from 3.0 to 5.4, while for 1913–1914 they averaged over 5.5 (for a much larger number), a level of 6 to 7 at the initial date seems realistic.[10]

If the initial ratio of total capital to product is between 6 and 7, an initial ratio for reproducible capital can be set between 3 and 4. Two types of evidence support this conclusion. First, the shares of nonreproducible assets, particularly land and subsoil assets, in total wealth at early dates range between a third and a half. Thus, for Great Britain, Deane and Cole estimate the share of land in national wealth to be over 50 percent in 1798, 1812, and 1832. An early estimate for the United States by Raymond Goldsmith sets the share of land and subsoil assets in total domestic wealth (excluding consumers' durables) at about a half in 1805; about 45 percent in 1850; and about four-tenths in 1880.[11] The share of land in private tangible wealth in Australia was almost two-fifths in 1903, declining to one-fifth in 1956.[12] The share of land in total wealth in Denmark in 1880 was 44 percent; in Norway in 1884 about 36 percent; in Sweden in 1885 about 42 percent; and in Italy the share in total private wealth was 45 percent (including mines and quarries) in 1908, and declined to 38 percent in 1924–1925.[13]

The second type of evidence in support of an initial reproducible capital–product ratio of 3 to 4, specifically for the older countries, is the inferrable net capital formation proportion in the premodern past. In a 1965 paper I set the probable growth rate of total product

9. See Raymond Goldsmith and Christopher Saunders, eds., *Income and Wealth, Series VIII* (London: Bowes and Bowes, 1959), table VI, pp. 30–31.

10. The 1950 data are from *ibid.*, table VII, p. 32; the 1913–1914 data, by Josiah Stamp, were summarized in Simon Kuznets, "Quantitative Aspects of the Economic Growth of Nations: IV. Distribution of National Income by Factor Shares," *Economic Development and Cultural Change*, vol. VII, no. 3, part II (April 1959), appendix table 3, p. 65.

11. See "The Growth of Reproducible Wealth of the United States of America from 1805 to 1950," in Simon Kuznets, ed., *Income and Wealth, Series II* (London: Bowes and Bowes, 1953), table II, p. 310.

12. See J. M. Garland and R. W. Goldsmith, "The National Wealth of Australia," in Goldsmith and Saunders, *Income and Wealth*, p. 355.

13. The estimates for Denmark and Norway are by Falbehansen and for Sweden by Fahlbeck, quoted in Corrado Gini, *L'Ammontare e la Composizione della Ricchezza delle Nazioni*, 2nd. rev. ed. by Antonino Giannone (Turin: Unione Tipografica Editrice Torinese, 1962), p. 360. The estimates for Italy, by Gini, are from *ibid.*, p. 401.

in developed Western Europe over the long period 1500–1750 at roughly 0.4 percent per year, or 4.1 percent per decade.[14] For the century from 1750 to 1850, the rate would have to be materially higher — if only because of population growth, and perhaps also because growth in per capita product accelerated markedly. The rate of population growth for the developed European countries between 1750 and 1950 was between 0.5 and 0.7 percent per year.[15] With a minimum rate of growth of per capita product of about 0.2 percent per year, the annual rate of increase in total product would be 0.8 percent per year, about a quarter to a fifth of that typical of most developed countries in the century that followed (the much greater acceleration occurred in the growth rate of per capita product, from about 2 percent to about 15–17 percent per decade). With a premodern growth rate of total product of 0.8 percent per year, the net capital formation proportion that would cumulate to an initial reproducible stock–product ratio of 3 would be (3×0.8), or 2.4 percent; for one of 4 it would be (4×0.8), or 3.2 percent. These net capital formation proportions seem low enough to have been feasible within the level and structure of product that prevailed over the period, although the relations between net and gross product in preindustrial centuries are so ambiguous that it is difficult to define and measure net capital formation with sufficient specificity to lend meaning to differences between net capital formation proportions of 2 and 3 percent.[16]

If we may assume an initial capital–output ratio of 6 to 7 for total capital, and one of 3 to 4 for reproducible capital; and a capital formation proportion that rises from 5 to 15 percent (Base III in Table 8), several conclusions can be drawn from the illustrative cases.

First, the growth rate of total capital would be greater than the growth rate of total product *only* if total product grew at less than 2 percent per year. But if the latter were 2 percent, it is highly unlikely that the net capital formation proportion would rise as steeply as we have assumed, or that its average level would be as

14. See Simon Kuznets, "Capital Formation in Modern Economic Growth (and Some Implications for the Past)," *Third International Conference of Economic History, 1965,* vol. I (Paris and The Hague: Mouton, 1968), esp. pp. 30–31.

15. The figures for 1750 are from B. Ts. Urlanis, *Growth of Population in Europe* (in Russian, Moscow: Gospolitizdat, 1941), pp. 414–415; those for 1950 are from United Nations, *Demographic Yearbook, 1963* (New York, 1964), table 4.

16. See discussion in Kuznets, "Capital Formation in Modern Economic Growth," referred to in note 14.

high as 10 percent, for this level and trend would imply a net incremental capital–output ratio of 5 to 1 — far exceeding those found in the long-term records for several developed countries. For the more likely combination of the assumed net capital formation proportion with a growth rate of total product of at least 3 percent per year, an initial total capital–output ratio of 6 to 7 would yield a growth rate in the total stock of capital well below that of total product. This means that the growth rate of the per capita supply of total capital would be about 35 to 45 percent short of the growth rate of per capita product. This shortfall for total capital would be the greater, the higher the growth rate of total product (see columns 5–6, lines 8, 12).

Second, for the same plausible combinations, and an initial reproducible capital–output ratio of 3, the growth rate of reproducible capital would exceed the growth rate of product when the latter is 3 percent per year — particularly when the net capital formation proportion shows an upward trend. But when the initial reproducible capital–product ratio is about 4, and the growth rate of total product is 3 percent per year, the growth in reproducible capital will also fall short of that of product, even with a marked upward trend in the net capital formation proportion.

This general finding that the growth rate of total, and even of reproducible, capital would probably be lower than that of total product results from the assumed initial capital–output ratios and assumed level and trend in the net capital formation proportion. The high initial capital stock output ratios are clearly associated with the dominant role of natural resources in the preindustrial capital structure; and partly with the probability that even reproducible capital did not generate rapid enough growth in total output in the premodern period to yield an initial low reproducible capital–output ratio. The limitations on the level and trend of the capital formation proportions are presumably imposed by deepseated factors that affect the allocation of product between the present and the future. Thus, like the low rate of growth of manhours per capita, the low rate of growth of capital compared with total product is the result of a variety of basic factors that not only affected capital structure in the preindustrial past but also determined capital accumulation proportions during modern economic growth.

Finally, I should comment briefly on long-term trends in the rate of utilization of net capital stock. The fact that average hours per worker declined substantially over time does not mean that the average hours of use of capital stock moved accordingly: for some stock, such as residential buildings, no such inference is possible; nor is it possible for many industries that operate on a twenty-four-hour basis for technological or social reasons, and the shares of these industries in total capital stock may well have risen. But the question of hours of use is irrelevant, unless longer hours mean greater noncurrent capital costs (that is, capital inputs) and shorter hours mean lower costs — which is hardly likely. Unless capital is over-driven in excessive time use, and loses thereby more than its regular depreciation rate (which is a function of technological progress rather than of chronological hours), capital costs are not affected by hours of use. When shorter hours represent involuntary failure to use capital because of social or technological inefficiency, capital inputs must still be counted fully, since such failure reduces residual productivity — as it should. In short, we may accept the growth rate of capital stock net of depreciation as a proper approximation to the growth rate of capital input into additional product, without allowing for secular trends in hours of use.

Combined inputs and residual productivity

The growth rates for labor and capital inputs are combined by weighting the former by the share of labor compensation and the latter by the share of returns on assets (capital) in total net product at factor cost — on the obvious premise that the contribution of the two factors is best measured by the economic rewards that society bestows on them. The implications as to the effectiveness of prices as a proper weighting system, without distortion by monopoly, ignorance, and so on, are analogous to those involved in using prices to weight output. Also no allowance is made for possible effects of scale, which is not reflected in rates of growth, or for the possibility that one or both factors have a specific relation to growth of output not reflected in a simple fractional coefficient. These problems, more closely related to productivity than to input, will be considered when sources of productivity are discussed.

The distribution of net product at factor cost between labor and capital involves the allocation of the income of individual entrepreneurs between the labor and capital components — and this problem weighs more heavily in the early phases of growth, when entrepreneurial income is a larger share of the total. But, when account is taken of the results of differing allocations of income of individual entrepreneurs, the general levels and trends in the shares of compensation of labor and income from assets can be fairly easily established.

Within the time range for which approximate data are available, mostly over the past century and a half, the share of labor varied from somewhat over 50 to close to 80 percent; and that of income from assets from well over 40 and perhaps close to 50 percent to about 20 percent. In the post-World War II period, 1950–1962, the shares in national income for nine Western countries range from 72 to 79 percent for labor income (for Italy and the United States respectively), with most of the countries showing shares of 73 to 74 percent; and the shares of income from assets lie between 21 and 28 percent.[17] The longer-term records show much higher shares of income from assets in the early periods, and a distinct decline to the recent levels. Thus, for the United Kingdom the share (average for the two methods of allocating entrepreneurial income) was 44 percent in 1860–1869, and declined to 24 percent in 1954–1960; for France it declined from about 36 percent (excluding corporate savings) in 1853 to about 18 percent in 1954–1960; for Germany it declined from about 35 percent in 1895 to about 25 percent in 1954–1960 (although with a change in territory).[18] The records are scanty, but the trend is unmistakable: one may reasonably argue that over the illustrative century of modern economic growth (which can be expanded to a century and a half without doing much violence to the historical trend) the share of labor income has risen, probably from about 55 to 75 percent, while that of income from assets has declined, probably from about 45 to about 25 percent.

These trends might have been expected, at least as far as direction, if not necessarily magnitude, is concerned. With the much greater rise in capital stock than in labor supply per capita, the price of, or return to, capital should have risen less or declined more than the price of, or return to, labor. Furthermore, as Table 8 suggests, one would have expected the average total capital–income ratio in most countries to have declined — since the growth rate of

17. See Denison, *Why Growth Rates Differ*, table 4–1, p. 38.
18. See Kuznets, *Modern Economic Growth*, table 4.2, pp. 168–170.

total capital stock was lower than that of total net product (the shift of the latter to the factor cost base would not affect the growth rate significantly). The share of income from assets in national or domestic product at factor cost equals the total capital stock–product ratio, multiplied by the rate of return on capital stock. If initially the capital–net product ratio was 6 to 7, and the rate of return on capital stock was, say, 7 percent, the share of income from assets should have been between 42 and 49 percent. If the total capital–net product ratio dropped to between 4 and 5, and the return on capital dropped to between 5 and 6 percent, the share of income from assets should have declined to between 20 and 30 percent. Although illustrative, all these figures are fairly realistic and indicate a substantial decline in the share of income from assets which resulted from the relative growth rates of labor, capital, and product.

Given these levels and trends in shares of labor income and income from assets, we can use the illustrative analysis in Table 8, together with the findings derived from Tables 6 and 7, to estimate the contribution of the growth of combined inputs per capita to the growth of per capita product. Let us assume an annual growth rate of total product of 3 percent; of population of 1 percent; and hence of per capita product of 1.98 percent. The estimated decline in man-hours per capita can be set at 3 percent per decade, or at 0.3 percent per year. By using Base III in Table 8 as the combination most favorable to a higher contribution of capital that is still realistic, and an initial capital–product ratio of 6, we would get a growth rate of total capital stock of 2.54 percent per year (growth factor of 12.3 in line 8, column 5 of Table 8, reduced to an annual basis), and of capital stock per capita of 1.52 percent per year. In combining the contributions of labor and capital over a century, we should take weights intermediate between the initial 55–45 and the terminal 75–25 distribution. If we weight the decline of manhours per capita of 0.3 percent per year by two-thirds, and the rise in capital stock per capita of 1.52 percent per year by one-third, we get a growth rate in combined inputs per capita of 0.49 percent per year, or about a quarter of the total growth rate of per capita product. The remaining three-quarters, or more correctly, (101.98) : (100.49), converted into a percentage, that is, 1.48 percent per year, represents the growth rate of productivity. A similar calculation, which assumes a 4 percent growth rate of total product but leaves all other assumptions the same, yields an annual growth rate of combined inputs per capita of 0.55 percent, compared with a growth rate of per capita product of 2.97 percent.

In short, despite a favorable allowance that triples the net capital formation proportion, combined inputs contribute a limited fraction, between a quarter and a fifth, of growth in per capita product. The balance can be attributed to the growth of productivity. And, given the assumptions of the accepted national economic accounting framework, and the basic demographic and institutional processes that control labor supply, capital accumulation, and initial capital–output ratios, this major conclusion — that the distinctive feature of modern economic growth, the high rate of growth of per capita product, is for the most part attributable to a high rate of growth in productivity — is inevitable.

In order to indicate that this finding is not the result of a choice of illustrative coefficients in Table 8, or of unrealistic assumptions concerning the growth of labor input, I present specific calculations of input and output rates of growth for long periods for five developed countries for which the data are available, plus a similar summary for the post-World War II decade for nine developed countries (Table 9).

It should be emphasized that the growth rates in column 3 refer to net stock of reproducible fixed capital, and are, therefore, somewhat too high. Also the post-World War II period was one of vigorous capital accumulation and full employment — full mobilization and utilization of factor inputs. Finally, the growth rates in column 1 should be for net rather than for gross output; in which case, they would have been slightly lower.

The interesting aspect of the evidence is that, with few exceptions, the growth rate of even fixed capital stock was lower than that of total product (for the long-term records, the only exceptions are for 1879 to 1899 for Norway, and 1889 to 1929 for the United States). And, with one or two exceptions, the contribution of the growth rate of factor inputs per capita was a minor fraction of the growth rate of per capita product.

Furthermore, in three of the five countries with long records (Norway, the United States, and Canada) the growth rate of productivity accelerated in the later period; in Canada and Norway this acceleration occurred despite higher growth rates in capital stock. With the rate of decline in hours greater since the early twentieth

Table 9. Long-term trends and post-World War II changes in rates of growth
of input and productivity, conventional economic accounting,
selected developed countries.

	Rates of growth per year (%)							
	Output (1)	Labor (2)	Capital (3)	Com- bined input (4)	Output per unit of input (5)	Popu- lation (6)	Output per capita (7)	Ratio of col. 5 to col. 7 (8)
A. Long-term changes								
United Kingdom, GDP								
1. 1855 to 1913	1.82	0.74	1.43	0.98	0.83	0.86	0.95	0.87
2. 1925–29 to 1963	1.93	0.82	1.77	1.09	0.83	0.47	1.45	0.57
France, GDP								
3. 1913 to 1966	2.33	−0.50	1.95	0.18	2.15	0.40	1.92	1.12
Norway, GDP								
4. 1879 to 1899	1.72	0.68	1.87	0.93	0.78	0.85	0.86	0.91
5. 1899 to 1956	2.80	0.25	2.47	0.72	2.07	0.79	1.99	1.04
United States, GNP								
6. 1889 to 1929	3.70	1.74	3.76	2.43	1.24	1.71	1.96	0.63
7. 1929 to 1957	2.95	0.53	1.01	0.64	2.30	1.24	1.69	1.36
Canada, GNP								
8. 1891 to 1926	2.96	1.82	2.74	2.02	0.92	1.93	1.01	0.91
9. 1926 to 1956	3.89	0.77	2.86	1.18	2.68	1.70	2.15	1.25
B. Changes from 1950 to 1962 (national income)								
10. United Kingdom	2.38	0.40	2.30	0.82	1.55	0.44	1.93	0.80
11. France	4.70	0.21	3.43	0.95	3.71	1.00	3.66	1.01
12. Belgium	3.03	0.45	1.51	0.74	2.27	0.54	2.48	0.92
13. Netherlands	4.52	0.85	4.00	1.67	2.80	1.29	3.19	0.88
14. Germany (FR)	7.26	1.71	5.36	2.67	4.47	1.13	6.06	0.74
15. Denmark	3.36	0.60	3.87	1.41	1.92	0.70	2.64	0.73
16. Norway	3.47	−0.12	3.44	0.80	2.65	0.91	2.54	1.04
17. Italy	5.95	0.78	2.50	1.26	4.63	0.60	5.32	0.87
18. United States	3.36	0.80	3.88	1.46	1.87	1.71	1.62	1.15

Lines 1–3: Population, output, and input are from R. C. O. Mathews and others,
"Economic Growth in the United Kingdom, 1855–1963," and E. Malinvaud and others,
"Croissance Française," both mimeographed preliminary reports for the Social Science
Research Council study of Postwar Economic Growth in Historical Perspective. Entries

in column 4 are averages of growth rates for labor (manhours) and capital (fixed capital only) weighted by 0.65 and 0.35 respectively for line 1, and 0.72 and 0.28 for lines 2 and 3 — these weights derived from the same sources.

Lines 4–9: Columns 1–4 are derived from N. H. Lithwick, *Economic Growth in Canada: A Quantitative Analysis* (Toronto: University of Toronto Press, 1967), tables 53-58, pp. 53–57. Manhours and fixed capital are used. Column 5 is derived by dividing (100 + column 1) by (100 + column 4). Column 6 for the early years is from M. C. Urquhart and K. A. H. Buckley, eds., *Historical Statistics of Canada* (Cambridge: Cambridge University Press, 1965), the United States Bureau of the Census, *Historical Statistics of the United States, Colonial Times to 1957* (Washington, D.C., 1961), and Central Bureau of Statistics of Norway, *Trends in Norwegian Economy, 1865–1960*, no. 16 of *Samfunnsøkonomiske Studier* (Oslo, 1966); for the recent years it is from the United Nations, *Demographic Yearbook, 1965.*

Lines 10–18: Columns 1–5 are based on Edward F. Denison, *Why Growth Rates Differ: Postwar Experience in Nine Western Countries* (Washington, D.C.: The Brookings Institution, 1967), tables 21-1, 21-5, 21-7, 21-9, 21-11, 21-13, 21-15, 21-17, 21-19 (pp. 298, 302, 304, 306, 308, 310, 312, 314, 316), for the growth rates of national income (adjusted) and the contributions of labor (excluding education) and capital, already weighted for combination in column 4. I used *ibid.*, table 4-1, p. 38, showing the shares of labor and capital in national income, to reconstruct the unweighted growth rates of labor and capital in columns 2 and 3.

Population is from the *Demographic Yearbook, 1965* and *1967*, table 4.

century, and the rise in the net capital formation proportion probably reaching some constant (if higher) level well before the end of our long period, the rate of growth of combined inputs per capita would decline — over and beyond the decline caused by the shift in the weights of labor income and income from assets (the rising share of labor income would mean greater weight of the more slowly growing input factor). While the growth rate of per capita inputs would thus decline, the findings in Chapter I indicate no retardation in the growth rate of product per capita. One might, thus, expect the growth rate of productivity in most countries to be higher in the twentieth century than in the nineteenth.

Nonconventional Costs: Current and Capital

The possibility that conventional national economic accounting treats some outputs that are really costs of production as *final* rather than as *intermediate* products requires serious scrutiny. This is particularly true in view of the differences in growth rates among the several productive branches of the economy which cause changes in the industrial structure of production (such as the decline in the share of agriculture or the rise in the share of manufacturing), shifts characteristic of modern economic growth, which will be examined in later chapters. Such changes in the structure of production are usually associated with, indeed require, changes in other aspects of social structure — not only economic but also political and in the long run even ideological.

In their effects on the scale and character of the firm and the occupational demands generated by the new technology, shifts in the structure of production produce significant changes in conditions of life and work of the members of society who participate actively in economic production — and this involves a large proportion of the members of a nation, and a most important activity for them and their dependents. If modern economic growth called for rapid urbanization, it must be recognized that urban life required more resources to satisfy the countryside level of wants for food, sanitation, recreation, transportation from home to job, and so on. Furthermore, the greater complexity of industrial and other economic units may have required larger inputs into governmental regulation and adjudication. Many of these extra outlays, extra inputs of real resources, appear in national economic accounts under either household or government consumption, and are treated as *final* product, as a component of unduplicated aggregate output. But to the extent that the outlays, either by households or by government, are current expenditures necessary for the adequate participation in or smooth operation of the modern production process, they are intermediate, not final product; their inclusion represents duplication; and if their proportion to total product rises over time, their inclusion exaggerates the growth rate of unduplicated economic product.

This overstatement will be reflected in the measure of productivity. But, in addition, effects of structural changes on conditions of work give rise to required inputs that may have been omitted in the calculation cited in the preceding section; and such omitted costs are more relevant than economies of scale and similar nonlinearities. As the expanding literature in this field indicates, these *required* inputs may lie in education and research and development — which are not included under capital formation in the conventional economic accounts, except when embodied in structures, equipment, or inventories. The basic assumption is that such additions to inputs — these extra resources (in education, for instance) — are required by the changing production system for augmenting its output, paralleling in a way the requirement for material capital. The same assumption could be made regarding at least part of other consumption expenditures — on health, recreation, housing, and so on — so long as it contributes to the improvement of quality of labor, and such improvement is a necessary (if not sufficient) condition of greater productivity.

If education and other outlays on improvement of quality of labor are viewed as capital investment, consequences flow for the measurement not only of inputs and productivity, but also of output or income, net of capital consumption. Since net output or income is the sum of final consumption (including government) and capital formation, several items — educational, health, and similar outlays, all or in part — must be shifted from consumption to capital formation. These now become analogous to capital purchases; but since they are gross capital formation, they should be reduced by current consumption of capital embodied in human beings. And the resulting reduction in net national product would be in addition to that caused by the allowance for higher real costs needed to offset changes in conditions of life imposed by changes in the structure of production. On the other hand, time devoted to formal education and to training on the job must be treated as investment — and the income foregone in these two uses of time added to national income, thus enlarging the total product beyond its conventional scope.

In identifying and measuring such nonconventional costs we face the difficult problem of distinguishing between productivity-raising by-products of changing patterns of life at large — which, while contributing to the growth of residual productivity of the type measured at the beginning of this chapter, are not "costs" — and the specific consumer expenditures made in response to changed conditions of work, where the outlay does represent costs, current or capital, geared specifically to an economic output. Over the long historical period of modern economic growth the marked rise in food supply and the improved health conditions should, all other conditions being equal, have made for a better quality of the body of workers. But if the additional food, health, and recreation outlays are treated as so many economic costs (rather than as final consumption), the implication would be that living is for work; and the distinction between final consumption, or product, and intermediate consumption, or costs, so basic in the ideological framework of modern society as well as in economic analysis and measurement, would be obliterated. However, if conditions of work under modern economic growth require some special outlays by consumers (either to protect health more than would otherwise be needed, or supply more food, or provide more recreation), now included under consumer outlay, these are clearly intermediate products, current costs, not final returns. Likewise, in the case of education, can we assume that it is all preparation for work and contains no element of ultimate consumption as part of life in general? There may be no question in the case of the highly specialized, work-oriented training secured in trade and professional schools, or in the case of training on the job — both of which seem to be geared to specific types of work. But is not the largest part of formal education preparation for living? The problems involved in distinguishing between final consumption, which despite its "finality" may contribute to productivity, and specific adjustments and responses to changed conditions of economic output, which represent current or capital costs, are difficult; and no hard and fast rules can be set. We face similar recalcitrant problems in attempting a functional analysis of government consumption (treated in conventional economic accounting as final product). Such an analysis would distinguish between direct services to business, costs of sustaining the social and economic fabric, and final products — material capital formation, mixed capital and consumer goods represented by public educational services, and final consumer goods in the form of government health and recreational services. But the fact that the difficulties in drawing the distinction are formidable is no reason for dismissing the major problems involved, as is done in conventional economic accounting; and for not attempting approximations — if only illustrative — to the quantitative implications.

What adjustments can be made in conventional growth rates to take account of the extra current and capital costs of modern economic growth? Rough as the answer to this question must be, I attempt to suggest the order of magnitude indicated by economic costs. In this attempt a clear distinction should be drawn between the effects of adjustments on the absolute level and structure of net product per capita, and those on the growth rates of per capita product and productivity. This distinction must be made because on some plausible assumptions the effects on level and structure are far greater than those on the growth rates. Thus if we start with a conventionally defined net product, we would: (a) subtract all extra consumption outlay imposed by extra costs of urbanization; (b) subtract all extra government outlays on goods (government consumption) associated with additional regulation, adjudication, and so on (caused in part by greater complexity of modern economic growth) or with greater costs of maintaining internal peace and external security; (c) shift outlays on education, by household or government, out of consumption and include them, together with income foregone in formal education and in training on the job, under *gross* capital formation (as educational investment), and then offset them in part by subtraction of current consumption of human capital, that is, of the stock of education, and so forth, embodied in the present labor force; and finally (d) reclassify that part of the resulting net total that represents net return on human capital stock, now included under labor compensation, as return on capital, analogous to net income from material capital assets. The reduction involved in the first two subtractions, by far the larger operations quantitatively, would depend upon the reference base used, the base in comparison with which extra current costs are calculated. If that base were in some hazy golden past before cities were established, when provision for the higher costs of urban life was not needed, and if it were to include an ideally minimal allowance for government consumption, free of the burdens of today's swollen military establishments and augmented civilian bureaucracies, the two sets of deductions would be enormous, absolutely and relatively, and the shift in functional shares within the reduced total (referred to under d) would also be marked. Such large adjustments should be borne in mind when comparisons are made between levels and structure of net product among developed and less developed countries in cross-section studies.[19]

But the effects of the adjustments on growth rates are less marked because the reference base in this case is the position of the country (now developed) at the initial phase of its growth; and the conventional net product at this early phase already contains some elements of duplication, some nonconventional current and capital costs. The adjustments of the growth rates are then limited to the

19. The shift in the developed countries to a higher share of returns from capital is particularly illuminating in comparisons between the developed and the less developed countries. While the former have a larger absolute *material* stock of capital per head, their ratio of total material capital to output is no greater than that in the less developed countries. The crucial difference lies in the greater absolute and *proportionate* stock of human capital — of investments in education, health care, feeding, and so on, of the population. If the stock of human capital, over and above the minimum level of unskilled laborers living on the bare necessities (as is true of much of the labor in the less developed countries) is included, both the capital–output ratio and the share of returns from such capital become much higher in the developed than in the less developed countries.

historical increase in the proportions of duplication, and so on, and do not allow for the total difference between reality and some ideal base suggested by absolute, if illuminating and plausible, criteria.

The effects on growth rates of the possible rise in the *proportion* of the intermediate products that represent nonconventional current costs, and of the shift to capital formation of items conventionally treated as consumption can be approximated. Much of the calculation that follows uses data for the United States because they are most easily available. While the United States is hardly a typical economic growth case (if any country can be that), it does illustrate some of the trends suggested.

(a) Urbanization over the last century and a half has been primarily a product of economic growth, a result of the technological changes that made large-scale operation and economies feasible. A large-scale plant implies a dense population community, and a shift of the working, hence total, population to the cities — which in turn involves an increase in economic inputs to attain the same level of satisfaction as in the countryside — for most needs, if not for those supplied by products of urbanized industry. This higher input cost is reflected either in higher prices in the city than in the countryside for the same product (such as food); or in outlay on additional "goods" required only because of the difference between rural and urban conditions of life (such as the need for more sanitation facilities in the cities because of greater population density). In approximating extra costs of city life, the distinction between higher prices for the same goods or greater outlays for the same satisfaction of needs is of some interest; but we are searching for the combined effect of the two.

Nathan Koffsky provided some information on comparative prices for 1941 of the same goods for the farm population, on the one hand, and all urban population, on the other. Even though, because of wide quality differentials, no price difference was assumed for rent, the proportional excess of prices in the city was either 14 percent (city expenditure weights) or 30 percent (farm expenditure weights).[20] Using these price data, but allowing roughly for differences in city size, I attempted an adjustment relevant to the move-

20. See his paper, "Farm and Urban Purchasing Power," in Conference on Research in Income and Wealth, *Studies in Income and Wealth*, vol. 11 (New York: National Bureau of Economic Research, 1949), table 8, p. 170.

ment of national income in the United States for 1870–1940, which indicated that the inflation of product over the seventy-year span would be about 10 percent; and that the growth rate would be reduced accordingly.[21] But this adjustment proved inadequate, because it took account only of price differences for identical goods; also it weighted the price differentials by population, not by volume of consumption (in current unadjusted prices), which made for an upward bias in the adjustment.

A more acceptable approximation is suggested by the method followed in Table 10. Here I take advantage of the studies on family expenditures in the United States, which distinguish farm, rural nonfarm, and urban families; and for 1935–1936 also distinguish four city-size groups. A comparison of consumption per capita for families with identical income per capita yields an approximation of the greater consumption in the cities because of higher costs (resulting either from higher prices or larger quantities to satisfy the same wants), assuming that the propensity to save is the same for the two groups. Since, in general, families of farm operators have a somewhat higher propensity to save at the same real income level, the estimate of greater consumption costs in nonfarm areas is somewhat exaggerated. But this bias makes the conclusion all the stronger.

The technique followed was to calculate income and consumption per person for the farm and other population groups, classified by income per family; and then apply the relation of consumption to income established for the farm families to the other groups to derive their *estimated* consumption — under the hypothetical living conditions of the countryside. The ratio of actual to estimated consumption for the nonfarm population groups, which is always above 1.0, is then an approximation to the relative costliness of nonfarm life (lines 5, 10). For 1935–1936, the data used are limited to nonrelief families and total income underlies the classification; but the exclusion of relief families affects the results slightly, since the difference in costliness of life is best measured for groups above the relief or poverty level (the latter also account for rather small proportions of total consumption). For 1960–1961 the data cover both families and individuals, and money income (after taxes) is

21. See Simon Kuznets, "Long-Term Changes in the National Income of the United States of America since 1870," in Kuznets, *Income and Wealth, Series II*, table 6, p. 61.

Table 10. Effects of urbanization on the relation of current consumption expenditures to income per capita, United States, 1870 and 1960.

A. Relation of current consumption expenditures to per capita income, farm, rural nonfarm, and four subgroups of urban population

	Farm (1)	Rural non-farm (2)	Urban (3)	Cities			
				Small (4)	Me-dium (5)	Large (6)	Metrop-olises (7)

1935–36 data, nonrelief families (of 2 or more)

	Farm (1)	Rural non-farm (2)	Urban (3)	Small (4)	Medium (5)	Large (6)	Metropolises (7)
1. Total income per capita ($)	286	426	568	447	490	622	773
2. Same, excluding gifts and direct taxes	279	409	539	436	471	614	727
3. Current consumption, per capita ($)	244	357	478	401	423	537	635
4. Line 3 as % of line 2	87.5	87.3	88.7	92.0	89.8	87.5	87.3
5. Ratio of actual to estimated consumption (on basis of farm)	1.00	1.17	1.34	1.23	1.26	1.38	1.52
6. Line 3 as ratio of farm level	1.00	1.46	1.96	1.64	1.73	2.20	2.60
7. Current consumption adjusted for internal price differentials, farm basis = 1.00 (line 6 : line 5)	1.00	1.25	1.46	1.33	1.37	1.59	1.71

1960–61 data, families and individuals, money income after taxes for groups with family income of $2,000 and over

	Farm (1)	Rural non-farm (2)	Urban (3)	Small (4)	Medium (5)	Large (6)	Metropolises (7)
8. Money income after taxes, per capita ($)	1,358	1,471	1,968	—	—	—	—
9. Current consumption per capita ($)	1,007	1,321	1,780	—	—	—	—
10. Ratio of actual to estimated consumption (on basis of farm)	1.00	1.25	1.47	—	—	—	—
11. Line 9 as ratio of farm level	1.00	1.31	1.77	—	—	—	—
12. Current consumption adjusted for internal price differentials, farm basis = 1.00 (line 11 : line 10)	1.00	1.05	1.20	—	—	—	—

Table 10 — continued

B. Effects of urbanization, based on division among rural farm, rural nonfarm, and urban population

	1870			1960		
	Farm (1)	Rural non-farm (2)	Urban (3)	Farm (4)	Rural non-farm (5)	Urban (6)
13. Shares in population (%)	44.6	29.8	25.6	7.6	22.6	69.8
14. Weights of consumption per capita	1.0	1.3	1.8	1.0	1.3	1.8
15. Shares in total current consumption (%)	34.46	29.93	35.61	4.67	18.07	77.26
16. Comparative cost (based on line 10)	1.0	1.2	1.45	1.0	1.2	1.45
17. Shares in consumption adjusted by line 16 (%)	34.46	24.94	24.56	4.67	15.06	53.28
18. Effects of urbanization (on conventional measures)	sum of columns 4–6, line 17, divided by sum of columns 1–3, line 17, or (73.01 : 83.96) = 0.870 — a reduction of 13%.					

C. Effects of urbanization, based also on distinction of four city-size groups

			Cities			
	Farm (1)	Rural non-farm (2)	Small (3)	Me-dium (4)	Large (5)	Over 1 million (6)
1870						
19. Shares in population (%)	44.6	29.8	10.5	4.4	10.7	0
20. Weights of consumption per capita	1.0	1.3	1.5	1.7	2.0	2.3
21. Shares in total current consumption (%)	34.85	30.27	12.31	5.85	16.72	0
22. Comparative cost index	1.0	1.2	1.3	1.35	1.54	1.7
23. Shares in consumption adjusted by line 22 (%)	34.85	25.23	9.47	4.33	10.86	0
1960						
24. Shares in population (%)	7.6	22.6	19.9	16.1	22.1	11.7
25. Shares in total current consumption (%)	4.60	17.77	18.06	16.56	26.73	16.28

Table 10 — continued

	(1)	(2)	(3)	(4)	(5)	(6)
26. Shares in consumption adjusted by line 22 (%)	4.60	14.81	13.89	12.27	17.36	9.58
27. Effects of urbanization	sum of line 26 divided by sum of line 23, or (72.51 : 84.74) = 0.856 — a reduction of 14.4%.					

—: information not available.

Small cities are those with 2,500 to 25,000 population; medium are those from 25,000 to 100,000; large cities are those from 100,000 to 1,500,000 in panel A and to 1,000,000 in panel C.

Lines 1–3, columns 1–3: Number of persons, distributed by family income groups, is from National Resources Planning Board, *Family Expenditures in the United States* (Washington, D.C., June 1941), table 362, p. 120. Aggregate income, consumption, and outlay on gifts and personal taxes, by family income groups are from *ibid.*, table 372, p. 123, for farm families; table 386, p. 127, for rural nonfarm families; and table 400, p. 130, for urban families. *Columns 4–7:* Line 1 is derived from National Resources Committee, *Consumer Incomes in the United States* (Washington, D.C., 1938), table 7, p. 23. Lines 2 and 3 are based on the sources cited below for line 5.

Line 5: The procedure is described in the text. For columns 1–3 the underlying data are given in the sources cited in the notes to lines 1–3. *Columns 4–7:* Average income, average consumption, and average outlay on gifts and personal taxes per family, by family income classes up to $10,000, are given in *Family Expenditures*, table 144, p. 51, for farm families; table 195, p. 66, for small-city families; table 197, p. 66, for medium-city families; table 199, p. 67, for large-city families; and table 201, p. 68, for families in metropolises. For families with incomes of $10,000 or more, average income, average income excluding gifts and personal taxes, and average consumption per family are assumed to be the same in the four city-size groups as for all urban families, as derived from *ibid.*, table 400. The number of families in each city-size group is given in *Consumer Expenditures*, table 9 B, p. 97, and the average number of persons per family for all cities, by family income classes, is given in *Family Expenditures*, table 362, p. 120. The preliminary distribution of number of persons, by family income classes, for the four city-size groups, based on these two sets of series, is adjusted to the total number of persons in each city-size group, derived from *Consumer Expenditures*, table 7, p. 23. Per capita income, income excluding gifts and personal taxes, and consumption were then calculated (for lines 1–3); and on the basis of per capita income excluding gifts and personal taxes and outlay on consumption by family income classes for farm families, derived from *Family Expenditures*, table 144, p. 51, and table 362, p. 120, consumption in the four city-size groups comparable with farm consumption was estimated by the procedure described in the text.

Lines 8–9: The underlying data are from "Consumer Expenditures and Income: Rural Farm Population, United States, 1961," *USDA Consumer Expenditure Survey Report no. 5* (Washington, D.C., April 1965), table 1, p. 14; "Consumer Expenditures and Income: Rural Nonfarm Areas in the United States, 1961," *BLS Report no. 237–88* (Washington, D.C., June 1964), table 1, p. 9; and "Consumer Expenditures and Income: Urban United States, 1960–61," *BLS Report no. 237–38* (Washington, D.C., April 1964), table 1A, p. 10. Families and single individuals, classified by money income after taxes, are shown for ten income groups. My calculations exclude units with income of less than $2,000, which accounted for 24.6 percent of farm units, 20.1 percent of rural nonfarm units, and 11.1 percent of urban units.

Line 10: Estimated by the procedure described in the text.

Lines 13, 19, 24: Underlying data are from the Bureau of the Census, *Historical Statistics of the United States, Colonial Times to 1967, Continuation to 1962 and Revisions* (Washington, D.C., 1965), series 34a–50a with farm population extrapolated from 1920 to 1870 by the movement of labor force in agriculture given in Kendrick, *Productivity Trends*, table A-VII, p. 308. The definition of urban population adopted in 1950 (to include suburban population with urban) was followed, and the additional population was apportioned between the large-city group and the group of cities with 1 million or more, proportionately to their population in 1960 before such inclusion.

Lines 14, 20: Line 14 was taken, by assumption, from the weights shown in line 11 (for 1960–61), rounded. Line 20 is the same as line 14, with the city group weights derived from lines 11 and 6.

Lines 16, 22: Based, by assumption, on lines 10 and 5. The cost index in line 10 (for 1960–61) underestimates slightly the relative costliness, because of omission of family units with income less than $2,000; but no adjustment is warranted. Line 22 is based on line 16, with the distinctions among city-size groups based on line 5.

the base of classification and the datum on incomes, but in the calculations I used only data for units with money income after taxes of $2,000 and over — minimizing the effects of omission of income in kind.

It is significant that the ratio of actual to estimated consumption (that is, the index of relative costliness of nonfarm life) shows a steady progression as we move from farm to rural nonfarm, then to cities of increasing size. We also find that consumption per person is higher in the cities than on the farms, and only partly because of higher costs. This means that when we apply the cost differentials to measure their impact in the earlier decades compared with the recent, we must allow for the higher per capita consumption of the nonfarm population. The final calculation, in panels B and C, indicates that the cumulative effect over the nine decades was to inflate the growth factor by a seventh or an eighth. Thus, if the growth factor for total consumption over the nine decades was, say, 10, the adjustment would reduce it to 8.56 or 8.70.

The approximation is crude, but there seems to be nothing in the procedure that would minimize this moderate adjustment. A downward bias in the adjustment could result if I exaggerated the differences in 1870 in favor of larger per capita consumption in the cities (that is, if weights in line 14, columns 2–3, or those in line 20, columns 2–6, are too high). But even on the extreme assumption — that per capita consumption is the same for all population groups so that we use population as weights — the adjustment ratio would be 0.856 in panel B and 0.854 in panel C, scarcely a significant change. Or there could be a downward bias because I am, in fact, underestimating the differences in cost of consumption in cities in the 1960's. Yet the procedure would yield a high estimate, since it includes under higher costs of consumption in the cities the possibly lower propensity to save of urban families. Finally, my allocation of population among farm, rural nonfarm, and city-size groups within urban population could be wrong, but this is unlikely since the base is provided by continuous population censuses, and suburbs are included with the large-city population in 1960.

It may be concluded that over the nine decades and for a country like the United States, the proportion of intermediate costs to terminal consumption was roughly 15 percent; or for an illustrative century back to the 1860's some 16 percent. Since the rate of urbanization was far higher in the United States than in Japan and the older developed countries of Europe, this is a generous allowance for the effects of higher costs of consumption and the resulting proportion of intermediate products in the conventional measure of total private consumption.

The adjustment above is for the effects of urbanization, and makes no allowance for possible trends in the proportion of intermediate products in total consumption by the *farm* population. Offhand, it seems unlikely that long-term rises in this proportion (other than for costs of education, considered separately below) in the course of modern economic growth could have been substantial. But a tested answer would require a detailed scrutiny of the changing composition of consumption by farm families, not feasible here. For the present the effects of economic growth on the structure of the consumption of farm population are neglected, and the adjustment is limited to differential effects of growing urbanization.

Since we are concerned with the effects on the growth rate of net national product, rather than on that of consumption, the adjustment should be shifted to reflect the increased proportion of intermediate products in terminal aggregate net product (net rather than gross to remove the duplication involved in capital consumption, and allow for expansion of the latter to reflect the shift of education to capital investment). This shift is most conveniently made in two steps. First, the share of consumption expenditures in GNP, in the 1960's and a century ago is established; then the share of capital consumption in GNP, in the 1960's and a century ago is estimated — and this permits the last step in the calculation.

For fifteen developed countries — Japan, the four overseas offshoots, and all of those in Europe — United Nations data show that the average share of private consumer expenditures in GNP in 1963–1967 is 60 percent. For seven of them (the United Kingdom, Germany, Italy, Norway, Sweden, Canada, and the United States) we can approximate the share of private consumption expenditures in GNP in the 1860's or (for Italy) at the beginning of industrialization. For these countries (for which the share of private consumption expenditures in GNP in 1963–1967 is also 60 percent), the average share about a century earlier was 83 percent.[22] We can then set the typical movement over the last century as a decline from about 83 to about 60 percent of GNP.

For fourteen developed countries, the share of capital consumption in GNP for 1963–1967 is, on the average, about 9.7 percent. For seven of them (the United Kingdom, Italy, Denmark, Norway, the United States, Canada, and Australia), for which the average ratio in the 1960's was 9.6 percent, the similar ratio about a century ago averaged about 5.5 percent.[23] We can, therefore, conclude that the increased proportion of intermediate products, associated with urbanization, amounted, over the illustrative century to the 1960's, to $[0.16 \times (60 \div 90.3) \div (83 \div 94.5)]$, or 12 percent of net national product.

(b) What are the effects of a possible increase in the nonconventional costs included in government consumption? *Total* government consumption in 1963–1967 was, on the average, about 14.7 percent of GNP for the fifteen developed countries. In the seven for which we have long-term series on the breakdown of GNP by use of product, the share of total government consumption in GNP in the 1860's or at the beginning of industrialization was 4.4 percent (see countries listed for the share of private consumption in the source quoted in note 22), compared with their 1960's average of 16.6 percent. This suggests an upward trend over a century in the share of total government consumption in GNP from roughly 4 percent to 14.7 percent.

But we are concerned with the intermediate costs of government — expenditures on administration, defense, and the like. The United Nations data for the 1960's show for nine countries (Australia, Denmark, Germany, Italy, New Zealand, Sweden, the United Kingdom, the Netherlands, and the United States) the major components of government consumption expenditures of which three (education and research, health, and miscellaneous welfare services) can be identified as final product; the remainder, largely general administration and defense, can be identified as intermediate. For

22. See Kuznets, *Modern Economic Growth,* table 5.3, pp. 236–239.
23. *Ibid.,* table 5.5, pp. 248–250 in conjunction with table 5.3.

these nine countries, the final product components (adjusted upward for the Netherlands and Germany to include miscellaneous welfare services not shown separately), averaged 7.1 percent of GNP, compared with 15.8 percent of GNP for total government consumption. This suggests a breakdown for the 1960's of the total government consumption share of 14.7 percent into 6.6 percent for final product, and 8.1 percent for intermediate product.

But how much of the total government consumption share of 4.0 percent of GNP a century ago represented final and intermediate components respectively? Since data are not readily available and the initial share of total government consumption is small, and since we should allow for the largest realistic adjustment, we set the share of intermediate products in government consumption a century ago at about half of the total (although it is about 55 percent today, despite the large increase in educational, health, and other services). This means a rise in the intermediate component of government consumption from 2.0 to 8.1 percent of GNP; or from 2.1 to 9.0 percent of net national product. This, combined with the adjustment effects of urbanization, would mean a reduction in the terminal net national product, and hence in the aggregate growth rate, of 18.9 percent.

(c) Two other sources of possible downward adjustment in the growth rate for net national product are net national capital formation (or net domestic, the levels and trends in the two being roughly the same in most developed countries); and the shift of outlays on education from consumption (private and government) to capital formation.

Since the typical shares of private consumer expenditures and of total government consumption in net national product, all conventionally defined, were 87.8 and 4.2 percent a century ago, then changed to 66.4 and 16.3 percent respectively in the middle 1960's, the share of net national capital formation, also conventionally defined, moved from 8.0 to 17.3 percent of NNP. Any adjustment in this component can, therefore, affect a total rise of only 9.3 percent in its proportion to NNP.

Two aspects of such an adjustment may be considered. First, material capital formation includes residential and related construction; and the value of the resulting capital stock may be considered to be inflated by urbanization, in the sense that if there had been no urbanization, a much smaller stock of residential and related capital would have been adequate. This adjustment would, however, be quite small. United Nations data show that for 1963–1967, the share of residential construction in gross domestic capital formation for twelve developed countries was about 21 percent; for lack of adequate detail, I assume that the percentage in net national capital formation would be the same (although it would probably be somewhat lower). For the United States in 1965, the gross value of nonfarm, nonindustrial construction, a group closely related to dwellings as servicing private households, was about a quarter of residential construction.[24]

Long-term trends in shares of residential construction in total capital formation are inconclusive, declining in some countries but remaining relatively constant in others.[25] Assuming a constant proportion, residential and related construction would rise from (0.262×0.08), or 2.1 percent of NNP, a century ago to (0.262×0.173), or 4.5 percent of NNP, in the middle 1960's — an increase of 2.4 percentage points. We have no information on the difference between urban and rural residential and related capital, relative to the need; but at the maximum the adjustment would be between 1 and 2 percentage points.

The other aspect of the adjustment in the net national capital formation proportion is the possibility that the greater cost of ultimate consumption (by private households and hence by the labor force) in the cities means a greater cost of labor input into capital formation. To be sure, this higher cost is offset by greater efficiency of scale; otherwise much of the capital formation would be produced in the countryside. If we were to apply the full consumption cost differential to the net capital formation proportion, the 17.3 percentage share in the middle 1960's would be divided by 1.45, the differential for urban communities given in Table 10. The rise in the conventional measure, 9.3 percent of NNP, would be cut to only 3.9 percentage points; and aggregate growth of NNP would be reduced another 5.4 percent. But this is an exaggeration. A fair compromise might be to assign a downward adjustment of 2 percentage points — which, combined with the 19 percentage point reduction accounted for under (a) and (b) brings the total downward adjustment to 21 percent.

24. See United States, Office of Business Economics, *The National Income and Product Accounts of the United States, 1929–1965: A Supplement to the Survey of Current Business* (Washington, D.C., 1966), table 5.2, pp. 80–81.

25. See Kuznets, *Modern Economic Growth*, table 5.6, pp. 252–256.

If we treat formal education as capital investment, outlays by private households and by government on education would be shifted to capital formation — but would not affect the net national product total. The latter might be changed if income foregone in formal education and in training on the job were added and the capital consumption representing consumption of educational capital stock embodied in human beings were deducted. The question is whether the proportion to conventional net national product (or to product as adjusted above) of the net balance of addition and subtraction just noted is positive or negative and has increased or diminished.

Unfortunately, data for estimating either the addition or the deduction are not available, and considerable time and effort will be expended before they are produced and tested. But the conjecture here, boldly advanced, suggests that the proportion of each to GNP or NNP is relatively small; and the net balance is likely to be no more than a minor fraction of aggregate product. Later it will be indicated that the total net stock of educational capital (both formal education and training on the job) falls appreciably short of net material reproducible capital in a country like the United States in the late 1950's; and that such educational capital has grown at a distinctly higher rate than material capital stock (even reproducible). Unless there are grounds for assuming the contrary, consumption of educational capital is probably somewhat smaller than consumption of material capital; and its proportion to conventional aggregate product (gross) has probably risen about 2 to 4 percentage points over the past century. The proportion of income foregone, the item to be added, could not have increased more than that. In order to avoid elaborate and unreliable calculation, which could result in a modification of only 1 to 3 percentage points in aggregate growth of conventionally defined product over a century, I shall assume that the net balance in question, as a proportion of aggregate product, conventional or adjusted, has changed so little that we can disregard it.

(d) In considering the effects on growth of productivity of an allowance for educational investment in quality of labor, two approaches can be followed, both illustrated by estimates for the United States. In the first we use estimates of different rates of compensation, paid presumably to workers in the same age and sex groups but differing with respect to formal education and skills acquired from training on the job. Kendrick's study of productivity trends in the United States provides long-term series on manhour inputs, and on labor input in which manhours are weighted by compensation per manhour in different industries, the weights held constant over the period for which inputs and productivity are being measured (his pp. 32–34). Since in general these interindustry differences in compensation per manhour reflect the combined effects of age-sex differentials (relatively minor) and differences in formal education and training on the job (relatively major), they provide a convenient approximation to what we need to supplement our indexes of manhours by an allowance largely for effects of education. Kendrick's estimates indicate that from 1869 to 1957 manhours grew at a rate of 1.63 percent per year, whereas labor input grew 2.01 percent per year — the addition thus being about one-quarter of the growth rate in manhours. But there were substantial differences in this relative addition among the several subperiods. From 1929 to 1957, manhours grew only 14.9 percent and labor input 29.4 percent; from 1909 to 1929 manhours and input grew 27.9 and 36.1 percent respectively; and between 1869 and 1909 the two growth factors were 182.3 percent and 228.1 percent.[26] The results are similar to Denison's, if we correct his series for exaggerated allowances for shorter hours and a longer school year (as indicated in note 26), at least for the period since 1929. Although the difference, about one-fourth of the growth rate of manhours, also allows for changing age-sex differentials, it can stand as a generous allowance for the effects of investment in training — relevant also to other countries.

The second approach begins with the estimates for the United States by Theodore W. Schultz. He shows a net stock of educational capital in labor force, including on-the-job training of males, of

26. See Kendrick, *Productivity Trends*, table A-XIII, pp. 316–317. The rates are for the series relating to the national economy.

Lithwick, in *Economic Growth of Canada*, adjusted Denison's estimates for 1929–1957 to exclude the doubtful allowances for effects of reduction of hours and lengthening of the school year on efficiency. With these adjustments, growth over the period in the Denison series is 17.5 percent in manhours; 2.8 percent for age-sex differentials; and 13.2 percent for education (see *ibid.*, table 6, p. 13). The ratio of the growth of the combined additions for education and age-sex differentials to that for manhours, that is, 16.0 to 17.5 percent, is almost the same as that shown in Kendrick for 1929–1957 (14.5 to 14.9 percent).

some $882 billion in 1957 (in 1956 prices), compared with a net stock of reproducible material capital of $1,270 billion.[27] Since total net wealth (including nonreproducible material assets) was about 1.23 of reproducible capital stock in 1955,[28] the ratio of educational capital in the labor force to total material capital was 0.56. With this ratio at 0.6 in the 1960's, and allowing a somewhat higher rate of return on educational capital (Schultz, note 12, p. 6, suggests a combined rate for educational capital in labor force and for on-the-job training of male workers, of about 4.8 percent, compared with one of 3.9 percent for reproducible tangible wealth), the returns on educational capital in the 1960's can be set at about 0.74 of the returns on total tangible capital — which would shift the weight of capital input in the 1960's to (0.25×1.74) or 0.435; and that of labor input to 0.565.

In going back to the 1860's, we should note that the growth rate of educational capital — which, according to Schultz, was two to three times higher than that of net tangible capital between 1929 and 1957 — was probably higher throughout the century. If we set this rate at twice the rate for tangible capital, as a generous allowance, the ratio of educational to tangible capital would dwindle to a small fraction in the 1860's; and even if we allowed for a higher rate of return on educational capital, the weight for total capital could not be more than 0.435, since the weight for tangible capital has been set at 0.333. I, therefore, set the weights of labor and capital in this new version at 0.565 and 0.435 respectively for the century as a whole; and raise the growth rate of total capital, to allow for the inclusion of a more rapidly growing component — which amounted to 0.6 of tangible capital in the 1960's and grew over the preceding century at twice the rate of tangible capital.

Table 11 illustrates, for a century of growth at the typical aggregate growth rate derived from conventional accounting, the growth rates of labor and capital inputs and the resulting growth rate of productivity; it also shows the effects of the various adjustments for nonconventional current and capital costs that have been discussed so far. The results are quite clear. In the conventional analysis, growth of net product per capita is close to 2 percent per year; and the growth of productivity, about 1.5 percent per year, ac-

27. See "Reflections on Investment in Man," *The Journal of Political Economy*, vol. LXXX, no. 5, part 2 (October 1962), table 1, p. 6. Further references in the paragraph, unless otherwise noted, are to the same source.
28. Goldsmith and Saunders, *Income and Wealth, Series VIII*, table I, p. 9.

Table 11. Adjustments for current and capital nonconventional costs, illustrative century of typical economic growth.

Assumed: annual growth rate of gross product (domestic or national) — 3.0%
annual growth rate of population — 1.0%

	Conventional calculation (1)	Adjusted for current costs (intermediate products) (2)	Adjusted also for capital costs	
			Var. I (3)	Var. II (4)
Growth rates per year (%)				
1. NNP	2.95	2.71	2.71	2.71
2. Labor input	0.80	0.80	1.00	0.80
3. Capital input	2.54	2.54	2.54	2.97
4. Combined inputs	1.38	1.38	1.51	1.74
5. Residual productivity	1.55	1.31	1.18	0.95
6. NNP per capita	1.93	1.69	1.69	1.69
7. Ratio of productivity growth to growth of NNP per capita	0.80	0.78	0.70	0.56

Line 1: Column 1 is calculated on the assumption that the capital consumption ratio to GNP is 5.5 percent at the beginning and 9.7 percent at the end of the century (see text). Columns 2–4 allow for the effects of the rising proportion of intermediate products, 21 percent of terminal NNP (conventionally measured; see text).
Line 2: Columns 1, 2, 4 are calculated on the assumption that manhours *per capita* decline 2 percent per decade (see discussion in the first part of this chapter). Column 3 is calculated on the assumption that investment in education adds one-fourth to the growth rate of manhours (see text).
Line 3: Columns 1–3 are based on the growth factor of capital given in Table 8, Base III, with the initial capital–product ratio of 6. For column 4 the growth rate is raised on the assumption that the additional capital component (education, etc.) grew at double the rate of tangible capital, and that, at the end of the century, its stock amounted to 0.6 of tangible stock (see text).
Line 4: Labor and capital input in columns 1–3 weighted by 2 and 1 respectively (see discussion at the beginning of this chapter); in column 4 the weights are 0.565 and 0.435 respectively (see text).
Line 5: [(100 + line 1) ÷ (100 + line 4) − 100].
Line 6: Derived from line 1 and the 1 percent growth rate assumed for population.
Line 7: Ratio of line 5 to line 6.

counts for eight-tenths of growth in per capita product. With the elimination of nonconventional current costs (column 2), amounting to 21 percent of terminal NNP, growth in per capita product drops to 1.7 percent per year, a reduction of only slightly over a tenth of the original rate (since the 21 percent reduction represents a cumulative adjustment over a century). The reduction in residual productivity is more significant, particularly in column 4 — where it is cut from 1.55 percent (in the conventional accounting) to

0.95 percent per year. But, by and large, the reductions are moderate, even though they are based on generous assumptions and the use of United States data, both of which tend to yield a high rather than a low adjustment.

In particular, if the adjustments are to be judged in terms of their effect on two of the major findings here — the much higher rate of growth of per capita product for the modern period, and the large contribution to this growth of the increase in productivity — their weights, based on the historical record, can hardly be sufficient to negate the findings. With the premodern rate of growth in per capita product less than 0.2 percent per year (which can be suggested for Western Europe back to year 1000),[29] an adjustment in the modern growth rates to match this low level would imply that as much as 1.8 percent of the 3 percent growth in total product, or six-tenths, would have to be written down as debits for intermediate products or for inadequate internal price adjustments. Likewise, a denial of significant growth in productivity would imply, on the assumption of even proportionality of labor input (unadjusted for quality changes) to total population, that *pure* consumption per capita (that is, consumption for consumption's sake and containing only insignificant elements of education, training, and so on, or of intermediate products) has failed to grow substantially. For any growth in per capita consumption would reflect pure productivity increase, since all the extra inputs into material or human capital and all intermediate products would have already been excluded, and since it cannot be assumed that some *net* draft was made on capital stock to sustain or increase this "pure" consumption.

My purpose in presenting these rather simple calculations is to urge that, once we accept the wide differentials between the growth rates in the conventionally defined total and per capita product in modern economic development and those in the premodern long

29. As Table 1 indicated, for per capita product the growth rate for most developed countries over the last century was between 14 and 24 percent per decade, with a typical value of 18 to 20 percent; and extrapolation of present levels in Table 2 (and other evidence) suggests that before entry into modern growth, per capita product in these developed countries (except Japan) was $200 or more in prices of the 1960's — the date roughly the middle nineteenth century. If we set $50 as the minimum in European conditions, and assume that it prevailed about the year 1000, the implicit growth rate for the period 1000–1850 is about 1.6 percent per decade, or about 0.16 percent per year.

periods, downward adjustments for costs omitted from the conventional measures (and associated with changes in conditions of life and work generated by structural changes in economic and social institutions) would have to be unrealistically large to do more than qualify the major findings. This is all the more important because these omitted costs are at the root of some current problems, which stand out conspicuously and may thereby blind us to the fact that they are only qualifications against the background of an enormous advance in net output, productivity, and pure consumption. At least this has been the record so far, and this broad conclusion would not be much affected by any reasonable modification that could be made in the details of the estimates above, such as raising the proportion of current costs represented by intermediate products from 21 to even 30 percent of terminal NNP, or attempting a more realistic allowance for investment in education.

The foregoing adjustments for nonconventional costs, which only deal with economically overt costs and involve for the most part a reclassification of items already covered in conventional economic accounts, may not go far enough — from the standpoint of a thorough evaluation of the costs and returns of modern economic growth. Although moving beyond recorded economic acts and transactions and estimates generated by economic accounting leads into realms of unquantifiable speculation, it is only proper at least to suggest the major costs omitted in the preceding adjustments.

The first are internal hidden costs, internal in that they concern the domestic society rather than external relations of the developed economies, and hidden in that they are not offset (or only negligibly offset) by the extra outlays of economic resources like those identified above as intermediate products or new types of capital. Some of these costs may be easily recognizable quasi-economic inputs. For example, the time spent in commuting to and from the job is not included in hours of work, yet commuting time must have increased significantly in the course of economic growth, with movement to the suburbs to escape some of the higher costs and greater discomfort of residence within the central city. Others may be deprivations and discomforts for which no economic price tag seems appropriate. These may range from such obvious and distasteful consequences of modern economic growth as air and water pollution to more subtle effects of urban civilization represented by the difficulties of maintaining privacy and of escaping from the vulgarities of mass media and from irrational domestic violence.[30]

One could estimate the economic cost, in terms of the resources needed to offset *some* of these negative consequences of modern economic growth, even though such offsets have not actually been made. But such estimates would be of potential, not actual, offsets, suggesting that society considers their priority too low to warrant the necessary inputs. One could argue, then, that such low priority results from obvious defects in economic and social institutions, and that, relevant to criteria superior to (or different from) those followed in real life, modern economic growth does have some ill effects, which should be assigned the proper negative economic values. For example, it is reasonable to argue that while diseconomies of scale resulting from mass use of passenger cars and transistor radios — in the way of air and sound pollution — are substantial, the failure to remedy the situation through economic inputs is caused not by a low priority but by the weakness of the relevant institutions: the private market and other institutions are far more efficient in supplying large numbers of people with cars and transistor radios than in supplying them with protection from the resulting air and sound pollution. But the fact remains that, because these are hidden costs not yet offset in reality, any estimate of their economic magnitude is subject to a wide margin of error — and we have no evidence to draw upon for comparative analysis.

The problem with the second group of omitted costs — those external and resulting from the association between modern economic growth and the enormous increase in the destructiveness of armed conflict — is even greater. Our record so far, despite its inclusion of two world wars (perhaps three, counting the Napoleonic), justifies the broad conclusion above as to the immense growth of product and productivity in the course of modern economic development. But the economic calculus is based upon keeping the stock of capital, that is, future capacity to produce, constant. If the potential destruction of an atomic holocaust means killing a substantial proportion of world population, affecting its genetic capacity for further growth, and making much of the world practically uninhabitable for decades, then, weighted by the probability of its occurrence, such destruction should be entered with a minus sign.

30. For a perceptive discussion see Ezra J. Mishan, *The Costs of Economic Growth* (London: Staples, 1967).

And if there is a significant connection between modern economic growth and the increased nationalism and tensions in international relations that make modern conflict probable, then the price paid for probable armed conflict should be debited as an omitted but significant cost of modern economic growth. The "ifs" in the two preceding sentences suggest the number and uncertainty of the links involved. But the comment is sufficient to suggest the enormity of the costs in question, and even enough to attach an aura of unreality not only to the rather moderate adjustments summarized in Table 11, but also to many of the findings.

For both the internal and external hidden costs, the analysis just given would require comparisons with the past — since, as indicated, measurement even of net growth is from a historical base. Thus, we would have to know the diseconomies of scale, not offset by economic inputs, that prevailed in the presently developed countries on the eve of their entry into modern economic growth; we would also have to know the dangers of armed conflict induced by antecedent economic growth that loomed in the background to threaten further capacity to survive and to grow. That some major diseconomies did exist is evident from even a superficial historical survey. The cities in the early nineteenth century, and more so in the eighteenth, did not suffer as much from pollution, but, unlike the cities of the 1960's, they were afflicted with high death and morbidity rates. Even the surviving population endured many discomforts of urban life which were later reduced either by new technology or by movement to the suburbs, and both the higher death and morbidity rates and the many discomforts were negative consequences of the premodern economic growth that resulted in the premodern cities. Likewise, such technical progress as was attained before modern economic growth increased the capacity for destruction by armed conflict — even if it protected the, by then, developed countries from invasions by economically less developed populations, like that which destroyed the Roman Empire and was a continuing threat to Western Europe until the end of the fifteenth century. None of this precludes the possibility that the external, if not the internal, omitted costs loom much larger today, absolutely and relatively, than they did in earlier epochs of economic growth.

The preceding comments suggest the importance of these negative aspects of modern economic growth, even though the magnitude of their effect on the latter is still an unknown quantity. Further analysis of these aspects calls for a level of discourse and type of data that I feel poorly equipped to handle; and it had better be left to more competent students in the field. However, I hope that the limited analysis of nonconventional but overt costs, represented by the adjustments discussed here, retains a value of its own and may provide some suggestions for the pursuit of the much more difficult task of a critical examination of all aspects of economic growth, not only those reflected in actual input and output.

III

Sectoral Shares
in Product:
A Cross-Section View

Several sectors within the production structure of a country's economy can be distinguished because they produce different goods by processes that differ in technology and organization. The goods turned out may be finished, that is, ready without further fabrication for use by household or durable capital purchasers, or they may be unfinished. Finished products may differ with respect to durability, priority of need they satisfy, responsiveness to changing economic levels, degree of complementarity with other products, and supply conditions. Unfinished products may differ in distance from the finished products and in the character of the finished products that they enter. The production processes, or inputs, may differ even for identical or similar goods, with respect to the technology used, reliance on natural resources, and the unit organizing the production process. An extremely wide variety of sectors can be distinguished by a combination of characteristics of output and production processes, particularly in a developed economy of some size.

Our interest here is in the differing responsiveness of the production sectors in the course of modern economic development, in their rates of growth, and in the consequent changes in their long-term shares in total output or input. This differential response is partly a function of the high rate of growth of per capita product, which, given different income elasticities of demand for different finished goods, means a high rate of change in the structure of

99

domestic demand. It is partly a function of the revolution in transport and communication which strengthened the trade and other ties among nations, affected their comparative advantages in world markets, and thus changed the structure of foreign demand and hence that of domestic production. It is partly a function of technological changes, which have had differing impact on the several production sectors, affecting their growth regardless of changes in the structure of domestic and foreign demand. Modern economic growth, with its rapid rise in per capita product, based largely on continuous changes in material and social technology and accompanied by increasing economic interdependence of nations, necessarily generates major differences in rates of growth of the several sectors in the production system, and hence rapid changes in the production structure of the economies undergoing such growth. The latter can hardly be understood unless the changes in the production structure are perceived and measured.

This chapter presents international comparisons for recent years; the next, a review of long-term trends. The results of the international cross-section comparisons may not provide a sound basis for projecting trends in production structure — either backward into the past or forward into the future. But any disparities that emerge between the results of cross section comparisons and those of direct observations of trends in the course of economic growth help identify the specific factors that operate in growth over time but are not reflected in cross-section data. Furthermore, the latter are of interest, in and of themselves, in that they reveal important differences in the current structure of the world.

Before turning to the findings, we deal briefly with the difficulties of securing acceptable measures of the production structure by a simple approach, making use of the shares of the different sectors in total output and in the total of a production factor like labor force. The problems particularly relevant to the study of economic growth and structure can best be perceived under three broad heads: (a) sectoral identity; (b) sectoral differences in measurability; and (c) supply of data.

(a) The problem of sectoral identity can be illustrated by asking whether, when we compare the shares of the agricultural sector of a developed country in the 1840's and in the 1960's, we are dealing with one and the same sector. Is such an approach realistic for agriculture in, say, the United States — first, in view of the vast differences in technology of operation and in the extent of dependence on other sectors (for such items as machinery, chemical fertilizers, or hybrid seeds); and second, in view of the marked differences in degree of specialization and the shift from the self-sufficient rural population of the early nineteenth century, capable of producing a variety of nonagricultural goods, to the specialized farmers of today? Likewise, when we compare the shares of the agricultural sector in the developed countries with those in the much less developed countries of Asia or SubSaharan Africa, is it realistic to treat them as one and the same sector, in view, again, of the vast differences in technology and degree of specialization? The same question arises in regard to manufacturing, which ranges from huge, large-scale, capital-endowed factories to home handicraft units; and to services, which range from highly skilled professional performance to unskilled menial work.

These questions may be answered by pointing out that agriculture supplies the essential foods for human consumption: it does so today in both developed and less developed countries, and it did in the early nineteenth century; that agriculture is tied to the soil, and is a relatively small-scale activity imposing a pattern of life on its participants that is different from the more concentrated urban pursuits — today in both developed and less developed countries, and in the former in the early nineteenth century. To the extent that this is true, agriculture does constitute a sector in regard to which developed and less developed countries and the developed countries today and in the nineteenth century can be compared. The same argument holds for manufacturing, or construction, or transport, or trade, or services. In this sense a clear identification of the sectors prevails despite marked differences in technology and specialization.

But it is also true that our classification, which fails to distinguish between traditional agriculture and modern agriculture, between handicraft manufacturing and animal transport, on the one hand, and modern manufacturing and mechanical transport, on the other, does understate, for that reason, the change in production structure associated with modern economic growth; it conceals much of the international disparity in production structure between the developed and less developed countries. A crude adjustment can occasionally be made for effects of differences in specialization. For example, in the treatment of a productive factor like labor it is possible to distinguish between fully employed wage and salary labor and unpaid family labor; and, of course, some of the differences emerge in comparisons of product per worker for one and the same sector — over time or across space. But the classification of productive sectors is particularly weak in indicating the extent of uses of technology, as contrasted with major differences in the nature of the product and of broad conditions of production. It is, therefore, important to remember that measures of the change in sectoral shares that accompanies modern economic growth understate — by a large margin — long-term changes in production structure and international differences in such structure between developed and less developed countries.

(b) Even with fairly precise identification of production sectors, measurability of product (and of inputs) is not equally easy, either for the same sector at different levels of development or for different sectors at the same level of development. For example, in the agricultural sector of some less developed economies, even gross output depends upon the yield of the preferred crop; and since markets are limited, producers may decide to let the inferior crop rot in the field rather than harvest it. Under such conditions, an adequate measure of total output of the sector requires knowledge of the disposition or use, rather than of the yield, of the production process. More important, differences in ease of measurability are produced by differences in complexity and quality of specific products. Consequently, a sector whose output is dominated by complex products that differ in quality is less susceptible to accurate measurement through available market prices than another with more "standardized" products. Contrasts in this respect between some service sectors — particularly those requiring advanced professional training or involving several functions not easily identifiable (for example, most government activities) — and an industry producing a commodity (such as wheat flour or bituminous coal), whose quality is reflected in market prices, are well-known, as are the difficulties in measuring "real" output of many service sectors and of industries producing complex fabricated products of rapidly changing and diverse quality. Similar difficulties are faced in the measurement of productive factors: capital and labor are of differing complexity and quality, and these differences are not always reflected in the quantitative terms that are feasible with the available market measures. It is for the more developed countries, which have a greater share of complex material products and a greater weight of the service sectors, that the problems of measurability seem to be more acute — "seem" because we may be insufficiently cognizant of the quality differentials within what seem to us the simpler economies of the less developed countries.

(c) The supply of countrywide quantitative data for economic analysis is a function partly of the ease of measurement and partly of the interest society takes in such data. On both counts the supply of economic data for the study of growth tends to be markedly biased in favor of the more developed countries and the more recent periods (except when withheld by deliberate decisions of authoritarian governments). This means that even total utilization of available data fails to yield a complete and unbiased picture of the growth process over time, or of international differences across the full range of development. In view of such limitations on the supply of data and the sensitivity of the structures studied, particularly in small countries, to many special factors, each of analytical interest, the resulting distributions cannot be effectively studied by formal statistical techniques based on some general characteristics of assumed variance. It is necessary to keep the individual units and the specific groups in continuous view, because the more efficient formal methods may yield results not easily recognizable as erroneous.

Association between Product per Capita and Sectoral Shares

Table 12 summarizes the shares of the three major production sectors and their subdivisions in aggregate output, predominantly gross domestic product at factor cost, for some fifty-seven countries grouped in increasing order of per capita product in 1958 (all such per capita product converted to U.S. dollars by relevant exchange rates). Data for 1958 rather than for a later year were used, partly because of greater supply of United Nations estimates of product converted to U.S. dollars, partly for comparability with the sectoral shares in labor force contained in the 1960–61 population censuses.

All countries for which the data are available are included, except for several significant omissions which represent analytical decisions and must be recognized. First, as in Chapter I, all Communist countries are excluded because their institutions, the price and market bases of measurement, the very definitions of product, are

Table 12. Shares of production sectors in gross domestic product at factor cost, fifty-seven countries grouped by 1958 GDP per capita, about 1958.

	Groups of countries in increasing order of 1958 GDP per capita							
	I (1)	II (2)	III (3)	IV (4)	V (5)	VI (6)	VII (7)	VIII (8)
1. Number of countries	6	6	6	15	6	6	6	6
2. GDP per capita ($)	51.8	82.6	138	221	360	540	864	1,382
3. Regional identity of countries	F-4	F-3	A-4	F-2	A-1	A-1	E-6	E-3
	A-2	A-2	L-2	A-3	L-3	L-3		S-3
		L-1		L-9	E-2	E-2		
				E-1				
Shares of major sectors (%)								
4. A	53.6	44.6	37.9	32.3	22.5	17.4	11.8	9.2
5. I	18.5	22.4	24.6	29.4	35.2	39.5	52.9	50.2
6. S	27.9	33.0	37.5	38.3	42.3	43.1	35.3	40.6
Subdivisions of I								
7. Mining and quarrying	1.1	1.3	1.3	2.0	3.3	0.7	2.2	2.2
8. Manufacturing	7.7	10.4	12.6	16.2	18.1	23.9	31.3	31.2
9. Construction	4.0	4.1	4.1	4.2	5.7	5.8	7.5	6.6
10. Electricity, gas, water	0.5	0.7	0.8	1.1	1.6	2.1	2.6	2.4
11. Transport and communication	5.2	5.9	5.8	5.9	6.5	7.0	9.3	7.8
Subdivisions of S								
12. Trade	12.8	11.8	13.5	15.3	14.9	13.5	11.3	14.2
13. Banking, insurance, and real estate	0.6	1.4	1.8	2.0	3.6	3.7	2.8	4.0
14. Ownership of dwellings	2.4	5.0	6.0	5.8	6.0	5.9	4.1	3.8
15. Public administration and defense	5.7	6.9	7.1	6.4	7.2	10.8	6.8	8.1
16. Other services	6.4	7.9	9.1	8.8	10.6	9.2	10.3	10.5

The A sector includes agriculture, forestry, hunting, and fishing. The I and S sectors comprise the subdivisions indicated in lines 7–11 and 12–16 respectively.

The fifty-seven countries covered are, in increasing order of per capita GDP: Malawi, Nigeria, Tanganyika, Burma, Uganda, Pakistan, India, Kenya, Thailand, Sudan, Haiti, United Arab Republic, South Korea, Ceylon, Taiwan, Paraguay, Syria, Ecuador, Honduras, Peru, Turkey, Philippines, Southern Rhodesia, Mauritius, Malaya, Dominican Republic, El Salvador, Colombia, Portugal, Guatemala, Nicaragua, Brazil, Mexico,

Spain, Greece, Jamaica, Costa Rica, Chile, Japan, Uruguay, Ireland, Italy, Israel, Puerto Rico, Argentina, Austria, Netherlands, Finland, West Germany, Belgium, Norway, United Kingdom, Denmark, France, Australia, Canada, United States.

Lines 1–2: Per capita gross domestic product, at factor cost for 1958, converted to U.S. dollars, is given in United Nations, *Yearbook of National Accounts Statistics, 1966* (New York, 1967), table 7A, pp. 725–729. For Japan, however, per capita GDP in 1958 was set at $400. The entries in line 2 are unweighted geometric means for the countries listed above and grouped as shown in line 1.

Line 3: The regions are identified by the following letters: F for Africa; A for Asia; L for Latin America; E for Europe; and S for overseas offshoots of Europe. Turkey is classified under A.

Lines 4–16: Entries are unweighted arithmetic means of the shares for individual countries calculated (except for Brazil and Costa Rica) from the country tables on the industrial origin of product, given in *ibid.* For the large majority of countries the shares are based on 1957–59 estimates of gross domestic product at current factor cost and exclude adjustments in totals. In a few instances the estimates are for product in constant or in market prices, or for net domestic product. For Brazil and Costa Rica the underlying data are unpublished estimates (in 1960 factor cost) supplied by the Economic Commission for Latin America.

For a few countries, full detail was not given on some subdivisions. Except for Brazil and Argentina, the shares for these were allocated on the basis of the average of the shares for other countries in the specific group. For Brazil, the combined share of trade and banking, insurance, and real estate was allocated on the basis of the shares of the two subdivisions in NDP derived from figures in the *Yearbook of National Accounts Statistics, 1965* (New York, 1966). For Argentina the combined share of banking, insurance, and real estate and ownership of dwellings was broken down on the basis of the estimates supplied by ECLA. The adjustments are minor, but make possible a consistent and complete industrial breakdown for the countries and groups of countries covered.

viewed as so different from those in the non-Communist countries that their inclusion would obfuscate the major features of economic structure within each of the two groups.

Second, with the single exception of Mauritius (included because so few less developed African countries are in the sample), I omitted all countries with population of less than one million. This seemed warranted because of the erratic character of the production structure of the heavily dependent splinter countries.

Third, several countries were excluded because their production structures were markedly affected by some single, largely exogenous factor, such as oil or a mineral deposit. In such cases the large share of the relevant subdivision, say mines and quarries, would automatically mean unusually small shares of other subdivisions and sectors. Since our interest is in establishing the important parameters of production structure in cross-section analysis for comparison with the trends over time, it seemed best to exclude the few countries whose structure was sharply affected by such exogenous factors. Any country in which the share of mines and quarries was raised by exceptional wealth to over 10 percent of total product was omitted, and a similar rule was applied to a few other countries. The "mining" exclusions were Iraq, South Africa, Zambia, Bolivia, and Venezuela. Other exclusions were Panama (the Canal); Jordan (heavy subsidization of government and Arab refugees); and Algeria, Cambodia, and Vietnam (war-affected countries). Omission of ten countries does not seem fatal, since their inclusion after some allowance for the sources of distortion in their structure would not affect the pattern of differences in production structure indicated by the fifty-seven countries included in Table 12.

If the averages in Table 12 are accepted as an approximation of production structure unaffected by major exogenous factors (war, extra sources of wealth, and so on), what pattern is revealed? The answer is fairly clear for the three major sectors. The share of the A sector, predominantly agriculture but including forestry, fisheries, and hunting, is inversely correlated with per capita product: it is more than 50 percent in the lowest income group and as small as 9 percent in the top group (line 4). The share of the I sector, which includes not only mining, manufacturing, electric power, gas, water, and construction — the usual components of the industry sector — but also transportation and communication, is closely and positively associated with per capita product: it is less than 20 percent of aggregate product in the lowest income group and more than 50 percent in the high income groups (line 5). The share of the S sector, which includes trade, banking, and so forth, income from dwellings, and public and private services of various kinds, tends to be positively associated with per capita product, rising from under 30 percent in the lowest income groups to over 40 percent in the high income groups (line 6). But the association for the S sector is weak and limited to the lower ranges of the total span in per capita product. Both the close and conspicuous association between the shares of the A and I sectors and per capita product; and the weak, if positive, association of the share of the S sector have been observed before, and should be quite familiar by now.[1]

The shares of the subdivisions of the I sector, except that of mining and quarrying which can be expected to behave erratically, are positively associated with per capita product — rising from the low to the high income countries (lines 7–11). Manufacturing is

1. See, for example, Hollis B. Chenery, "Patterns of Industrial Growth," *The American Economic Review*, vol. L, no. 4 (September 1960), pp. 624–654, esp. table 3, p. 634.

the dominant subdivision, and the fourfold rise in its share is distinctly greater than that of the share of the I sector as a whole, which barely triples; it is matched only by the large relative rise in the small share of the electricity, gas, and water subdivision.

Among the subdivisions of the S sector only the share of banking, insurance, and real estate shows a striking rise as we shift from low to higher income countries, but the subdivision is small (lines 12–16). The two substantial shares, those for trade and public and private services combined, move within a narrow range: the former shows little association with per capita product, and the latter shows a positive association rising from about 12 to about 19 percent with some fluctuation. Obviously, the limited response of the S sector to the wide differences in per capita product results from a similarly limited response of the shares of its major subdivisions rather than from a combination of a close and positive association for one subdivision with offsetting marked and negative association for another.

Another aspect of the relation between differences in the shares of various sectors and subdivisions and those in per capita product is suggested in Table 13. Here the dispersion of shares in the sample is measured by the range between the averages for the six countries with the largest and the six countries with the smallest shares — the countries arranged with no regard to per capita product (columns 1, 2, 4); and this range is related to the average share for all fifty-seven countries (columns 3, 5). The share of the A sector shows the widest dispersion, is matched only by that for the small subdivision of banking, insurance, and real estate, and is followed, at some distance, by that for manufacturing (lines 1, 8, 4). These findings contrast with the much narrower dispersion in the shares of trade (line 7) and of the S sector as a whole (line 3). While the less developed countries are underrepresented in the sample, the broad difference in dispersion would probably be confirmed with more complete coverage. Similar differences were found, in a slightly different grouping of sectors and subdivisions, for the shares about 1950.[2]

Table 13 gives two measures of the association between differ-

---

2. See Simon Kuznets, "Quantitative Aspects of the Economic Growth of Nations: II. Industrial Distribution of National Product and Labor Force," *Economic Development and Cultural Change,* supplement to vol. V, no. 4 (July 1957), tables 1–5, pp. 8–12.

Table 13. Relation between dispersion of sectoral shares in product and their association with product per capita (based on data underlying Table 12).

	Average shares in product (%)			Range in shares, % (col. 1 — col. 2) (4)	Range divided by AM (col. 4 ÷ col. 3) (5)	Range in Table 12 as propor- tion of col. 4 (6)	E — 1 (7)
	Highest six coun- tries (1)	Lowest six coun- tries (2)	All coun- tries (3)				
Major sectors							
1. A	58.0	6.7	29.2	51.3	1.8	0.86	−0.56
2. I	55.3	16.7	33.4	38.6	1.2	0.82	0.34
3. S	49.5	23.2	37.4	26.3	0.7	0.48	0.13
Subdivisions of I							
4. Manufacturing	35.3	5.7	18.5	29.6	1.6	0.80	0.49
5. Construction	9.2	2.0	5.1	7.2	1.4	0.36	0.16
6. Transport and communication, electricity, gas, and water	13.9	4.1	8.0	9.8	1.2	0.46	0.20
Subdivisions of S							
7. Trade	23.6	8.1	13.7	15.5	1.1	0.09	0.04
8. Banking, insurance, and real estate	5.3	0.5	2.4	4.8	2.0	0.70	0.68
9. Ownership of dwellings	9.0	1.5	5.0	7.5	1.5	0.19	0.16
10. Public services	12.8	3.8	7.2	9.0	1.2	0.27	0.12
11. Other services	14.2	3.9	9.1	10.3	1.1	0.39	0.16

Columns 1–2: Unweighted arithmetic means of shares of the six individual countries with the highest and lowest shares for the respective sectors and subdivisions.

Column 3: Arithmetic means of shares for all countries.

Column 6: The difference between columns 1 and 8 of Table 12, regardless of the position of the highest and lowest shares among the eight per capita product groups distinguished, related to the range in column 4. This ratio suggests the explanatory effect of the differences in per capita product, on the assumption of a continuous, unidirectional association.

Column 7: E is the ratio of the percentage difference in the per capita output of a given sector (contribution to GDP) to the percentage difference in per capita product. It represents the response of a given sector (or subdivision) to relative per capita product differences. It is calculated for a standard per capita product difference of 20 percent, and is the average for the full income range in Table 12, that is, from $51.8 to $1,382 (see lines 9 and 18 of Table 14).

ences in per capita product and those in the shares of sectors and subdivisions. The first compares the range in Table 12, between the groups of countries with the lowest and highest per capita product, with that observed in groups of countries with the smallest and largest shares (column 6). This simple measure of the extent to which per capita product "accounts for" the variance of the sectoral shares confirms our observation in Table 12: the conspicuous association with the A and I sectors, the manufacturing subdivision, and the small banking and insurance subdivision; and the weak association with the other components of the S sector, particularly trade, and with the S sector as a whole.

The second measure, E, represents, in its basic form, the average ratio of the percentage difference in the sector's (or subdivision's) absolute contribution to GDP (per capita) when total GDP per capita increases 20 percent. Here the average is for the full range of per capita product differences in Table 12, in other words, from $51.8 to $1,382 (the measures are presented in detail in Table 14). The more E deviates from 1.0, the greater the impact of per capita product differences on the share of a sector. Hence the larger the entry in column 7, sign disregarded, the greater the impact of per capita product differences on the shares of sectors and subdivisions. It can be observed that differences in the value of $(E-1)$ for the various sectors and subdivisions agree with differences in column 6 and with the earlier observations of Table 12.

Of particular interest in Table 13 is the clear relation between the dispersion in the shares of the sectors or subdivisions and the association of the shares with differences in per capita product (or the magnitude of the impact of the latter). The sectors and subdivisions whose shares are greatly affected by differences in per capita product (the A sector; manufacturing; and banking, insurance, and real estate) also show the widest dispersion in shares; those sectors and subdivisions whose shares appear to be least affected by differences in per capita product (trade, other service components, and the S sector as a whole) show narrower dispersion of shares. In other words, if the complex of factors represented by per capita product significantly affects the share of a given sector or subdivision, international differences in this share will be wide — corresponding to the internationally wide differences in per capita product. If the international differences in per capita product have a limited effect on shares, international differences in the shares will be narrow. The implication is that, at least for the sectors and subdivisions shown here, the complex of factors represented by per capita product differences, is the major determinant of international differences in production structure. Other forces are present, but apparently have much less effect.

For purposes of comparative analysis, the grouping and the shares in Table 12, representing as they do simple averages of raw data for individual countries (small groups at that), must be reduced to some reasonably useful benchmark values of per capita product and corresponding shares. This can be done in two ways. The first would involve setting up an equation connecting per capita product and the shares; and then by means of this equation calculating estimated shares for any desired set of values of per capita product. This approach requires a defensible analytical model and, what is more difficult, formal assumptions concerning variance of the distribution (for proper fitting and calculation of parameters). These assumptions cannot be readily accepted since they result in the loss of identity of units and groups. I consider the second approach preferable: to take three-group moving averages of the successive groups in Table 12; and estimate the shares corresponding to selected benchmark values of per capita product by simple interpolation (Table 14, lines 1–5, 10–14). The pattern revealed is naturally similar to that shown in Table 12, but with more systematic movements.

As already indicated, the E value measures the elasticity of response of the output of a sector to a change or difference in per capita product, and represents the percentage change in the sectoral output associated with the percentage change in per capita product. Thus, an E value of less than 1 means that the sector's output changes by a smaller ratio than per capita product, and if the latter increases, the sector's share declines. Since E varies with the size of the total percentage change or difference in per capita product, it was calculated for a standard increase of 20 percent.

The E value for the A sector is below 1, reflecting the marked drop in its share as we move from lower to higher per capita income; it is compensated by E values above 1 for the other sectors, and most subdivisions within them. Furthermore, as one would expect, the elasticity of response of the major sectors and most of their subdivisions diminishes as we move to higher product per

Table 14. Shares of production sectors in gross domestic product at benchmark values of 1958 GDP per capita, and elasticity of response (E) of sectoral output to relative differences in product per capita.

	Major sectors			Subdivisions of I		
						Transportation and communication, electricity,
				Manufac-	Con-	gas, and
	A	I	S	turing	struction	water
	(1)	(2)	(3)	(4)	(5)	(6)
Shares at benchmark values of GDP per capita (%)						
1. $70	48.4	20.6	31.0	9.3	4.1	6.1
2. $150	36.8	26.3	36.9	13.6	4.2	6.9
3. $300	26.4	33.0	40.6	18.2	5.0	7.8
4. $500	18.7	40.9	40.4	23.4	6.1	9.4
5. $1,000	11.7	48.4	39.9	29.6	6.6	10.4
E values for a standard increase in GDP per capita of 20 percent						
6. $70 to 300	0.56	1.37	1.21	1.53	1.16	1.19
7. $300 to 1,000	0.30	1.36	0.98	1.46	1.25	1.26
8. $70 to 1,000	0.44	1.36	1.11	1.50	1.21	1.22
9. $51.8 to 1,382	0.44	1.34	1.13	1.49	1.16	1.20

			Subdivisions of S			
		Banking,		Banking, insurance, real estate, and	Public	Public administration
		insurance,			adminis-	and other
		and real	Dwell-	dwell-	adminis-	Other	services
	Trade	estate	ings	ings	tration	services	services
	(1)	(2)	(3)	(4)	(5)	(6)	(7)
Shares at benchmark values of GDP per capita (%)							
10. $70	12.7	1.0	3.7	4.7	6.2	7.3	13.5
11. $150	13.8	1.9	5.7	7.5	6.8	8.8	15.6
12. $300	14.6	2.9	5.9	8.8	7.7	9.5	17.2
13. $500	13.6	3.3	5.5	8.8	8.2	9.9	18.1
14. $1,000	13.4	3.6	4.4	8.0	8.4	10.1	18.5
E values for a standard increase in GDP per capita of 20 percent							
15. $70 to 300	1.10	1.83	1.37	1.49	1.16	1.20	1.18

Table 14 — continued

	(1)	(2)	(3)	(4)	(5)	(6)	(7)
16. $300 to							
1,000	0.92	1.22	0.73	0.92	1.08	1.06	1.07
17. $70 to 1,000	1.02	1.55	1.07	1.22	1.12	1.14	1.13
18. $51.8 to							
1,382	1.04	1.68	1.16	1.33	1.12	1.16	1.14

Lines 1–5, 10–14: The shares at benchmark values are estimated by interpolation of series based on Table 12 (calculated to two decimal places). These series are successive three-group means of the geometric means of the group averages of per capita product and of the arithmetic means of the group shares and include the single terminal groups. The differences in percentage shares are then apportioned in accordance with the proportional differences in the logarithms of the mean per capita product.

Lines 6–9, 15–18: The equation used to compute E from relative differences in per capita product and sectoral shares is $E_i = a_i + [(a_i - 1)/r]$, where E_i refers to sector i; a_i is the ratio of the sector's share at the end of the interval to its share at the beginning of the interval (so that usually it is less than 1.0 for the A sector and more than 1.0 for the I sector); and r is the fraction by which per capita product increases over the interval (see Simon Kuznets, *Modern Economic Growth: Rate, Structure, and Spread* [New Haven: Yale University Press, 1966], p. 99, and discussion on pp. 98–100). In the calculation I adopted a standard r of 20 percent, and, by dividing the logarithms of the actual $(1 + r)$ by the logarithm of 1.20, calculated the relevant number of standard interval units. Thus, the range from $70 to $300 yielded roughly 8 standard interval units, that from $300 to $1,000 roughly 6.6, and that from $51.8 to $1,382 yielded about 18. I then divided the logarithm of the actual a_i by the relevant number of standard units, took the antilog of the result, and substituted it for a_i in the above equation to derive E_i.

capita (see lines 6, 7). The intriguing exceptions are the construction and public utility subdivisions of the I sector.[3]

One other aspect of the table deserves explicit mention. In the span from $70 to $300, the share of the A sector drops markedly, with a correspondingly large rise in the share of the I+S sector.

3. Professor Chenery's analysis for 1950–1955, in "Patterns of Industrial Growth," yields similar results when the E values for similar benchmark ranges of per capita product are estimated. For this purpose I had to estimate NDP values in 1953 prices corresponding to GDP values in 1958 prices since Professor Chenery's sample and equation are based on 1953 prices. Having the benchmark values, I derived shares in product corresponding to those used in Table 14; and for major sectors treated shares in NDP as comparable with those in GDP. The E values thus derived from Professor Chenery's analysis (using the equations in his table 3, and setting the coefficient of the size factor at 0) are:

	$70 to 300	$300 to 1,000	$70 to 1,000
A sector	0.55	0.40	0.48
I sector as defined in Table 14	1.47	1.30	1.39
S sector	1.18	1.01	1.10

Except for the greater decline in the coefficient for the I sector, these E values and their movements are fairly close to those shown in Table 14.

But within the nonagricultural part of the economy, the shares of the I and S sectors do not shift much, the former accounting for 40 percent of the non-A total at the $70 benchmark and for 45 percent at the $300 benchmark. By contrast, between the $300 and $1,000 benchmark values, the share of the I sector in the non-A total shifts from 45 percent to 55 percent. If one draws a distinction between the shift from agriculture to nonagriculture within the production structure, and the shift within the nonagricultural sector, the suggestion is that, for the lower spans of per capita product, where the share of the nonagricultural sectors rises rapidly, the structure within it may shift only moderately; whereas at the higher levels of per capita product the shifts in structure among the nonagricultural sectors and divisions are more marked.

This suggestion is supported by the association found between per capita product and the structure of manufacturing (Table 15). Since manufacturing is the subdivision for which the share in gross domestic product increases most as we move from low to high per capita product groups, it is interesting to observe the branches of manufacturing that contribute most to this rising contribution of manufacturing — a rise that is more than half of the decline in the share of the A sector. The data on subdivisions of manufacturing come from sources other than the national economic accounts (for most countries), and relate to value added, not to the net (or gross of capital consumption) contribution to national or domestic product. However, these shares of manufacturing branches in total manufacturing value added may be linked with the share of manufacturing in gross domestic product, to derive shares of manufacturing branches in the latter. This was done for Table 15, separately for 1953 and 1963, and the use of the two years was dictated by an interest, explained in Chapter IV, in changes over time in cross-section relations. For the present purposes, however, we use averages of the two cross-sections to approximate the levels for 1958, the mid-year of the span.

Both the detailed and broader classifications reveal that for the span between about $92 and $306 per capita product (in 1958 prices), the shifts in the structure of manufacturing value added are quite limited (lines 1–19). For the six major groups the total shift between columns 1 and 3 (the sum of changes in shares), signs disregarded, amounts to 11.0 percentage points; for the thirteen branches the total shift is 20.6 percentage points. But from the 1958

Table 15. Shares of branches of manufacturing in manufacturing value added and in gross domestic product, at benchmark values of GDP per capita (average of cross-section shares for 1953 and 1963).

	Benchmark values of GDP per capita					
1953$:	81	135	270	450	900	1,200[a]
1958$:	91.7	153	306	510	1,019	1,359
	(1)	(2)	(3)	(4)	(5)	(6)
A. Shares in manufacturing value added (%)						
1. Food, beverages, and tobacco	33.8	37.4	34.8	27.2	17.6	15.5
2. Textiles	18.3	14.2	10.5	9.4	7.1	5.6
3. Clothing and footwear	4.8	6.3	7.8	7.5	6.3	5.5
4. Wood products and furniture	6.9	5.4	4.9	5.1	5.7	5.4
5. Paper and paper products	0.9	1.3	1.9	2.9	3.9	4.3
6. Printing and publishing	2.5	2.6	2.9	3.5	4.7	5.3
7. Leather products (excluding footwear)	1.1	1.3	1.2	1.1	0.8	0.7
8. Rubber products	1.2	1.4	1.2	1.3	1.4	1.4
9. Chemicals and petroleum products	8.7	9.3	9.7	9.6	8.9	9.3
10. Nonmetal mineral products	5.4	5.5	4.9	4.8	4.7	4.5
11. Basic metals	4.0	3.5	4.3	5.2	5.7	6.0
12. Metal products	10.4	9.9	13.7	19.8	29.8	32.8
13. Miscellaneous	2.0	1.9	2.2	2.6	3.4	3.7
Major groups						
14. Food, beverages, and tobacco	33.8	37.4	34.8	27.2	17.6	15.5
15. Textiles and clothing (lines 2–3)	23.1	20.5	18.3	16.9	13.4	11.1
16. Wood, paper, printing, and leather (lines 4–7)	11.4	10.6	10.9	12.6	15.1	15.7
17. Rubber, chemicals, and petroleum (lines 8–9)	9.9	10.7	10.9	10.9	10.3	10.7

Table 15 — continued

	(1)	(2)	(3)	(4)	(5)	(6)
18. Industrial raw materials (lines 10–11)	9.4	9.0	9.2	10.0	10.4	10.5
19. Fabricated metal products (lines 12–13)	12.4	11.8	15.9	22.4	33.2	36.5
B. Shares in GDP (%)						
20. Total manufacturing	11.6	14.1	19.9	25.2	29.5	30.0
21. Food, beverages, and tobacco	4.0	5.2	6.9	6.8	5.2	4.6
22. Textiles	2.2	2.0	2.1	2.4	2.1	1.7
23. Clothing and footwear	0.5	0.9	1.6	1.9	1.9	1.6
24. Wood products and furniture	0.8	0.8	1.0	1.3	1.7	1.6
25. Paper and paper products	0.1	0.2	0.4	0.7	1.1	1.3
26. Printing and publishing	0.3	0.4	0.6	0.9	1.4	1.6
27. Leather products (excluding footwear)	0.1	0.2	0.2	0.3	0.2	0.2
28. Rubber products	0.1	0.2	0.2	0.3	0.4	0.4
29. Chemicals and petroleum products	1.0	1.3	1.9	2.4	2.6	2.8
30. Nonmetal mineral products	0.6	0.7	1.0	1.2	1.4	1.4
31. Basic metals	0.5	0.5	0.9	1.3	1.7	1.8
32. Metal products	1.2	1.4	2.7	5.0	8.8	9.9
33. Miscellaneous	0.2	0.3	0.4	0.7	1.0	1.1
Major groups						
34. Food, beverages, and tobacco	4.0	5.2	6.9	6.8	5.2	4.6
35. Textiles and clothing (lines 22–23)	2.7	2.9	3.7	4.3	4.0	3.3
36. Wood, paper, printing, and leather (lines 24–27)	1.3	1.6	2.2	3.2	4.4	4.7

Table 15 — continued

	(1)	(2)	(3)	(4)	(5)	(6)
37. Rubber, chemicals, and petroleum (lines 28–29)	1.1	1.5	2.1	2.7	3.0	3.2
38. Industrial raw materials (lines 30–31)	1.1	1.2	1.9	2.5	3.1	3.2
39. Fabricated metal products (lines 32–33)	1.4	1.7	3.1	5.7	9.8	11.0

ᵃ Based on 1963 alone, but the structures for 1953 and 1963 at the benchmark level of $900 (in 1953 prices) are quite similar.

The procedure used in deriving the shares is that described in the notes to Table 14.

Per capita GDP, needed for grouping the countries, was derived by extrapolating the per capita GDP in U.S. dollars, given for 1958 in the *Yearbook of National Accounts Statistics, 1967*, table 7B, either by the per capita GDP derived by dividing GDP in constant prices, given in *ibid.*, country tables, by population given in the *Demographic Yearbook, 1965*, table 4 for 1953, and *1967*, table 4 for 1963, or by the index of real product per capita, given in the Organisation for Economic Co-operation and Development, *National Accounts of Less Developed Countries, 1950–1966* (Paris, July 1968), table E. The latter method of extrapolation was used for all countries in the listing below of countries in the sample except those followed by (YNAS), for which the former method was used.

The GDP per capita estimates in 1958 dollars were then shifted to the 1953 base by the price index implicit in GNP for the United States, given in the *Economic Report of the President* (Washington, D.C., February 1968), table B-3, p. 212.

Lines 1–13: The underlying estimates of shares in value added in total manufacturing are unpublished figures kindly supplied by the United Nations Statistical Office. The countries included in the sample are in increasing order of GDP per capita in 1953: Nigeria, Tanzania, Burma, Mozambique, India, Pakistan, Kenya, Thailand, Congo Republic, Taiwan, United Arab Republic, South Korea, Paraguay, Ceylon, Syria, Tunisia, Ecuador, Peru, Brazil, Philippines, Morocco, Honduras, Turkey, Dominican Republic, El Salvador, Colombia, Nicaragua, Guatemala, Mexico, Spain, Greece, Japan (YNAS), Costa Rica, Chile, Italy (YNAS), Argentina, Ireland (YNAS), Uruguay, Austria (YNAS), France (YNAS), Belgium (YNAS), Norway (YNAS), Denmark (YNAS), United Kingdom (YNAS), Australia (YNAS), Switzerland (YNAS), New Zealand (YNAS), Sweden (YNAS), Canada (YNAS), and the United States (YNAS).

The subgroups are based on the two-digit SITC classification and the numbers corresponding to lines 1–13 are 20–22, 23, 24, 25–26, 27, 28, 29, 30, 31–32, 33, 34, 35–38, 39.

Line 20: The underlying data are from the *Yearbook of National Accounts Statistics, 1967* except for the Philippines (for which the data are taken from the 1966 issue) and Jamaica (GDP per capita based on OECD sources). The countries included are in increasing order of GDP per capita in 1953: Nigeria, Burma, Pakistan, Thailand, Taiwan, South Korea, Paraguay, Ceylon, Ecuador, Peru, Philippines, Honduras, Turkey, Dominican Republic, Portugal, Colombia, Jamaica, Greece, Japan, Costa Rica, Chile, Italy, Puerto Rico, Argentina, Austria, Israel, Netherlands, Finland, West Germany, France, Belgium, Norway, Denmark, United Kingdom, Australia, Sweden, Canada, and the United States.

Lines 21–33: Averages of the shares for 1953 and 1963, based on the shares underlying lines 1–13, 20.

dollar benchmark of $306 to that of $1,019, also a multiple of 3.3, the total shift in the shares is 45.4 percentage points for the six major groups, and 47.0 for the thirteen branches. Within the lower span of per capita product, while the share of manufacturing in total product rises rapidly, the changes in the internal structure of manufacturing are quite limited; whereas at the higher levels of per capita product the familiar shifts within manufacturing away from food, clothing, and wood products, toward chemical and metal products, become conspicuous.

The shares of manufacturing in GDP, derived for some thirty-eight countries in Table 15, are quite similar at the benchmark levels in 1958 prices, to those in Table 14 (compare Table 15, line 20 with Table 14, column 4, lines 1–5, allowing for the differences in benchmark values). The average for 1953 and 1963 in Table 15, like the share for 1958 in Table 14, shows a rise from about 10 percent at the lowest benchmark value to about 30 percent at the highest.

The combination of the internal shifts within manufacturing with the rise in its share in product, particularly rapid in the lower ranges of per capita product, results in a distinctive pattern of changes of shares of branches of manufacturing in aggregate product (lines 21–39). All major branches contribute heavily to the rise in the share of manufacturing in total product over the lower per capita product spans, that is, within the range from about $92 to about $500 (in 1958 prices, from column 1 to column 4); and it is only in the brackets above $500 per capita that the shares of some major branches of manufacturing, such as food, and textiles and clothing, decline. Thus, of the rise in the manufacturing share in total product of some 13.6 percentage points between the benchmark values of $92 and $500, food and textiles and clothing alone contribute 4.4 percentage points, or a third; whereas the shares of these two branches in total product *decline* 3.2 percentage points over the range from $500 to over $1,300 per capita product. The distribution among the thirteen branches provides more detail on the association, but the conclusion remains that the shift in the structure of manufacturing between the lower benchmark values of per capita product differs substantially from that between the higher per capita product values, causing differences in the contribution of the various branches to the increase in total product.

Effect of Size

Given the marked association between per capita product and sectoral shares in total output, the question still arises whether a country's size is a significant factor affecting sectoral structure. A country's size bears heavily upon the proportion of foreign trade to total product and hence upon the effects of foreign demand and supply on structure of domestic output.[4] Size also may determine feasible economies of scale, thereby shaping the structure of domestic output, regardless of foreign trade effects. Finally, since size and level of economic development (the latter as indicated by per capita product) are *not* significantly associated, the former constitutes an additional and separate variable, and its effects should be approximated.

In its bearing on both foreign trade proportions and the size of the domestic market relevant to economies of scale, an appropriate simple measure of size would be the magnitude of total output. But since effects of size should be measured independently of those of per capita product, differences in size will be observed at identical or similar levels of per capita product — in a double cross-classification of the two variables. This specific cross-classification was adopted, despite its cumbersomeness, in order to avoid the assumptions and anonymity of a multiple regression procedure applied to the type of data under analysis. For identical levels of per capita product, however, relative differences in size as measured by total product and by population are the same, and population was used as the criterion, with the dividing line set at ten million, and countries allocated to two groups — large (over ten million) and small (under ten million).

The dividing line was drawn so as to have enough cases in each group to allow adequate analysis of effects of per capita product within each group, hence of the size effects at the same benchmark levels of per capita product. Table 16, in which the basic sample for 1958 is divided into twenty-two large and thirty-five small countries, shows that large countries accounted for a large proportion within seven of the eight groups classified by per capita product — reflecting the lack of association between size and per capita product; and

4. See, for example, Simon Kuznets, "Quantitative Aspects of the Economic Growth of Nations: IX. Level and Structure of Foreign Trade: Comparisons for Recent Years," *Economic Development and Cultural Change,* vol. XIII, no. 1, part II (October 1964).

Table 16. Large and small countries in sample, grouped by 1958 GDP per capita.

	Groups of countries in increasing order of 1958 GDP per capita							
	I (1)	II (2)	III (3)	IV (4)	V (5)	VI (6)	VII (7)	VIII (8)
1. Total number of countries (see Table 12)	6	6	6	15	6	6	6	6
2. Number of large countries	3	3	1	5	2	2	2	4
3. GDP per capita, large countries ($)	56.5	84.3	121	229	359	583	845	1,500
4. Regional identity of large countries	F-1 A-2	F-1 A-2	A-1	A-2 L-3	A-1 E-1	L-1 E-1	E-2	E-2 S-2
5. Number of small countries	3	3	5	10	4	4	4	2
6. GDP per capita of small countries ($)	47.4	80.9	141	217	361	520	873	1,174
7. Regional identity of small countries	F-3	F-2 L-1	A-3 L-2	F-2 A-1 L-6 E-1	L-3 E-1	A-1 L-2 E-1	E-4	E-1 S-1

	Groups of large countries by GDP per capita				
	I (1)	II (2)	III (3)	IV (4)	V (5)
8. Number	5	4	5	4	4
9. GDP per capita ($)	62.9	149	294	702	1,500
10. Average population (millions)	119.2	25.0	46.9	33.1	72.2
11. Regional identity	F-1 A-4	F-1 A-3	A-1 L-3 E-1	L-1 E-3	E-2 S-2

	Groups of small countries by GDP per capita						
	I (1)	II (2)	III (3)	IV (4)	V (5)	VI (6)	VII (7)
12. Number	5	5	5	5	5	5	5
13. GDP per capita ($)	58.1	122	193	226	337	546	1,039

Table 16 — continued

	(1)	(2)	(3)	(4)	(5)	(6)	(7)
14. Average population (millions)	7.5	5.8	3.9	4.8	3.9	3.3	6.3
15. Regional identity	F-5	A-3	F-2	A-1	L-4	L-2	E-4
		L-2	L-3	L-3	E-1	A-1	S-1
				E-1		E-2	

Based on data underlying Table 12, and on population estimates for 1958, taken from United Nations, *Demographic Yearbook, 1965*. Large countries have a GDP of $1,200 million or more and a population of 10 million or more in 1958. GDP per capita (lines 3, 6, 9, 13) is the geometric mean for each group; and population (lines 10, 14) is the arithmetic mean.

that the contrast with respect to size was quite substantial, the averages for groups among the large countries ranging from 25 to 119 million, and those among the small countries, from 3.3 to 7.5 million (lines 10, 14). The other detail of interest, partially revealed by the averages in Table 16 (particularly line 10), is that the truly large countries, say with populations of about 50 million or more, tend to cluster at the extremes of the per capita product range. As the regional identity entries indicate, most of these countries are in Asia (India, Pakistan, Indonesia, and Japan), disregarding here Mainland China, with one in Africa (Nigeria) and one in Latin America (Brazil); and all except Japan are at the lower end of the per capita product range (line 11). The other large countries (the United States, the United Kingdom, France, Germany, and Italy) are at the upper end of the per capita product range. Practically no truly large countries fall between the two extremes. This suggests that the international contrasts in per capita product are even more striking when weighted by population at either end rather than by number of countries; but the bearing upon the specific question at hand — the effect of size on structure of domestic production — is not clear enough to warrant pursuing this clue further.

The effects of grouping countries by size on the shares of the major sectors and their subdivisions, at the benchmark levels of per capita product in 1958, are shown in Table 17. The procedures followed for each of the two size groups were the same as those used for the total sample in Table 14; but since fewer countries are covered, the approximations are subject to greater errors (or rather, greater effects of some elements peculiar to individual countries).

Table 17. Shares of production sectors in gross domestic product at benchmark values of GDP per capita, large and small countries, 1958.

	Benchmark values of GDP per capita ($)					Average, cols.
	70 (1)	150 (2)	300 (3)	500 (4)	1,000 (5)	1–5 (6)
A. Population (millions)						
1. Large countries	59.0	38.4	30.3	34.5	44.0	40.1
2. Small countries	6.1	4.0	3.2	3.5	5.6	4.3
B. Shares in GDP (%)						
Major sectors						
A						
3. Large countries	45.8	36.1	26.5	19.4	10.9	27.8
4. Small countries	50.7	37.0	26.7	20.4	14.2	29.8
				(20.5)	(14.6)	
I						
5. Large countries	21.0	28.4	36.9	42.5	48.4	35.4
6. Small countries	21.1	26.5	31.4	38.1	48.7	33.2
				(37.7)	(47.2)	
S						
7. Large countries	33.2	35.5	36.6	38.1	40.7	36.8
8. Small countries	28.2	36.5	41.9	41.5	37.1	37.0
				(41.8)	(38.2)	
Subdivisions of I						
Manufacturing						
9. Large countries	10.4	15.8	22.2	26.4	30.7	21.1
10. Small countries	8.3	13.5	16.9	21.0	27.1	17.3
Construction						
11. Large countries	3.6	4.0	4.2	4.6	5.5	4.4
12. Small countries	4.9	4.4	5.0	6.1	7.4	5.6
Transport and communication and electricity, gas, and water						
13. Large countries	5.9	6.7	7.9	8.7	9.4	7.7
14. Small countries	6.8	7.0	7.4	9.2	12.7	8.6
				(8.6)	(10.6)	
Subdivisions of S						
Trade						
15. Large countries	15.8	13.7	12.8	13.6	14.0	14.0
16. Small countries	10.2	13.8	15.8	14.4	12.8	13.4
Banking, insurance, and real estate and income from dwellings						
17. Large countries	4.9	6.9	7.4	7.3	7.6	6.8
18. Small countries	3.9	7.5	8.8	9.0	8.1	7.5

Table 17 — continued

	(1)	(2)	(3)	(4)	(5)	(6)
Public and private services						
19. Large countries	12.5	14.9	16.4	17.2	19.1	16.0
20. Small countries	14.1	15.2	17.3	18.0	16.2	16.2

Lines 1–2: Population estimated by interpolation procedure similar to that used to estimate the shares corresponding to benchmark values. The averages in column 6 are geometric means.

Lines 3–20: Based on data underlying Table 12. The entries in parentheses in columns 4–5, lines 4, 6, 8, 14, exclude Norway, which, because of the large share of its transport and communication, affects significantly the estimated values at the $500 and $1,000 benchmark levels. The averages in column 6 are arithmetic means.

The interpolated population averages in lines 1–2 indicate the differences in size at each benchmark level of per capita product; if the relative difference in size is most relevant, the population ratio of large to small countries, which varies from 8–1 to 10–1, that is, within a fairly narrow range, suggests that differences in size are not associated with differences in per capita product.

Certain effects of the size breakdown are sufficiently consistent to warrant explicit mention. First, in general, at the same level of per capita product, the share of the A sector tends to be larger in the small countries than in the large, with the differences notably marked at the extreme per capita product levels (lines 3–4). Conversely, the share of the I sector tends to be larger in the large countries than in the small — because of the larger share of manufacturing in the large countries — with the shares of both construction and transport and public utilities being smaller in the large countries (lines 5, 6, 9–14).

Although the shares of the S sector for the large and small countries are roughly the same on the average, about 37 percent of GDP, the patterns of change as we move from the lower to the higher levels of per capita product are different. For the large countries, the share rises fairly steadily through the full range of the benchmark levels, from 33.2 percent at the $70 level to 40.7 percent at the $1,000 level (line 7). For the small countries the share rises only within the lower part of the income range, from 28.2 percent at the $70 level to 41.9 percent at the $300 level, then declines at the higher income levels (line 8). Obviously the pattern of movement for the full sample, that is, a rise in the share to $300 and stability or decline at higher income levels results from the pattern of movement in the small countries (see Table 14, lines 1–5, column 3).

Finally, the difference between the large and the small countries in the movement of the share of the S sector with differences in per capita product is found also in such major subdivisions as trade, and public plus private services. For the former the share in the small countries rises from the $70 to the $300 benchmark level, for the latter to the $500 level, and both decline at the higher levels; even for the much smaller financial subdivision, the share rises to the $500 level and then declines (lines 16, 18, 20). In the large countries, the share of trade is roughly constant at 13–14 percent over most of the range in per capita product, with the doubtful exception of a 16 percent share at the lowest income level ($70). Also, in the large countries the share of services other than trade and finance rises steadily and significantly from 12.5 percent at the $70 level to 19.1 percent at the $1,000 level; and is significantly lower than in the small countries at the lower income levels and higher at the upper income levels (lines 19, 20).

The differences between large and small countries in the levels and patterns of shares of sectors and subdivisions just summarized may prove of interest in more intensive analysis. But by far the dominant conclusion suggested by Table 17 is that the effects of per capita product on differences in shares of various sectors and subdivisions persist almost in full force *within* both major size groups; and that, compared with these, the effect of size on the differences in the shares of sectors and their subdivisions is minor. This is especially true of the major sectors and large subdivisions. Thus, for the A sector the difference between columns 1 and 5 (by per capita product) is 35 percentage points for the large countries, and 36 percentage points for the small (compared with 37 percentage points in Table 14, column 1, lines 1–5); and the average difference between large and small countries is just 2 percentage points. For manufacturing, the one major subdivision for which the shares differ consistently between the large and the small countries, the average difference between the two groups is 3.9 percentage points, whereas the differences in the shares between the extreme benchmark levels of per capita product are 20 points for the large countries and 17 for the small.

The size factor appears to have a somewhat greater effect on the structure of manufacturing (Table 18). Manufacturing in the large

Table 18. Shares of major branches of manufacturing in manufacturing value
added and in gross domestic product, at benchmark values of GDP
per capita, large and small countries (averages of cross-section shares
for 1953 and 1963).

	Benchmark values of GDP per capita (1958 $)					
	91.7 (1)	153 (2)	306 (3)	510 (4)	1,019 (5)	Average, cols. 1–5 (6)
A. Shares in manufacturing value added (%)						
Large countries (twenty-two)						
1. Food, beverages, and tobacco	33.5	29.3	23.3	19.4	14.7	24.0
2. Textiles and clothing	22.0	21.3	18.7	16.0	13.2	18.2
3. Wood, paper, printing, and leather	12.3	11.4	11.1	11.7	12.9	11.9
4. Rubber, chemicals, and petroleum products	11.0	12.5	13.6	13.6	12.7	12.7
5. Industrial raw materials	8.2	9.5	10.8	11.5	11.4	10.3
6. Fabricated metal products	13.0	16.0	22.5	27.8	35.1	22.9
7. Shifts in shares	29.4[a]		30.0[b]		55.2[c]	
Small countries (thirty-three)						
8. Food, beverages, and tobacco	33.9	39.5	37.4	31.5	20.3	32.5
9. Textiles and clothing	21.4	20.5	19.0	17.0	13.1	18.2
10. Wood, paper, printing, and leather	11.2	10.4	11.5	13.5	16.9	12.7
11. Rubber, chemicals, and petroleum products	10.3	9.3	9.1	9.0	8.8	9.3
12. Industrial raw materials	11.1	9.4	8.7	8.9	9.4	9.5
13. Fabricated metal products	12.1	10.9	14.3	20.1	31.5	17.8
14. Shifts in shares	12.0[a]		46.6[b]		50.2[c]	
B. Shares in GDP (%)						
Large countries						
15. Total manufacturing in 1958	12	16	22	26	31	21.4
16. Food, beverages, and tobacco	3.8	4.7	5.1	5.1	4.6	4.6
17. Textiles and clothing	2.6	3.4	4.1	4.2	4.1	3.7

Table 18 — continued

	(1)	(2)	(3)	(4)	(5)	(6)
18. Wood, paper, printing, and leather	1.2	1.8	2.5	3.0	4.0	2.5
19. Rubber, chemicals, and petroleum products	1.5	2.0	3.0	3.5	3.9	2.8
20. Industrial raw materials	1.2	1.5	2.4	3.0	3.5	2.3
21. Fabricated metal products	1.7	2.6	4.9	7.2	10.9	5.5
22. Rise in shares (lines 16–18 compared with line 15)	4.1 out of 10[a]		2.0 out of 9[b]		5.1 out of 19[c]	

Small countries

	(1)	(2)	(3)	(4)	(5)	(6)
23. Total manufacturing in 1958	12	14	17	21	27	18.2
24. Food, beverages, and tobacco	4.1	5.5	6.3	6.6	5.5	5.6
25. Textiles and clothing	2.6	2.9	3.2	3.6	3.5	3.2
26. Wood, paper, printing, and leather	1.3	1.5	.2.0	2.8	4.6	2.4
27. Rubber, chemicals, and petroleum products	1.2	1.3	1.6	1.9	2.4	1.7
28. Industrial raw materials	1.3	1.3	1.5	1.9	2.5	1.7
29. Fabricated metal products	1.5	1.5	2.4	4.2	8.5	3.6
30. Rise in shares (lines 24–26 compared with line 23)	3.5 out of 5[a]		3.7 out of 10[b]		5.6 out of 15[c]	

[a] Column 1 to column 3.
[b] Column 3 to column 5.
[c] Column 1 to column 5.
For the countries covered and sources of data in lines 1–6, 8–13, and the coverage of the major groups see the notes to Table 15. For the basis of classification of large and small countries see the notes to Table 16.
Lines 15, 23: Based on the 1958 cross-section shares of manufacturing in GDP given in Table 17, lines 9–10.
Lines 16–21, 24–29: Derived by multiplying the shares in manufacturing value added by the share of total manufacturing in gross domestic product.
For the meaning of lines 7, 14, 22, 30, see discussion of Table 15.

countries is characterized by a distinctly lower share of the food group, and distinctly higher shares of the chemicals and fabricated metal product groups (column 6, lines 1–6, 8–13). Moreover, in the large countries the movement away from the food products industries toward the chemicals and metal products starts in the span from $92 to $300; and the relative stability of the structure of manufacturing within the lower span of per capita product, noted in connection with Table 15, is observed here for the smaller countries alone. In the large countries, the shift in structure of manufacturing is as large in the lower income span as it is in the higher — about 30 percentage points; whereas in the small countries, the shift in structure is only 12 percentage points in the former compared with over 45 points in the latter (lines 7, 14). However, it should be noted that, in association with an identical movement in benchmark values of per capita product, the total shift in the structure of manufacturing (from column 1 to column 5) is almost as great for the small countries as for the large.

Panel B shows the shares of the major branches of manufacturing in total product, using rough estimates of the shares of manufacturing in GDP for large and small countries, derived from Table 17. The differences in structure to be expected from panel A are present but much reduced; and the general pattern of movements of the shares in total product is much the same for the large and small countries, while the differences in level are minor compared with the rise in the share as we move along the income scale. Thus, the shares of the food and textiles and clothing groups in the total product rise to the $510 benchmark and decline at the higher levels of per capita product in both the large and small countries (lines 16–17, 24–25). The shares of the chemical, industrial raw materials, and fabricated metal products groups rise consistently in both large and small countries (lines 20–22, 27–29). And the difference between the average shares of, say, the metal products group in the large and small countries, 1.9 percentage points, is small compared with the product-associated range in the share of this group: 9.2 percentage points for the large and 7.0 for the small countries (lines 21, 29).

More detailed analysis of the size factor is of interest,[5] but in view of the dominance of the association of shares of major sectors and subdivisions with per capita product, and the limited weight of the size factor, the size variable is omitted from further discussion.

5. See Hollis B. Chenery and Lance Taylor, "Development Patterns: Among Countries and Over Time," *The Review of Economics and Statistics,* vol. L, no. 4 (November 1968), pp. 391–416. However, as the discussion in Chapters IV and VI indicates, cross-section parameters are sensitive to changes over time; and since the latter affect significantly the applicability of cross-section values to time trends, there is a question as to the effect on conclusions in this paper of the pooling of time series and cross-section data.

Comments on the Cross-Section Association

Several groups of factors might explain the dominant association between per capita product and shares of sectors and subdivisions in total output, even after the size factor is taken into account. The structure of demand, that is, the differential response of demand for various goods to greater per capita income, is one. The technological involvement, by its impact on scale of plant and enterprise and hence on conditions of life of the population, would also affect demand differently at low and high levels of per capita product; and furthermore, the different input–output relations among sectors would have a differential impact on the *net* output of various sectors, even gross of capital consumption (as distinct from the full value of final product, important from the standpoint of demand structure). Indeed, the lines of connection are numerous since most of the correlates of per capita product — not only the purely economic, like those already mentioned, but also the noneconomic concomitants in demographic, political, and other social institutions — might have some bearing on production structure. Although some of these may not significantly affect the shares of major sectors, they may be relevant to the explanation of patterns for the shares of some subdivisions, for example, of income from dwellings or of the public services subdivision.

To attempt an adequate explanation of the association between differences in per capita output and the variety of production structure by sector and subdivision would involve a proper measure of the weights of the proximate factors and tests of the persistence of the relations in cross-sections at different dates, and is beyond the scope of this book. But, bearing in mind a concern with long-term trends in production structure in the course of modern economic growth, it is appropriate to comment on one major point: the relation between the findings for the A and I sectors and the Engel and similar "laws" concerning cross-section income or expenditure elasticities of demand for consumer goods (and saving). Any conclusions reached would have some relevance for the association between per capita product and the shares of other sectors and subdivisions.

The income or expenditure elasticities of demand for various products relate per capita income or expenditures (for individuals and households) to the proportions of income or expenditures spent on various categories of consumer goods or devoted to saving. In considering elasticity of demand for goods, the relation is between personal disposable income or total expenditures per capita and the proportions spent on consumer goods at final cost to the purchasers (at market prices). And the many studies of family expenditures reveal the consistent decline in the proportion spent on foods as per capita income and expenditures rise. Since foods are the main product of the A sector, this low propensity to consume them may be a major factor in the decline in the share of the A sector in total product from about 50 percent at the $70 benchmark level to about 10 percent at $1,000 (see Table 14). Likewise, the high income and expenditure elasticities of demand for clothing and durable consumer goods (and for savings, which are translated into manufactured producer goods or construction) may account for the increase in the share of the I sector from about 20 percent at the $70 benchmark level to about 50 percent at $1,000.

But the relations of the type observed in Table 14 differ from the proper measure of income elasticity of demand in at least five respects. Even when these sources of differences are removed, a major question remains as to whether the properly measured income elasticity of demand reflects some set of priorities of human wants invariant to differing technological and institutional conditions, or is a variable reflection of the latter.

(a) GDP per capita at factor cost (used for Table 14) differs from personal disposable income per capita, relevant to income elasticity of demand. GDP at factor cost includes profits of private enterprises (gross of capital consumption) and government income, either from enterprises, etc. or from direct taxes; and the share of GDP not represented by personal disposable income ranged in the 1950's between 15 percent for the less developed countries and about 20 percent for the more developed countries.[6] We do not know whether business firms and governments in the less developed and more developed countries apportion their gross profits and other income differently between the A and I sectors. But this is a substantial proportion of total product (distributed among the A, I, and S sectors) on which household propensity to consume has no bearing. Furthermore, we know that the share of personal dispos-

6. See Simon Kuznets, *Modern Economic Growth: Rate, Structure, and Spread* (New Haven: Yale University Press, 1966), table 8.1, lines 84–93, p. 406. The comparison is between countries with 1958 per capita GDP of less than $200 and of more than $575.

able income in GDP declines over time, and consequently a different or changing disposition of the increasing remainder may have a bearing on the movements over time of the A and I sector shares in GDP.

(b) Even if the independent variable were personal disposable income, the range in the shares of the products of the A and I sectors in the consumption or output in international comparisons would be significantly affected by the size distribution of income, particularly in the low income countries — and differently from the way in which it is affected in typical cross-section studies among individuals and families within a single country. In a single country, the units are grouped by size of income (whether or not adjusted for transitory elements); and unmeasured variations in inequality are confined within relatively narrow income-size classes. This is not true of international comparisons where the units are countries, and where two countries with the same low per capita income can have markedly different size distributions of income.

The possible effect on the range of shares in series like those in Table 14 can be seen from a simple illustration. Assume that in one low income country, 99 percent of the population receive 70 percent of total income, and their average propensity to use the products of the A sector is 0.6, while the propensity of the top 1 percent of the population, which receives 30 percent of total income, is 0.1 for the same products. The total average propensity (the share of the A sector output, assuming no foreign trade balances, and so on) is then $(0.70 \times 0.6) + (0.30 \times 0.1)$, or 45 percent. Assume that in the other low income country the distribution is equal, so that the lower 99 percent of the population receive 99 percent of the income, and their average income is 41.4 percent higher. With this change in the income distribution, the average share spent on A products becomes 0.55 (for all income groups), declining for the low income groups and rising for the top group. Thus, with the same average per capita income, and a similar internal propensity to consume, the share of expenditures on the A products would be 45 percent in one country and 55 percent in the other.

The example is extreme and could easily be modified, but the point is obvious. While the size distribution of income at the higher levels of per capita product can usually have only a limited effect on consumption and savings propensities and on the differential impact on the A and I sectors, it can have a perceptible effect at the lower per capita income levels. This means that any observed international difference in the range of shares of the A and I sectors (or similar size-of-income-sensitive sectors and subdivisions) is partly based upon some implicit size distribution; and could change perceptibly for the *same* range of per capita income, with substantial changes in the size distribution at the lower end of the income array. Even at the higher income levels, modifications of the size distribution, if substantial enough, could have a perceptible effect on the share of the A sector, especially if the latter has dropped to an absolutely low level.

(c) Domestic output (which is what Table 14 reflects) differs from domestic consumption or private consumption expenditures (which is what income elasticity of demand reflects). The discrepancy lies in the addition of imports and subtraction of exports, in the flow from domestic output to domestic consumption; and the differences between developed and less developed countries in the structure of exports and imports with respect to A and I sector products are well-known. But available data suggest that the quantitative contribution of this factor to changes in shares in Table 14 is rather limited (Table 19). The significant feature of Table 19 — and it would probably not be changed even if a more elaborate adjustment were made — is that in both the small and large countries, products of the A sector are a sizable fraction of total exports, even at the higher per capita product levels; and in both groups of countries, products of the A sector are a substantial proportion of imports, even at the lowest per capita product levels. The net balances, which are of most interest here, at the several benchmark levels of per capita product, differ too slightly to produce a significant shift from the range of shares in domestic output to that in shares in flow into domestic use. Thus, for the large countries, the share of the A sector in domestic output declines from 45.8 to 10.9 percent, roughly from 4.2 to 1; the share in flow into domestic use declines from 42.0 to 11.3, or roughly from 3.7 to 1. The adjustment for the net balance of A or I exports and imports has, in general, a fairly limited effect, even if it does contribute a minor fraction to the association between the shares of the A and I sectors and per capita product — a fraction not connected with the domestic propensities to consume or save.

(d) The difference between the concept of a sectoral share in the case of production structure (as in Table 14) and in the case of final

Table 19. Structure of commodity exports and imports, and the shift from domestic output to flow into domestic use, A and I sectors (percentages at three benchmark levels of per capita product).

	A sector			I sector		
	$70 (1)	$300 (2)	$1,000 (3)	$70 (4)	$300 (5)	$1,000 (6)
Large countries						
1. Share in commodity exports	87	69	39	13	31	61
2. Share in commodity imports	39	38	44	61	62	56
3. Net balance (line 2 − line 1)	−48	−31	5	48	31	−5
4. Line 3 as % of GDP	−3.8	−2.5	0.4	3.8	2.5	−0.4
5. Share in GDP (from Table 17)	45.8	26.5	10.9	21.0	36.9	48.4
6. Share in flow into domestic use (line 4 + line 5)	42.0	24.0	11.3	24.8	39.4	48.0
Small countries						
7. Share in commodity exports	81	74	60	19	26	40
8. Share in commodity imports	58	37	36	42	63	64
9. Net balance (line 8 − line 7)	−23	−37	−24	23	37	24
10. Line 9 as % of GDP	−5.5	−8.9	−5.8	5.5	8.9	5.8
11. Share in GDP (from Table 17)	50.7	26.7	14.2	21.1	31.4	48.7
12. Share in flow into domestic use (line 10 + line 11)	45.2	17.8	8.4	26.6	40.3	54.5

Lines 1–3, 7–9: The underlying data are from Simon Kuznets, "Quantitative Aspects of the Economic Growth of Nations: IX. Level and Structure of Foreign Trade: Comparisons for Recent Years," *Economic Development and Cultural Change*, vol. XIII, no. 1, part II (October 1964). Appendix table 7, pp. 99–103, shows the structure of exports and imports, mostly for 1957–60, for seventy-odd countries. The food group and unfinished consumer goods are identified as originating largely in the A sector (disregarding the minor amounts of fabrication involved, and the mining products entering unfinished consumer goods); and all other categories (finished consumer goods, finished and unfinished producer goods, fuel, and unallocated) as originating in the I sector. Only those

countries were used for which both export and import structure were given; again the countries with uncommonly high shares for mining or other industries reflecting exogenous bounties were omitted. The fifty countries were then classified as large (twenty-one) or small (twenty-nine), arranged by their 1958 GDP per capita, and the percentage shares shown in lines 1–2 and 7–8 were interpolated by the usual procedure.

Lines 4, 10: I assumed that the shares of either imports or exports in total product were 10 percent for large countries and 30 percent for small countries (see *ibid.*, table 2B, column 3, p. 10, in which the proportion of imports plus exports varies from 19 to over 60 percent). But these shares relate to the final values of exports and imports, including distribution and transportation charges. Table 14 shows that the ratio of total transport, etc. and trade to the sum of total product of the A sector and the exportable product of the I sector (i.e., mining and manufacturing) ranges at the three benchmark values from about 32 to 55 percent; but this ratio should be scaled down for the present purpose since retail trade and electricity, gas, and water are not relevant. Assuming 20 percent for distribution and transportation charges in international trade, the 10 and 30 percent were reduced to 8 and 24 percent respectively for lines 4 and 10.

demand (as in measuring income elasticity of demand for the products of the A and I sectors) is of far greater weight. In the latter we are dealing with demand for foods purchased by households at final market prices and in the form in which they are purchased by ultimate consumers; in the former, with net and gross value product originating in a given sector (gross of consumption of fixed capital alone, and net in all other respects).

Two major factors contribute to this difference between finished product at final market value and the contribution of a sector to aggregate output. First, the value of a finished product at full market cost to the final consumer includes, *in addition* to the *gross* value of the product as it emerges from a given sector, possible contributions of other sectors. Thus, the cost of food to a household that is not itself a food producer, say an urban family, includes not only the gross value of the food at the farm (the contribution of the A sector) but also the costs of transportation, possible fabrication (such as preserving or canning), and distribution (the contributions of the I and the S sectors). This difference between the cost of a finished good to ultimate consumers and the gross value of that good when it leaves the sector of origin is significant, not only in such international differences as are represented by the comparisons in Tables 12 and 14, but also in trends over time. The shift of population toward the cities, the urbanization process that accompanies modern economic growth, produces a substantial rise in the proportion of fabrication, transportation, and distribution charges included in the final cost of goods, especially with respect to products of the A sector; and urban consumers account for a rapidly increasing proportion of demand (as indicated in Chapter II). Since the 1870's the proportion of non-A sector components in the final price of food has risen from about 0.3 to about 0.5 in Sweden, and to about 0.6 in the United States; and, whereas the ratio of final costs of food to primary input (gross value at the farm) was 1.8 and 2.3 in recent decades in these two countries, in a country like India this ratio may well have been only 1.3.[7]

The effect of such a differential in the ratio of final costs to primary input for foods on the share of the A sector can easily be illustrated. Disregard the effects of foreign trade and assume: that agriculture produces only foods; that at the benchmark value of $70 per capita the ratio under discussion is 1.3, whereas at the $1,000 benchmark value it is 2.3; and, to sharpen the effect, that the income share spent on foods, at final costs, is 0.5 at both benchmark values. Food at final costs will then be 50 percent of total product at both benchmark values. But, in terms of the total value of product, the share of the A sector will be $(0.5 \div 1.3)$, or 38 percent of GDP at the $70 level, and $(0.5 \div 2.3)$, or 22 percent at the $1,000 level. Thus, the difference in the ratio of final costs to primary input alone would cause, under the illustrative conditions given, a drop of some 16 points in the share of the A sector, despite the assumption that in final costs the same proportion is spent on food at the high and low per capita income levels, an assumption that contradicts Engel's law.

But the shares just derived are for the full value of food products as they emerge from the A sector — not the *net* contribution to NDP (or the contribution, gross of fixed capital consumption, to GDP). Here the other source of discrepancy between the final cost to ultimate consumers and the productive contribution of a sector becomes evident. Assume that in the low per capita income countries the A sector produces food largely with its own resources — purchasing no chemical fertilizers, machinery, construction materials, or fuel from other sectors. On this assumption, the ratio of output to gross value of product (net or gross of capital consumption charges) will be high. By contrast, the A sector in the high per capita product countries is likely to be much more mechanized, and much more dependent on purchases of production inputs from other sectors. No data are at hand for estimating the differences

7. See Simon Kuznets, "Quantitative Aspects of the Economic Growth of Nations: VII. The Share and Structure of Consumption," *Economic Development and Cultural Change*, vol. X, no. 2, part II (January 1962), table 13, p. 43, and discussion on pp. 46–48.

involved, but let us assume that the ratio of the contribution of the A sector product to GDP to its full value is 95 percent in the less developed countries, and 70 percent in the high per capita product countries.[8] The share of the A sector, based on the contribution to GDP recorded in Table 14, would then become, to continue this illustration, (0.38 × 0.95), or about 36 percent at the $70 benchmark value, and (0.22 × 0.70), or 15.4 percent at the $1,000 benchmark value. Thus, still without regard for the Engel law, the adjustment for the differences between final costs of finished goods and unduplicated contribution of the A sector yields an illustrative decline in the share of the A sector in GDP of 20 percentage points (in percent of GNP) — well over half of the range of some 37 percentage points shown in Table 14.

While this calculation is illustrative, it is not unrealistic, and two comments are appropriate. The sources of difference that yielded this decline in the share of the A sector as we moved from lower to higher per capita product countries would also raise the shares of the I and S sectors. The greater share of the fabrication and transportation costs in the final cost of foods would automatically raise the share of the I sector — even if the elasticity of demand for finished foods were 1 and remained there. Also, unlike the A sector, modern industry has tended to become less dependent on other sectors (at least those outside the I sector), in part a reflection of the shift in the structure of manufacturing away from branches dependent on raw materials from the A sector.[9] Thus, as one moves

8. Since cross-section data are not available, I used the time series ratios derived from Östen Johansson, *The Gross Domestic Product of Sweden and Its Composition, 1861–1955* (Stockholm: Almqvist and Wiksell, 1967), table 3, pp. 42–43. The ratio of the contribution to gross domestic product to total output of the A sector (excluding duplication within the A sector proper) was 94.9 percent in 1861–1865 and 73.0 percent in 1951–1955.

There was a similar decline in the ratio of farm output, net of purchases from other sectors, to gross farm output in the United States. According to John W. Kendrick, *Productivity Trends in the United States* (Princeton: Princeton University Press for the National Bureau of Economic Research, 1961), table B-1, p. 347, this ratio (for output in 1929 dollars) was 89 percent in 1869 and 64 percent in 1957.

9. According to Johansson, table 16, pp. 68–71, for the combined sector of mining, manufacturing, and electric light and power, the ratio of the contribution to gross domestic product to its total output (excluding duplication within the combined sector proper) was 39 percent in 1861–1865 and rose to 68 percent in 1951–1955.

This rise appears to be untypically large. For the United States comparison of value added with gross value of manufacturing output indicates a relatively minor rise — from 36 percent in 1880 to 41.0 percent in 1914, and 39.3 percent in 1948 (based on volumes in 1929 prices; see Daniel Creamer, Sergei P. Dobrovolsky, and Israel Borenstein, *Capital in Manufacturing and Mining: Its Formation and Financing* [Princeton: Princeton University Press for the National Bureau of Economic Research,

from the low to the high per capita product countries, the differences that reduce the share of the A sector increase the shares of the I and S sectors, despite an assumption of income elasticity of demand equal to 1 for the products of all the sectors.

Second, and more important, the effects of the factors involved here over time are particularly conspicuous and help to explain, not only such cross-sections as are shown in Tables 12 and 14, but also the movements of the shares over time to be discussed in Chapter IV. The factors that made for the rise in the ratio of final costs to primary inputs lie essentially in urbanization, which is in turn closely associated with shifts in production structure and technological changes; and the growing dependence of the A sector on the other sectors is also an effect of changes in technology, as a result of which the I sector provided far more efficient inputs than the A sector could itself originate. The shifts from the mule, horse, and donkey to the tractor, from natural to chemical fertilizers, from scarecrows to plastic covers and chemical pesticides were the result of the technological change which is at the source of modern economic growth; and technological change is marked by a bias toward replacing the slowly acting biological processes typical of agriculture with the faster acting mechanical and synthetic processes typical of the I sector.

(e) Of the groups of differences between the international comparisons in Table 14 and cross-section income elasticity of demand derived from family expenditure studies the most difficult to appraise is that arising from valuation problems, as applied both to per capita GDP and to the relative structure of prices of A and I products affecting the A and I sector shares. Presumably, when the effects of differences in income on demand for groups of goods are studied, per capita income differentials are expressed in some acceptable purchasing power equivalents and the relative prices are roughly the same for purchasers at different real income levels, so that income propensity to consume reflects priorities of wants for

---

1960], table A-10, pp. 252–258). For Canada, the ratio of value added to gross value of production, for manufacturing in current prices, moves from 43.2 percent in 1870 to 47.8 percent in 1910 and 44.1 percent in 1956–1958 (see M. C. Urquhart and K. A. H. Buckley, eds., *Historical Statistics of Canada* [Cambridge: Cambridge University Press, 1965], series Q 1–11, p. 463).

The ratio of net to gross output of manufacturing is far lower than that for any other major branch of production activity. This suggests that trends in manufacturing must be scrutinized separately for gross value of output, for value added, and for contribution to product (net or gross of fixed capital consumption).

people at different real income levels who can choose among identical or comparable goods at the same prices. Actually, even in family expenditure studies within one country, personal disposable income in current prices cannot be assumed to have the same purchasing power for different income groups, even for the same bundle of goods; nor is the price structure among the same sets of goods the same for different income groups. But, at least within a country at a given point of time, such differences are minimized because the markets are interconnected and because there are no legal and few institutional restrictions on the mobility of goods and resources. In international comparisons the problems of converting different currencies to equivalent purchasing power are far more complex; and the differences in price structure of the relevant groups of goods (for example, as between products of the A and I sectors) are likely to be far more conspicuous.

The data at hand are scanty and not too closely geared to the needs of analysis. The few studies that compare prices of identical or similar goods in countries at different levels of per capita income established by exchange rate conversion indicate that these directly comparable prices, weighted by the average quantities of the United States and other countries, yield significantly narrower international per capita income differences than those based on per capita incomes converted by exchange rates.[10] Exchange rates apparently underestimate purchasing power and more in the lower income countries. The magnitude of the adjustment required would vary from one group of countries to another; and, in fact, its precise measurement calls for more data and analysis than are presently available. For whatever it is worth, the evidence suggests an allowance that would set the ratio of purchasing power conversion to the exchange rate conversion at 2.0 at the benchmark level of $70 and at 1.25 at the benchmark level of $1,000 — both benchmarks set by exchange rate conversion.

Data on sectoral price structure are even scantier than those used in general purchasing power conversions of national currencies; but, with the help of rather heroic assumptions, they can be gleaned from the same sources. Table 20 assembles the relevant data, but it must be stressed that the grouping of prices to correspond to major

10. See a brief review in Kuznets, *Modern Economic Growth,* table 7.3, pp. 376–377, and its discussion, pp. 374–384.

Table 20. Sectoral price structure, selected European countries, 1950, and Latin American cities, 1962 (with United States structure as base).

	European countries, 1950			Latin American capital cities, 1962 (related to Los Angeles-Houston)		
	I prices A prices (1)	S prices A prices (2)			I prices A prices (3)	S prices A prices (4)
1. United Kingdom	1.26	0.75		11. Buenos Aires	1.91	1.54
2. France	1.48	0.73		12. Montevideo	1.53	1.50
3. West Germany	1.45	0.76		13. Santiago de		
4. Geometric mean,				Chile	1.61	1.92
lines 1–3	1.39	0.75		14. Geometric mean,		
5. Belgium	1.18	0.99		lines 11–13	1.68	1.64
6. Netherlands	1.53	0.76		15. Mexico City	1.29	1.02
7. Denmark	1.43	0.83		16. Rio de Janeiro	1.80	1.45
8. Norway	1.26	0.83		17. Lima	1.32	1.29
9. Geometric mean,				18. Geometric mean,		
lines 5–8	1.34	0.85		lines 15–17	1.45	1.24
10. Italy	1.43	0.50				

The I/A and S/A price ratios for the United States in 1950 and for the combination of Los Angeles and Houston in 1962 equal 1.00. Those underlying the 1950 structure are geometric means of prices weighted by domestic and U.S. quantities; those underlying the 1962 structure are weighted by a common set of Latin American quantities.

Columns 1–2: The sources are Milton Gilbert and Irving B. Kravis, *An International Comparison of National Products and the Purchasing Power of Currencies* (Paris: OEEC, 1954); and Milton Gilbert and Associates, *Comparative National Products and Price Levels* (Paris: OEEC, 1958). The ratios are based on detailed binary comparisons, for the United Kingdom, France, Germany, and Italy in the 1954 volume, tables 27–30, pp. 113–120; for Belgium, the Netherlands, Denmark, and Norway in the 1958 volume, tables 38–41, pp. 99–106.

The A sector includes foods; the I sector includes clothing and household textiles, fuel, light and water, household goods, transport equipment and services, communication services, producers' durables, and construction; the S sector includes housing, household and personal services, recreation and entertainment, health, education, miscellaneous consumer services, and general government administration. Because their prices do not properly reflect factor costs, or because the group could not be easily allocated to one of the three major sectors, alcoholic beverages, tobacco, inventories, net exports, and the defense component of government were excluded.

Columns 3–4: The basic data are from United Nations, "A Measurement of Price Levels and the Purchasing Power of Currencies in Latin America, 1960–62," *Economic Bulletin for Latin America*, vol. VIII, no. 2 (October 1963), pp. 195–235, in particular the data on weights in table 10, pp. 216–217, and on units of currencies equivalent to $1 U.S. for various groups of commodities and services in June 1962, table 22b, p. 232. The 1960 quantity weights in table 10 were used for the 1962 comparison.

The following groups were allocated to the three major sectors: food to the A sector; clothing, textiles, transport and communications, total of construction, producers' equipment, and transport equipment to the I sector; housing, personal care, and recreation to the S sector. Beverages and tobacco were excluded. The basic source excludes price information on government expenditures on goods.

sectoral price indexes and ratios is approximate. Indeed, the approximate character of the procedure is imposed by the difference between the full value of finished goods (to which prices refer in studies aimed at purchasing power conversions of national currencies) and the contribution of a sector to total product (gross or net of capital consumption, at factor cost or at market prices) which is a *netter* concept. The prices of food, which in Table 20 we take to represent the prices of products of the A sector, reflect a fabrication and transportation component that is part of the I sector, and a trade component that is part of the S sector. Likewise, the prices of textiles, clothing, and furniture, which we take to represent the prices of the I sector, reflect a raw material component (cotton or wool in textiles and clothing, or wood in furniture) that is part of the A sector. The price comparisons are thus for overlapping categories, not for neatly separated sectoral contributions; and perhaps a neater separation of consumer goods prices would yield wider differences in price structure than those suggested in Table 20. For the present, however, this is all that we have in the way of readily available data.

As might have been expected, the ratio of I sector prices to A sector prices is distinctly higher in the lower per capita product countries than in the United States. For the European countries in 1950, this ratio (United States = 1.00) varies from 1.2 to 1.5; for the Latin American capital cities in 1962, in comparison with Los Angeles-Houston, the I/A ratio varies from 1.3 to 1.9. This scanty evidence suggests that the I/A price ratio is significantly greater in all other countries than in the United States, and perhaps the greater, the lower the country's per capita product. The evidence on the relative prices for the S sector is inconsistent. The S/A price ratios for the European countries are all below 1, range from as low as 0.5 for Italy to close to 1 for Belgium, and suggest that, in comparison with the United States, the prices of the S sector are distinctly below those of the A sector, let alone the I sector. For the Latin American cities — and it is difficult to assay the weight of such *interurban* comparisons — the S/A price ratio is well above 1, except for Mexico City where it is close to 1, but in most cases it is lower than the I/A price ratio. Thus, compared with the United States, the prices of the S sector are higher than those of the A sector but lower than those of the I sector. This inconsistency in the evidence for the S sector prices may reflect not only the limitations of the Latin American sample, but also the qualitative differences in the S sector products among countries at different levels of per capita income that are more difficult to measure than those in the tangible commodities and services of the A and I sectors. Granted that the prices of government and education services in countries other than the United States are lower (or higher) relative to the prices of wheat, rice, coal, and electrical power, what of the possibly wide quality differentials in administrative and educational services?

The evidence, although limited and contradictory, suggests that disparities caused by the method of conversion and the differences in sectoral price structure loom large in the international comparisons represented in Table 14. As a result, the association between differences in per capita product and the shares of sectors in total product might assume different parameters if the required adjustments were made.

Since our primary interest is in the relevance of cross-sections to long-term changes over time, the obvious question is: are the value bases reflected in the cross-sections derived — which make no adjustment for international differences in price structure or for the inadequate conversions by exchange rates — comparable with those implicit in the long-term records on product and its sectoral components? I shall consider this question in the next chapter, where I compare cross-section associations with the associations between long-term trends in per capita product and in sectoral shares in product.

(f) Assuming that all the differences between the measures in Table 14 and the proper bases for measuring income elasticity of demand were eliminated, and we have measures of personal disposable income, with the same distribution by size, and domestic consumption at final cost with adequate adjustments for purchasing power and internal price structure comparabilities, some questions remain. Does income elasticity of demand, so measured, reflect sets of preferences, of wants, sufficiently invariant to technological and institutional changes to constitute relatively immutable "laws," presumably of human nature? And, if so, would they yield a relation that would persist through the long stretch of economic growth? Could one then establish, on the basis of the cross-section, with appropriate adjustments, an acceptable pattern of association and growth over time? That these questions are answered in the negative may seem like urging the obvious; but it is important to stress the technological and institutional elements in this relation, even after the elimination of the differences discussed under the five preceding points. For the presence, and indeed dominance, of the technological and institutional elements even in these "pure" measures, is also likely to mean that the relation will be variable in space and changeable over time.

A decline in the share of a commodity in expenditures as we shift toward a higher per capita income presumably reflects a decision to use the additional income for other goods, or to use less of it proportionately than was used before the addition. This preference may have nothing to do with *how* the addition to per capita income is secured; in which case, it reveals priorities independent of sources of income, a structure of demand independent of the conditions of supply. But usually the factors that make additions to per capita income possible — often new or different material or social technology — also affect the structure of demand, either creating new needs and implicitly lowering the relative priority of the old needs, or creating new means of satisfying old needs, and lowering the priority of the old means of satisfying these old needs. In either case the resulting structure of demand, the propensity to consume and to save, is not an expression of scales of human wants invariant to differences in material technology, but is greatly affected by the latter. The effects of technological changes on conditions of life have been discussed in Chapter II, in connection with non-conventional current costs or intermediate products, and there is no need for further comment.

The new point here relates to the substitution of commodities provided by the more advanced technology for those of the old in satisfying the old needs, for example, the replacement of "natural" vegetable products (fertilizers, rubber, and the like) by synthetic industrial products. And other substitutions not as obvious — such as synthetic drugs that supply the essential vitamins and proteins, if not the calories — have reduced the demand for natural food products, the output of the A sector. In other words, if the propensity to consume foods is x at a given level of per capita product; and if foods are products of the A sector alone, the propensity to consume the latter is also x. But even if the propensity to consume food (at the same prices, and so on) is also x at higher per capita product levels, and part is satisfied by vitamin pills, a product of the I sector, the propensity to consume food products of the A sector must be less than x. Thus, the structure of demand, in terms of recognizable categories of wants, is different from that in terms of specific products relevant to these categories. Even the categories of wants are not independent: if shelter and clothing provide greater protection against cold, the demand for food as a source of heat (calories) is affected; and one can conceive of the partial replacement of the demand for the food products of the A sector by the demand for other types of internal fuel, the products of the I sector.

All this may seem like a semantic quibble; like contending with a straw-man interpretation of the structure of demand, envisaging it as an expression of some technologically and socially invariant set of wants, provided by a rational group of individuals with an identical store of knowledge. But it is important, for reasons already indicated, to recognize not only the straw-man aspects of the concept of an invariant or stable structure of demand, but also the various ways in which institutional and technological changes penetrate into and affect the structure of demand — even when we deal with the demand response of individuals to their personal income (current or long-term) under assumptions of stable purchasing power and internal price structure.

One final comment is appropriate. The discussion in this section, which dealt with the factors involved in the international cross-section association between per capita product and the shares of the A and I sectors, applies with equal relevance to the association between per capita product and shares of other sectors and subdivisions. The difference between total personal income and gross domestic product; the effect, even though minor, of foreign trade; the different input-output relations among sectors, reflecting different levels of technology; the adjustments in the exchange rate conversion to a common monetary unit and the differences in internal price structure; and the differential impact of substitution effects produced by technology are all relevant to the ties between per capita product and the shares in product of other sectors and subdivisions. If the institutional, technological, and price elements are important in the association between per capita product and the

A sector, which provides the goods of prime necessity perhaps most closely related to physiological needs, they are likely to be even more important for other goods, which are not prime necessities and are probably more sensitive to differences in technology and in institutional determinants of final demand.

IV

Sectoral Shares
in Product:
Long-Term Trends

Having observed in the cross-section for 1958 the dominant association between per capita product and the shares of the A and I sectors and of some subdivisions of the S sector, and having discussed some of the factors involved, we would expect to find, as per capita product increased with growth over time, long-term changes in shares in product similar to differences in the cross-section. Whether or not this expectation is fulfilled, the directly observed long-term changes are of interest in and of themselves. The two questions of most concern can be answered reliably only by the time series. What have been the generally observed long-term trends in sectoral shares in product, associated with economic growth in the developed countries? Are similar shifts in the sectoral structure of aggregate output observed in other countries, especially in those showing no marked growth and no significant rise in per capita product? Only after these two questions have been explored, can we examine the relation between the long-term changes in shares over time and their conformity to the cross-section associations.

Changes in Shares: The Three Major Sectors

Table 21 summarizes changes in the shares of the three major sectors in thirteen developed countries, and in a few less developed countries for which long records are available. The following findings may be suggested.

(a) The distinction between shares in current and in constant price product should be significant in the long run, since one may

143

Table 21. Long-term changes in shares of major sectors in gross domestic product (percentages).

	Shares in current price volumes			Shares in constant price volumes		
	A (1)	I (2)	S (3)	A (4)	I (5)	S (6)
Great Britain–United Kingdom						
Great Britain, NDP, 1865 and 1885 prices						
1. 1801/11	34.1	22.1[a]	43.8[a]	33.2	23.0[a]	43.8[a]
2. 1851/61	19.5	36.3[a]	44.2[a]	19.3	36.4[a]	44.3[a]
3. 1907	6.4	38.9[a]	54.7[a]	6.7	37.0[a]	56.3[a]
4. Change, 1801/11 to 1907	−27.7	+16.8[a]	+10.9[a]	−26.5	+14.0[a]	+12.5[a]
Great Britain, GDP						
5. 1907	6.4	48.9	44.7	—	—	—
6. 1924	4.2	53.2	42.6	—	—	—
United Kingdom, GDP						
7. 1924	4.4	55.0	40.6	—	—	—
8. 1955	4.7	56.8	38.5	—	—	—
9. 1955	4.7	56.2	39.1	—	—	—
10. 1963–67	3.4	54.6	42.0	—	—	—
11. Change, 1907 to 1963–67	−3.2	+4.5	−1.3	—	—	—
France						
GDP, 1954 prices						
12. 1896	—	—	—	25.0	46.2	28.8
13. 1963	—	—	—	8.4	51.0	40.6
14. Change, 1896 to 1963	—	—	—	−16.6	+4.8	+11.8
Belgium						
GDP, 1953 and 1963 prices						
15. 1910	—	—	—	8.9	45.9	45.2
16. 1953–55	—	—	—	8.1	50.0	41.9
17. 1953–55	—	—	—	8.4	47.0	44.6
18. 1963–67	—	—	—	6.2	49.8	44.0
19. Change, 1910 to 1963–67	—	—	—	−3.0	+6.9	−3.9
Netherlands						
National income						
20. 1860	25.0	75.0		—	—	—
21. 1910	15.3	84.7		—	—	—

Table 21 — continued

	(1)	(2)	(3)	(4)	(5)	(6)
NDP						
22. 1913	18.8	36.8	44.4	—	—	—
23. 1950	14.9	47.2	37.9	—	—	—
24. 1950	14.2	48.6	37.2	—	—	—
25. 1963–67	8.0	49.9	42.1	—	—	—
26. Change, 1913						
to 1963–67	−10.1	+11.7	−1.6	—	—	—
Germany						
Pre-World War II, NDP, 1913 prices						
27. 1850–59	40.9	59.1		44.8	22.8	32.4
28. 1935–38	13.6	84.4		16.2	56.3	27.5
29. Change, 1850–59						
to 1935–38	−27.3	+27.3		−28.6	+33.5	−4.9
Federal Republic, excluding Saar and West Berlin, NDP, 1936 prices						
30. 1936	13.4	58.0	28.6	13.4	58.0	28.6
31. 1950	12.4	59.9	27.7	11.1	57.3	31.6
GDP, 1954 market prices						
32. 1950	10.4	56.6	33.0	10.3	54.5	35.2
33. 1960	6.3	59.7	34.0	6.6	61.8	31.6
Including Saar and West Berlin						
34. 1960	6.0	59.8	34.2	6.3	61.9	31.8
35. 1963–67	4.5	57.8	37.7	5.4	62.4	32.2
36. Change, 1936						
to 1963–67	−5.6	+1.1	+4.5	−4.6	+7.8	−3.2
Denmark						
NDP, 1929 prices						
37. 1870–79	45.0	55.0		41.4	58.6	
38. 1950–51	19.6	80.4		18.7	81.3	
39. Change, 1870–79						
to 1950–51	−25.4	+25.4		−22.7	+22.7	
GDP, 1955 prices						
40. 1950–51	20.4	45.0	34.6	19.5	45.4	35.1
41. 1963–67	10.9	49.5	39.6	14.0	50.1	35.9
42. Change, 1950–51						
to 1963–67	−9.5	+4.5	+5.0	−5.5	+4.7	+0.8
Norway						
GDP, market prices						
43. 1865	33.8	31.9	34.3	—	—	—
44. 1950	13.8	53.1	33.1	—	—	—

Table 21 — continued

	(1)	(2)	(3)	(4)	(5)	(6)
GDP, 1963 prices						
45. 1950	14.9	55.7	29.4	15.1	50.8	34.1
46. 1963–67	8.3	55.9	35.8	8.0	57.1	34.9
47. Change, 1865 to 1963–67	−26.6	+21.4	+5.2	—	—	—
Sweden						
GDP, 1913 prices						
48. 1861–70	38.3	22.6	39.1	34.6	21.6	43.8
49. 1951–55	9.8	58.3	31.9	6.8	60.2	33.0
GDP, 1959 prices						
50. 1951–55	12.7	54.6	32.7	9.2	50.9	39.9
51. 1963–67	6.5	54.5	39.0	5.6	54.9	39.5
52. Change, 1861–70 to 1963–67	−34.7	+35.6	−0.9	−31.4	+42.6	−11.2
Italy						
GDP, 1938 prices						
53. 1861–70	54.3	20.3	25.4	46.1	19.6	34.3
54. 1891–1900	47.4	22.0	30.6	41.7	23.4	34.9
55. 1950–52	25.8	45.5	28.7	22.4	43.6	34.0
56. 1951–52	22.7	43.4	33.9	20.2	36.0	43.8
57. 1963–67	13.1	47.1	39.8	13.7	47.9	38.4
58. Change, 1891–1900 to 1963–67	−31.2	+27.2	+4.0	−25.8	+32.1	−6.3
Japan						
NDP, market prices, 1934–36 prices						
59. 1879–83	62.5	37.5		65.6	34.4	
60. 1904–13	40.6	59.4		38.6	61.4	
61. 1924–33	22.4	77.6		23.3	76.7	
62. 1951–54	20.2	79.8		16.1	83.9	
63. 1959–61	13.6	86.4		11.9	88.1	
64. Change, 1879–83 to 1959–61	−48.9	+48.9		−53.7	+53.7	
65. 1952–53	22.4	39.4	38.2	—	—	—
66. 1963–67	11.9	45.3	42.8	—	—	—
67. Change, 1952–53 to 1963–67	−10.5	+5.9	+4.6	—	—	—

Table 21 — continued

	(1)	(2)	(3)	(4)	(5)	(6)
United States						
National income, 1859 prices						
68. 1839	42.6	25.8	31.6	44.6	24.2	31.2
69. 1889/99	17.9	44.1	38.0	17.0	52.6	30.4
GNP, 1929 prices						
70. 1889/99	—	—	—	25.8	37.7	36.5
71. 1919/29	—	—	—	11.2	41.3	47.5
72. 1953	—	—	—	5.9	48.4	45.7
GDP, 1963 market prices						
73. 1953	5.5	47.2	48.3	4.3	45.3	50.4
74. 1963–67	3.3	43.5	53.2	3.3	44.3	52.4
75. Change, 1839 to 1963–67	—	—	—	−48.5	+38.1	+10.4
Canada						
GDP, 1949 prices						
76. 1870	45.3	54.7		—	—	—
77. 1920	24.5	75.5		—	—	—
78. 1919–23	20.8	42.4	36.8	—	—	—
79. 1951–55	11.5	49.6	38.9	—	—	—
80. 1951–55	11.5	49.6	38.9	13.6	48.9	37.5
81. 1963–67	6.6	47.8	45.6	9.7	54.6	35.7
82. Change, 1919–23 to 1963–67	−14.2	+5.4	+8.8	—	—	—
Australia						
GDP, 1910–11 prices						
83. 1861–80	25.1	31.0	43.9	22.5	30.7	46.8
84. 1935–38 (F)	22.6	32.8	44.6	24.9	29.6	46.4
85. 1935–38 (F)	22.6	31.8	45.6	—	—	—
86. 1955–59 (F)	14.7	47.1	38.2	—	—	—
87. 1956–58 (F)	14.6	48.7	36.7	—	—	—
88. 1963–66 (F)	11.9	49.8	38.3	—	—	—
89. Change, 1861–80 to 1963–66 (F)	−13.8	+18.2	−5.1	—	—	—
Argentina						
GDP, 1950 prices						
90. 1900–04	—	—	—	33.3	24.8	41.9
91. 1935–39	—	—	—	24.3	36.0	39.7

Table 21 — continued

	(1)	(2)	(3)	(4)	(5)	(6)
GDP, 1960 prices						
92. 1935–39	—	—	—	26.2	37.9	35.9
93. 1950–54	17.0	42.7	40.3	19.9	43.5	36.6
94. 1963–67	16.4	49.3	34.3	16.9	48.4	34.7
95. Change, 1900–04						
to 1963–67	—	—	—	−18.3	+21.7	−3.4
Honduras						
GDP, 1960 prices						
96. 1925–29	—	—	—	63.4	12.5	24.1
97. 1960–64	—	—	—	43.0	24.7	32.3
98. Change, 1925–29						
to 1960–64	—	—	—	−20.4	+12.2	+8.2
Philippines						
Gross value added, 1939 prices						
99. 1918	—	—	—	60.4	39.6	
100. 1961	—	—	—	33.6	66.4	
101. Change, 1918						
to 1961	—	—	—	−26.8	+26.8	
Egypt						
GNP and GDP, 1939 prices						
102. 1895–99	—	—	—	44.4	55.6	
103. 1959–62 (F)	—	—	—	28.0	72.0	
104. Change, 1895–99						
to 1959–62 (F)	—	—	—	−16.4	+16.4	

(F): fiscal year beginning July 1.

—: information not available.

[a] The I sector excludes and the S sector includes transport and communication. Unless otherwise indicated, underlying product estimates are at factor cost.

When years in the stubs are connected by a slash (/), data are for the single years indicated; when connected by a dash (–), they are for all the years in the interval.

The changes in shares are sums of changes in overlapping series except in those cases indicated in the stubs. For the post-World War II changes the shares are derived from the country tables in the United Nations, *Yearbook of National Accounts Statistics, 1968* (New York, 1969), and unpublished data supplied by the United Nations, unless otherwise indicated in the country notes below.

United Kingdom

Lines 1–6: Underlying data are from Phyllis Deane and W. A. Cole, *British Economic Growth, 1688–1959*, 2nd. ed. (Cambridge: Cambridge University Press, 1967), table 37, p. 166, and table 40, p. 175, for current price volumes. Constant price volumes are derived by means of the Rousseaux price indexes given in Brian R. Mitchell, *Abstract of British Historical Statistics* (Cambridge: Cambridge University Press, 1962), pp. 471–473, three-year averages for 1801 and 1811, and five-year averages centered on the years indicated for 1851, 1861, and 1907.

Lines 7–8: Underlying data are from Deane and Cole, table 41, p. 178.

France

Lines 12–13: Underlying data are from E. Malinvaud and others, *Sources et origines de la croissance française au milieu du xxème siècle*, a mimeographed preliminary report for the Social Science Research Council study of Postwar Economic Growth in Historical Perspective (Paris, June 1965), table 8, p. 29.

Belgium

Lines 15–16: Underlying data are from Claude Carbonnelle, "Recherches sur l'évolution de la production en Belgique de 1900 à 1957," *Cahiers économiques de Bruxelles*, vol. I, no. 3 (April 1959), table 1, p. 358, and the 1953 weights given in the appendix, pp. 375–378.

Netherlands

Lines 20–23: Underlying data are from J. B. D. Derksen, "Het national incomen naar bedrijfstakken in Nederland en enkele andere landen," *Statistische en Econometrische Onderzoekingen*, 3rd. quarter, 1960 (Hague: Zeist, 1960), table 2, p. 134.

Germany

Lines 27–28: Underlying data are from Walther G. Hoffmann, *Das Wachstum der Deutschen Wirtschaft seit der Mitte des 19. Jahrhunderts* (Berlin: Springer Verlag, 1965), table 122, pp. 506–509, and table 103, pp. 454–455.

Lines 30–31: Underlying data are from the United Nations, *Statistical Papers*, Series H, no. 9 (New York, May 1965), table 3, p. 20.

Denmark

Lines 37–38: Underlying data are from Kjeld Bjerke and Niels Ussing, *Studier over Danmarks Nationalprodukt, 1870–1950* (Copenhagen: G. E. C. Gads, 1958), table II, pp. 144–145. The A share is for agriculture only.

Norway

Lines 43–44: Underlying data are from the Central Bureau of Statistics, *Trends in Norwegian Economy, 1865–1960*, no. 16 of *Samfunnsøkonomiske Studier* (Oslo, 1966), table 24, p. 55, table 20, p. 53, and table 22, p. 54, the last for the approximation of the share of transport and communication, which were shifted from the S to the I sector.

Sweden

Lines 48–49: Underlying data are from Östen Johansson, *The Gross Domestic Product of Sweden and Its Composition, 1861–1955* (Stockholm: Almqvist and Wiksell, 1967), table 55, pp. 150–151, and for constant price volumes from the tables for individual sectors, which give the gross value of output and the contribution to gross domestic product in current prices and the former in 1913 prices. The difference between the two in current prices was adjusted for price changes: for the A sector on the basis of the price index for gross value of output of the I sector; for the I and S sectors on the basis of price indexes for the gross value of output of the A and I sectors combined. The resulting estimates were subtracted from the gross value of output in 1913 prices.

Italy

Lines 53–55, columns 1–3: Underlying data through 1950 are from Istituto Centrale di Statistica, *Annali di Statistica*, Series VIII, vol. 9 (Rome, 1957), table 32, pp. 237–238, for gross value added in public administration and defense, and table 35B, pp. 245–246, for the private sectors. The item representing duplication (unallocated intermediate goods) is distributed among the branches of the private sector proportionately to gross volume.

For 1951–52, the underlying current price volumes for the private sector are the product of the constant price series and the implicit price indexes, given in Giorgio Fuà, *Notes on Italian Economic Growth, 1861–1964* (Milan: Giuffrè, 1965), tables 1. 2, 5, 6, pp. 56–59, 65–68. For 1951–52 value added in public administration and defense is given in Istituto Centrale di Statistica, *Annali di Statistica, Series VIII*, vol. 12 (Rome, 1960), table 13, p. 135; and the duplicating item, from table 15, p. 136, is distributed among the branches of the private sector as described in the paragraph above.

Lines 53–55, columns 4–6: Underlying data are from Fuà, tables 1, 2, pp. 56–59, with the branches of the private sector adjusted for duplication by proportionate allocation of banking services and government services to enterprises, as given in *ibid.*, tables 3–4, pp. 60–64.

Japan

Lines 59–63: Underlying data for current price volumes are from the unpublished Hitotsubachi series. For the constant price shares (column 4) column 1 was modified by the ratio of prices of agricultural product to the general price index. The latter is from Kazushi Ohkawa, Miyohei Shinohara, and Mataji Umemura, eds., *Estimates of Long-Term Economic Statistics of Japan since 1868*, vol. 8, *Prices* (Tokyo: Toyo Keizai Shinpo Sha, 1967), table 1, p. 134, and the former from table 10, col. 4, p. 165.

United States

Lines 68–69: Underlying data for current price volumes are from Robert E. Gallman and Thomas J. Weiss, "The Service Industries in the Nineteenth Century," in Victor R. Fuchs, ed., *Production and Productivity in the Service Industries*, vol. 34 of *Studies in Income and Wealth* (New York: Columbia University Press for the National Bureau of Economic Research, 1969), tables 2, A-1, pp. 291, 306; in combination with estimates of commodity product in Robert E. Gallman, "Commodity Output, 1839–1899," in William N. Parker, ed., *Trends in the American Economy in the Nineteenth Century*, vol. 24 of *Studies in Income and Wealth* (Princeton: Princeton University Press for the National Bureau of Economic Research, 1960), table A-1, p. 43, variant A.

Constant price volumes are from the same sources, but I had to calculate the share of transport and communication for inclusion in the I sector. The price indexes used are from Gallman-Weiss, table 3, p. 292, and the current dollar values are from the statistical appendix (table A-1).

Lines 70–72: Underlying data are from John W. Kendrick, *Productivity Trends in the United States* (Princeton: Princeton University Press for the National Bureau of Economic Research, 1961), table A-IV, pp. 302–303, which shows indexes of output for the A and I sector components; and table A-XXI, p. 332, which shows the index of real net product. The weights used in conjunction with these indexes are the Department of Commerce estimates given in the Bureau of the Census, *Long Term Economic Growth, 1860–1965* (Washington, D.C., 1966), series C132 to C209, pp. 228–235. The share of the S sector is derived as a residual.

Canada

Lines 76–77: Underlying data are from M. C. Urquhart and K. A. H. Buckley, eds., *Historical Statistics of Canada* (Cambridge: Cambridge University Press, 1965), series E 214–224, p. 141.

Lines 78–79: Underlying data are from *ibid.*, series E 130–142, p. 138, for net domestic income for 1919–26, and series E 45–65, p. 133, for gross domestic product for 1926–60. The two sets of series are linked in 1926.

Australia

Lines 83–84: Underlying data are from N. G. Butlin, *Australian Domestic Product, Investment and Foreign Borrowing, 1861–1938/39* (Cambridge: Cambridge University Press, 1962), table 2, pp. 10–11, and table 269, pp. 460–461. Government business undertakings, which are primarily railroads, harbors, and public utilities, are included in the I sector.

Lines 85–86: Underlying data are revisions of the Butlin series, comparable with the official estimates for recent years, supplied by Bryan D. Haig, Research School of Social Science, Australian National University. Transport and communication was shifted to the I sector on the basis of line 84 for line 85, and line 87 for line 86.

Argentina

Lines 90–91: Underlying data are from Alexander Ganz, "Problems and Uses of National Wealth Estimates in Latin America," in Raymond Goldsmith and Christopher Saunders, eds., *Income and Wealth, Series VIII* (London: Bowes and Bowes, 1959), table XVIII, p. 247.

Lines 92–93: Underlying data are from unpublished estimates by the Economic Commission for Latin America, Division of Research and Statistics. The 1950–54 estimates agree with the United Nations figures.

Honduras

Lines 96–97: Underlying data are from unpublished estimates by ECLA.

Philippines

Lines 99–100: Underlying data are from Richard W. Hooley, "Long-Term Economic Growth in the Philippines," in International Rice Research Institute, Growth of Output in the Philippines, mimeographed papers presented at a Conference, December 9–10, 1966, tables 1, 2, pp. 4–10, 4–14.

United Arab Republic

Lines 102–103: Based on the data underlying Table 3. The share of the A sector in 1945–49, given in Donald Mead, *Growth and Structural Change in the Egyptian Economy* (Homewood, Ill.: Richard Irwin, 1967), table I-A-6, p. 286, was extrapolated back by the ratio of the index of agricultural output to the index of GDP, and forward by gross product by industrial origin.

plausibly assume (although it is only a guess) that technological changes resulted in a greater reduction of relative prices of net product (or product gross of consumption of fixed capital) in the I than in the A sector. But comparison for the countries for which estimates are available for shares in both current and constant price volumes reveals no marked differences in changes over the long periods — with the exception of the United States for 1839–1899, where the sharp reduction in prices of transportation resulted in a much greater rise in the share of the I sector in constant than in current prices (see columns 2, 5, lines 68, 69). If marked sectoral price differentials do exist, the price indexes used to adjust the estimates assembled here are far too crude to reflect them adequately.

In this respect the time series are similar to the cross-section data used: the latter are not adjusted for differences in intersectoral price levels between the low and the high per capita product countries (for example, the likely higher ratio of A sector to I sector prices in the developed industrialized countries than in the less developed, lower per capita product countries). In either case, and particularly for the long time series, it is almost impossible to construct adequate sectoral price indexes, so we must use what we have, bearing in mind that a better correction for sectoral price trends might reveal an even greater drop in the share of the A sector and a greater rise in the shares of the I sector and of some subdivisions of the S sector than we find now.

(b) For several developed countries the share of the A sector in total product at the earlier dates is as high as the share in recent years for the least developed countries. In Germany in the 1850's, in Denmark in the 1870's, in Italy in the 1860's (and much later), in the United States in the 1840's, in Canada in the 1870's, and in Japan in the 1880's the share of the A sector ranged from 40 percent of total product to over 60 percent; and the same was true of England and Wales in the mid-eighteenth century.[1] The cross-section analysis for 1958 shows shares of the A sector as high as these in the two groups with the lowest per capita product — $52 and $83 respectively in 1958 prices (see Table 12, columns 1–2). It is not surprising that the share of the A sector in the product of presently developed countries was high in the nineteenth (or in some cases in the eighteenth) century; but it is intriguing because these countries, except for Japan, had a per capita product at the time of at least $200, in 1958 prices.[2]

Two implications of this finding should be noted. The first flows from the plausible argument that the share of the A sector in any sizable economy's total product, no matter what the level of eco-

1. In Phyllis Deane and W. A. Cole, *British Economic Growth, 1688–1959*, 2nd. ed. (Cambridge: Cambridge University Press, 1967), table 37, p. 166, the share of the A sector in the national income of Great Britain is estimated at 32.5 percent in 1801. Extrapolation back to the eighteenth century by means of indexes of real output in England and Wales for agriculture and other branches (by decades, see table 19, p. 78) yields a share of the A sector of 52 percent in 1700, of 48 percent in 1740/50, and of 32.5 percent in 1800.

2. See Table 2, which shows the GDP per capita for the developed countries in the early and mid-nineteenth century, in 1965 prices. To shift to the 1958 price base, these per capita estimates should be divided by 1.109, the ratio of the 1965 price index implicit in United States GNP to that for 1958. With this adjustment, per capita GDP in 1958 prices was over $200 for Great Britain in 1765–1785, and at its lowest, $194, for Sweden in 1861–1869 (always excluding Japan).

nomic development, has an upper limit well below 100 percent. Some services (government, professional, personal, and distributive) must be provided in the way of a social infrastructure, and some urban population must exist. Judging by the least developed, lowest per capita product countries today, this limit to the share of the A sector can be set reasonably at 70 percent — and there is no ground for assuming that it was significantly higher in the nineteenth or even the eighteenth century world.[3] Therefore, the international range in the share of the A sector in product can be put at about 25 to 70 percent, with some of the high product countries of that time having shares of 40 percent or over. Today, the international range is much wider: in some large less developed countries the share of the A sector is between 60 and 70 percent; at the other extreme, in most of the developed countries it is well below 10 percent. This means that the international disparity in product structure, at least with respect to the share of the A sector, has widened considerably over the last century to century and a half, concurrently with growing international disparity in per capita product.

The second implication concerns the speed of the movement of the shares of the three sectors, and in particular the decline of the share of the A sector. If the typical trend over the last century and a quarter was a decline in the share of the A sector from 40 percent or more to 10 percent or less, the rate of this decline must have been a large multiple of that observed for the older developed countries in the centuries preceding modern economic growth. Judging by the ratios for the African and Asian countries in the late 1950's and early 1960's, the share of the A sector in the medieval counterparts of the presently developed countries must have been between 50 and 60 percent in the ninth and tenth centuries, before the emergence and growth of medieval cities. If the movement thereafter can be visualized as a long-term shift away from agriculture, the trend between A.D. 1000 and the first half of the nineteenth century was from 60 percent at the highest to 40 percent at the lowest (excluding such exceptionally early starters as the Netherlands and Great Britain). This decline of 20 percentage

3. The highest shares of the A sector in GDP in the late 1950's or early 1960's are those for several countries in SubSaharan Africa: Ethiopia, 66 percent in 1963; Lesotho, 69 percent in 1964; Nigeria, 69 percent in 1958; Uganda, 64 percent in 1958 (see United Nations, *Yearbook of National Accounts Statistics, 1967* [New York, 1968], table 3, pp. 790 ff.). The only country outside of Africa that had as high a share was Nepal, with 66 percent in 1958. The shares in the larger countries of Asia ranged from 51 percent for India in 1960 to 55 percent for Indonesia in 1963.

points over some eight centuries can be compared with a drop of some 30 percentage points in a century to a century and a half. A similar, and more telling, comparison will be made later for changes in the distribution of the labor force among the three major sectors. The important point is that the acceleration in the rate of growth in per capita product, characteristic of modern economic growth, was accompanied by an equally conspicuous acceleration in the rate of change in production structure — illustrated here by the share of the A sector in total product, but probably relevant also to the shifts in a more detailed classification of production branches within which total product originated.

(c) In all the developed countries, the share of the A sector in total product declined substantially over the long periods covered. In most countries the decline amounted to between 20 and 30 percentage points, except of course when the share was already quite low in the initial period (for example, see the United Kingdom, line 11; Belgium, line 19; the Netherlands, line 26). As a result, by the early or middle 1960's, the share of the A sector in most developed countries is well below 10 percent, and in a few (Denmark, Italy, and Australia) somewhat over 10 percent. The minus signs in the appropriate lines in columns 1 and 4 indicate the prevalence of this decline. One is struck by the low level to which the share declined in the United Kingdom, Germany, the United States, and Canada; and the last two countries still have a surplus of agricultural products.

Australia is the single exception to this widespread decline of the share of the A sector among the developed countries. The share for 1948 (not given in the table) is about the same as in 1935–1938, and only slightly lower than the share in the 1860's (lines 83–85). This pattern may have characterized other small overseas offshoots of Europe, which benefited from a highly productive agricultural establishment with ready markets in the metropolitan countries, and for a long time saw little advantage in development *away* from the A sector.

(d) The few series in Table 21 for the less developed countries suggest a far more intriguing pattern. In the developed countries, the generally observed decline in the share of the A sector accompanied an equally general long-term rise in per capita product — although the rate of the latter differed among countries, and the relation between it and the decline in the share of the A sector is still to be explored. But in several of the less developed countries, selected here to document the point, although per capita product failed to rise significantly, the share of the A sector declined quite markedly. This is true of Honduras, the Philippines, and Egypt, for which the records cover periods varying from four to six decades (lines 96–104). For the periods shown, the share of the A sector in total product declined about a third in Honduras, and two-fifths or more in the Philippines and Egypt. Yet in all three countries product barely changed over these same long periods.[4] The evidence for India, for the period between the middle 1920's and the early 1950's, suggests the same association, but a tested series of national product that provides a consistent estimate of the distribution between A and the other sectors is not available.[5]

4. For the estimates for value added or total product for the Philippines and Egypt, see Table 3, and the notes to it. The estimates of GDP at 1960 factor prices for Honduras were prepared by the Division of Statistics, Economic Commission for Latin America (kindly provided by Mr. Loeb); by using the population estimates in United Nations, *Demographic Yearbook, 1960* and *1963*, I calculated the per capita product to be 363 lempira in 1925–1929 and 365 in 1960–1964.

5. The most relevant data are in Kshitimohon Mukerji, *Levels of Economic Activity and Public Expenditure in India* (Bombay: Asia Publishing House, 1965). The two estimates of national income for the Indian Union presented by Mr. Mukerji differ in the weight assigned to trends in agricultural and industrial output: in Variant I, the index for agriculture is taken to represent not only agriculture but also the "small enterprises and 'other commerce and transport,' to use the National Income Committee's classification"; in Variant II the weight assigned to the index of agricultural output is the contribution of "agriculture, animal husbandry and ancillary activities," which in 1948–49 accounted for 49.1 percent of national income (p. 56). The trend of industrial activity is assumed to represent the remainder of national income.

The results most relevant here may be summarized as follows:

	Variant I		Variant II	
	National income per capita (1948–49 rupees) (1)	Share of A sector (%) (2)	National income per capita (1948–49 rupees) (3)	Share of A sector (%) (4)
1900–04 (fiscal)	262	67.7 (implicit)	222	81.2 (implicit)
1925–29 "	293	58.3 "	273	63.5 "
1950–52 "	268	48.7 (observed)	272	48.7 (observed)

Columns 1 and 3 are from Mukerji, table G, pp. 57–58. Columns 2 and 4 for 1950–1952 are from United Nations, *Yearbook of National Accounts Statistics, 1957* (New

True, the sample underlying this finding is small, but the total number of countries with stagnant per capita product over the recent long period is also small. And yet the result is not surprising. In many less developed countries, where population has grown and the agricultural sector has been stagnant, some modern industries and services have emerged, reducing the share of the A sector even though overall per capita product may have failed to rise. Also, in some small less developed countries that have exported a good part of their agricultural products in the past, foreign markets may have shrunk and the recession in the markets for products of the A sector may have barred a significant rise in total per capita product despite the rise in the shares of the I and S sectors. Thus, although we find this combination of stagnant per capita product with a marked decline in the share of the A sector in only a few countries, the finding and its implications are important. If total product per capita failed to rise, product *per worker* could hardly have risen significantly. In view of the contrast usually found between low per worker product in the A sector and higher per worker product in the I+S sector, observed especially in the less developed countries (see Chapter V), the combination of a decline in the share of the A sector with constancy of aggregate product per worker might mean an absolute decline in product per worker in the A sector (if there was no shift of labor from that sector to produce a corresponding reduction of its share in labor force). Alternatively, product per worker in the I+S sector might decline (if there was a shift of labor from agriculture, causing a rise in the share of the I+S sector in the labor force). Or it could mean a combination of absolute decline in per worker product in the A sector with either constancy or decline in per worker product in the I+S sector. Other combinations can easily be formulated; the most plausible is an absolute decline in per worker product in the A sector resulting from increased pressure of population on land under conditions of relatively stagnant agricultural technology, and some rise in per worker

---

York, 1958). For the earlier years the share was extrapolated by the ratio of the index of agricultural output (Mukerji, table 1, pp. 83–84) to that of the relevant variant of national income.

Mr. Mukerji prefers Variant II, but it implies an implausibly high share for the A sector in 1900–1904. In both variants the share declines from 1925–1929 to 1950–1952, while per capita national income either declines or is stagnant.

product in the I+S sector resulting from a growth of modern components in industry and services.

Whether or not this hypothesis of underlying duality between the stagnant traditional A sector and the more modern I+S sector is valid (and this will be explored in Chapter V), the fact is that the combination of constant (or declining) per capita product with a marked decline in the share of the A sector represents a significant exception to the close association found in the recent cross-section between positive differences in per capita product and declines in the share of the A sector.

Another significant exception — the combination of constant or rising per capita product with an increasing share of the A sector in total product — can be suggested although I have no data to support it. This could be the case for a small less developed country in the early period of its entry into the network of international trade, provided that its exportable surpluses originated in the A sector. If in these early decades the emerging agricultural exports were attained without reducing the output of peasant agriculture, and without raising unduly the output of the I and S sectors (through greater trade activity or, less likely, more domestic manufacturing), the sharp increase in total agricultural output resulting from the newly opened export markets should result in a combination of rising per capita product with a rising share of the A sector.[6]

(e) In most of the developed countries in Table 21 for which the shares of the I and S sectors are distinguished, the share of the I sector rises substantially — largely or entirely offsetting the decline in the share of the A sector — and the share of the S sector rises or declines slightly. In the exceptions — France in the twentieth

6. There is some suggestion of a rising share of the A sector in the total product of Ceylon for the period 1881–1911. According to Donald R. Snodgrass, *Ceylon: An Export Economy in Transition,* Economic Growth Center of Yale University (Homewood, Ill.: Richard Irwin, 1966), the share of the A sector in labor force remained about the same: 68.2 percent in 1881 and 68.9 percent in 1911. However, during the same period, the share within the agricultural labor force of workers on plantations, with a distinctly higher per worker product than workers in the peasant economy, rose appreciably — from less than 25 percent of total labor force in 1881 to somewhat over 34 percent in 1911; while the ratio of peasant population to land remained constant, suggesting no increase of pressure on land in the peasant economy (derived from Snodgrass, table A-26, pp. 322–323 and table 2-8, p. 48). These trends within the A sector, combined with the constant share of the A sector in total labor force, should have led to both a rise in per capita product and an increase in the share of the A sector in total product, unless there were counteracting trends in per worker product in the I+S sector. I have no data on per worker product before about 1950.

century (line 14); the United States (line 75); and possibly Canada in the twentieth century (line 82) — the share of the S sector did rise substantially, in comparison with the decline in the A sector. In Great Britain, allowing for a rise of 5 percentage points in the share of the transport and communication subdivision, the share of the I sector, properly defined, rises about 22 percentage points between 1801/11 and 1907, and about 27 percentage points between 1907 and 1963–1967, leaving only a minor rise in the share of the S sector, properly defined.

The typical trend in the share of the I sector is a rise from 22 to 25 percent before entry into modern economic growth to between 47 and almost 60 percent. This rise of 25 to over 30 percentage points is roughly the same as the decline in the typical share of the A sector. Given the associations observed in the cross-section analysis, such a rise in the share of the I sector, and the absence of any conspicuous trend in the share of the S sector, should have been expected. However, we must explore further to see whether the parameters of association suggested by the cross-section apply (or merely agree in sign or direction of movement).

There are some puzzling aspects about the trends and levels of the I and S sector shares. The shares of the S sector for the United States and Canada did rise significantly, and at the terminal dates are distinctly higher than those in the European countries closest with respect to per capita product. The opposite is true of the shares of the I sector. In Sweden, the European country with the highest per capita product and the most impressive record of long-term growth, the share of the S sector declined over the long period, if it moved at all; in the middle 1960's it was about four-tenths of GDP compared with over 50 percent for the United States, while the share of the I sector was almost 55 percent in Sweden and less than 45 percent in the United States. In general, all the European countries, except France in the twentieth century, show a much greater concentration of growth in the share of the I sector and little growth in the share of the S sector; and until recent years, a much larger share of product originating in the I sector and a much smaller share for the S sector than the United States and Canada show. Whether this is a real difference in the production structure or only the result of some differences in statistical procedure is a question that requires much more intensive study of disaggregated data than is feasible here. But the sources of the differences may well lie in internal price structure since the prices of services are relatively much higher in the United States.[7] The analysis of the labor force in Chapter VI will provide a partial check on this conjecture.

Changes in Shares: Subdivisions of the I and S Sectors

In distinguishing the subdivisions, first of the I sector (Table 22), we limited ourselves almost entirely to the records of the developed countries, including only one less developed country, Argentina. As might have been expected, manufacturing, the major component of the I sector, dominates the observed rises in the sector shares, although the greater detail in Table 23 shows that the share of manufacturing for France did not rise (from the end of the nineteenth century), and for some other countries (the United Kingdom and Norway) rose only slightly in the later periods. But Table 22 shows that over the full periods, the share of manufacturing (sometimes including mining or electricity, gas, and water) in all seven countries shows a substantial rise. The typical initial share of manufacturing ranges between 11 and 15 percent of total product, and it rises to between 30 and 40 percent. Moreover, the rise in the share of manufacturing accounts for at least half of the total rise in the share of the I sector, and in some countries for much more. But this is only to be expected, since at the initial level the manufacturing share is already about half of that of the I sector.

The patterns of movement in the shares of the other subdivisions are diverse. The share of mining, like that of any other natural resource sector, declines if in the early periods of modern economic growth the country enjoyed some advantage reflected in a relatively high share of mining (say, well above about 2 percent of total product) — as was the case in the United Kingdom (line 3), and Australia (lines 39, 42). Such a decline is to be expected, since the

7. Using the OEEC data underlying Table 20, I calculated the ratio of the S prices to I prices for European countries, with the United States structure as base (for 1950, the year for the original field study).

For the eight European countries the S/I price ratio, relative to that for the United States (taken as 1), averaged roughly 0.55 (geometric unweighted mean of the ratios for the individual countries). The validity of this comparison for other years (1950 was still fairly close to the end of the war, and was also affected by rent controls), or for a comparison of net value product originating (rather than of value of finished goods, to which the price comparisons apply), is a matter for further scrutiny. But the data do suggest that the price structure is a significant factor.

Table 22. Long-term changes in shares of subdivisions of the I sector in gross domestic product (percentages).

	Mining (1)	Manufac- turing (2)	Construc- tion (3)	Electricity, gas, and water (4)	Transpor- tation and com- munica- tion (5)	Total I (6)
United Kingdom						
Current prices						
1. 1907	6.3	27.1	3.9	1.6	10.0	48.9
2. 1963–67	2.3	33.8	7.0	3.2	8.3	54.6
3. Change, 1907 to 1963–67	−4.0 (−4.2)	+6.7 (+6.1)	+3.1 (+3.0)	+1.6 (+1.6)	−1.7 (−2.0)	+5.7 (+4.5)
Germany						
1913 prices						
4. 1850–59	1.0	18.5	2.5	0	0.8	22.8
5. 1935–38	3.1	39.9	5.0	2.3	6.0	56.3
6. Change, 1850– 59 to 1935–38	+2.1	+21.4	+2.5	+2.3	+5.2	+33.5
Sweden						
Current prices						
7. 1861–70	13.8[a]		5.8	[a]	3.0	22.6
8. 1951–55	44.1[a]		7.9	[a]	6.3	58.3
9. Change, 1861– 70 to 1951–55	+30.3[a]		+2.1	[a]	+3.3	+35.7
Italy						
Current prices						
10. 1861–70	0.5	15.9	2.1	0.1	1.7	20.3
11. 1891–1900	0.8	14.6	2.2	0.5	3.9	22.0
12. 1950–52	1.1	32.3	3.5	2.6	6.0	45.5
13. Change, 1891– 1900 to 1950–52	+0.3	+17.7	+1.3	+2.1	+2.1	+23.5
1938 prices						
14. 1861–70	1.1	15.9	1.3	0	1.3	19.6
15. 1891–1900	1.2	17.9	1.4	0.1	2.8	23.4
16. 1950–52	0.9	27.5	2.2	3.6	9.4	43.6
17. Change, 1891– 1900 to 1950–52	−0.3	+9.6	+0.8	+3.5	+6.6	+20.2

Table 22 — continued

	(1)	(2)	(3)	(4)	(5)	(6)
Current prices						
18. 1951–52	1.0	29.2	4.7	2.2	6.3	43.4
19. 1963–67	0.8	28.3	8.2	2.7	7.1	47.1
20. Change, 1951–52 to 1963–67	−0.2	−0.9	+3.5	+0.5	+0.8	+3.7
1963 prices						
21. 1951–52	0.7	21.2	6.0	2.2	5.9	36.0
22. 1963–67	0.8	29.7	7.4	2.9	7.1	47.9
23. Change, 1951–52 to 1963–67	+0.1	+8.5	+1.4	+0.7	+1.2	+11.9
United States						
Current prices						
24. 1839	0.6	14.3	4.5	6.4		25.8
25. 1889/99	2.2	25.4	7.0	9.5		44.1
26. Change, 1839 to 1889/99	+1.6	+11.1	+2.5	+3.1		+18.3
1859 prices						
27. 1839	0.4	10.7	6.3	6.8		24.2
28. 1889/99	2.1	24.2	4.7	21.6		52.6
29. Change, 1839 to 1889/99	+1.7	+13.5	−1.6	+14.8		+28.4
1929 prices						
30. 1889/99	2.1	21.1	6.3	8.2		37.7
31. 1919/29	2.4	23.8	4.1	11.0		41.3
32. 1953	1.6	29.6	3.7	13.5		48.4
33. Change, 1889/99 to 1953	−0.5	+8.5	−2.6	+5.3		+10.7
National income, current prices						
34. 1953	2.9	30.8	4.5	2.0	7.0	47.2
35. 1963–67	2.0	28.3	4.5	2.4	6.3	43.5
36. Change, 1953 to 1963–67	−0.9	−2.5	0	+0.4	−0.7	−3.7
Australia						
Current prices						
37. 1861–80	9.7	7.6	10.3	3.4		31.0
38. 1935–38 (F)	3.0	17.0	6.3	6.5		32.8
39. Change, 1861–80 to 1935–38 (F)	−6.7	+9.4	−4.0	+3.1		+1.8

Table 22 — continued

	(1)	(2)	(3)	(4)	(5)	(6)
1910/11 prices						
40. 1861–80	9.1	8.7	11.3		1.6	30.7
41. 1935–38 (F)	2.3	15.4	5.9		6.0	29.6
42. Change, 1861–						
80 to 1935–38 (F)	−6.8	+6.7	−5.4		+4.4	−1.1
Argentina						
1960 prices						
43. 1935–39	0.5	27.1	3.3	0.7	6.3	37.9
44. 1963–67	1.5	34.1	3.5	1.9	7.4	48.4
45. Change, 1935–						
39 to 1963–67	+1.0	+7.0	+0.2	+1.2	+1.1	+10.5

(F): fiscal years beginning July 1.
a Electricity, gas, and water included in column 1.
When years in the stubs are connected by a slash (/), data are for the single years indicated; when connected by a dash (–), they are for all the years in the interval.
For sources of underlying data see notes to Table 21.
The figures in parentheses in line 3 are the sums of changes from 1907 to 1924, 1924 to 1955, and 1955 to 1963–67.

growth process itself would produce a larger rise in the shares of production branches *not* dependent on natural resources. By contrast, if a country begins its growth with a rather low share for mining, the latter may rise, since technological progress means new techniques for exploiting natural endowments and may thereby add to the stock of natural resources. Thus in some countries we find a rise in the share of mining (Germany, line 6; the United States, lines 26, 29; and Argentina, line 45), although it never reaches sizable proportions, and may even decline after an initial rise.

The share of the construction subdivision rises in most countries — a trend which should have been expected in view of the effects of urbanization on housing and related construction, and of the possibly rising share of construction in capital formation in the early stages of development. The estimates may also reflect a shift toward more specialized contract construction activity, away from construction done on own account by farm and other enterprises (and often not recorded as construction in the estimates). It is interesting that in the United States and Australia, where population growth was retarded sharply in the twentieth compared with the nineteenth century, the rather high initial share of construction declines (lines 29, 33, 42). Presumably, in other countries (like Canada and New Zealand) similarly "empty" in the earlier decades, a decline in the rates of population growth and construction of the basic infrastructure should also have meant a decline in the share of construction. But for the small sample in Table 22 the dominant trend is upward.

The share of the transport and communication subdivision, one of the most dynamic components in modern economic growth, rises quite consistently — in most countries substantially from a rather low initial level. The decline for the United Kingdom in the twentieth century may reflect both a change in relative prices and a recession in importance of shipping. But this is a minor exception to the general picture of substantial rise — particularly in the shares based on constant price volumes (in Italy, lines 13, 17; in the United States, lines 26, 29) — rises that are even more striking on a relative basis than those in the share of manufacturing.

Because of the large contribution of manufacturing to the rise in the share of the I sector and to growth of product we assembled some long-term records on branches of manufacturing. These usually provided the shares in manufacturing value added (sometimes only in total output); and those were linked with shares of manufacturing in total product to derive the shares of branches of manufacturing in the latter (Table 23). The long-term records for various countries yield shares different from those based on the recent series (for example, Italy, lines 18–19; Sweden, lines 27–28; the United States, lines 33–34); and the classification of branches is not as clear-cut as that for recent years used in Chapter III. But the inconsistencies are limited, and the classification is adequate.

The most uniformly observed finding in Table 23 is the rise in the shares of two branches: chemicals and petroleum products and the metal products group (which here includes both basic metals and the fabricated metal industries). In all ten countries these shares rise; and the rise for the metal products group actually dominates the rise in the share of all manufacturing in total product. Indeed, in France and Norway the former is larger than the latter. In most other countries, it accounts for more than three-quarters of the rise in the share of all manufacturing in total product.

A third group whose share in total product rises almost as uni-

Table 23. Long-term changes in shares of branches of manufacturing in gross domestic product (percentages).

	Total manufacturing (1)	Food, beverages, and tobacco (2)	Textiles and clothing (3)	Wood products (4)	Paper and printing (5)	Chemicals and petroleum products (6)	Nonmetal minerals (7)	Metal products (8)	Miscellaneous, leather, and rubber (9)
Great Britain–United Kingdom									
Great Britain, GDI, current prices									
1. 1907	27.1	4.5	8.4	1.1	1.7	1.2	—	8.6	1.6
2. 1924	30.4	6.8	7.7	0.9	2.3	1.9	—	8.3	2.5
United Kingdom, GDP, current prices									
3. 1924	31.5	7.1	8.1	—	2.4	2.0	—	8.5	3.4
4. 1955	36.8	3.9	5.2	—	2.8	3.1	—	17.9	3.9
5. 1953	35.2	3.9	5.1	1.1	2.3	2.9	1.4	16.8	1.7
6. 1963	33.6	3.9	3.6	1.0	2.7	3.5	1.3	15.7	1.9
7. Change, 1907 to 1963[a]	+7.3	−0.9	−4.8	—	+1.3	+2.3	—	+8.2	+1.2
France									
GDP, constant prices									
8. 1896	35.2	5.6	16.3	—	—	0.8	1.7	6.4	4.4
9. 1929	34.8	5.2	10.6	—	—	2.0	1.7	11.0	4.3
10. 1963	34.8	5.1	5.0	—	—	4.2	1.5	15.1	3.9
11. Change, 1896 to 1963	−0.4	−0.5	−11.3	—	—	+3.4	−0.2	+8.7	−0.5

Germany

NDP, constant prices

12. 1875	28.0	6.2	10.2	2.9	0.4	0.9	2.5	4.9	—
13. 1911–13	34.6	6.9	7.8	2.9	1.2	2.8	2.5	10.5	—
14. 1936–38	40.4	8.3	6.5	2.2	1.0	4.5	2.1	15.8	—
15. Change, 1875 to 1936–38	+12.4	+2.1	−3.7	−0.7	+0.6	+3.6	−0.4	+10.9	—

Italy

GNI, current prices

16. 1861–70	15.9	5.7	⎫ 7.7		0.5	0.1	0.3	1.6	b
17. 1901–10	17.0	4.3	⎪ 6.7		1.0	0.3	0.6	4.1	b
18. 1952–54	29.8	5.7	⎪ 6.2		2.7	4.0	1.2	10.0	b
19. 1953	27.4	5.3	⎪ 5.4		2.3	4.1	1.2	9.1	b
20. 1963	29.2	3.2	⎭ 6.5		2.8	3.3	2.0	11.4	b
21. Change, 1901–10 to 1963	+14.6	−0.7	+0.6		+2.2	+2.9	+1.4	+8.2	b

Norway

GNP, current prices

22. 1930	23.0	7.5	2.8	1.2	3.9	2.0	0.8	4.4	0.4
23. 1960	24.2	3.9	2.4	1.6	3.5	2.3	1.0	9.2	0.3
24. Change, 1930 to 1960	+1.2	−3.6	−0.4	+0.4	−0.4	+0.3	+0.2	+4.8	−0.1

Table 23 — continued

	(1)	(2)	(3)	(4)	(5)	(6)	(7)	(8)	(9)
Sweden									
GDP, current prices									
25. 1861–70	13.8	5.0	1.4	2.5	0.3	0.6	0.2	3.4	0.4
26. 1901–10	25.8	8.4	2.9	3.1	1.9	1.0	1.2	6.0	1.3
27. 1951–55	42.6	7.6	4.0	3.4	5.5	2.7	1.4	16.5	1.5
28. 1953	30.9	3.6	3.5	2.2	4.6	1.8	1.4	12.7	1.1
29. 1963	33.2	3.4	2.8	2.1	4.5	1.8	1.4	16.0	1.2
30. Change, 1861–70 to 1963	+31.1	+2.4	+1.9	+0.8	+5.1	+2.1	+1.2	+16.4	+1.2
United States									
NI, current prices									
31. 1839	14.3	2.1	2.6	1.7	1.0	0.7	0.7	3.1	2.4
32. 1879	21.1	3.2	4.3	2.3	1.8	1.1	0.8	5.3	2.3
33. 1929	30.5	3.1	4.8	1.1	4.1	3.1	1.1	10.8	2.4
34. 1929	25.5	2.8	3.5	1.8	2.5	2.4	0.9	9.8	1.8
35. 1965	30.7	2.8	2.2	1.3	2.6	3.1	1.0	16.1	1.6
36. Change, 1839 to 1965	+21.4	+1.0	+0.9	−1.1	+3.2	+3.1	+0.5	+14.0	−0.2
Canada									
GDP, current prices									
37. 1870	19.5	3.4	2.0	4.1	0.7	0.9	0.6	4.8	3.0

Australia

GDP, current prices

38. 1910	22.8	4.4	2.8	3.7	1.5	1.0	1.0	6.6	1.8
39. 1953	29.1	4.3	2.6	2.1	4.1	2.4	0.9	11.1	1.6
40. 1953	29.1	4.5	2.9	2.1	4.0	2.5	0.8	10.9	1.4
41. 1963	25.9	4.1	2.3	1.5	3.4	2.4	0.9	10.0	1.3
42. Change, 1870 to 1963	+6.4	+0.5	0	−2.6	+2.8	+1.4	+0.4	+5.4	−1.5
43. 1911–13 (F)	14.1	2.8	2.5	2.7	0.9	0.8	°	3.7	0.7
44. 1953 (F)	27.3	4.1	4.1	3.1	1.8	2.1	°	10.8	1.3
45. 1953 (F)	27.1	4.1	4.0	3.1	1.8	2.1	°	10.7	1.3
46. 1963 (F)	27.8	3.9	3.1	2.9	2.1	2.5	°	12.1	1.2
47. Change, 1911–13 to 1963 (F)	+13.9	+1.1	+0.7	+0.2	+1.2	+1.7	°	+8.5	+0.5

Argentina

GDP, 1950 prices for lines 48–49; current prices for lines 50–51

48. 1900–04	13.0	4.5	2.5	1.5	0.5	0.9	1.8	0.4	0.9
49. 1955	22.0	4.8	3.8	0.8	1.2	2.9	1.2	5.8	1.5
50. 1953	26.7	6.3	5.7	1.3	1.3	3.1	1.2	6.5	1.3
51. 1963	31.1	7.0	3.1	0.5	1.7	5.1	1.3	9.1	3.3
52. Change, 1900–04 to 1963[d]	+12.5	+0.8	−0.8	−1.3	+1.0	+3.6	−0.5	+7.5	+2.2

(F): fiscal year beginning July 1.
—: information not available.

a Using 0.8 of change in lines 5–6.
b Included in column 5.
c Included in column 4.
d Using 0.8 of change in lines 50–51.

United Kingdom

Lines 1–4: From Deane and Cole, *British Economic Growth*, tables 40, 41, pp. 175, 178.

Lines 5–6: Column 1 is from the United Nations, *Yearbook of National Accounts Statistics, 1967* (New York, 1968). Columns 2–9 are based on unpublished United Nations data.

Line 7: Cumulated total, adjusted for overlap in lines 2–3. Columns 4 and 7 are included in column 9.

France

Lines 8–11: From Malinvaud and others, "Sources et origines de la croissance française," table 8, p. 29. Column 4 is included in column 7; column 5 in column 9; and leather in column 3.

Germany

Lines 12–14: Column 1 is from Hoffmann, *Das Wachstum der Deutschen Wirtschaft*, table 103, pp. 454–455, adjusted to exclude electricity, gas, and water and construction on the basis of the weights shown in table 76, pp. 390–395. Columns 2–9 are derived by means of the weights and annual indexes shown in table 76 (the index for paper products interpolated roughly when not given). Since no mention is made of printing and miscellaneous products, column 5 is for paper only and column 9 is not available.

Italy

Lines 16–18: Column 1 is from the Istituto Centrale di Statistica, *Annali . . . Series VIII*, vol. 9, tables 15, 36, pp. 217, 249–250, for present boundaries. Columns 2–9 are based on the estimates for changing boundaries in *ibid*, tables 12–14, pp. 212–215. Columns 3–4 include leather; column 5 includes rubber and miscellaneous.

Lines 19–20: Column 1 is from the *Yearbook of National Accounts Statistics, 1967*. Columns 2–9 are based on unpublished United Nations data. Subgroups are comparable with those in lines 16–18.

Norway

Lines 22–23: From Norway, Central Statistical Bureau, *National Accounts, 1865–1960* (Oslo, 1965), table 2, pp. 68–69. Column 8 includes miscellaneous products; column 9 covers leather and rubber.

Sweden

Lines 25–27: Column 1 is based on Johansson, *The Gross Domestic Product of Sweden*, table 55, pp. 150–151. Indirect taxes and customs duties were excluded from the total to approximate GDP. Mining is included in the metals group (column 8). Power stations, gas, and water, included by Johansson with manufacturing, is excluded on the basis of gross output, shown in Johansson, tables 15–16, pp. 66–69. Columns 2–9 are based on the shares of the subgroups in gross output of manufacturing, given in Johansson, tables 7–14, 16, pp. 50–65, 68–69.

Lines 28–29: Column 1 is based on the *Yearbook of National Accounts Statistics, 1967.* Columns 2–9 are based on unpublished United Nations data. Mining is excluded.

United States

Lines 31–32: Column 1 is calculated from Gallman and Weiss, "The Service Industries," table 2, p. 291, and Gallman, "Commodity Output," table A-1, p. 43, variant A. Columns 2–9 are based on unpublished estimates by Professor Gallman; professional instruments and ordnance are included in column 8.

Line 33: Column 1 was extrapolated from line 32 by the change in the share derived from the Bureau of the Census, *Long Term Economic Growth,* series C 111 to C 121, pp. 224–227. Columns 2–9 were extrapolated from line 32 by the change in shares derived from Daniel Creamer, Sergei P. Dobrovolsky, and Israel Borenstein, *Capital in Manufacturing and Mining: Its Formation and Financing* (Princeton: Princeton University Press for the National Bureau of Economic Research, 1960), table A-10, pp. 252–258.

Lines 34–35: From the Department of Commerce, *The National Income and Product Accounts of the United States, 1929–1965: A Supplement to the Survey of Current Business* (Washington, D.C., 1966), table 1.12, pp. 18–21. The total excludes income from the rest of world.

Canada

Lines 37–39: Column 1 is from Urquhart and Buckley, *Historical Statistics of Canada,* series E 214–44, E 46–65. Columns 2–9 are from *ibid.,* series Q 1–11, Q 30–137 (value added).

Lines 40–41: Column 1 is from the *Yearbook of National Accounts Statistics, 1967.* Columns 2–9 are based on unpublished United Nations data.

Australia

Lines 43–44: Column 1, line 44, was derived from unpublished data supplied by Bryan D. Haig of the Australian National University; and for line 43 was extrapolated by linking in 1935–38 to Butlin, *Australian Domestic Product,* table 2, pp. 10–11 (and unpublished revisions). Columns 2–9 were derived from A. Maizels, "Trends in Production and Labour Productivity in Australian Manufacturing Industries," *Economic Record,* vol. XXXIII, no. 65 (August 1957), table I, p. 166, which gives indexes to the base 1947/48–1949/50. I applied these to the 1953/54 distribution of manufacturing underlying line 45.

Lines 45–46: Column 1 is from the *Yearbook of National Accounts Statistics, 1967.* Columns 2–9 are based on unpublished United Nations data regrouped for comparability with lines 43–44: leather is included in column 3, not in column 9, and stone, clay, and glass are combined with wood in column 4.

Argentina

Lines 48–49: Column 1 is from the United Nations, *Análisis y Proyecciones del Desarrollo Económico de la Argentina, II. Los Sectores de la Producción* (Mexico, 1959), part I, table 15, pp. 116–117. Columns 2–9 are from the mimeographed preliminary report of the same title, table XV, p. 147.

Lines 50–51: Column 1 is from the *Yearbook of National Accounts Statistics, 1967.* Columns 2–9 are based on unpublished United Nations data.

formly is paper and printing. Of the nine countries for which this group is distinguished, only Norway shows a slight drop (line 24). In all other countries the rise is substantial relatively, and in several countries even absolutely.

Long-term changes in the shares of other branches show considerable diversity. That of food, beverages, and tobacco declined in Great Britain–United Kingdom, France, Norway, and Italy, but rose in other countries. The share of textiles and clothing declined in most of the countries for which it was distinguished, but rose in Sweden, the United States, and Australia. It was constant in Canada. The shares of the wood products and the nonmetallic mineral groups also show diverse trends, with a balance toward declines in the former and rises in the latter. Further detail could be provided, but the summary in Table 23 is sufficient to indicate that the conspicuous rise in the share of manufacturing in total product was led largely by the metal products, chemicals and petroleum, and paper and printing branches, with the trends in the shares of the other branches in total product more variable. Additional evidence will be given in Chapter VI when long-term trends in the shares of manufacturing branches in countrywide labor force are discussed.

Coverage of the subdivisions of the S sector (Table 24), limited to six developed and one less developed country, is further qualified by divergent definitions of subdivisions and plagued by difficult valuation problems. Some trends can be discerned, but they are subject to a wide margin of error.

In the United Kingdom, Germany, Sweden, Italy (over the long period), and Argentina the share of the S sector in total product declines; in the United States it rises; in Australia, for volumes in current prices it rises slightly, for volumes in constant prices it declines slightly. Against this background, the only trend that is somewhat general is the rise in the share of public administration services (government and defense) — although even here Australia is an exception. Yet, in view of the growing importance of government in the developed economies, the finding is plausible.

The only other semblance of consensus, with the exception of Argentina, is in the decline in the share of the finance and dwellings category. This decline may be caused partly by recent controls of residential rent, or there may be other reasons for the downward

Table 24. Long-term changes in shares of subdivisions of the S Sector in gross domestic product (percentages).

	Trade (1)	Finance and dwellings (2)	Other private services (3)	Government and defense (4)	Total S (5)
United Kingdom					
Current prices					
1. 1907	18.9[a]	7.9[a]	14.7	3.2	44.7
2. 1963–67	13.9[a]	4.4[a]	17.0	6.7	42.0
3. Change, 1907 to 1963–67	−5.0[a] (−4.6)	−3.5[a] (−3.9)	+2.3 (+1.1)	+3.5 (+6.1)	−2.7 (−1.3)
Germany					
1913 prices					
4. 1850–59	7.1[b]	2.9[b]	22.4		32.4
5. 1935–38	9.4[b]	4.5[b]	13.6		27.5
6. Change, 1850–59 to 1935–38	+2.3[b]	+1.6[b]	−8.8		−4.9
Sweden					
Current prices					
7. 1861–70	21.8[c]	13.7[c]	[c]	3.6	39.1
8. 1951–55	20.3[c]	3.7[c]	[c]	7.9	31.9
9. Change, 1861–70 to 1951–55	−1.5[c]	−10.0[c]	[c]	+4.3	−7.2
Italy					
Current prices					
10. 1861–70	6.4	5.5	7.8	5.7	25.4
11. 1891–1900	8.7	8.3	7.5	6.1	30.6
12. 1950–52	8.9	5.7	4.2	9.9	28.7
13. Change, 1891–1900 to 1950–52	+0.2	−2.6	−3.3	+3.8	−1.9
1938 prices					
14. 1861–70	10.8	11.0	6.7	5.8	34.3
15. 1891–1900	10.9	12.6	6.3	5.1	34.9
16. 1950–52	11.0	9.2	3.9	9.9	34.0
17. Change, 1891–1900 to 1950–52	+0.1	−3.4	−2.4	+4.8	−0.9

Table 24 — continued

	(1)	(2)	(3)	(4)	(5)
Current prices					
18. 1951–52	10.4	6.4	7.2	9.9	33.9
19. 1963–67	9.8	9.7	7.9	12.4	39.8
20. Change, 1951–52 to 1963–67	−0.6	+3.3	+0.7	+2.5	+5.9
1963 prices					
21. 1951–52	9.6	9.6	9.3	15.3	43.8
22. 1963–67	9.7	9.5	7.5	11.7	38.4
23. Change, 1951–52 to 1963–67	+0.1	−0.1	−1.8	−3.6	−5.4

United States

	(1)	(2)	(3)	(4)	(5)
Current prices			⎧‾‾‾‾‾‾‾‾‾⎫		
24. 1839	11.5	11.6	8.5		31.6
25. 1889/99	14.1	10.5	13.4		38.0
26. Change, 1839 to 1889/99	+2.6	−1.1	+4.9		+6.4
27. 1929	15.7	14.9	10.3	5.9	46.8
28. 1963–67	16.2	13.6	10.4	13.0	53.2
29. Change, 1929 to 1963–67	+0.5	−1.3	+0.1	+7.1	+6.4

Australia

	(1)	(2)	(3)	(4)	(5)
Current prices					
30. 1861–80	13.0	15.6	10.1	5.2	43.9
31. 1935–38 (F)	18.5	11.1	10.4	4.6	44.6
32. Change, 1861–80 to 1935–38 (F)	+5.5	−4.5	+0.3	−0.6	+0.7
1910/11 prices					
33. 1861–80	13.5	13.9	12.8	6.6	46.8
34. 1935–38 (F)	19.7	12.1	10.1	4.5	46.4
35. Change, 1861–80 to 1935–38 (F)	+6.2	−1.8	−2.7	−2.1	−0.4

Table 24 — continued

	(1)	(2)	(3)	(4)	(5)
Argentina					
1960 prices					
36. 1935–39	20.0	3.7	6.9	5.3	35.9
37. 1963–67	16.7	4.1	7.1	6.8	34.7
38. Change, 1935–39 to 1963–67	−3.3	+0.4	+0.2	+1.5	−1.2

(F): fiscal year beginning July 1.
ᵃ Finance is included with trade.
ᵇ Finance and hotels are included with trade.
ᵉ Finance and private services are included with trade.
When years in the stubs are connected by a slash (/), data are for the single years indicated; when connected by a dash (–), they are for all the years in the interval.
See the notes to Table 21 for the sources of the underlying data.
The figures in parentheses in line 3 are the sum of changes from 1907 to 1924, 1924 to 1955, and 1955 to 1963–67.
The allocation of the total for trade and other services (commercio e servizi vari) in current prices in lines 10–12 is based on the constant price series and the implicit price indexes given in Fuà, *Notes on Italian Economic Growth*, tables 1, 5, pp. 56–58, 65–67.
The underlying data for lines 27 and 28 are the official estimates, for 1929 taken from the Bureau of the Census, *Long Term Economic Growth*, series C 132 to C 209, pp. 228–235, and for 1963–67 from the United Nations, *Yearbook of National Accounts Statistics, 1968*, vol. I. *Individual Country Data* (New York, 1969).

drift of the proportion of this category of almost pure property income to total product.

No clear trends are shown by the shares of other subdivisions. The share of trade rises in Germany (where it is unusually low compared with other countries), Italy (over the long period to the 1950's), the United States, and Australia; but it declines in the United Kingdom (inclusive of finance), Sweden, and Argentina. The share of private services rises in the United Kingdom, and slightly in the United States (in the twentieth century) and Australia (for volumes in current but not in constant prices); it apparently declines in other countries. Such diversity of trends in the shares of trade and services other than government may be real, rather than one created by inadequate coverage and questionable accuracy of the estimates. But the sample is small and the estimates subject to wide margins of error, so it would be well to suspend judgment pending examination of the shares in labor force.

Time Trends and Cross-Sections: General Comments

Several of the findings in the preceding discussion have some bearing on conformity of long-term changes with those indicated in the cross-section for a recent year. On the one hand, in some less developed countries in which per capita product failed to rise over the long period, the share of the A sector declined appreciably — whereas the 1958 cross-section (or any other cross-section within the modern period) would indicate no change in the share of the A sector for a fixed per capita product (and, in fact, the size factor, given the likely loss in relative size of countries with stagnant per capita product, suggests a minor *rise* in the share of the A sector). On the other hand, in all the developed countries, with per capita product rising significantly over the long periods, the changes in the shares of the sectors and subdivisions conform quite well with the 1958 cross-section for the appropriate ranges of per capita product — that is, from about $150 to over $1,000 in 1958 prices: the share of the A sector declines markedly; those of the I sector and, particularly, of the manufacturing and transport subdivisions rise markedly; that of the S sector changes little and erratically. Within manufacturing, the uniform and conspicuous rise in the shares in total product of the metal products, chemical, and paper and printing branches is what we would expect from the cross-section; the same is true of the rise within the S sector of the share of government and defense. Yet, against this broad conformity, the quantitative relation between growth in per capita product and changes in shares, as compared with that between differences in per capita product and differences in shares in the cross-section, remains to be explored.

Before doing so it would be well to consider more explicitly why and under what conditions conformity between the temporal and cross-section associations should be expected. This discussion assumes that changes in both per capita product and sectoral shares are measured in dollar units and price structure comparable with those involved in the cross-section — so that neither, particularly the temporal changes in price structure, affects conformity (whether valuation bases are, in fact, the same in the cross-section and time series is discussed toward the end of this section). The association of the cross-section with movement over time should also be considered for *groups* of countries, and the association among groups in cross-section should not be compared with relations over time for individual countries.

With all this assumed, we can say that if the cross-section differentials in per capita product and in sectoral shares are viewed as the cumulative result of past growth, when such growth is observed in time series it should show the same association between changes in per capita product and changes in sectoral shares as is revealed by the accumulated differences in product per head and in the sectoral shares in a comparison for a recent year. But this viewpoint — that a given cross-section should yield a correct estimate of past trends because it is the accumulated result of past growth — is valid only under certain conditions. And these conditions suggest why in so many cases the cross-section does not lead to a correct backward projection.

One obvious condition is that, for the full range of the sample covered by the cross-section, the growth in the past over which changes over time will be measured for comparison with the cross-section must dominate the picture; and the initial levels of per capita product and the associated initial differences in shares must be relegated to insignificance. If we start with such an insignificant initial position, a kind of *tabula rasa,* the cross-section must be, by assumption, the result of cumulated past growth. Hence, measurement of the growth process in the past should yield average parameters identical with those found in the cross-section — provided that we cover the full period of growth back to the zero initial starting point.

Needless to say, this situation is unrealistic. Any cross-section sample that includes the less developed countries cannot be interpreted as one in which past growth within any reasonable historical period was so large as to dwarf the initial levels and structure. After all, one important feature of the less developed countries is that they failed, over a long-term past, to sustain high rates of growth and structural transformation. And even in the developed countries, the levels of per capita product at the beginning of the long periods of a century to a century and a half, were in most cases between a fifth and a sixth of current levels — hardly a negligible fraction. Yet this unrealistic condition immediately yields two suggestive implications. First, *ceteris paribus,* the current cross-section for groups of countries with high growth rates may yield a better estimate of past temporal changes than the cross-section for countries with low growth rates in the observed past. Second, given cumulation to greater growth over longer periods, the longer the period studied, the more closely will the current cross-section serve to describe temporal changes — unless extension of the period allows changes in the trends.

The second, more relevant, condition of conformity between cross-section and time changes applies directly to the kinds of comparison usually drawn. If the initial levels are high enough to affect the cross-section at the *end* of any observed period of long-term changes, this terminal cross-section will correctly reveal the income-share relations over the period with respect to both size of share and magnitude of changes *only* if it is identical with the initial one. Any change between the initial and terminal cross-sections will necessarily mean a discrepancy in the relations between income and sectoral shares, between the changes over time and either of the cross-sections that frame the period for which the temporal changes are observed.

To illustrate: assume that the sample includes only five countries, and that the cross-section at the beginning of the period yields the following shares for the A sector at our customary benchmark values of product per capita:

	$70	$150	$300	$500	$1,000
		Initial Cross-Section (I)			
Share of A (%)	50	40	30	20	10

Assume further that at the end of the period these five countries yield the same shares for the A sector at the same benchmark values of comparable dollars, with a single exception — at the $300 level:

	$70	$150	$300	$500	$1,000
		Terminal Cross-Section (II)			
Share of A (%)	50	40	25	20	10

The total number of possible movements over time, that is, between cross-sections I and II (including a country's remaining at the same level), and the number of relations between pairs of per capita product values and shares of the A sector within each cross-section (including the pairing of a country with itself) will both equal (n × n), or 25 in this illustration. Strict conformity between cross-section and changes over time will be assured only if all 25 possible moves *between* the two cross-sections can be matched by the 25 moves *within* a single cross-section (either I or II) — for only under these conditions will a single cross-section forecast or "back-cast" the correct relation between changes in per capita product and changes in shares. The single change in this illustration introduces some nonconformity. The relations between income and shares resulting from 5 of the 25 possible moves over time will not match those in the initial cross-section (moves from I-70, I-150, I-300, etc. to II-300); and the results of 5 other moves will not match relations in the terminal cross-section (moves from I-300 to II-70, II-150, II-300, and so on). If the per capita product range is the same in the initial and terminal cross-sections, and if the same countries are represented throughout the period connecting the two cross-sections, the identity of the latter is the required condition for full conformity between cross-section and time changes, not merely of the sign but also of the magnitude of the relations between product per capita and sectoral shares.

In substantive research, the strict conditions of the illustration and argument may be relaxed, and the conclusion qualified though not denied. For example, country coverage need not be identical for the two cross-sections and changes over time. The argument still holds for three different samples — one for the initial cross-section, a second for the long-term changes, and a third for the terminal cross-section — if all three are representative of the universe under study, and the sampling errors (or some other recognizable errors) in qualifying them can be properly appraised.

Finally, I again emphasize that the cross-sections are either averages of varying degrees of complexity, or are described by mathematically defined regression equations between per capita product and sectoral shares; and that they must, therefore, be compared with averages of changes over time for groups of countries (or some equation fitted to temporal changes in a group of countries). To be sure, if the cross-section relation is close, and the variance of relations for individual countries around the averages (or regression lines) is narrow, the errors of comparison between a single country's changes and a cross-section relation are also limited; but they are present and must be remembered in testing the relations and in using the cross-section association to estimate changes over time.

If comparisons are made for individual countries (as in Table 25), the average result for the group, rather than the individual country results, must be stressed.

Granted that differences between initial and terminal cross-sections produce some nonconformity in the relations between changes in per capita product and total shares over time and the relations between per capita product differences and sectoral shares in either cross-section, should one expect changes in the cross-sections at successive dates? The answer depends, in the first place, on the meaning of such differences in successive cross-sections. This meaning can be most directly suggested by saying that a change from one cross-section to the next signifies that over the intervening period the relation between changes in per capita product and the sectoral shares was different from the cumulative effect of changes in per capita product and sectoral shares *antecedent* to the initial cross-section. The latter represents the cumulative result of preceding changes, which have specifically determined the relations within this initial cross-section. Thus if 0 denotes the initial date at which the values (for both product and sectoral shares) were completely overshadowed by changes over time that occurred between years 0 and I (at which point the initial cross-section I appears), differences between cross-sections I and II mean that the relations between per capita product and sectoral shares in the changes over the period from I to II differed from the relations in the changes over the period from 0 to I — since these changes over the period from I to II differ from the association in the initial cross-section I. Of course the pattern of changes and relations between per capita product and sectoral shares over the period from I to II may be similar to that over part of the period from 0 to I, say a period from $(0 + x)$ to I. But this would only mean that the change in the pattern of movement over time was between the periods from 0 to $(0 + x)$ and from $(0 + x)$ to II, rather than between the periods from 0 to I and from I to II. The point remains that differences among successive cross-sections signify a secular *change* in the relations between changes over time in per capita product and sectoral shares in the course of long periods of growth, assuming that the cross-sections are compared in a long-period succession.

The conclusion, which perhaps should have been obvious from the start, is that the validity of a cross-section for a recent year in

gauging past changes over time in the response of sectoral shares
to changes in per capita product depends upon the temporal stability of these relations. If through the long periods associated with
economic growth, the share of the A sector at the $70 benchmark
value (with constant purchasing power) was always 50 percent,
whereas at the $150 benchmark value it was always 40 percent,
then this segment of the successive cross-sections would show these
same values, and would correctly reflect the historical relations in
the movement of the shares within the specified range of per capita
product. But, if in some periods the response of the A sector to
rises in per capita product from $70 to $150 accelerated, and its
share declined from 50 to 35 rather than to 40 percent, no single
cross-section would yield a proper measure of past changes in sectoral shares (a dependent variable) for the rises in per capita product within this range (the independent variable). Thus judgment
of the reliability of cross-section relations as a guide to past changes
and associations, not merely with respect to sign but also with respect to size, depends upon judgment of the temporal stability of
the relations — in this instance between changes over time in per
capita product and sectoral shares; in other cases for other pairs of
complexes of variables.

This judgment could be explored in the light of our knowledge
of the factors linking level of per capita product (and the structural
aspects of economic growth connected with it) and shares of production sectors — to see how much stability in the relations over
time can be expected. Some of the discussion in the last part of
Chapter III on the cross-section association is of direct relevance
here; but to push it further does not promise to be rewarding.
Since per capita product and shares of various sectors are connected
either via the structure of final demand (in response to per capita
product), or via the input-output structure of industries (in response to comparative advantages depending upon differential technological attainment), and since so little is known about the technological changes which are so crucial at all levels of linkage between
per capita product and shares of sectors, the data for the analysis
of the temporal pattern of the relations being explored are hardly
likely to be available. In view of the vast and rapidly changing
flow of innovations in material and social technology, we could conclude that the chances of temporal stability in the quantitative relations between per capita product and shares of sectors in total

product are not high; and that accordingly cross-section relations are not likely to be a reliable base for inferring changes over time. But this would be merely an impression which cannot carry us far. It may be more useful, for the present, to turn to the statistical data and compare the relations within current cross-sections with those in observed long-term changes.

At this point we must return to the question of the bases for conversion of per capita product, and the sectoral price structure, used in cross-sections like those in Tables 12 and 14; and ask whether we need to adjust for them in comparisons of the cross-section parameters with those revealed by trends over time. This question can be answered readily with respect to the internal sectoral price structures. As shown in Table 20, the I/A price ratios are higher in the low per capita product developed countries. One would assume that this relationship would also hold over time, in that economic growth would lower prices of I sector products relative to those of A sector products; and if so, the share of the A sector over long periods would decline more when estimated for volumes in constant prices than when measured for volumes in current prices — with an opposite result for the rise in the share of the I sector in constant and current price volumes. Yet Table 21, which shows the sectoral shares in both constant and current price totals for several countries, reveals no such difference. This failure can probably be blamed on the sectoral price indexes: a more sensitive adjustment might reveal the expected shift over time in the sectoral price structure toward a declining ratio of I sector prices to A sector prices. But since the available records show no such trends, the time series should be compared with cross-section differences measured in the sectoral price structure *without* adjustment, as they are in Tables 12 and 14.

The answer to the question becomes more problematical when the comparability of international cross-section differences in per capita product with trends in per capita product over time is considered. The estimates of product over long periods are usually adjusted for price changes by indexes for as many components as possible; and are based on prices for identical or comparable goods at successive points of time. In this sense, conversion to a common base is more similar to an approximation of purchasing power equivalents than to the use of exchange rates. Consequently, one could argue that for comparisons with change over time, the cross-section association between sectoral shares and per capita product should be derived from per capita product converted by some approximation to direct price equivalents, not by exchange rates.

Yet this inference is subject to doubts. In the first place, as just indicated, the available historical series, adjusted for price changes and related to product in constant prices, do not reflect the expected shift in sectoral price structure, in the ratio of A prices to I prices or to I+S prices. We can therefore eliminate one possible source of differentials between exchange rate and direct price comparison conversions. If the latter is used, the higher ratio of A prices to I+S prices tends to narrow the gap between the per capita product of the less developed countries and that of the more developed countries (particularly when the prices of the latter are used as weights). Secondly, the shift from exchange rate to purchasing power conversion (based on the prices of the United States), which as suggested in Chapter III would at least double per capita product at the low levels, would yield unrealistic results in comparison with the per capita product of the presently developed countries in the nineteenth century (shown in Table 2, in 1965 prices). For example, per capita GNP of India, set at $73 in 1958 and equivalent to $81 in 1965 prices, would be adjusted to $162, just about a fifth short of per capita GNP of Sweden in 1861–1869.[8] This estimate is highly doubtful, in view of the greater climatic and other requirements in Sweden, and its economic position in the middle nineteenth century. Similarly, the per capita GNP of the United Arab Republic, set in 1958 at $124, and equivalent to $138 in 1965 prices, would be adjusted to $276 — about a third higher than the per capita GNP of Sweden in the 1860's. With all due allowance for the introduction of nuclei of modern industry in India and the United Arab Republic, the results are implausible.

Given the levels of per capita product for the presently developed countries in the middle of the nineteenth century, any significant

8. GNP per capita in 1958 dollars is from United Nations, *Yearbook of National Accounts Statistics, 1968*, vol. II. *International Tables* (New York, 1969), table 2C. The shift from 1958 to 1965 prices (by a ratio of 1.109) is based on the index implicit in GNP for the United States (see the *Economic Report of the President* [Washington, D.C., February 1968], table B-3, p. 212).

Many other less developed countries could be cited with similarly implausible estimates as a result of the adjustment (for example, Indonesia, with a 1958 GNP of $89 per capita, convertible to $99 in 1965 prices, and to $198 with the adjustment; or South Korea, with a GNP per capita in 1958 of $141, or $156 in 1965 prices, adjusted to as high as $312).

upward adjustment of per capita product in the underdeveloped countries, particularly those in Asia and SubSaharan Africa, would yield questionable results. It may well be that the growth rates for the developed countries have been overestimated, and, as a result, their per capita product levels in the nineteenth century are underestimated; but, given our long-term records and the inadequate adjustment for quality changes, it is difficult to accept such an inference. The trouble is more likely to lie with the attempts to adjust for purchasing power equivalence. At any rate, for present purposes it seemed best not to adjust the per capita product estimates in Table 14, but this possibility should be borne in mind when the results of comparison with long-term trends become apparent.

Comparisons of Long-Term Changes with Cross-Section Differentials

The first comparison is presented in Table 25. Even if valuation bases in the cross-section and time series are assumed comparable, the long-term changes should be in prices of the same year as that employed in the cross-section. Thus, if the 1958 cross-section is used to estimate changes in sectoral shares that should have occurred over time in association with observed changes in per capita product, the estimates of long-term changes in product should be in 1958 dollars; and those of the levels and proportional changes in shares should also reflect the 1958 sectoral price structure. Furthermore, the cross-section and the time changes should both be for representative samples of the universe; and the calculation of expected and observed changes should be for groups of countries, since the group relations in the cross-section yield expected changes in shares only for groups of countries (for individual countries the margin of error would have to be further estimated).

The available data on long-term changes in product and sectoral shares do not fully satisfy these requirements. Table 25 includes only nine countries, hardly a representative sample comparable with the more than fifty countries included in the 1958 cross-section; the comparison is limited to countries for which changes in the share of the A sector can be observed in volumes in constant prices, but not necessarily in 1958 prices and with the 1958 price structure. However, two checks can be made; and some suggestive results derived, for whatever value they may have in other tests, with richer data.

The 1958 cross-section is used to estimate the expected proportional changes in the shares of the A and I+S sectors, given the per capita product levels and changes (in 1958 prices) shown in columns 1 and 2 for each country covered in the table. These expected proportional changes appear in columns 4 and 7. However, the observed changes (columns 3, 6), which should be for shares in volumes in 1958 prices, are calculated from the shares in constant price volumes with the base years given. For Denmark and Italy the observed changes in shares in 1929 and 1938 price volumes respectively can be checked against those in 1958 price volumes, the latter derived by extrapolating the 1958 shares used in Tables 12 and 14 (see lines 4–5, 7–8). The differences are slight and scarcely affect the broad results; and the long-term proportional changes in sectoral shares would probably not differ widely because of differences in the base year. Second, a rough calculation of the 1958 cross-section for the nine countries in Table 25 can be compared with the one based on over fifty countries in Tables 12 and 14. The share of the A sector at the benchmark levels of $500 and $1,382 would be 18.0 and 8.3 percent respectively, compared with 18.7 and 9.2 percent in Tables 12 and 14. These two checks suggest that errors resulting from failure to use the 1958 price structure and from the small size of the sample in Table 25 are not large enough to invalidate general conclusions drawn from the table.

These conclusions, for the nine countries, may now be stated. First, the broadest measure of the ratio of the expected to the observed proportional changes, that in column 9, is less than 1 for all nine countries. This finding, which is not an algebraic necessity, means that the decline in the share of the A combined with the rise in that of the I+S sector was greater in these countries than expected from the 1958 cross-section. The geometric mean ratio for the countries (using line 5 for Denmark, line 8 for Italy, and line 10 for the United States) is about 0.6; but this average is misleading, since the ratio for three major countries (the United States, Japan, Argentina) is 0.5 or less. Even at that, the underestimation of observed changes over periods as long as those covered in Table 25 is substantial, implying even greater underestimation for shorter subperiods for some of these countries. For example, while the ratio for Sweden for the full period is 0.97, for 1861–1870 to 1911–1915

Table 25. Observed and estimated long-term proportional changes in shares of the A and I+S sectors, product in constant prices.

	Initial GDP per capita (1958 $) (1)	% rise in GDP per capita (2)	Proportional changes in shares						
			Decline in A		Col. 4/ Col. 3 (5)	Rise in I+S		Col. 7/ Col. 6 (8)	Geometric mean, cols. 5, 8 (9)
			Observed (3)	Estimated (4)		Observed (6)	Estimated (7)		
Great Britain, 1865 and 1885 prices									
1. 1801/11 to 1907	183	303	0.80	0.56	0.70	0.40	0.29	0.72	0.70
France, changing bases, linked									
2. 1896 to 1963	442	200	0.66	0.54	0.81	0.22	0.14	0.63	0.71
Germany, 1913 prices									
3. 1850–59 to 1910–13	190	136	0.48	0.39	0.81	0.39	0.19	0.50	0.64
Denmark, 1870–79 to 1958									
4. 1929 prices	274	298	0.59	0.60	1.02	0.42	0.23	0.56	0.76
5. Shifted to 1958 prices	274	298	0.59	0.60	1.02	0.39	0.23	0.61	0.79
Sweden, 1913 prices									
6. 1861–70 to 1951–55	137	728	0.80	0.72	0.90	0.43	0.44	1.04	0.97
Italy, 1861–69 to 1960–64									
7. 1938 prices	193	242	0.68	0.52	0.77	0.58	0.25	0.44	0.58
8. Shifted to 1958 prices	193	242	0.68	0.52	0.77	0.58	0.25	0.44	0.58

United States								
9. 1834–43 to 1894–1903, 1859 prices	372	142	0.65	0.45	0.69	0.52	0.14	0.26	0.42
10. 1869/79 to 1919/29, 1929 prices	581	142	0.69	0.47	0.69	0.40	0.10	0.24	0.41
Japan, 1934–36 prices								
11. 1879–83 to 1959–61	69	598	0.81	0.60	0.74	1.56	0.57	0.36	0.52
Argentina, 1960 prices								
12. 1900–04 to 1960–64	376	77	0.53	0.31	0.60	0.30	0.09	0.32	0.44

When years in the stubs are connected by a slash (/), data are for the single years indicated; when connected by a dash (–), they are for all the years in the interval.

For the sources of observed proportional changes in shares see the notes to Table 21. For the *estimated* shares see explanation in the text. The terminal periods for Denmark and the United States (see lines 4–5, 10) were set prior to the most recent dates available because a later date would yield too high a per capita product to permit proper estimation from the 1958 cross-section.

The estimates in column 1 were extrapolated from GDP in current 1958 dollars in United Nations, *Yearbook of National Accounts Statistics, 1966*, table 7A, by linking them with the series on per capita product in constant prices derived from the sources underlying Table 1. The latter also provided the estimates of percentage rise in per capita product in column 2. In general, linear interpolations between logarithms of quinquennial or decennial averages were used to estimate any single year figure.

The estimates of shares in lines 5 and 8 were derived by extrapolating back the shares in 1958 prices (used also for Tables 12 and 14) by the movement of shares in constant price volumes.

it is 1.43, and for 1911–1915 to 1951–1955 it is 0.59; for Germany, the ratio for the full period is 0.64, that for 1850–1859 to 1880–1889 is 0.78, and that for 1880–1889 to 1910–1913 is 0.54.[9]

Second, the underestimation, based on the cross-section, of the rise in the share of the I+S sector is, in most countries, more conspicuous than that of the decline in the share of the A sector. In all the countries except Great Britain and Sweden the ratios in column 8 are significantly below those in column 5. Since in most countries the share of A estimated from the 1958 cross-section is lower than the observed share at the initial date, while the opposite is true of the initial share of the I+S sector, and these differences are made up by a greater decline (toward 1958) of the observed A share and a greater rise of the observed I+S share than of the estimated, the ratio of the latter to the former must be lower for the I+S than for the A share.[10] So it is with respect to the I+S share, especially its dynamically growing components, that the ratio of estimated to actual rise is likely to be lowest.

Third, this consistent and sizable underestimation of observed changes implies that the shares of the A and I+S sectors have changed, in response to rises in per capita product, at higher rates during the periods covered in Table 25 than during other periods that could have affected the 1958 cross-section — presumably preceding ones in most countries. The implied acceleration in the shifts between the A and I+S sectors in response to growth in per capita product applies of course only to those countries for which the period covered terminates in or close to 1958 — but this includes most countries in the sample. This acceleration in structural

9. In "Development Patterns: Among Countries and Over Time," *Review of Economics and Statistics*, vol. L, no. 4 (November 1968), Hollis B. Chenery and Lance Taylor cite the "proportion of the historical decline (in share of primary sector) explainable by the present-day regression in each country" as follows: United States, 80 percent; United Kingdom, 66 percent; France, 80 percent; Germany, 74 percent; Italy, 86 percent; Sweden, 86 percent; Norway, 80 percent; Canada, 67 percent; Japan, 86 percent (note 22, p. 402). The proportions for Sweden and the United Kingdom are lower but those for the United States, France, Germany, Italy, and Japan are higher than those in Table 25. The reasons for these differences are not clear.

10. This may be seen if we designate d as expected (estimated) decline in the A share; (d+a) as observed decline, in which a is the excess of the observed over the estimated share of the A sector at the initial point of time. The estimated proportional decline is d/A, where A is the estimated initial share of the A sector; and the observed proportional change is (d+a)/(A+a). The observed proportional change in the share of the I+S sector is (d+a)/(100−A−a); and the estimated proportional change is d/(100−A). The ratio in column 5 (for the share of the A sector) is then (d/A): [(d+a)/(A+a)], or [(d)/(d+a)]. [(A+a)/A)]; whereas the ratio in column 8 is [(d)/(d+a)]. [(100−A−a)/(100−A)]. Obviously, the second ratio must be smaller than the first.

shifts could have been expected since the rate of technological change has probably been higher in the more recent decades than in the earlier.

Because the sample of countries in Table 25 is so small and because the time spans for several of the countries are so long, a larger sample of countries was used for a shorter and more recent period of historical change. The results of this comparison of cross-section relations (for 1953) with changes over time (from 1953 to 1965) are summarized in Table 26.

For thirty-two countries with a fairly wide range of per capita product, we have both the shares for the initial and terminal years in constant and current prices, and measures of gross domestic product per capita in constant prices. We calculated the cross-section relations in 1953 prices; estimated the expected changes in shares from 1953 to 1965 on the basis of this cross-section (or the moving averages underlying it); established the observed changes in shares in 1953 prices by carrying them forward by the constant price volume shares; and compared the observed and estimated proportional changes — not for individual countries but for the very groups used to establish the cross-section relations.

Several features of the computations for Table 26 and related calculations should be recognized in interpreting the findings. First, the cross-section relations and those between product per capita and levels of and changes in shares over time were computed for an identical sample of countries. Consequently, the empirical bases are the same for both the cross-section and time-series changes and relations. Second, while for Table 26 the 1953 cross-section was extrapolated forward to 1965, similar calculations (not shown) in which the 1965 cross-section in 1965 prices was extrapolated back to 1953 yield similar results. The broad findings would therefore stand, whether for forward or backward extrapolation. Third, while the initial and terminal values are for single years, this could not have affected the group averages much, since the total period, 1953–1965, was well after the end of World War II and long enough to represent long-term changes.

The following findings are suggested.

(a) For all six groups of countries the proportion of changes in shares estimated from the cross-section to observed changes ranged from about a half to two-thirds, reflecting a significant shortfall. The results are not too different from those in Table 25 where the

Table 26. Observed and estimated changes in shares of major sectors and manufacturing in gross domestic product, 1953 to 1965 (thirty-two countries grouped in increasing order of GDP per capita in 1953 and 1965).

A. Groups of countries and average shares (%)

	Groups					
	I (1)	II (2)	III (3)	IV (4)	V (5)	VI (6)
1. Number of countries	5	5	5	6	6	5
Grouping by 1953 per capita product						
2. GDP per capita (1953$)	53.3	120	165	281	551	959
Shares in product (%)						
3. A sector	52.5	43.5	40.3	24.6	16.0	12.0
4. I sector	16.5	21.2	25.5	33.1	48.2	50.8
5. S sector	31.0	35.3	34.2	42.3	35.8	37.2
6. Manufacturing	7.5	11.3	14.3	17.9	31.7	29.4
Grouping by 1965 per capita product						
7. GDP per capita (1953$)	65.2	140	198	405	903	1,378
Shares in product (%)						
8. A sector	46.7	42.4	30.2	16.1	10.4	8.9
9. I sector	21.4	24.8	29.1	42.4	54.4	55.2
10. S sector	31.9	32.8	40.7	41.5	35.2	35.9
11. Manufacturing	11.0	13.3	16.1	23.6	36.4	32.9

B. Proportional change in shares, 1953 to 1965, observed and estimated from the 1953 cross-section

	Rise in GDP per capita (%) (1)	Proportional change in share				
		A (2)	I+S (3)	I (4)	S (5)	Manufacturing (6)
Group I						
12. Observed	22.3	−0.111	0.123	0.295	0.031	0.457
13. Estimated	22.3	−0.042	0.047	0.087	0.025	0.146
Group II						
14. Observed	20.9	−0.113	0.087	0.227	0.003	0.245
15. Estimated	20.9	−0.075	0.055	0.083	0.037	0.098

Table 26 — continued

	(1)	(2)	(3)	(4)	(5)	(6)
Group III						
16. Observed	22.9	−0.222	0.150	0.225	0.094	0.327
17. Estimated	22.9	−0.097	0.058	0.119	0.014	0.159
Averages, groups I–III (geometric means)						
18. Observed	22.0	−0.150	0.120	0.249	0.042	0.340
19. Estimated	22.0	−0.072	0.053	0.096	0.025	0.134
20. Ratio, line 19 to line 18		0.48	0.44	0.39	0.60	0.39
Group IV						
21. Observed	57.2	−0.294	0.096	0.241	−0.017	0.201
22. Estimated	57.2	−0.266	0.102	0.192	0.019	0.199
Group V						
23. Observed	45.2	−0.271	0.052	0.091	−0.002	0.124
24. Estimated	45.2	−0.204	0.042	0.096	−0.020	0.073
Group VI						
25. Observed	39.9	−0.293	0.040	0.091	−0.030	0.115
26. Estimated	39.9	−0.263	0.036	0.076	−0.019	0.060
Averages, groups IV–VI (geometric means)						
27. Observed	47.3	−0.286	0.062	0.139	−0.016	0.146
28. Estimated	47.3	−0.245	0.060	0.120	−0.007	0.109
29. Ratio, line 28 to line 27		0.86	0.97	0.86	0.44	0.75
30. Average, lines 20 and 29 (geometric mean)		0.64	0.65	0.58	0.51	0.54

C. Shares at benchmark values of GDP per capita (1953$), 1953 and 1965 cross-sections (%)

	A (1)	I+S (2)	I (3)	S (4)	Manufacturing (5)
$65					
31. 1953	50.3	49.7	17.9	31.8	8.6
32. 1965	46.7	53.3	21.4	31.9	11.0
$135					
33. 1953	40.7	59.3	23.9	35.4	12.8
34. 1965	38.0	62.0	26.3	35.7	14.2

Table 26 — continued

	(1)	(2)	(3)	(4)	(5)
$270					
35. 1953	28.5	71.5	34.1	37.4	20.1
36. 1965	26.3	73.7	35.1	38.6	20.0
$450					
37. 1953	20.2	79.8	41.7	38.1	24.9
38. 1965	18.1	81.9	43.0	38.9	26.0
$900					
39. 1953	12.6	87.4	50.1	37.3	29.1
40. 1965	11.1	88.9	51.7	37.2	31.4

The underlying shares in product were calculated from United Nations, *Yearbook of National Accounts Statistics, 1966*, supplemented by earlier issues. The product per capita in 1953 prices was estimated by extrapolating the 1958 GDP per capita by the movement of GDP per capita in constant prices, calculated from the *Yearbook of National Accounts Statistics* (for total product) and from the *Demographic Yearbook* (for population); or from the OECD Development Center, *National Accounts of Less Developed Countries* (Paris, February 1967); or from unpublished ECLA tabulations of GDP in constant factor costs for most Latin American countries. The estimates, in 1958 U.S. dollars, were then shifted to 1953 U.S. dollars by the implicit price deflator for gross national product (see *Economic Report of the President* [Washington, D.C., February 1968], table B-3, p. 212).

Only those countries were taken for which the sectoral shares were available in both current and constant prices, for the full period or for a period within it not much shorter than a decade. The base year for the constant price series was 1960, or around 1960, except for a few countries with a base of the mid-1950's. The arithmetic means in lines 3–6 are based on current price shares for the initial year (1953 in all but a few countries). The shares for 1965 were estimated for each country by adding to the 1953 shares relative changes in the shares in constant prices, adjusted to add out to 100 (for relatively minor discrepancies). Given these estimated shares for 1965 (in initial year prices), the group averages were calculated (by the 1953 ranking) and then the observed proportional changes in lines 12, 14, 16, 21, 23, and 25 were derived. The shares for 1965, grouped by the 1965 ranking, are shown in lines 8–11.

The countries included in this calculation are, in increasing order of their 1953 per capita GDP and with the period indicated when it differed from 1953–65: Burma (1953–64), Nigeria (1953–63), Uganda (1955–65), Pakistan (1953–64), Thailand, South Korea, Ceylon (1956–65), Paraguay, Ecuador, Peru (1953–63), Philippines, Turkey, Honduras, Dominican Republic (1953–64), Portugal, Colombia, Jamaica, Greece, Chile, Italy, Puerto Rico, Austria, Argentina, Uruguay, Germany (FR), Finland, France, Belgium, Norway, Denmark, United Kingdom, Canada.

The estimated shares in both initial and terminal years, corresponding to the geometric mean product per capita for each group, were calculated from group means for 1953 computed in the manner followed for Table 14, and including the thirty-two countries listed in the preceding paragraph. From these averages we also calculated the shares at benchmark values of GDP per capita in 1953 prices for 1953; and followed the same procedure for the benchmark values for 1965.

changes over much longer past periods for nine countries were compared with the 1958 cross-section. But here it cannot be argued that the time span between the date of the cross-section and the initial date for the temporal changes may contribute to the failure of the cross-section to "predict" the full magnitude of the changes over time.

(b) This substantial understatement of changes over time emerges, even though the two cross-sections in panel C — one for the beginning of the period and the other for the end — differ only slightly. Of course, the differences only *seem* minor in comparison with the absolute magnitudes of the shares at the benchmark levels. They are, however, substantial enough when the proper comparison is made. Thus, in the movement over time from $65 to $135, the share of the A sector changes from 50.3 to 38.0 percent (column 1, lines 31, 34), or over 24 percent of the initial value — not from 50.3 to 40.7 (in the 1953 cross-section), nor from 46.7 to 38.0 (in the 1965 cross-section), both less than 20 percent of the initial value.

(c) The two cross-sections in panel C can be taken to represent the observed relations, in 1953 and 1965 respectively. We could then ask how estimated values for 1965 based on the 1953 cross-section would look in comparison with the actual values in 1965 (represented by the cross-section for that year in 1953 prices). For an assumed rise over the period of a third in per capita product — from benchmark levels in 1953 of $65, 135, 270, 450, and 675 to $86.7, 180, 360, 600, and 900 respectively — the changes estimated in this way fall short of the observed changes: ratios of estimated to observed changes average 0.64 for the share of the A sector, 0.67 for the share of the I sector; and 0.50 for the share of the S sector. Similarly, backward projection can be made where we begin with the 1965 cross-section as given, and ask what the estimated shares in 1953 would be on the assumption that per capita product was a quarter smaller for each benchmark level. For benchmark levels in 1965 of $86.7, 180, 360, 600, 900, and 1,200 (and 1953 levels of $65, 135, 270, 450, 675, and 900 respectively), the average ratios of estimated to observed changes are 0.59 for the share of the A sector, 0.63 for the share of the I sector, and 0.19 for the share of the S sector. The results are similar to those derived in panel B of Table 26, but because of the assumption of the *same* rate of increase for all per capita product groups, and the inadequacy of the partition values for the low income groups, one of the more interesting findings in Table 26 is not revealed.

(d) This finding is the difference in the relation between the cross-section and changes over time for the three low product per capita groups of countries, compared with the three high product per capita groups. The less developed countries show a distinctly lower rate of growth in per capita product over the period (panel B, column 1) — ranging between 21 and 23 percent, with an average of 22 percent, whereas the rates for the more developed countries range between 40 and 57 percent and their average is 47 percent. But the declines in the share of the A sector and rises in the shares of the I sector and of manufacturing in the low per capita product, less developed countries, were far greater than might have been expected from the cross-section (either 1953 or 1965); the ratio of estimated to observed changes is less than half for the three low per capita product groups of countries for all major sectors except S, where it is 0.6 (line 20). By contrast, the declines in the share of the A sector and rises in the share of the I, for the three groups of high per capita product countries, are far closer to what could have been expected from the cross-section: the ratio of expected to observed change ranges well above 0.7. For the share of the S sector, this ratio is only 0.44 (line 29). If the low ratios of expected to observed proportional changes mean an acceleration in the rate of response of structural changes to rises in per capita product, such acceleration during the period under discussion appears to have been — relative to the past — much greater among the less developed than among developed countries.

Since Table 26 suggests a substantial discrepancy between cross-section and time series movements for the share of manufacturing, I repeated the comparison for the major branches within manufacturing (Table 27). Here the sample for 1953 and 1963 underlying Table 15 is used. Table 27 shows the cross-sections for 1953 and 1963 (the average of which was shown in Table 15), and it may be observed that, for the share of all manufacturing in total product, the levels and shifts from 1953 to 1963 (lines 7a–7b) are not unlike those for the smaller sample in Table 26 (panel C, column 5, allowing for the differences in benchmark values).

As in Table 26, the *estimated* changes in Table 27 fall short of the observed; but here the shortfall is limited to the lower spans of per capita product (from $81 to $108, and from $135 to $180). For

Table 27. Observed and estimated changes in shares of major branches of manufacturing in gross domestic product (current prices), 1953 to 1963 (based on 1953 and 1963 cross-sections).

	A. Shares in manufacturing value added and in GDP at benchmark values of GDP per capita					
	Benchmark values (1953$)					
	81 (1)	135 (2)	270 (3)	450 (4)	900 (5)	1,200 (6)
Shares in manufacturing value added (%)						
1. Food, beverages, and tobacco						
(a) 1953 cross-section	36.1	37.5	34.8	26.4	17.9	—
(b) 1963 cross-section	31.6	37.4	34.8	28.1	17.2	15.5
2. Textiles and clothing						
(a) 1953 cross-section	23.1	22.4	19.2	17.1	13.7	—
(b) 1963 cross-section	23.1	18.5	17.4	16.8	13.2	11.1
3. Wood, paper, printing, and leather						
(a) 1953 cross-section	13.1	10.9	11.5	13.3	15.7	—
(b) 1963 cross-section	9.7	10.2	10.4	11.7	14.5	15.7
4. Rubber, chemicals, and petroleum products						
(a) 1953 cross-section	9.0	9.3	9.7	10.2	9.5	—
(b) 1963 cross-section	10.7	12.1	12.1	11.6	11.3	10.7
5. Industrial raw materials						
(a) 1953 cross-section	7.2	8.8	9.3	10.4	10.1	—
(b) 1963 cross-section	11.6	9.3	9.0	9.6	10.6	10.5
6. Fabricated metal products						
(a) 1953 cross-section	11.5	11.1	15.5	22.6	33.1	—
(b) 1963 cross-section	13.3	12.5	16.3	22.2	33.2	36.5
Shares in GDP (%)						
7. Total manufacturing						
(a) 1953 cross-section	9.7	12.9	19.8	25.5	29.7	—
(b) 1963 cross-section	13.6	15.3	20.0	24.9	29.3	30.0
8. Food, beverages, and tobacco						
(a) 1953 cross-section	3.5	4.8	6.9	6.7	5.3	—
(b) 1963 cross-section	4.3	5.7	7.0	7.0	5.0	4.6
9. Textiles and clothing						
(a) 1953 cross-section	2.2	2.9	3.8	4.4	4.1	—
(b) 1963 cross-section	3.1	2.8	3.5	4.2	3.9	3.3
10. Wood, paper, printing, and leather						
(a) 1953 cross-section	1.3	1.4	2.3	3.4	4.7	—
(b) 1963 cross-section	1.3	1.6	2.1	2.9	4.2	4.7

Table 27 — continued

	(1)	(2)	(3)	(4)	(5)	(6)
11. Rubber, chemicals, and petroleum products						
(a) 1953 cross-section	0.9	1.2	1.9	2.6	2.8	—
(b) 1963 cross-section	1.5	1.9	2.4	2.9	3.3	3.2
12. Industrial raw materials						
(a) 1953 cross-section	0.7	1.1	1.8	2.6	3.0	—
(b) 1963 cross-section	1.6	1.4	1.8	2.4	3.1	3.2
13. Fabricated metal products						
(a) 1953 cross-section	1.1	1.5	3.1	5.8	9.8	—
(b) 1963 cross-section	1.8	1.9	3.2	5.5	9.8	11.0

B. Observed and estimated changes in shares in GDP, 1953 to 1963
(percentages, changes for standard rise of a third in GDP per capita)

	Total manu-facturing (1)	Food, bever-ages, and to-bacco (2)	Tex-tiles and clothing (3)	Wood, paper, printing, and leather (4)	Rubber, chem-icals, and petro-leum products (5)	Indus-trial raw mate-rials (6)	Fabri-cated metal products (7)
$81 in 1953 to $108 in 1963							
Observed shares and changes							
14. Share, 1953	9.7	3.5	2.2	1.3	0.9	0.7	1.1
15. Share, 1963	14.6	5.1	2.9	1.5	1.7	1.5	1.9
16. Change	+4.9	+1.6	+0.7	+0.2	+0.8	+0.8	+0.8
Estimated changes							
17. Forward (using 1953 cross-section)	+1.8	+0.7	+0.4	+0.1	+0.2	+0.2	+0.2
18. Backward (using 1963 cross-section)	+1.0	+0.8	−0.2	+0.2	+0.2	−0.1	+0.1
$135 in 1953 to $180 in 1963							
Observed shares and changes							
19. Share, 1953	12.9	4.8	2.9	1.4	1.2	1.1	1.5
20. Share, 1963	17.3	6.2	3.1	1.8	2.1	1.6	2.5
21. Change	+4.4	+1.4	+0.2	+0.4	+0.9	+0.5	+1.0
Estimated changes							
22. Forward	+2.9	+0.8	+0.4	+0.4	+0.3	+0.3	+0.7
23. Backward	+1.9	+0.5	+0.3	+0.2	+0.2	+0.1	+0.6

Table 27 — continued

	(1)	(2)	(3)	(4)	(5)	(6)	(7)
$270 in 1953 to $360 in 1963							
Observed shares and changes							
24. Share, 1953	19.8	6.9	3.8	2.3	1.9	1.8	3.1
25. Share, 1963	22.8	7.0	3.9	2.6	2.7	2.1	4.5
26. Change	+3.0	+0.1	+0.1	+0.3	+0.8	+0.3	+1.4
Estimated changes							
27. Forward	+3.2	−0.1	+0.3	+0.6	+0.4	+0.5	+1.5
28. Backward	+2.8	0	+0.4	+0.5	+0.3	+0.3	+1.3
$450 in 1953 to $600 in 1963							
Observed shares and changes							
29. Share, 1953	25.5	6.7	4.4	3.4	2.6	2.6	5.8
30. Share, 1963	26.7	6.2	4.0	3.5	3.0	2.7	7.3
31. Change	+1.2	−0.5	−0.4	+0.1	+0.4	+0.1	+1.5
Estimated changes							
32. Forward	+1.7	−0.6	−0.1	+0.5	+0.1	+0.1	+1.7
33. Backward	+1.8	−0.8	−0.1	+0.5	+0.2	+0.3	+1.7
$675 in 1953 to $900 in 1963							
Observed shares and changes							
34. Share, 1953	28.0	5.9	4.2	4.1	2.7	2.9	8.2
35. Share, 1963	29.3	5.0	3.9	4.2	3.3	3.1	9.8
36. Change	+1.3	−0.9	−0.3	+0.1	+0.6	+0.2	+1.6
Estimated changes							
37. Forward	+1.7	−0.6	−0.1	+0.5	+0.1	+0.1	+1.7
38. Backward	+1.8	−0.8	−0.1	+0.5	+0.2	+0.3	+1.7
$900 in 1953 to $1,200 in 1963							
Observed shares and changes							
39. Share, 1953	29.7	5.3	4.1	4.7	2.8	3.0	9.8
40. Share, 1963	30.0	4.6	3.3	4.7	3.2	3.2	11.0
41. Change	+0.3	−0.7	−0.8	0	+0.4	+0.2	+1.2
Estimated changes							
42. Backward	+0.7	−0.4	−0.5	+0.5	−0.1	0	+1.2
Average change							
Two lower per capita product groups (lines 14–23)							
43. Observed	+4.65	+1.5	+0.45	+0.3	+0.85	+0.65	+0.9
44. Estimated (average of forward and backward projections)	+1.9	+0.7	+0.2	+0.2	+0.2	+0.2	+0.4

Table 27 — continued

	(1)	(2)	(3)	(4)	(5)	(6)	(7)
Three higher per capita product groups (lines 29–42)							
45. Observed	+0.9	−0.7	−0.5	+0.1	+0.5	+0.2	+1.4
46. Estimated (average of forward and backward projections)	+1.4	−0.6	−0.2	+0.5	+0.1	+0.1	+1.5

—: information not available.

For the countries included in the sample, sources of data, and the procedures used in deriving the cross-section values in lines 1–13 see the notes to Table 15.

For the method of deriving *estimated* changes by forward and backward projections as well as for the derivation of the *observed* changes, both derivations resting upon the cross-sections for 1953 and 1963, see discussion in the text.

In averaging estimated changes for lines 44 and 46, the results of the forward and backward projections were weighted equally for each per capita product group, and then averaged once more.

the highest span of per capita product, however, the estimated change in the share is distinctly larger than the observed. The contrast between the findings for the lower and the upper levels of per capita product is, however, the same as in Table 26.

Of primary interest here are the findings for the branches, conveniently summarized in lines 43–46. For the lower per capita product spans, the estimated changes fall short of the observed — the latter, all rises — for all six major branches distinguished. For the higher per capita product spans ($450 to $600, and higher), the estimated rise in the share of all manufacturing in total product is larger than the observed, not so much because of greater estimated rises for the various branches (although that in the wood, paper, and leather group is marked) as because of lesser estimated declines for the food products, and particularly the textiles and clothing group.

One can also observe that there are persistent differences among the major branches with respect to the disparities between the estimated and observed changes. Thus, for the chemicals branch the estimated rises are consistently short of the observed, barely more than a quarter of them. In the food products branch, on net balance, the estimated changes fall short of the observed, but in the textiles and clothing and wood branches they do not. But the data do not lend themselves to too detailed a study: the main point, that for the postwar decade the cross-section estimates of changes fall short of the observed — and in different ways at different per capita levels — for major branches of manufacturing, let alone total manufacturing, is clearly revealed.[11]

No general conclusions can be claimed on the basis of the limited samples covered in Tables 25, 26, and 27; and judgment should be suspended in any case until the relations between cross-sections and changes over time in shares of sectors in labor force are observed in Chapter VI. However, the preceding discussion suggests that, while cross-sections can reveal the directions of the association over time between rises in per capita product (and similar key synthetic variables) and changes in the shares of sectors and subdivisions (and other aspects of the structure of the growing economy), they are not likely to provide a firm basis for estimating the relevant parameters.

One could go back at this juncture to the discussion of valuation problems at the end of the preceding section, and argue that the parameters of the cross-section and of the changes over time can be reconciled — by assuming that the per capita product range in the cross-section is exaggerated, relative to the changes in per capita product over time. If, accordingly, the per capita product range in the cross-section were reduced, there would be greater movements of sectoral shares corresponding to the same per capita product differences; and the cross-section estimates might not fall short of the observed changes in shares over time. But if the significant discrepancies between cross-section estimates and changes over time are to be effectively removed by such a procedure, the adjustments in

11. A. Maizels, in *Industrial Growth and World Trade* (Cambridge: Cambridge University Press, 1963), table 2.5, p. 53, reveals equally major differences between the cross-section and time-trends parameters in the association between per capita income and growth rates of major branches of manufacturing, the cross-section relating to 1955 and the time trends to 1899–1957. The regression equations used, in double log form, were fitted to manufacturing value added per head (in constant prices) as the dependent variable, and real product per head and population size (the latter for the cross-section only) as the independent variables. The regression coefficients on per capita product (which dominated the regression) were roughly the same for the cross-section and the time trends only for the metals and metal product branches. For food, beverages, and tobacco, the two sets of regression coefficients (listing the cross-section first) were 1.10 and 0.78, an overestimate of the time trends of some 40 percent; for chemicals they were 1.31 and 2.44, an underestimate of the time trends by about a half; for textiles they were 0.93 and 0.59, an overestimate of the time trends of almost three-fifths; and for other manufacturing industries (largely the wood, paper, and printing group) they were 1.50 and 1.16, an overestimate of the time trends by about three-tenths. All of these discrepancies were large multiples of the standard errors. Several of them (particularly for chemicals and the "other manufacturing" group) are similar to those shown in Table 27.

the cross-section per capita differentials would have to be quite different at the several ranges of per capita product. Thus, by reference to Table 26 one can see that the needed adjustments in the cross-section would have to assume that, for an increase of about 20 to 25 percent of per capita product (over time), the range in per capita product would have to be reduced by fully a half at the low per capita product levels (from $53 to $163, in 1953 prices); but at levels of roughly $300 or more, and for growth of close to 50 percent, the adjustment would have to be limited to barely a tenth. At present, we see no rationale for such differentiated adjustments in the cross-section; they are merely ad hoc modifications devised to reconcile the parameters of the cross-section with those of temporal changes. Similar problems would be faced in justifying the differentiated adjustments in per capita product in the cross-section required to remove the discrepancies between estimated and observed changes in Table 27.

It may well be that the discrepancies are analytically significant, reflecting as they do changes over time in the pattern of relations between per capita income and shares of sectors — an inference that is suggested by the continuously changing technological and institutional framework within which modern economic growth takes place. The discrepancies are, therefore, to be studied — not removed. To put it paradoxically, the value of the cross-section may lie *not* in its capacity to predict correctly the magnitude of changes over time; but rather in its revelation of the discrepancy between its implication and the observed historical change — a discrepancy indicating that temporal changes must have occurred in the relations. But the proper identification of such temporal changes requires the evidence of long-term records.

V

Sectoral Shares
in Labor Force:
A Cross-Section View

Association between Product per Capita and Sectoral Shares

Differences in shares of sectors in product do not imply similar differences in their shares in productive resources. Thus the finding that in 1958 the share of the A sector in GDP was 48.4 percent at the benchmark value of $70 GDP per capita, while it was only 11.7 percent at the benchmark value of $1,000 (see Table 14), does not mean that the shares of the A sector in labor force, at the two benchmark levels of GDP per capita, were also 48.4 and 11.7 percent; or that the difference between them was the same. Another relationship can easily be visualized, especially since the proportion of labor force to total population is roughly the same throughout the per capita product range, and therefore the proportional difference between the benchmark levels of $70 and $1,000 *per capita* would be the same as that in GDP *per worker* at comparable levels. To illustrate: assume that at the lower level the share of the A sector in labor force was 48.4 percent, the same as its share in GDP, thus implying that per worker output in the A sector was the same as countrywide output per worker. Assume further that in the shift to the $1,000 level, output per worker in the A sector rose to only 4 times its initial level, while countrywide product per capita and per worker rose to 14.29 times (1,000 ÷ 70). The implicit share of the A sector in labor force at the $1,000 level would be 41.8 percent — not much lower than at the $70 level. The high and low per capita (or per worker) product countries would differ greatly in the share of the A sector in total output but little in its share in labor force;

199

Table 28. Shares of production sectors in labor force, fifty-nine countries grouped by 1958 GDP per capita, about 1960.

	Groups of countries in increasing order of 1958 GDP per capita							
	I (1)	II (2)	III (3)	IV (4)	V (5)	VI (6)	VII (7)	VIII (8)
1. Number of countries	5	6	6	18	6	6	6	6
2. GDP per capita ($)	72.3	107	147	218	382	588	999	1,501
3. Regional identity of countries	A-3	A-3	A-1	A-4	A-1	A-1	E-6	E-2
	F-2	F-2	F-4	F-2	L-4	L-2		S-4
		L-1	L-1	L-10	E-1	E-3		
				E-2				
Shares of major sectors (%)								
4. A	79.7	63.9	66.2	59.6	37.8	21.8	18.9	11.6
5. I	9.9	15.2	16.0	20.1	30.2	40.9	47.2	48.1
6. S	10.4	20.9	17.8	20.3	32.0	37.3	33.9	40.3
Subdivisions of I								
7. Mining and quarrying	1.2	1.2	0.9	1.1	1.2	0.8	1.5	1.0
8. Manufacturing	5.7	7.5	9.0	11.6	17.4	24.2	29.3	29.7
9. Construction	1.4	2.9	2.8	3.9	6.0	8.5	8.3	8.5
10. Electricity, gas, and water	0.2	0.5	0.6	0.4	0.9	1.4	0.8	1.4
11. Transport, storage, and communication	1.4	3.1	2.7	3.1	4.7	6.0	7.3	7.5
Subdivisions of S								
12. Commerce	4.7	6.9	8.4	7.4	11.8	14.5	13.7	17.8
13. Services	5.7	14.0	9.4	12.9	20.2	22.8	20.2	22.5

See the notes to Table 12 for the coverage of the A, I, and S sectors, for the regional identification letters, and for the sources and procedure followed for the 1958 per capita GDP. Here the subdivisions of the S sector are limited to commerce and services.

The fifty-nine countries included are, in increasing order of per capita GDP: Pakistan, Sierra Leone, India, Thailand, Sudan, Indonesia, Haiti, United Arab Republic, Libya, South Korea, Taiwan, Paraguay, Syria, Tunisia, Ivory Coast, Ghana, Morocco, Liberia, Ecuador, Honduras, Turkey, Peru, Sabah and Sarawak, Philippines, Mauritius, Dominican Republic, Malaya, El Salvador, Colombia, Portugal, Guatemala, Nicaragua, Brazil, Mexico, Spain, Greece, Jamaica, Costa Rica, Chile, Japan, Uruguay, Ireland, Italy, Israel, Puerto Rico, Argentina, Netherlands, Finland, Germany (FR), Belgium, Norway, Denmark, France, Australia, Switzerland, New Zealand, Sweden, Canada, and the United States.

The sectoral shares in labor force, excluding persons not allocated by industry, are arithmetic means of the shares for individual countries calculated, except for Colombia and Haiti, from the absolute data reported in the United Nations, *Demographic Yearbook,*

1964 (New York, 1965), table 12, supplemented by *ibid.*, table 9, and by the International Labour Office, *Yearbook of Labour Statistics, 1966* (Geneva, n.d.), table 2A. The data in the majority of cases are for 1960. For Colombia and Haiti they are from ECLA sources and are for 1962.

For Brazil, the one country for which full detail was not given, electricity, gas, and water was combined with finance. We assumed that the former was 1 percent of total labor force and transferred the balance to commerce.

and "industrialization" of output would not be accompanied by "industrialization" of labor force.

The discussion here concentrates on sectoral shares in labor force, rather than in capital stock. One obvious reason is that available data on the sectoral distribution of the labor force permit adequate analysis, which is not the case with capital stock (although figures on sectoral destination of current capital formation are in good supply). But there is a more substantive reason for emphasizing shares in labor force, and it may explain the greater abundance of data on the distribution of labor force. The sectoral structure of production is of interest because active participation in specific sectors imposes specific patterns on the lives of the participants (and those of their dependents), affects the kind of enterprise and occupational status that the participants share, and determines the activity that they engage in. Since active work within the economy plays a dominant role in the lives of the people so engaged (and their dependents), and since the pattern of life and work imposed on the participants differs greatly among sectors, it is no exaggeration to say that these effects of production structure on the lives of the active participants (and their dependents) are its most important aspect; and the effects of the differentials in production structure among countries are consequently also important. It is little wonder that information on the economic activity and the major sectoral attachment of the economically active population is one of the oldest and most commonly collected types of data — whatever the difficulties in using it in a meaningful fashion.

Table 28 relates to shares of the major sectors and their subdivisions in total labor force around the year 1960, for countries grouped by their 1958 GDP per capita. The definitions of sectors and subdivisions are identical with those used for total product; and the countries omitted in the analysis of product because of the distorting effects of too high a share of an exogenous source or because of politically disturbed conditions are excluded here also. The labor force, or gainful workers, or economically active population (the terms are used interchangeably since the minor differences among them are of little concern here) is defined as "all persons of either sex who furnish the supply of labour available for the production of economic goods and services." [1] Like all such definitions, this one conceals a host of difficulties that are a source of equally numerous incomparabilities in international usage. These difficulties are caused by the differences among countries in the lower age limits set for inclusion in labor force, in the treatment of unpaid family workers, in the handling of partially engaged and of the armed forces, and so on. The problems particularly relevant to the analysis will be noted later in this chapter, when various adjustments are discussed. For the present, we shall use labor force as given — to obtain a general view of the sectoral shares at different levels of economic performance, or of GDP per capita.

Table 28 reveals that the assumptions made in the illustration above are not realistic. If, as we move from the lower to the higher per capita product countries, the share of the A sector in total product drops markedly, its share in labor force drops even more. And in general the impression conveyed by Table 28 is that the shares of the sectors and subdivisions in labor force change markedly in response to differences in per capita product — more than their shares in product.

A more effective comparison of shares in labor force and output requires reduction to identical benchmark levels; and the shift to the latter for shares in labor force is presented in Table 29, which also gives the estimated sectoral shares in labor force about 1950, for benchmark values comparable to 1958 GDP per capita.

One reason for the comparison of 1950 and 1960 shares is to see whether a large error is involved in using 1960 shares in labor force for countries grouped by 1958 GDP per capita. The use of the 1958 GDP per capita for grouping countries was dictated by the availability of total and per capita product in terms of United States dollars for the largest number of countries. On the other hand, the estimates of sectoral shares in labor force are based on census of population data, the most recent ones for 1960 for most countries; and *annual* sectoral distributions of labor force are available for very few countries.

Table 29 suggests that for the decade of the 1950's, the change

1. United Nations, *Demographic Yearbook, 1964* (New York, 1965), note to table 9, p. 28.

Table 29. Shares of production sectors in labor force at benchmark values of 1958 GDP per capita, about 1960, about 1950, and estimated for 1958 (percentages).

	Benchmark values of 1958 GDP ($)				
	70 (1)	150 (2)	300 (3)	500 (4)	1,000 (5)
A. Shares for 1960					
Major sectors					
1. A	80.5	63.3	46.1	31.4	17.0
2. I	9.6	17.0	26.8	36.0	45.6
3. S	9.9	19.7	27.1	32.6	37.4
Subdivisions of I					
4. Mining and quarrying	1.2	1.0	1.0	1.1	1.1
5. Manufacturing	5.5	9.3	15.5	21.4	27.9
6. Construction	1.3	3.2	5.4	7.1	8.4
7. Electricity, gas, water	0.2	0.5	0.8	1.0	1.2
8. Transport, storage, and communication	1.4	3.0	4.1	5.4	7.0
Subdivisions of S					
9. Commerce	4.5	7.6	10.3	12.5	15.5
10. Services	5.4	12.1	16.8	20.1	21.9
B. Shares for 1950					
11. A	79.3	65.0	45.7	31.5	20.8
12. I	7.8	16.9	27.2	37.0	44.1
13. Commerce	5.6	5.7	8.8	11.3	13.9
14. Services	7.3	12.4	18.3	20.2	21.2
C. Shares for 1958					
15. A	80.3	63.7	46.0	31.4	17.7
16. I	9.2	17.0	26.9	36.2	45.3
17. Commerce	4.7	7.2	10.0	12.2	15.2
18. Services	5.8	12.1	17.1	20.2	21.8

Lines 1–10: The underlying data are from Table 28. The procedure followed is that described in the notes to Table 14.

Lines 11–14: The underlying shares for individual countries are from Simon Kuznets, "Quantitative Aspects of the Economic Growth of Nations: II. Industrial Distribution of National Product and Labor Force," *Economic Development and Cultural Change*, supplement to vol. V, no. 4 (July 1957), appendix table 3, pp. 75–81, except for Ceylon and Greece. The data for Ceylon are from Donald R. Snodgrass, *Ceylon: An Export Economy in Transition*, Economic Growth Center of Yale University (Homewood, Ill.: Richard Irwin, 1966), table A-26, pp. 322–323 (average of shares for 1946 and 1953); for Greece (for 1951) the data are from United Nations, *Demographic Yearbook, 1956* (New York, 1956). Most of the data are for about 1950, ranging from 1947 to 1953.

The 1950 per capita GDP was estimated for individual countries by extrapolating the 1958 level by one of various indexes. The major sources of the latter, based on GDP either at constant factor cost or at constant market prices were: (1) United Nations, *Yearbook of National Accounts Statistics, 1966* and *1964*, tables for individual countries; (2) OECD, Development Center, *National Accounts of Less Developed Countries* (Paris, February 1967), particularly table B, pp. 9–12; (3) special estimates of GDP at constant 1960 factor cost for the Latin American countries provided by the Research Division of ECLA. Population figures used in conjunction with the sources under (1) and (3) were taken from the United Nations, *Demographic Yearbook, 1965* (New York, 1967), table 4.

With the shares for the individual countries, and their per capita GDP in 1958 prices available, the shares for benchmark values of GDP per capita in 1958 prices like those in panel A, were estimated by the procedure used for Table 14.

Lines 15–18: Estimated by straight-line interpolation between 1950 and 1960.

per year in the sectoral shares in labor force, at the same levels of 1958 per capita GDP, was in fractions of 1 percent. If we estimate the 1958 shares in labor force by simple linear interpolation between 1950 and 1960, the results differ slightly from the shares for 1960. Hence, for most purposes we can use the 1960 shares in labor force to represent the 1958 shares; or, alternatively, use the 1958 shares as interpolated for panel C. Comparison of the sector shares in labor force with those in GDP, at the same levels of 1958 GDP per capita (Tables 29 and 14) reveals the following similarities and differences.

(a) The shares of the A sector in labor force are generally higher than those in product — the former ranging from 80 to 18 percent, the latter from 48 to 12. Conversely, the shares of the I and S sectors in the labor force are distinctly below their shares in product. The implications of these differences for output per worker are discussed in connection with Table 31.

(b) As we move from the low to the high per capita product countries, the decline in the share of the A sector in labor force is at least as marked as in its share in output. The absolute decline in the former, some 63 percentage points, is naturally greater than that in the latter, some 37 points; but even the proportional decline is somewhat greater.

(c) The greater change in the share in labor force than that in product, associated with the change in per capita product, is even more conspicuous for the I sector: the share in labor force rises 36 percentage points, from a *lower* initial level than the share in output, which rises only 28 points. The difference between the changes in the shares of manufacturing is not as large: for the labor force,

22 points; for product, 20. For construction and for transportation and public utilities the differences are greater: the share of the former in labor force rises 7.1 percentage points, its share in product rises only 2.5 points; for the latter the share in labor force rises 6.6 percentage points, and its share in product rises only 4.3 points.

(d) The most striking difference, however, is between the shares of the S sector, particularly if we exclude the finance and real estate subdivisions, for which comparison with the labor force is not relevant. We observed in Chapter III the puzzling failure of the share of trade in output to rise as we moved from the low to the high income countries; and even the rise of only about a third in the share of services was surprising in view of the greater relative demand for services with rising per capita product and urbanization. The share of commerce in labor force more than triples, and that of services quadruples as we move from the lowest to the highest benchmark levels of per capita product.

(e) One significant consequence of the greater responsiveness of the shares of the S sector and its subdivisions in labor force to differences in per capita product is that the shift of labor force from agriculture is distributed more equally between the I and S sectors than the shift of product from the A sector. Thus, in Table 29, the share of the A sector in labor force declines 62.6 percentage points over the full range from the $70 to the $1,000 benchmark value, the share of the I sector rises 36.1 points, and the share of the S sector rises 26.5, or more than four-tenths of the decline in the share of the A sector (lines 15–18). In the case of product, the share of the S sector rises only 8.9 percentage points, or less than a fourth of the total decline of 36.7 percentage points in the share of the A sector (see Table 14, lines 1–5).

Although in general shares in labor force seem to be more responsive to differences in per capita product than shares in GDP, in the case of manufacturing the two are almost equally responsive. Its share in the labor force rises 22.4 percentage points (Table 29, line 5); and its share in product rises 20.3 points (see Table 14). For the sample covering manufacturing branches, the finding is similar: for total manufacturing the share in labor force rises 20.6 percentage points (Table 30, line 20), and the share in GDP rises 18.4 points (Table 15, line 20).

The close similarity in the pattern of movement in the shares of

Table 30. Shares of branches of manufacturing in manufacturing labor force
and in total labor force at benchmark values of GDP per capita
(average of cross-section shares for 1953 and 1963).

	Benchmark values of GDP per capita					
1953$:	81	135	270	450	900	1,200[a]
1958$:	91.7	153	306	510	1,019	1,359
	(1)	(2)	(3)	(4)	(5)	(6)
A. Shares in manufacturing labor force (%)						
1. Food, beverages, and tobacco	28.4	29.5	28.5	22.8	15.2	14.0
2. Textiles	20.3	17.5	11.9	10.5	8.4	6.6
3. Clothing and footwear	8.0	12.2	15.3	13.9	11.2	10.0
4. Wood products and furniture	12.2	9.4	8.4	8.0	7.9	7.4
5. Paper and paper products	0.5	0.8	1.4	2.2	3.1	3.3
6. Printing and publishing	1.9	2.2	2.7	3.3	4.3	4.8
7. Leather products (excluding footwear)	1.3	1.4	1.4	1.3	1.0	0.9
8. Rubber products	1.0	1.0	0.9	1.0	1.2	1.3
9. Chemicals and petroleum products	4.4	4.6	4.4	4.8	4.9	5.0
10. Nonmetal mineral products	6.1	6.1	4.8	4.7	4.3	4.1
11. Basic metals	3.0	2.3	2.4	3.5	4.6	4.8
12. Metal products	10.8	11.0	15.6	21.2	30.2	33.7
13. Miscellaneous	2.1	2.0	2.3	2.8	3.7	4.1
Major groups						
14. Food, beverages, and tobacco	28.4	29.5	28.5	22.8	15.2	14.0
15. Textiles and clothing (lines 2–3)	28.3	29.7	27.2	24.4	19.6	16.6
16. Wood, paper, printing, and leather (lines 4–7)	15.9	13.8	13.9	14.8	16.3	16.4
17. Rubber, chemicals, and petroleum (lines 8–9)	5.4	5.6	5.3	5.8	6.1	6.3
18. Industrial raw materials (lines 10–11)	9.1	8.4	7.2	8.2	8.9	8.9
19. Fabricated metal products (lines 12–13)	12.9	13.0	17.9	24.0	33.9	37.8
B. Shares in total labor force (%)						
20. Total manufacturing	8.3	10.5	16.3	21.9	28.1	28.9
21. Food, beverages, and tobacco	2.4	3.1	4.7	5.0	4.3	4.0
22. Textiles	1.7	1.8	1.9	2.3	2.4	1.9
23. Clothing and footwear	0.7	1.3	2.5	3.0	3.1	2.9
24. Wood products and furniture	1.0	1.0	1.4	1.8	2.2	2.1

Table 30 — continued

	(1)	(2)	(3)	(4)	(5)	(6)
25. Paper and paper products	b	0.1	0.2	0.5	0.9	1.0
26. Printing and publishing	0.2	0.2	0.4	0.7	1.2	1.4
27. Leather (excluding footwear)	0.1	0.2	0.2	0.3	0.3	0.2
28. Rubber products	0.1	0.1	0.2	0.2	0.3	0.4
29. Chemicals and petroleum products	0.3	0.5	0.7	1.1	1.4	1.5
30. Nonmetal mineral products	0.5	0.6	0.8	1.0	1.2	1.2
31. Basic metals	0.2	0.2	0.4	0.8	1.3	1.4
32. Metal products	0.9	1.2	2.5	4.6	8.5	9.7
33. Miscellaneous	0.2	0.2	0.4	0.6	1.0	1.2
Major groups						
34. Food, beverages, and tobacco	2.4	3.1	4.7	5.0	4.3	4.0
35. Textiles and clothing (lines 22–23)	2.4	3.1	4.4	5.3	5.5	4.8
36. Wood, paper, printing, and leather (lines 24–27)	1.3	1.5	2.2	3.3	4.6	4.7
37. Rubber, chemicals, and petroleum (lines 28–29)	0.4	0.6	0.9	1.3	1.7	1.9
38. Industrial raw materials (lines 30–31)	0.7	0.8	1.2	1.8	2.5	2.6
39. Fabricated metal products (lines 32–33)	1.1	1.4	2.9	5.2	9.5	10.9

a Based on 1963 but the structures for 1953 and 1963 at the benchmark level of $900 (in 1953 prices) are quite similar.

b Less than 0.05 percent.

Lines 1–13, 21–33: For countries included in the sample, sources, and procedures, see notes to Table 15.

Line 20: Countries covered are, in increasing order of GDP per capita in 1953: India, Pakistan, Thailand, Haiti, United Arab Republic, Paraguay, Peru, Philippines, Morocco, Honduras, Turkey, Dominican Republic, Portugal, El Salvador, Colombia, Nicaragua, Mexico, Spain, Jamaica, Greece, Japan, Costa Rica, Chile, Italy, Puerto Rico, Argentina, Ireland, Austria, Israel, Netherlands, Finland, West Germany, France, Belgium, Norway, Denmark, United Kingdom, Australia, Switzerland, New Zealand, Sweden, Canada, and United States. For the two methods for deriving GDP per capita in 1953 and 1963 see the general note to Table 15. For Haiti, the one country not covered in Table 15, GDP per capita was based on the OECD publication cited there.

The share of manufacturing is the manufacturing labor force as a percentage of total labor force excluding those not classified by industry. Shares for two census or survey years were calculated and interpolated or extrapolated along a straight line for 1953 and 1963. The sources used were: United Nations, *Demographic Yearbook, 1955* and *1956* (for the earlier censuses); *1964* (for the more recent census); International Labour Office, *Yearbook of Labour Statistics,* for years beginning with 1956 and through 1968; and for Haiti in 1962, ECLA sources.

the manufacturing branches in labor force and in product over the range of benchmark values of per capita product is more interesting. Like Table 15, Table 30 suggests the limited shift in the structure of manufacturing among branches at the lower ranges of per capita product (that is, from about $92 to about $300 in 1958 prices, from column 1 to column 3), compared with the more marked shift at the higher per capita product ranges. Here again the shares in countrywide labor force of labor attached to the paper, printing and publishing, rubber products, chemicals and petroleum, basic metals, and fabricated metals products branches rise markedly and consistently; and the shares of food products, textiles, clothing, wood, and leather products show a different trend, rising to the $500 or $1,000 level, and then declining. To be sure, there are some differences between the levels and movements of the shares of manufacturing branches in total product and in countrywide labor force, but it is the similarity that stands out. The differences, however, will emerge when product per worker is discussed.

Sectoral Product per Worker

The differences in levels and movements of sectoral shares in labor force and in gross domestic product mean sectoral differences in per worker output. The results of the calculations, based on Tables 29 and 14, are shown in Table 31.

By dividing the share of a given sector in total output by its share in total labor force we obtain the sector's output per worker expressed as a ratio to countrywide product per worker. If O_i and O_t are designated as output in the i sector and in the total economy respectively, and L_i and L_t as the labor force in the i sector and in the total economy, the share of the i sector in output is O_i/O_t and its share in labor force is L_i/L_t. Dividing the former share by the latter yields $O_i L_t : O_t L_i = (O_i/L_i):(O_t/L_t)$. Thus, product per worker in the A sector at the $70 benchmark value is 63 percent of countrywide product per worker (line 1, column 1).

However, before the ratios were calculated, the shares in total GDP were adjusted to exclude banking, insurance, and real estate, and income from ownership of dwellings. Both are relatively pure property incomes; and the former can be conceived as originating in almost any sector or subdivision. In any case, it did not seem sen-

Table 31. Sectoral product per worker and related measures at benchmark values of GDP per capita, about 1960.

A. Sectoral product per worker (countrywide product per worker, excluding banking, insurance, and real estate, and income from ownership of dwellings = 1.00)

	Benchmark values of 1958 GDP per capita ($)				
	70 (1)	150 (2)	300 (3)	500 (4)	1,000 (5)
Major sectors					
1. A	0.63	0.63	0.63	0.65	0.75
2. I+S	2.53	1.64	1.32	1.16	1.05
3. I	2.25	1.67	1.35	1.24	1.15
4. S	2.80	1.61	1.29	1.06	0.93
Subdivisions of I					
5. Manufacturing	1.75	1.58	1.28	1.20	1.15
6. Construction	3.23	1.42	1.04	0.95	0.85
7. Transport, storage, and communication, and electricity, gas, and water	4.18	2.15	1.75	1.60	1.38
Subdivisions of S					
8. Trade	2.97	1.96	1.55	1.19	0.94
9. Services	2.65	1.39	1.13	0.99	0.92
Intersectoral ratios					
10. (I+S)/A (line 2:line 1)	4.02	2.60	2.10	1.78	1.40
11. S/I (line 4:line 3)	1.24	0.96	0.96	0.85	0.81
12. Trade/services (line 8:line 9)	1.12	1.41	1.37	1.20	1.02
Measures of inequality in sectoral product per worker					
13. Three major sectors	59.4	47.1	34.5	21.8	13.9
14. All subdivisions	59.4	47.1	34.5	23.2	16.4

B. Contribution of intrasectoral change in product per worker and of intersectoral shifts to differences in GDP per worker

	Successive intervals in benchmark values ($)				
	70 to 150 (1)	150 to 300 (2)	300 to 500 (3)	500 to 1,000 (4)	70 to 1,000 (5)
Ratio of terminal value to initial value					
15. GDP per capita (same as GDP per worker)	2.14	2.00	1.67	2.00	14.29

Table 31 — continued

	(1)	(2)	(3)	(4)	(5)
16. GDP, excluding banking, insurance, real estate, and income from ownership of dwellings, per worker	2.08	1.97	1.67	2.02	13.79
17. Output per worker, A	2.08	1.97	1.72	2.33	16.41
18. Output per worker, I	1.54	1.59	1.53	1.87	7.05
19. Output per worker, S	1.20	1.58	1.37	1.77	4.58
20. Output per worker, manufacturing	1.88	1.60	1.56	1.93	9.06
Shares of intrasectoral changes and of intersectoral shifts, three major sectors					
21. Intrasectoral changes	0.68	0.79	0.82	0.92	
22. Intersectoral shifts	0.32	0.21	0.18	0.08	

Lines 1–9: Shares in GDP in Table 14, adjusted to exclude banking, insurance, and real estate and income from ownership of dwellings, divided by shares in labor force in Table 29.

Lines 13–14: Sum, signs disregarded, of differences between shares in product (excluding banking, insurance, and real estate, and income from ownership of dwellings) and in labor force.

Lines 15–20: Calculated on the assumption that the proportion of labor force to total population is the same at the successive benchmark values. The product of the share of GDP excluding banking, insurance, and real estate, and income from dwellings in total GDP (from Table 14) and the benchmark values of GDP per capita yields the entries in line 16; and the product of the relatives (panel A, lines 1, 3, 4, and 5) and GDP excluding banking, insurance, and real estate, etc. per worker (line 16) yields the entries in lines 17–20.

Lines 21–22: The total contribution of intrasectoral changes is the sum of the differences in per worker product over the interval for each of the three sectors, weighted by the average share of each sector in labor force for that interval. The total contribution of intersectoral shifts is the sum of changes (signs regarded) in the share of each sector in the labor force over the interval, weighted by the absolute deviation of the average per worker product — the averages being derived as arithmetic means of per worker product at the beginning and end of the interval. The sums of the intra- and inter-components thus derived are quite close to the total change in countrywide per worker product over each interval, and it is their shares in the total change that are given here.

sible to include these items in output in the calculation of gross product per worker.[2]

One implication of this calculation should be made explicit; we are assuming that the shares at the benchmark values in Tables 14 and 29 are acceptable estimates for the universe of non-Communist

2. In making this exclusion I modified the procedure used in Simon Kuznets, "Quantitative Aspects of the Economic Growth of Nations: II. Industrial Distribution of National Product and Labor Force," *Economic Development and Cultural Change*, supplement to vol. V, no. 4 (July 1957), pp. 32–50.

countries, omitting the few cases with structures distorted by unusually high shares of exogenous income sources or by political perturbations (wars, revolutions, and so on). Hence, despite the differences in size and composition of the two samples, the two sets of shares are assumed to be comparable. And, in fact, this assumption will be verified by means of a calculation involving a sample of identical countries, for each of which shares in both product and labor force, with most of the adjustments, are available (see the following section).

The evidence in Table 31 concerning the sectoral differences in product per worker can now be summarized. First, relative product per worker in the A sector is, for all benchmark values, well below the countrywide product per worker (line 1). In contrast, the relatives of product per worker for the I sector, for manufacturing, and for the public utilities (electric power, gas, water, transport and communications) are all larger than the countrywide product per worker at all benchmark levels (lines 3, 5, 7). This is also true for the S sector and the trade and services subdivisions, except at the very top (lines 4, 8–9).

Second, there are, consequently, wide intersectoral differences in product per worker — at every benchmark level. The most important intersectoral ratio, that between the A sector and all the others in the economy, indicates that per worker product in the non-A sectors is from 4 to 1.5 times as high as that in the A sector (line 10).

Third, and perhaps most significant, the intersectoral difference in product per worker between the A and the other sectors narrows steadily as we move from the low to the high per capita product countries. This drop would also be evident in the I/A and S/A ratios. Furthermore, the ratios for the subdivisions of both the I and the S sectors also tend to converge.

Fourth, because of the sharp decline in the dominant (I+S)/A ratio and the convergence in the ratios for the various subdivisions, as we move from low to high per capita income countries, the inequality in product per worker is narrower at the higher benchmark levels than at the lower (lines 13–14). The measure of inequality used here is the sum, signs disregarded, of the differences between the shares of the sectors in total product and in total labor force respectively. It is equivalent to the average of deviations of sectoral relatives of product per worker from 1 (signs disregarded), the deviations weighted by the shares of the sectors in total labor force (the proper weight for such deviations).[3] The measures in line 13 (based on the three major sectors) and line 14 (allowing for the distinction of subdivisions) show a definite narrowing in the amplitude of intersectoral differences in product per worker — most conspicuous for the upper benchmark levels, that is, between $300 and $1,000.

The narrowing of intersectoral differences in product per worker in panel A of Table 31 is not an algebraic necessity, in that the formal structure of the measure does not necessarily yield a contraction. It can be demonstrated that the intersectoral differences need not change as we move from the lower to the higher benchmark levels. Let us consider the most important intersectoral ratio, $(I+S)/A$. With the share of the A sector in GDP, excluding the two property income components, declining from 50.8 percent at the $70 level to 12.7 percent at $1,000 (see Table 14), we can determine the change in the share of the A sector in labor force that would yield the same $(I+S)/A$ ratio at the $1,000 level as at the $70 level, that is, 4.02 (line 10, column 1). From the equation $4.02 = \dfrac{(1 - 0.127)\,x}{(1 - x)\,0.127}$, the required share (x) of the A sector in labor force at the $1,000 level works out to 0.369. The required share would thus be 36.9 percent, rather than 17.0 percent as shown in Table 29, line 1, column 5. With the share in labor force 36.9 percent, the relative product per worker for the A sector becomes 0.344 (instead of 0.75, now given in Table 31, line 1, column 5); the relative product per worker for the $I+S$ sector becomes 1.384 (rather than 1.05, now given in Table 31, line 2, column 5); and the $(I+S)/A$ ratio is $1.384/0.344$, or 4.02, the same as at the $70 level (rather than 1.40, now shown in line 10, column 5). Note, however, that even though the high intersectoral ratio of 4.02 is preserved, the share of the A sector in labor force still drops markedly, from 80.5 percent at $70 to 36.9 percent at $1,000.[4]

3. Using the notation already employed, the difference between shares in product and in labor force for a given i sector can be expressed as $(O_i/O_t) - (L_i/L_t)$, or $(O_iL_t - O_tL_i)/O_tL_t$. The deviation from 1 of relative product per worker for sector i is $[(O_i/O_t : L_i/L_t) - 1]$. Weighting it by L_i/L_t, we get $(O_iL_t - O_tL_i)/O_tL_t$.

4. If we designate: W_N as the relative product per worker for the $I+S$ sector at the lower level, and W_A as the relative product per worker for the A sector at the lower level, and use W'_N and W'_A to denote relatives at the higher per capita product level, it can be shown that: $W'_N/W'_A = (W_N/W_A)\,[(a_{0N}/a_{LN}) : (a_{0A}/a_{LA})]$ where the a terms in the right-hand brackets are the ratios of terminal to initial shares of the $I+S$ and

Some interesting implications of the differential movements of the sectoral shares in product and in labor force in Tables 14 and 29 and panel A of Table 31 can be shown if we again assume fairly realistically that the proportion of labor force to population is roughly the same for all benchmark values of per capita product. With this assumption, changes between successive benchmark values of GDP per capita and GDP per worker are identical (panel B, line 15). And with exclusion of the two property income components omitted in the comparison of shares in product and in labor force, interval changes for the slightly modified product per worker (line 16) can be calculated.

Since the entries for sectoral product per worker in panel A are relatives of countrywide product per worker for which the changes are shown in line 16, the changes over the same benchmark intervals in product per worker for each sector or subdivision can be calculated. This was done for the three major sectors and manufacturing (lines 17–20), and the result necessarily follows from the downward movement of the intersectoral ratios in panel A. The significant finding is that, as we move from the lower to the higher per capita and per worker countries, the proportional rise in per worker product is consistently and significantly larger in the A sector than in the I and S sectors, and would be even larger than that for the I and S sectors combined. Over the full range of benchmark values, product per worker in the A sector rises by a factor of 16.4, more than twice that of 7.1 for the I sector, and almost four times that of 4.6 for the S sector (column 5, lines 17–19). The rise in per worker product for the A sector over the full range of the benchmark values is, in fact, larger than that for any other sector or subdivision, even manufacturing, for which the factor is 9.1 (line 20, column 5). Putting it differently, the gross labor productivity disparities among countries, at different levels of per capita or per worker product,

A sectors in output and labor force respectively over the range from the lower to higher per capita product.

For the intersectoral (I+S)/A ratio to remain constant, the expression in the right-hand brackets has to equal 1. This means that the relative discrepancy between the changes in shares in product and labor force must be the same for both the I+S and A sectors.

The fractions are obviously not equal, particularly when calculated for the full range from $70 to $1,000. For the A sector the share in labor force declines more than the share in output; for the I+S sector the share in labor force rises appreciably more than the share in output.

are widest for the A sector; and the underdeveloped countries are more backward with respect to labor productivity in the A sector than in the other sectors of the economy.

The second and less important implication of this analysis is revealed in lines 21–22. Since sectors differ in the *level* of per worker product at successive benchmark values of countrywide per capita or per worker product, and since their shares in labor force shift, changes in countrywide per worker product between one benchmark value and the next can be produced not only by intra-sectoral changes in per worker product, but also by intersectoral shifts, that is, shifts of the labor force among sectors differing in per worker product. Since intersectoral shifts are away from the A sector toward higher per worker product sectors, they must contribute to the total rise in per worker product between benchmark levels.

This intersectoral factor is revealed indirectly by the intrasectoral change factors in lines 17–19, most of which are smaller than the total change factor in line 16. But it is shown directly by the calculation that distinguishes the contribution of the intrasectoral changes in per worker product from that of intersectoral shifts. Except for the interval from $500 to $1,000, the intersectoral shifts contribute about a fifth or more to the total movement in per worker product. The contribution of the intersectoral component would probably be significantly greater if based on a more detailed disaggregation than the three major sectors.

The sample relating to manufacturing branches, summarized in Tables 15 and 30, yields product per worker *within* manufacturing. The estimates, for the eight branches that should be distinguished because of the different levels of per worker product that character-ize them, are given in Table 32.

The measures of value added per worker, in lines 1–8, reveal differences among branches that are almost as wide as those in Table 31. The low value added branches — textiles, clothing and footwear, and wood products — are characterized by large propor-tions of females in their labor force or by the rural character of activity (as in wood), while capital intensity, that is, supply of capital per worker, is not exceptionally high. The higher capital intensity and the raising of value added by indirect taxes might ex-plain why the food, beverage, and tobacco group, also with a higher-than-average proportion of women, shows value added per worker above the average for all manufacturing. The branches

Table 32. Relative product per worker at benchmark values of GDP per capita, selected branches of manufacturing (based on the average of cross-sections for 1953 and 1963).

	Benchmark values of GDP per capita (1958$)					
	91.7 (1)	153 (2)	306 (3)	510 (4)	1,019 (5)	1,359 (6)
A. Value added per worker (VA per worker for manufacturing = 1.00)						
1. Food, beverages, and tobacco	1.19	1.27	1.22	1.19	1.15	1.11
2. Textiles	0.90	0.81	0.88	0.89	0.85	0.85
3. Clothing and footwear	0.60	0.51	0.51	0.54	0.57	0.55
4. Wood products and leather	0.59	0.62	0.62	0.66	0.73	0.74
5. Paper and printing	1.39	1.27	1.20	1.17	1.17	1.17
6. Rubber, chemicals, and petroleum products	1.84	1.90	2.06	1.87	1.70	1.69
7. Industrial raw materials	1.03	1.09	1.27	1.22	1.17	1.18
8. Fabricated metal products	0.96	0.91	0.89	0.93	0.98	0.97
Measures of inequality in value added per worker						
9. Eight groups above	22.5	29.2	29.3	24.5	18.7	17.7
10. Thirteen branches	23.9	30.4	29.3	24.5	18.7	17.7
B. Relative product per worker (countrywide product per worker, excluding banking, insurance, and real estate, and income from dwellings = 1.00)						
11. Total manufacturing	1.49	1.45	1.34	1.26	1.14	1.13
12. Food, beverages, and tobacco	1.77	1.84	1.63	1.50	1.31	1.25
13. Textiles	1.34	1.17	1.18	1.12	0.97	0.96
14. Clothing and footwear	0.89	0.74	0.68	0.68	0.65	0.62
15. Wood products and leather	0.88	0.90	0.83	0.83	0.83	0.84
16. Paper and printing	2.07	1.84	1.61	1.47	1.33	1.32
17. Rubber, chemicals, and petroleum products	2.74	2.76	2.76	2.36	1.94	1.91
18. Industrial raw materials	1.53	1.58	1.70	1.54	1.33	1.33
19. Fabricated metal products	1.43	1.32	1.19	1.17	1.12	1.10
20. Unweighted sum of deviations from 1.00, lines 12–19	5.11	4.87	4.56	3.65	2.58	2.49

Lines 1–8: Derived by dividing shares in value added in panel A of Table 15 by shares in labor force in panel A of Table 30 (both for total manufacturing).

Lines 9–10: Sum of differences, signs disregarded, between shares in manufacturing value added and in manufacturing labor force.

Line 11: Derived from line 20, Table 15 and line 20, Table 30, the former adjusted to exclude the estimated shares of the finance and dwelling components on the basis of the cross-section for 1958 in Table 14.

Lines 12–19: Lines 1–8 multiplied by line 11.

with high value added per worker — paper and printing, and chemicals and petroleum products — are distinguished by very high capital intensity and limited proportions of women workers (which is also true of basic metals).

The marked convergence of interbranch differences in value added per worker within manufacturing, like the intersectoral differences in product per worker within the economy at large, as we move from the low to the higher per capita product countries, is reflected in the measures of inequality in lines 9 and 10. However, in this sample such convergence only begins to appear at per capita product above the $300 benchmark value.

The relative of per worker product for manufacturing as a whole, for the sample in Table 32, declines steadily as we move from the lower to higher per capita product countries (line 11). Of the eight branches of manufacturing, only clothing and wood products show product per worker, relative to countrywide, below 1; and these two branches are the only ones in which the relatives do not converge toward 1 as we move from the lower to the higher per capita product levels. Only the branches with higher-than-average per worker product show such convergence and this finding goes far to explain the decline of the relative per worker product for manufacturing as a whole toward 1, as we move from the low to the high per capita product ranges.

Adjustments for Coverage of Labor Force Data

The basic data on labor force by the three major sectors and their subdivisions are drawn from the censuses of population and occupations. Two aspects of the definition of labor force used in the primary census data are of concern here. The first is scope — particularly the treatment of unpaid family workers, of females within the *paid* labor force, and of the paid male labor force at extreme (young and old) ages. The questions raised by these specific groups have to do with their equivalence (with respect to hours of work, experience, and other qualities) to the full-time male paid labor force in the prime ages from twenty to sixty-five. A complete answer to these questions requires data on hours of work, and on differences in experience and quality as reflected in hourly rates of compensation. But even without such data — and they are lacking on a wide comparative basis — rough equivalence weights applied to census data on sex, age, and labor force status of the active population in a number of countries provide useful adjustments for differences in intensity of employment and in quality of the major components of the labor force. The second set of questions concerns the sectoral classification of the labor force. Is the industrial attachment shown in the censuses representative, or does it conceal possible uses of A (non-A) sector labor force in non-A (A) sector work, even away from agriculture (nonagriculture)? While the questions concerning scope can be answered on the basis of fairly abundant census data, information on any overlapping within the sectoral classification of the labor force is hard to come by, and the comments on this aspect will be speculative.

Adjustment for scope

The evidence on variants in the scope of the labor force about 1960 is presented in Table 33. It contains a summary of data for forty-eight countries on the proportions of total labor force classified as unpaid family workers and on the proportions of the *paid* labor force accounted for by women, both sets of proportions for the country as a whole and for the three major sectors. It also summarizes data for a smaller sample, some twenty-six countries, on the proportions of males aged fifteen to nineteen and sixty-five and over among *all* male workers (including unpaid family workers, who cannot be distinguished but can be assumed to constitute small proportions), for the country and the three major sectors; and application of these proportions to total *paid* male workers yields estimates of paid male workers, aged twenty through sixty-four, for the country and for the three major sectors.

The countries were grouped in Table 33 by the share of the A sector in total labor force. I also experimented with the grouping by per capita product, but found the association between the proportions of the special groups distinguished in Table 33 and the share of the A sector in total (unadjusted) labor force to be closer. Yet the latter is associated with per capita product, as can be seen from lines 3 and 25. The successive columns in the table are, therefore, of groups not only in declining order of the share of the A sector in total labor force, but also in roughly rising order of per capita product.

The findings suggested by Table 33 can now be summarized.

Table 33. Association between shares of unpaid family workers, of female
workers, and of extreme age groups (male) within sectoral labor
force, and the shares of the major sectors in total labor force, about
1960.

A. Shares of unpaid family workers and of female workers, forty-eight countries, grouped in descending order of share of A sector in total labor force

	Groups of countries					
	I (1)	II (2)	III (3)	IV (4)	V (5)	VI (6)
1. Number of countries	8	8	8	8	8	8
2. Regional identity of countries	A-5	A-3	A-2	A-1	A-1	E-5
	F-2	F-2	F-1	F-2	L-2	S-3
	L-1	L-3	L-4	L-1	E-4	
			E-1	E-4	S-1	
3. GDP per capita, 1958 ($)	113	189	200	318	718	1,267
4. Labor force as % of population	41.1	31.9	32.3	37.4	37.9	40.8
5. Percent of labor force unallocated by sector or by status	4.6	5.8	4.6	3.8	3.7	3.5
Shares in total labor force, excluding unallocated (%)						
6. A sector	78.2	63.2	55.3	37.8	21.1	10.6
7. I sector	10.3	16.3	21.2	32.8	42.3	49.9
8. S sector	11.5	20.5	23.5	29.4	36.6	39.5
Unpaid family workers as percent of labor force, excluding unallocated						
9. Total for country	34.7	15.9	16.5	11.3	5.0	3.6
Within each sector						
10. A sector	42.3	23.6	27.3	24.2	16.9	20.5
11. I sector	6.0	3.0	2.8	3.2	1.0	0.8
12. S sector	8.2	2.7	3.4	3.7	2.7	2.8
Shares in labor force, excluding unallocated and unpaid family workers (%)						
13. A sector	69.0	57.4	48.1	32.3	18.4	8.7
14. I sector	14.8	18.9	24.7	35.8	44.1	51.3
15. S sector	16.2	23.7	27.2	31.9	37.5	40.0
Female workers as percent of labor force, excluding unallocated and unpaid family workers						
16. Total for country	14.3	19.8	14.8	23.2	26.7	27.8
Within each sector						
17. A sector	13.3	11.2	7.8	11.8	11.9	7.9
18. I sector	9.7	18.8	12.4	17.6	19.5	17.5
19. S sector	22.7	41.6	29.5	40.9	42.5	45.4

Table 33 — continued

	(1)	(2)	(3)	(4)	(5)	(6)
Shares in male labor force, excluding unallocated and unpaid family workers (%)						
20. A sector	69.8	63.6	52.1	37.1	22.1	11.1
21. I sector	15.6	19.1	25.4	38.4	48.5	58.6
22. S sector	14.6	17.3	22.5	24.5	29.4	30.3

B. Shares of extreme age groups in male labor force, twenty-six countries grouped in descending order of share of A sector in total labor force

	Groups of countries				
	I (1)	II (2)	III (3)	IV (4)	V (5)
23. Number of countries	4	5	6	6	5
24. Regional identity of countries	A-2	A-2	A-1	L-2	E-2
	F-1	F-1	F-1	E-3	S-3
	L-1	L-1	L-1	S-1	
		E-1	E-3		
25. GDP per capita, 1958 ($)	180	191	337	695	1,398
26. Share of A sector in total allocated labor force (%)	69.3	58.4	39.7	22.7	11.0
Shares in male labor force, excluding unpaid family workers (%)					
27. A sector	65.4	51.5	37.8	22.9	12.7
28. I sector	19.7	24.3	38.5	48.1	54.7
29. S sector	14.9	24.2	23.7	29.0	32.6
Males fifteen through nineteen, as percent of all male workers					
30. Total for country	12.5	11.0	9.6	9.1	7.5
Within each sector					
31. A sector	14.0	12.7	10.2	10.5	9.1
32. I sector	10.6	11.0	9.8	9.9	6.8
33. S sector	8.1	7.2	8.5	6.7	7.9
Males sixty-five and over as percent of all male workers					
34. Total for country	4.1	4.5	5.1	3.5	3.9
Within each sector					
35. A sector	5.0	6.0	8.7	6.6	8.7
36. I sector	2.0	2.3	2.3	1.9	2.4
37. S sector	2.8	3.6	3.8	3.6	4.4

Table *33* — continued

	(1)	(2)	(3)	(4)	(5)
Shares in male labor force, twenty through sixty-four, excluding unpaid family workers (%)					
38. A sector	63.5	49.5	36.0	21.7	11.7
39. I sector	20.6	24.9	39.7	48.5	56.0
40. S sector	15.9	25.6	24.3	29.8	32.3

See the notes to Table 12 for the coverage of the A, I, and S sectors; for the regional classification letters; and for the sources of and procedure followed for the 1958 GDP per capita.

The forty-eight countries included in *lines 1–22* are, in descending order of the share of the A sector in labor force: Thailand, Liberia, Sabah and Sarawak, Turkey, Sierra Leone, India, Pakistan, Honduras, South Korea, Philippines, Dominican Republic, Morocco, Ghana, El Salvador, Nicaragua, Malaya, Ecuador, United Arab Republic, Syria, Taiwan, Greece, Mexico, Peru, Costa Rica, Portugal, Libya, Jamaica, Mauritius, Ireland, Finland, Spain, Japan, Chile, Italy, Puerto Rico, Austria, France, Denmark, New Zealand, Israel, Sweden, Canada, Switzerland, Australia, Germany (FR), the Netherlands, Belgium, and the United States.

Lines 3, 25: Geometric means of GDP per capita for individual countries.

Lines 4–8, 10–12, 17–19: Arithmetic means of percentages for individual countries calculated from data given in United Nations, *Demographic Yearbook, 1964* (New York, 1965), table 12, supplemented by the International Labour Office, *Yearbook of Labour Statistics, 1966,* table 2A.

Lines 9, 16: Weighted means of the shares in lines 10–12 and 17–19 respectively, the weights being the shares in lines 6–8 and 13–15 respectively.

Lines 13–15: Calculated from lines 6–8 and 10–12, thus allowing for the different sectoral ratios of unpaid family workers in labor force (excluding unallocated).

Lines 20–22: Calculated from lines 13–15 and 16–19.

The twenty-six countries included in *lines 23–40* are: Turkey, Honduras, Philippines, Ghana, El Salvador, Malaya, United Arab Republic, Syria, Greece, Peru, Portugal, Mauritius, Ireland, Finland, Japan, Chile, Italy, Puerto Rico, Austria, France, New Zealand, Sweden, Canada, Australia, Netherlands, and the United States.

Lines 26–29, 31–33, 35–37: Arithmetic means of percentages for individual countries calculated from data given in United Nations, *Demographic Yearbook, 1964,* table 12 for lines 26–29, and table 9 for lines 31–33, 35–37.

Lines 30, 34: Weighted means of the shares in lines 31–33 and 35–37 respectively, the weights being the shares in lines 27–29.

Lines 38–40: Calculated from lines 27–37, by allowing for different sectoral ratios of male workers fifteen through nineteen and sixty-five and over to total male labor force (excluding unallocated), these ratios being assumed to hold for male workers excluding unallocated and unpaid family labor (that is, for lines 27–29).

(a) Unpaid family workers constitute substantial proportions of total labor force in the A sector — in all groups of countries, even when the share of the A sector is small and per capita product high (line 10). This proportion, which ranges from 17 to 42 percent of total labor force in the A sector, also affects the structure of countrywide labor force, contributing a large component of unpaid family labor in those countries where agriculture looms large and per capita product is low. The proportions of unpaid family workers in the I sector, with a range from 1 to 6 percent, and in the S sector, with a range from 3 to 8 percent, are appreciably lower (lines 11–12). Exclusion of unpaid family workers, therefore, substantially reduces the share of the A sector in labor force, and raises the shares of the I and S sectors. Comparison of lines 6–8 with lines 13–15 reveals that the share of the A sector excluding unpaid family labor drops substantially for all groups of countries; and the shares of the I and S sectors rise substantially, except in column 6 where, because the share of the A sector is small, the adjustments have a slight effect.

(b) With unpaid family workers (mostly female) excluded, the proportion of females among paid workers increases as we move toward the countries with lower shares of the A sector and high per capita product (line 16). In general, the proportion of women in the paid labor force in the A sector is low, after unpaid family labor is eliminated (line 17). In contrast, the share of females among paid workers in the S sector is appreciably higher than in the other sectors; and the difference is particularly notable in the upper income countries (line 19). The share of women in the paid labor force in the I sector falls between the low proportions for the A and the high proportions for the S sector (line 18). Consequently, when we exclude women and limit our view to the *paid male* labor force, the share of the A sector is larger; the share of the S sector is smaller; and that of the I sector remains about the same as in the total paid labor force, except in the higher per capita product groups where it is larger (compare lines 13–15 with lines 20–22).

(c) Considering next the extreme age groups within the paid male labor force, we find that in general the proportions of the young (fifteen through nineteen) and old (sixty-five and over) subgroups are highest in the A sector, the proportion for the two groups combined ranging between 17 and 19 percent (line 31 plus line 35). The range in the proportion (again combined) for the I sector is between 9 and 13 percent (line 32 plus line 36); for the S sector, between 10 and 12 percent (line 33 plus line 37). Thus, in the shift from total paid male labor force to paid males aged twenty through sixty-four, the share of the A sector is reduced; and those of the I and S sectors are raised — by a few percentage points (compare lines 27–29 with lines 38–40).

Before applying the findings of Table 33 to the estimates of sectoral differences in the unadjusted labor force, we should emphasize some general impressions conveyed by them. First, the specific subgroups within total labor force just distinguished loom large; their weights in the several sectors are quite different; and the resulting modifications in the structure of labor force are also quite different as we move from countries with large shares of the A sector and low per capita product to those with small shares of the A sector and high per capita product. Thus, if we take the two extreme groups in panel A of Table 33, in both of which total unadjusted labor force is roughly 41 percent of total population (line 4) and that excluding unallocated workers would be about 39 percent (line 5), the elimination of unpaid family workers reduces the labor force to about 25 percent of total population in column 1 and to about 38 percent in column 6; in addition the exclusion of women from labor force would mean a proportion of paid male labor force to total population of about 21.5 percent in column 1 and of about 27.5 percent in column 6; and the final allowance for the extreme age groups would yield a proportion of paid male workers aged twenty through sixty-four to total population of about 18.0 percent in the lowest per capita product group of countries and about 24.5 percent in the highest. The groups eliminated account for between four-tenths and more than half of the total labor force. They also have different weights in the agricultural lower per capita product countries and in the industrialized high per capita product countries, as is evident from the shift from rough equality in the proportion of total labor force to population of about 39 to 41 percent to a labor force proportion to total population that is more than a third larger in the high than in the low per capita product group.

Second, the different proportions of these subgroups in labor force in the different sectors at the several levels of industrialization and per capita product reflect major differences in pattern of life and participation in economic activity, partly imposed by the technological peculiarities of the sectors. The small-scale organization and the close association between family life and work in the A sector are reflected in the high proportions of unpaid family workers and of the extreme age groups, even among paid male workers, whereas the limited proportions in other sectors may reflect tighter age constraints on paid employment and greater educational requirements. The specific character of many jobs in the S sector, and the change in social practices associated with urbanization in the high per capita product countries are reflected in the high proportion of females in the paid labor force of the S sector, particularly in the high per capita product group. Further ramifications of the adjustment of the labor force to different conditions of life and work associated with the several sectors at different levels of economic development would probably have been revealed if additional labor force subgroups within a more detailed sectoral distribution could have been analyzed.

Third, despite their magnitude, the adjustments based on the elimination of the several subgroups within labor force distinguished in Table 33 do not modify the sectoral shares in labor force enough to obscure the differences among them, or even to reduce the significance of these differences. In comparison with the structure of total unadjusted labor force, in which the share of the A sector ranged from 80 percent at the per capita level of $70 to 12 percent for a per capita of about $1,500; and the shares of the I and S sectors ranged from 10 to 48 and 10 to 40 percent respectively (see Table 28, lines 4–6), the adjustments suggested in Table 33 look moderate indeed. Thus, after adjustments for unpaid family and women workers, the share of the A sector still ranges from 70 to 11 percent, for a range in per capita product of $113 to $1,267; and the shares of the I and S sectors range from 16 to 59 and from 15 to 30 percent respectively (lines 20–22). After adjustment for the extreme age groups among paid male workers, the share of the A sector would probably range from about 68 to about 9 percent; and those of the I and S sectors would range from 17 to 60 and from 15 to 31 percent. Thus, even for labor force more narrowly defined and limited to paid male workers twenty through sixty-four years of age, the range of differences in the sectoral shares in association with different levels of per capita product is still almost as wide as that in the shares in total labor force.

This impression must be checked by applying the adjustments to the earlier estimates of sectoral shares in labor force at the familiar benchmark values of 1958 GDP per capita. This can be done by deriving from Table 33 rough estimates of the difference produced by the different proportions of the various subgroups in the several sectors at given levels of the share of the A sector in total labor force, and applying these to the shares of corresponding benchmark values of GDP per capita in Table 29. The results are assembled in Table 34.

Table 34. Shares of major sectors in labor force, unadjusted and adjusted for
shares of unpaid family workers, female workers, and extreme age
groups (male), at benchmark values of 1958 GDP per capita, about
1960 (percentages).

	Benchmark values of 1958 GDP per capita ($)					Arithmetic mean, cols. 1–5 (6)
	70 (1)	150 (2)	300 (3)	500 (4)	1,000 (5)	
A. Complete omission of specified categories						
Share of A sector						
1. Unadjusted	80.5	63.3	46.1	31.4	17.0	47.7
2. Adjusted U	73.3	56.4	39.6	26.6	14.5	42.1
3. Adjusted UF	75.7	60.2	43.6	30.3	17.6	45.5
4. Adjusted UFA	74.1	58.3	41.7	28.7	16.6	43.9
Share of I sector						
5. Unadjusted	9.6	17.0	26.8	36.0	45.6	27.0
6. Adjusted U	13.3	20.4	30.0	38.5	47.2	29.9
7. Adjusted UF	13.6	21.2	31.9	41.5	51.8	32.0
8. Adjusted UFA	14.4	22.1	32.9	42.6	52.8	32.9
Share of S sector						
9. Unadjusted	9.9	19.7	27.1	32.6	37.4	25.3
10. Adjusted U	13.4	23.2	30.4	34.9	38.3	28.0
11. Adjusted UF	10.7	18.6	24.5	28.2	30.6	22.5
12. Adjusted UFA	11.5	19.6	25.4	28.7	30.6	23.2
B. Partial omission of specified categories						
Share of A sector						
13. Adjusted U	74.7	57.8	40.9	27.5	15.0	43.2
14. Adjusted UF	75.6	59.3	42.5	29.0	16.3	44.6
15. Adjusted UFA	74.9	58.3	41.5	28.3	15.8	43.7
Share of I sector						
16. Adjusted U	12.6	19.7	29.4	38.0	46.9	29.3
17. Adjusted UF	12.7	20.0	30.1	39.2	48.7	30.1
18. Adjusted UFA	13.0	20.4	30.6	39.7	49.1	30.6
Share of S sector						
19. Adjusted U	12.7	22.5	29.7	34.5	38.1	27.5
20. Adjusted UF	11.7	20.7	27.4	31.8	35.0	25.3
21. Adjusted UFA	12.1	21.3	27.9	32.0	35.1	25.7

Adjusted U: adjusted to exclude unpaid family workers (fully or partially).

Adjusted UF: adjusted to exclude unpaid family workers and female workers (fully or partially).

Adjusted UFA: adjusted to exclude unpaid family workers, female workers, and paid male workers in the extreme age groups (fully or partially).

Lines 1, 5, 9: From Table 29, lines 1–3.

Lines 2, 6, 10: Lines 1, 5, 9, adjusted by factors read from the trend lines of the ratios of lines 13–15 of Table 33 to lines 6–8 of Table 33, respectively.

Lines 3, 7, 11: Lines 2, 6, 10, adjusted by factors read from the trend lines of the ratios of lines 20–22 of Table 33 to lines 13–15 of Table 33, respectively.

Lines 4, 8, 12: Lines 3, 7, 11, adjusted by factors read from the trend lines of the ratios of lines 38–40 of Table 33 to lines 26–28 of Table 33, respectively.

Lines 13–21: The procedure is that followed for lines 2–4, 6–8, 10–12, except that only eight-tenths of the adjustment factor for unpaid family workers, four-tenths of the adjustment factor for female workers, and five-tenths of the adjustment factor for extreme age groups were deducted from the shares in lines 1, 5, 9 — to allow for some contribution by these categories of labor to GDP. The weights of 0.2 (for unpaid family workers), 0.6 (for paid female workers), and 0.5 (for extreme age groups among paid male workers, about 0.4 for males fifteen through nineteen and 0.6 for males sixty-five and over) were derived from Edward F. Denison, *Why Growth Rates Differ: Postwar Experience of Nine Western Countries* (Washington, D.C.: The Brookings Institution, 1967), table 7-3, p. 72, and table 7-4, p. 73.

Panel A shows the adjustment based on complete exclusion of the specified categories, that is, the complete omission of unpaid family workers, women workers, and paid male workers beyond the twenty-through-sixty-four age range. When compared with the shares in unadjusted total labor force, the results presumably show the total change that could be expected from this modification in the definition of the labor force. This is retained as an extreme variant in the calculation of adjusted relatives of sectoral product per worker.

Obviously, complete exclusion of the specified categories is unrealistic, since it implies that unpaid family workers, paid female workers, and paid male workers aged fifteen through nineteen or sixty-five and over contribute nothing to sectoral product; and even the assumption that the error involved is proportionately the same for all three sectors is no more realistic than the other. Undoubtedly, an unpaid family worker does contribute, although probably much less than a paid worker; a female worker, especially if paid, also contributes; and so do the very young and the very old male workers. The problem is to find the proper equivalents. The ones used here (and in Table 4) are the only ones readily available; they have been derived from the experience in developed countries, and imply an equivalent value of 0.2 per unpaid family worker, 0.6 per female paid worker, 0.4 per paid male worker fifteen through nineteen years of age, and 0.6 per paid male worker sixty-five and over — all in terms of the paid male worker twenty through sixty-four as 1.0. The adjustments based on these crude equivalence ratios are shown in panel B of Table 34.

Since these adjustments are taken from Table 33 — except that they are roughly fitted to the shares of the A sector in total labor force corresponding to the five benchmark values of per capita GDP — Table 34 confirms our impressions of Table 33. But having the shares in the unadjusted total labor force (lines 1, 5, 9), we can see the effects of the adjustments. With complete omission of the specified categories, the average share of the A sector drops only about 4 percentage points, that of the I sector rises 6 points, and that of the S sector declines 2 (column 6, lines 1, 4; 5, 8; 9, 12). With the partial adjustment, the change in average levels is even more moderate.

What is more crucial, the *difference* in the shares from one benchmark level of per capita product to the next is only slightly affected — despite the fact, already noted, that the specified categories account for from four-tenths to over a half of total labor force. Consider the difference in the shares between the lowest and the highest benchmark levels. The share of the A sector in the unadjusted total declines 63.5 percentage points, and the shares of the I and S sectors rise 36.0 and 27.5 points respectively. With the partial adjustment, the share of the A sector drops 59.1 percentage points and the shares of the I and S sectors rise 36.1 and 23.0 points respectively. The decline in the share of the A sector is reduced less than a tenth; the rise in the share of the S sector is reduced less than a sixth; and the increase in the share of the I sector shows practically no change. With the unrealistically high complete omission, the share of the A sector declines 57.5 percentage points, and the shares of the I and S sectors rise 38.4 and 19.1 points respectively. The major effect here is on the rise in the share of the S sector which is reduced from 27.5 to 19.1 percentage points, or almost a third. The far larger changes in the shares of the A and I sectors are much less affected.

Using the adjusted shares of the three sectors in labor force and the shares in gross domestic product (excluding banking, insurance, and real estate, and income from ownership of dwellings), we can derive adjusted relatives of sectoral product per worker and related measures (Table 35). Table 35 parallels Table 31, except that

Table 35. Sectoral product per worker and related measures at benchmark values of 1958 GDP per capita, labor force adjusted for proportions of unpaid family workers, female workers, and extreme age groups (male), about 1960.

A. Sectoral product per worker (countrywide product per worker, excluding banking, insurance, and real estate, and income from dwellings = 1.00)

	Benchmark values of 1958 GDP per capita ($)				
	70 (1)	150 (2)	300 (3)	500 (4)	1,000 (5)
Complete omission of specified categories in labor force					
Sectoral product per worker					
1. A sector	0.69	0.68	0.69	0.71	0.77
2. I+S sector	1.90	1.44	1.22	1.11	1.05
3. I sector	1.51	1.29	1.10	1.05	1.00
4. S sector	2.39	1.62	1.37	1.21	1.14
Intersectoral ratios					
5. (I+S)/A (line 2:line 1)	2.75	2.12	1.77	1.56	1.36
6. S/I (line 4:line 3)	1.58	1.26	1.25	1.15	1.14
Measure of inequality in sectoral product per worker					
7. Three sectors	46.5	37.0	25.6	16.4	8.3
Partial omission of specified categories in labor force					
Sectoral product per worker					
8. A sector	0.68	0.68	0.70	0.73	0.80
9. I+S sector	1.96	1.44	1.22	1.11	1.04
10. I sector	1.66	1.40	1.19	1.13	1.07
11. S sector	2.27	1.49	1.25	1.08	0.99
Intersectoral ratios					
12. (I+S)/A (line 9:line 8)	2.88	2.12	1.74	1.52	1.30
13. S/I (line 11:line 10)	1.37	1.06	1.05	0.96	0.93
Measure of inequality in sectoral product per worker					
14. Three sectors	48.0	37.1	25.3	15.5	6.9

B. Contribution of intrasectoral change in product per worker and of intersectoral shifts to differences in GDP per worker

	Successive intervals in benchmark values ($)				
	70 to 150 (1)	150 to 300 (2)	300 to 500 (3)	500 to 1,000 (4)	70 to 1,000 (5)
Complete omission of specified categories in labor force					
Ratio of terminal value to initial value					
15. GDP, excluding banking, insurance, real estate, and ownership of dwellings, per worker	1.98	1.79	1.57	1.84	10.24

Table 35 — continued

	(1)	(2)	(3)	(4)	(5)
16. Output per worker, A	1.95	1.81	1.62	1.99	11.40
17. Output per worker, I	1.69	1.52	1.50	1.75	6.76
18. Output per worker, S	1.34	1.51	1.39	1.73	4.87
Shares of intrasectoral changes and intersectoral shifts					
19. Intrasectoral changes	0.77	0.83	0.88	0.94	
20. Intersectoral shifts	0.23	0.17	0.12	0.06	

Partial omission of specified categories in labor force

Ratio of terminal value to initial value					
21. GDP, excluding banking, insurance, and real estate, and ownership of dwellings, per worker	2.08	1.69	1.57	1.85	10.21
22. Output per worker, A	2.08	1.74	1.64	2.03	12.02
23. Output per worker, I	1.75	1.43	1.49	1.75	6.58
24. Output per worker, S	1.36	1.41	1.36	1.70	4.45
Shares of intrasectoral changes and intersectoral shifts					
25. Intrasectoral changes	0.78	0.80	0.87	0.94	
26. Intersectoral shifts	0.22	0.20	0.13	0.06	

Lines 1–4: Shares in GDP in Table 14, adjusted to exclude banking, insurance, real estate, and income from ownership of dwellings, divided by shares in labor force in Table 34, lines 4, 8, 12.

Lines 7, 14: Sums, signs disregarded, of differences between shares in product and in labor force, both as adjusted for lines 1–4.

Lines 8–11: See notes to lines 1–4. The shares in labor force are from Table 34, lines 15, 18, 21.

Lines 15, 21: See notes to lines 15–20 of Table 31. The change was calculated from the indexes of GDP, excluding banking, insurance, and real estate, and income from ownership of dwellings (from Table 14), and the indexes of ratios of labor force to total population, with either complete or partial omission of the specified categories in the labor force. The latter indexes were derived from lines 4, 9, 16, 30, 34 of Table 33. The combination of the two sets of indexes yields GDP, excluding the two property income components, per worker, excluding the specified categories.

Lines 16–18, 22–24: Calculated by applying to lines 15 and 21 respectively, the relatives in lines 1 and 3–4, and 8 and 10–11.

Lines 19–20, 25–26: See notes to lines 21–22 of Table 31.

for the latter I used unadjusted shares in total labor force and for the former, shares adjusted for the specific categories distinguished. Comparison of the two tables, therefore, reveals the effect of the adjustment for scope of labor force on intersectoral inequalities in product per worker, on change in per worker product within the sectors, and on the contribution of intersectoral shifts to the differences at various benchmark levels in countrywide product per worker.

The comparison yields four results.

(a) The adjustment reduces intersectoral inequality, at least between A and I and S combined. The (I+S)/A ratio in Table 31 ranges from 4.02 at the $70 benchmark level to 1.40 at the $1,000 level (line 10); in Table 35 the range is from 2.75 to 1.36 or from 2.88 to 1.30 (lines 5, 12). Yet the reduction in the range is relatively moderate, and over the full span of benchmark values of per capita product it is still more than 2 to 1. The S/I ratio is affected somewhat more: whereas it ranged from 1.24 to 0.81 in Table 31 (line 11), it ranges from 1.58 to 1.14 or 1.37 to 0.93 in Table 35 (lines 6, 13). The adjustment for the high proportion of women (and to some extent, of unpaid family labor at the lower income levels) in the S sector raises its per worker product and therefore the ratio of its per worker product to that of the I sector.

(b) The persistence in Table 35 of a marked reduction in the (I+S)/A ratio and of a decline in the S/I ratio as we move from the low to the higher per capita product countries means not only that intersectoral inequality is reduced (reflected in lines 7, 14) but also that, as we move from low to high per capita product countries, the increase in per worker product is appreciably larger in the A sector than in the I and S sectors, and in the I sector, than in the S sector. Per worker product in the A sector increases by a factor of either 11.4 or 12.0, a factor almost twice as large as that for the I and even larger than that for the S sector; and per worker product in the I sector, which increases by a factor of either 6.8 or 6.6, is greater than the factor for the S sector, 4.9 or 4.4 (lines 16–18, 22–24, column 5).

(c) The rise between the benchmark values in the countrywide product per worker is distinctly smaller in Table 35 (lines 15, 21) than in Table 31 (line 16). The reason for this is that for the latter a constant proportion of labor force to total population was assumed, whereas the elimination of the specified categories raises the proportion of the adjusted labor force to total population as we move to the higher per capita product countries. It is significant that part of the higher per capita product in the developed than in the less developed countries is the result, therefore, of a higher ratio of labor force (reduced to equivalent units) to total population, a larger supply of labor units per capita. The fraction thus contributed is about a fourth, judging by the increase factors of 10.2 in Table 35 and 13.8 in Table 31.

(d) The intersectoral shifts account for smaller proportions of the total difference in per worker product when labor force is adjusted, dropping from over a fifth for the lowest benchmark interval to about a twentieth for the highest. As already indicated, this contribution could be greater with a more detailed subdivision of sectors, and the importance of such shifts in the different segments of the range of per capita product differentials could also change.

This survey of the adjustments for scope may be concluded with one final review. The analysis to this point combines shares in product and in labor force (the latter adjusted and unadjusted), derived from different samples of countries. Although there is little reason to assume that these samples do not represent the same universe, the analysis is repeated for a sample of countries for which *both* the shares in product and the shares in labor force, with the major adjustments in the latter (for unpaid family labor and paid female workers), are available. This sample includes only thirty-five countries, but it permits us to calculate the shares and sectoral ratios separately for each country; and therefore observe not only the average levels but the distributions of individual country ratios (Table 36). The countries are combined into four groups in increasing order of 1958 per capita GDP, ranging from $113 to $1,163. Although the range is distinctly narrower than those for the separate samples, all the findings established on the basis of the two separate samples are confirmed.

Two additional items of information deserve note. The first is the detail on the trade and service subdivisions of the S sector, for which shares in adjusted labor force have not previously been shown. The trade/services ratio rises from 1.4 to 1.8, then drops to 1.0 as we move from low to high per capita product countries (lines 22, 25); whereas the corresponding ratio, based on shares in unadjusted labor force, moves from 1.1 to 1.4 at the intermediate benchmark levels, then drops to 1.0 (see Table 31, line 12). The adjustments, particularly that for female workers, tend to yield a higher relative per worker product in trade than in the services.

Second, the distributions of the three intersectoral ratios permit us to observe the relative frequency of excess or deficiency. Al-

Table 36. Sectoral product per worker and related measures, thirty-five countries with data for both GDP and labor force, adjusted for unpaid
family and female workers, about 1960.

	Groups of countries in increasing order of 1958 GDP per capita			
	I (1)	II (2)	III (3)	IV (4)
1. Number of countries	9	8	9	9
2. GDP per capita ($)	113	215	446	1,163
3. Regional identity of countries	A-6	A-2	A-2	E-6
	F-1	F-1	L-3	S-3
	L-2	L-4	E-4	
		E-1		

Shares in GDP, excluding banking, insurance, and real estate and income from dwellings, at factor cost (%)

4. A sector	41.3	38.8	19.0	11.6
5. I sector	27.9	30.2	45.0	54.3
6. S sector	30.8	31.0	36.0	34.1
7. Trade	13.7	15.6	15.3	14.6
8. Services	17.1	15.4	20.7	19.5

Shares in labor force, adjusted (partial omission of unpaid family labor and female workers) (%)

9. A sector	59.4	57.3	27.8	13.6
10. I sector	18.7	22.3	40.9	50.1
11. S sector	21.9	20.4	31.3	36.3
12. Commerce	8.1	7.5	12.3	15.5
13. Other services	13.8	12.9	19.0	20.8

Relatives of sectoral product per worker (GDP per worker, excluding banking, insurance and real estate and income from dwellings = 1.00)

14. A sector (line 4 ÷ line 9)	0.70	0.68	0.68	0.85
15. I+S sector (lines 5 + 6 ÷ lines 10 + 11)	1.45	1.44	1.12	1.02
16. I sector (line 5 ÷ line 10)	1.49	1.35	1.10	1.08
17. S sector (line 6 ÷ line 11)	1.41	1.52	1.15	0.94
18. Trade (line 7 ÷ line 12)	1.70	2.09	1.24	0.94
19. Services (line 8 ÷ line 13)	1.24	1.19	1.09	0.94

Intersectoral ratios

20. (I+S)/A (line 15 ÷ line 14)	2.07	2.12	1.65	1.20
21. S/I (line 17 ÷ line 16)	0.95	1.13	1.05	0.87

Table 36 — continued

	(1)	(2)	(3)	(4)
22. Trade/services				
(line 19 ÷ line 18)	1.37	1.76	1.14	1.00

Intersectoral ratios (geometric means of ratios for individual countries)

	(1)	(2)	(3)	(4)
23. (I+S)/A	2.14	2.18	1.62	1.19
24. S/I	0.94	1.10	1.03	0.87
25. Trade/services	1.37	1.73	1.10	1.01

Size distributions of ratios

Size of ratio classes

	2.50 and over (1)	1.67–2.49 (2)	1.25–1.66 (3)	1.00–1.24 (4)	Under 1.00 (5)
(I+S)/A					
26. Group I	2	6	1	0	0
27. Group II	2	5	0	1	0
28. Group III	2	2	0	5	0
29. Group IV	0	1	3	2	3

Size of ratio classes

	1.25 and over (1)	1.00–1.24 (2)	0.85–0.99 (3)	0.71–0.84 (4)	Under 0.71 (5)
S/I					
30. Group I	0	5	2	1	1
31. Group II	3	1	3	1	0
32. Group III	1	4	3	1	0
33. Group IV	0	1	4	3	1

Size of ratio classes

	2.00 and over (1)	1.60–1.99 (2)	1.30–1.59 (3)	1.00–1.29 (4)	0.80–0.99 (5)	Under 0.80 (6)
Trade/services						
34. Group I	0	3	2	3	1	0
35. Group II	3	1	1	3	0	0
36. Group III	1	1	0	3	3	1
37. Group IV	0	0	1	3	5	0

The thirty-five countries for which both product and labor force data are available include, in increasing order of 1958 GDP per capita: Pakistan, India, Thailand, United Arab Republic, South Korea, Taiwan, Syria, Ecuador, Honduras, Peru, Turkey, Mauritius, Dominican Republic, Malaya, El Salvador, Portugal, Nicaragua, Spain, Greece, Jamaica, Chile, Japan, Italy, Israel, Puerto Rico, Austria, the Netherlands, Finland, Germany (FR), Belgium, Denmark, France, Australia, Canada, and the United States.

Lines 2–8: See notes to Tables 12 and 28 for sources and procedures.

Lines 9–13: See notes to Table 28 for sources and to Table 33 for the percentages of unpaid family and female workers omitted.

Lines 23–25: Geometric means of the ratios calculated separately for the individual countries.

Lines 26–37: Distributions of ratios underlying lines 23–25.

though the sample is small and the frequency distributions are not very detailed, they suggest that the differences in intersectoral inequality among low and high per capita product countries are *not* due to the inclusion of one or two unusually high or low ratios. Thus, in fifteen of the seventeen lower income countries, the $(I+S)/A$ ratio is 1.67 or more; whereas it is more than 1.67 in only one of the nine top income countries (lines 26, 27, 29). In nine of the seventeen low per capita product countries the S/I ratio is more than 1.0, whereas in eight of the nine in the highest income group it is less than 1.0 (lines 30, 31, 33). The trade/services ratio in all but one of the seventeen lower per capita product countries is 1.0 or more, and in ten it is 1.30 or more; whereas in eight of the nine top income countries it is less than 1.30 (lines 34, 35, 37). Despite the exceptions, inevitable in view of the special factors that can affect shares of sectors and subdivisions in product and labor force, the evidence suggests that the intersectoral ratios found in the earlier analysis represent dominant tendencies.

Problems of classification

Even after labor force has been adjusted for scope, or converted to equivalent units, the component classified as attached to the A sector may still include workers who spend some time in productive activities outside the A sector; and similar part-time engagement in another sector (or subdivision) may be true of workers classified under the non-A sectors (and subdivisions). To the extent that workers migrate periodically or temporarily from one production division to another, or hold several jobs at one time, cutting across sectoral or subdivisional boundaries, the available classification of the labor force does not properly mesh the sectors in labor force with those in product.

Unquestionably, some seasonal or temporary migration of workers from the A sector to others, or engagement in the countryside in non-A activities, takes place, especially in the less developed countries, even before the ultimate cityward migration. Unquestionably, in all countries there is some multiple job holding, part of which cuts across sectoral or subdivisional boundaries. The relevant question is to what extent the resulting biases in the labor force classification affect sectoral product per worker, and in particular, intersectoral inequalities at the several levels of countrywide per capita product.

As already suggested, data on this classification problem are scanty, and a plausible answer would require a long search and evaluation, not feasible here. However, the preceding discussion leads to the conclusion that these classification biases would have to be improbably, indeed impossibly, great to have a significant effect on the intersectoral inequalities that have been established.

This conclusion is supported by the illustration in Table 37, which provides an answer to the following question. How much non-A product would have to be turned out by the labor force attached to the A sector, in order for the per worker products of the A and I+S sectors to be equal? This question is posed by design in terms of the most important intersectoral ratio, (I+S)/A, but it could be repeated in terms of any intersectoral ratio. And the answer is given for the five benchmark values of 1958 per capita product.

Two assumptions can be made concerning this required additional product. First, we can assume that it is already included in the I+S component of GDP; in which case, in assigning it to the A sector labor force, we would have to *subtract* it from the I+S share, now assigned to the I+S labor force. This assumption underlies lines 5–7. Second, we can assume that the non-A product turned out by the A labor force is not included in the I+S component of product, and thus not included in GDP at all; in which case the additional output should not be subtracted from the I+S output of the I+S labor force. This assumption underlies lines 8–10.

The first assumption is less plausible than the second. Since it is common practice, especially in the less developed countries, to use the number of workers to estimate output in some production branches, the chances are that the non-A output of the labor force attached to the A sector is more frequently omitted than included

Table 37. Shifts or additions required to attain equality in sectoral product per worker, A and I+S sectors.

	Benchmark values of 1958 GDP per capita ($)				
	70 (1)	150 (2)	300 (3)	500 (4)	1,000 (5)
Shares in GDP (excluding banking, insurance, etc.) % *(based on Table 14)*					
1. A sector	50.8	39.8	28.9	20.5	12.7
2. I+S sector	49.2	60.2	71.1	79.5	87.3
Shares in labor force (partial adjustment) % *(from Table 34)*					
3. A sector	74.9	58.3	41.5	28.3	15.8
4. I+S sector	25.1	41.7	58.5	71.7	84.2
Shifts required, assuming transfer of product from I+S to A sector					
5. Addition to A, or subtraction from I+S, as % of GDP (line 3 − line 1, or line 2 − line 4)	24.1	18.5	12.6	7.8	3.1
6. Transfer as ratio to original product of A sector (line 5:line 1)	0.47	0.47	0.44	0.38	0.24
7. Transfer as ratio to original product of I+S sector (line 5:line 2)	0.49	0.31	0.18	0.10	0.04
Additions required, assuming no transfer from I+S sector					
8. Addition to A, as % of original GDP[a]	95.5	44.5	21.6	10.8	3.7
9. Addition as ratio to original product of A sector (line 8:line 1) 1.88	1.12	0.75	0.53	0.29	
10. Addition as ratio to original product of I+S sector (line 8:line 2)	1.94	0.74	0.30	0.14	0.04

[a] Derived from the equation: (share of the A sector in GDP + X) divided by (1 + X) = (share of the A sector in labor force), X being the required addition expressed as a ratio to the original GDP. The entry in line 8 is X multiplied by 100.

under the I+S sector. I suspect the truth lies somewhere between the two assumptions, but much closer to the second than to the first.

The main suggestion of the illustrative calculation is that, for countries at the lower benchmark levels of per capita product and possibly through the $500 level, the shifts or additions of non-A output by the A labor force in order to equalize per worker product in the A and I+S sectors are far too large to be likely. Thus, under the first assumption, at the $70 per capita level sectoral equality would require a shift of almost half of the product of the I+S component now assigned to the I+S labor force — which would increase the product of the A labor force by almost half of its original output. Under the more plausible assumption of addition rather than transfer, equality would be attained only if the non-A output of the A labor force were almost *twice* as large as its A output; and this addition of non-A output, presumably not covered in the present estimate, would also be almost twice as large as the covered I+S output, and would almost double countrywide product.

Of course, we need not insist on complete A and I+S equality of per worker product. But the calculation does suggest that any plausible guesses concerning the proportional additions of non-A output by the A labor force would have little effect on the presently measured intersectoral inequalities — for countries with per capita product ranging from $70 through $500. Thus, if we assume that the non-A output by the A labor force is, plausibly, no more than 10 percent of the original output of the A labor force, the (I+S)/A ratio for column 1, now 2.88 (see Table 35, line 12), would drop to 2.33 on the assumption in lines 5–7, and to 2.62 on the assumption in lines 8–10; whereas the ratio for column 5 would be 1.15 or 1.17 respectively. Thus, on the assumption that substantial additional non-A output is an addition, not a transfer, the range of the intersectoral ratio is from 2.62 to 1.17, only slightly narrower than the original range of 2.88 to 1.30.

Intersectoral Inequality in Product per Worker

Five major findings relating to the shares in labor force and sectoral product per worker are suggested by our discussion.

First, with the most reasonable conversion of special groups in labor force (unpaid family workers, paid women workers, and so on) to equivalent units, the share of the A sector in total labor force ranges from 75 percent at the $70 benchmark level to about 16 percent at the $1,000 level, while the shares of the I and the S sectors rise markedly (see Table 34, lines 15, 18, 21).

Second, the share of the A sector in labor force is generally higher than its share in product; and the differential is greater in the low than in the high per capita product countries. Consequently, per worker product in the A sector is significantly lower than that in the I+S sector (and those in the I and S sectors taken separately);

and intersectoral inequality in per worker product is greatest at the low per capita product levels and smallest at the high per capita product levels. The relevant (I+S)/A ratio is 2.88 at the $70 benchmark level and declines to 1.30 at the $1,000 level (see Table 35, line 12). This finding is confirmed by cruder calculations for 1950 and by the International Labour Office, which in an analysis of the 1950 labor force data comments on the fact that "a feature common to nearly all the countries is that the share of agriculture in the net domestic product falls notably short of its share of the labour force. This shortfall appears to be particularly marked in the less developed countries." [5]

Third, the level of the (I+S)/A ratio and its decline from the low to the high benchmark level of per capita product may both be reduced somewhat by allowances for possible understatement of non-A product turned out by the A labor force, and for the possible differences in sectoral price structure between the less developed and more developed countries. If we allow for a possible omission of non-A product amounting to 10 percent of total output of the A labor force and for an adjustment to comparable sectoral price structure which may add another tenth to the share of the A sector in product — both at the $70 but not at the $1,000 benchmark level — the (I+S)/A ratio at the $70 benchmark level drops to 2.4 and that at the $1,000 level remains at 1.3. Despite the crudity of all the adjustments, it is reasonable to suggest that the (I+S)/A ratio would drop from well over 2.0 at the $70 benchmark level to somewhat over 1.0 at the $1,000 level and above.

Fourth, the ratio of per worker product in the S to that in the I sector is 1.4 at the $70 benchmark level, and declines to less than 1 at the $1,000 level (see Table 35, line 13). The higher per worker product of the S sector reflects the much higher per worker product of the trade subdivision than that of services. The ratio of the former to the latter is 1.4 to 1.7 at the low per capita product levels and then drops to about 1 (see Table 36, lines 22, 25). The higher per worker product in the trade subdivision, and the convergence of these ratios to about 1 at the higher levels of per capita product, were also found in the analysis of the 1950 data in the paper cited in note 2.

5. The 1950 calculations are given in Kuznets, "Quantitative Aspects . . . Industrial Distribution," pp. 33–39. The quotation is from "The World's Working Population: Its Industrial Distribution," *International Labour Review,* vol. LXXXIII, no. 5 (May 1956), p. 520.

Fifth, with the classification by sectors and subdivisions used here, intersectoral inequality in product per worker, dominated by the difference between I+S and A, but also affected by the differences between I and S and those within the S sector, shows marked contraction, a rapid convergence toward equality as we move from low to high per capita product countries. The weighted measure of intersectoral inequality in product per worker (based on the three major sectors) drops from 48 points at the $70 benchmark level to 7 points at the $1,000 level (see Table 35, line 14).

Several explanations of the intersectoral differentials in per worker product may be suggested; but discriminating tests of these explanations require data and analysis that are not at hand. We can only list the more obvious explanations, suggest their likely weight, and consider the requirements for an adequate test. The discussion is limited to the major (I+S)/A differential, but much of it applies *pari passu* to the other intersectoral differentials.

(a) Since the product figures underlying the per worker estimates are gross of capital consumption and returns on capital, the higher per worker product in the I+S sector could be the result of either a greater supply of material capital per worker or a greater return per unit of capital, or both. For this explanation to be operative, the difference between the I+S sector and the A sector in supply of capital per worker, or return per unit of capital, or both, would have to be much greater in the less developed, low per capita product countries than in the developed group. In this case, subtraction of returns on capital (per worker) from product per worker would mean greater deductions from the share of the I+S than from that of the A sector in total product; and this difference in the shift from total product to the service income component would be greater in the less developed than in the developed countries. As a result, the differentials in labor income per worker between the A and I+S sectors would be much narrower than those in total product per worker; and with this greater contraction of the differentials in the less developed countries, the inequality in sectoral labor income per worker might be almost the same at all levels of per capita product.

We do have scanty data on the stock of material capital, reproducible and total, for a few countries in recent years, from which we can exclude dwellings (since income from the latter is omitted in the calculation of sectoral product per capita) and within which we can distinguish, at least for fixed capital if not for inventories, between agriculture and other sectors.[6] The data suggest that the share of the A sector in *total* capital, including nonreproducible components but excluding dwellings, is no lower than its share in labor force. Thus for India in 1950 the share of agriculture in this total stock was about 72 percent, and that in labor force was about 71 percent, and for the four developed countries for which this estimate is available (the Netherlands in 1950, Norway in 1953, West Germany in 1950, and the United States in 1955), the average share of agriculture in total fixed stock is over 22 percent, higher than the share in labor force which is roughly 19 percent. This means that the supply of *total* capital, excluding dwellings, per worker is as high in the A sector as in the I+S sector. To be sure, the supply of *reproducible* fixed capital per worker is lower in the A sector. Thus, the share of agriculture in reproducible capital is only about 39 percent in India, 12.5 percent in Mexico in 1950, 31 percent in Colombia in 1953; and the average share is less than 10 percent for five developed countries (the four listed above, plus Canada for 1955). The supply of fixed reproducible capital per worker in the A sector is probably not more than half that in the I+S sector in the developed countries; and perhaps somewhat less in the underdeveloped countries. But this differential would only affect the allocation of capital consumption, not of total income from assets, a far larger figure. Although the evidence is scanty, it does not suggest a significantly lower supply of total capital (that is, of the capital that yields capital returns) per worker in the A than in the I+S sector, either in the less developed, or even more so, in the developed countries.

Hence, if the return on capital contributes to the explanation of the (I+S)/A ratio of product per worker and its decline as we move from the less to the more developed countries, it must be because of differences in return *per unit* of material capital (even the distribution of inventories would favor an adequate share of capital in the A sector, perhaps greater per worker than in the other sectors). Such returns per unit of material capital must be

6. See Raymond Goldsmith and Christopher Saunders, eds., "A Summary of National Wealth Estimates," *Income and Wealth, Series VIII* (London: Bowes and Bowes, 1959), table I, pp. 8–11.

much higher in the I+S than in the A sector in the less developed countries; and this differential must diminish rapidly as we move to the more developed countries.

In the present state of our knowledge, it is not possible to say whether sectoral differentials in return per unit of material capital exist in the less developed countries, and if they do, how large they are. In another connection I argued that such returns, on *equity* of individual entrepreneurs in the A sector in the less developed countries, must be much lower than the apparent return on total capital in the I+S sector.[7] But this conclusion was reached by assuming a labor return per entrepreneur equal to the countrywide compensation per employee. To make the same assumption here would be to assign, by definition, all of the sectoral differentials in product per worker to differences in the return per unit of material capital, a premise that can be tested only by direct evidence.

Even without direct evidence, two observations can be made in regard to sectoral differentials in return per unit of material capital in the less developed countries. First, if the proportions of returns from assets in total product, for both less and more developed countries, are known, the effect of the differentials in return per unit can be approximated. The returns from assets are about 20 percent of national income, in both high and low per capita product countries.[8] With capital consumption ranging from 6.6 to 8 percent of GNP and hence roughly from 7 to 9 percent of national income, the shares of capital returns plus capital consumption in total GDP would range from 27/107, or 25 percent, to 29/109, or 27 percent. We would then subtract from these the shares of banking, insurance, and real estate and income from ownership of dwellings to obtain the final proportions of income from assets (including capital consumption) in the total of GDP used in the calculation of sectoral product per worker. The proportions at the extremes of the product per capita scale would therefore be $(25 - 4.7)/95$ and $(27 - 8.0)/92.0$, or 21.3 and 20.7 percent respectively. If we assume that in the developed countries return per unit of capital is the same in the A and I+S sectors, it would mean, when combined

7. See Simon Kuznets, "Quantitative Aspects of the Economic Growth of Nations: IV. Distribution of National Income by Factor Shares," *Economic Development and Cultural Change,* vol. VII, no. 3, part II (April 1958), pp. 23–28.

8. Simon Kuznets, *Modern Economic Growth: Rate, Structure, and Spread* (New Haven: Yale University Press, 1966), table 8.1, line 68, p. 405. The figures on capital consumption cited in the next sentence are derived from lines 85–86, p. 406.

with equal stock of material capital per worker, that labor returns per worker in the A and I+S sectors are equal or differ by the same proportion as total product per worker. And if we assume that at the lowest benchmark level of per capita product the return per unit of capital is five times as high in the I+S sector as in the A sector, the shares of the A and I+S sectors in labor return (that is, total product excluding returns on assets plus capital consumption) would be, if we use the shares in total product in Table 37, (50.8 minus one-sixth of 21.3) divided by 78.7 for the share of the A sector, and (49.2 minus five-sixths of 21.3) divided by 78.7 for the share of the I+S sector, or 60.0 and 40.0 percent respectively of the total labor return, or service income. The use of these shares with the shares in labor force in Table 37 (reflecting the adjustment for special groups) would yield an (I+S)/A ratio of labor return per worker of 1.99 instead of 2.88 for the unadjusted shares — a substantial reduction but one that still leaves the intersectoral ratio in the less developed countries close to 2, compared with close to 1 for the developed countries. Incidentally, even the most extreme assumption that there are *no* capital returns in the A sector, would yield shares in service income of 64.5 and 35.5 percent for the A and I+S sectors respectively, and an intersectoral (I+S)/A ratio of over 1.6.

Second, and far more important, the assumption of wide sectoral differentials in return per unit of material capital in the less developed countries implies a dual structure. Presumably, if such large differentials per unit of material capital are maintained, there must be some obstacles to the movement of capital from the locus of low returns to that of high returns, and these may be connected with obstacles to the movement of other productive factors and other institutional peculiarities that create a dual structure, and thus prevent an effective equalization of productivity and returns in two or more segments of the economy. To be sure, the assumed disparity in return per unit of material capital between the I+S and A sectors may be the *proximate* cause and explanation of at least part of the (I+S)/A differential in total product per worker. But the disparity in these rates of return must stand for a duality of structure, at least in the sense that there are two capital markets isolated from each other, with one likely to be dominant in the A sector, and the other dominant in the I+S sector.

(b) A somewhat similar conclusion emerges when we consider

another possible explanation of the (I+S)/A differentials, this time having to do with possible differences in *quality of labor,* whether or not they result from the volume of per worker input into life, health, and education (in other words, into human capital). Even though estimates of shares in labor force were adjusted by conversion of unpaid family labor, paid female workers, and extreme age groups among paid male workers to comparable equivalents, significant differences in quality of the labor force must still remain. The resulting possible *sectoral* differences in quality might be in favor of the I+S sector, and much more in the less developed than in the more developed countries. If this is so, a large part of the sectoral differences in labor income per worker would be explained by such quality differences in the sense that if such income were related to standard quality units, the (I+S)/A differentials might be reduced significantly, and far more sharply in the underdeveloped than in the developed countries.

Such differences in quality of labor, over and above those associated with employment status (unpaid family labor), sex, and age, may flow from two distinct sources. The first is associated with greater investment of resources in human beings, in raising the general capacity of individuals as workers by better health and education. The implication of this hypothesis is that the I+S sector employs workers who represent a much greater investment of such productivity-raising inputs per worker than the A sector — and much more so in the underdeveloped than in the developed countries. The second source is inherited natural capacities, which might generate differences in quality of labor regardless of investment in health and education (or more correctly, given an adequate minimum to permit survival and activity in general). The implication of this hypothesis is that the I+S sector recruits workers with greater natural ability than the A sector, and much more so in the underdeveloped than in the developed countries. Of course, the two sources of quality differences, like the two hypotheses of sectoral differentials in return per unit of material capital, may be complementary rather than competitive.

Whether or not we could demonstrate that the I+S sector secures labor of higher quality, in the way either of better health and more education, or greater natural ability, or both, than the A sector, and that this selection is productive of much greater quality differentials in the underdeveloped countries, is a moot question. Offhand, the hypothesis seems plausible — since, if, as the estimates clearly indicate, average service income per worker is so much higher in the I+S than in the A sector, the compensation at the margin is also likely to be higher and in choosing additions or replacements, the I+S sector can presumably command higher quality labor. But even if one accepts the claim of higher quality of labor in the I+S than in the A sector, particularly in the underdeveloped countries, the implication with respect to the structure of these countries must be considered explicitly.

The consideration should be in terms of marginal return to labor, and cannot be easily joined to our estimates of *average* service income per worker for rather wide categories. We may, however, assume first that marginal compensation per worker is proportional to the average, so that we can apply the estimated sectoral differentials in average service income per worker to marginal service income per worker, that is, compensation of additional entrants into the labor force at a given minimum quality level. If so, why should there be such large (I+S)/A differentials in compensation, and hence presumably large quality differentials of labor entering the two sectors at the minimum quality level in both, and in the underdeveloped much more than in the developed countries? Presumably, a large potential supply of labor of somewhat poorer quality is available to the I+S sector at somewhat lower rates — and a rational calculation would show that unless other constraints not mentioned so far exist, a+d new workers may be employable at a compensation of w−x per worker, and these additional workers may produce somewhat more than the a workers at a rate of w per worker. In this type of calculation, without significant technological constraints on what is essentially substitution of labor for capital, the marginal compensation per worker in the I+S sector should not exceed the marginal compensation in the A sector by more than the cost of moving, if the latter is involved (such cost presumably spread out over the discounted future of the I+S employment). If, as the estimates suggest, the proportional differences in marginal (average) returns per worker in the I+S sector over the A sector far exceed any reasonably estimated moving cost, some constraints in the I+S sector must bar the addition of more labor of somewhat poorer quality to the other factors of production. These constraints may be associated with the limited choices in modern technology available to less developed countries in the I+S sector.[9] Thus, in a modern steel mill, increase in employment beyond a fairly narrow limit would add little to product; and since this limited quantity of labor is used effectively in combination with heavy fixed investment, a fairly high minimum quality of labor must be assured to avoid neglect, misuse, or other problems that would interfere with the effective use of the capital equipment. In this example, there is no choice between a large labor force of somewhat inferior quality and a smaller labor force of high quality: the latter is the only pattern feasible. And the illustration suggests that wide differentials in marginal labor quality and compensation between the I+S and A sectors in underdeveloped countries may be imposed by the technological constraints of the modern components in the I+S sector — constraints that are apparently far greater than any that apply to labor in the A sector in the underdeveloped countries. This quality differential may not be as great in the developed countries, since the modern technology applied in the A sector also imposes constraints on the minimum quality of labor to be added, which is not true of the traditional technology that dominates the A sector in the underdeveloped countries.

If we reject the marginal approach and assume compensation and quality of labor at the margin to be equal in the I+S and the A sectors even in the underdeveloped countries, the argument would shift to the structure of labor and its quality *above* the minimum entering level. If the average compensation and quality per worker are so much higher in the I+S than in the A sector, while the marginal compensation and quality are equal, the implication is that the distribution of quality (and compensation) above the marginal minimum is much more biased in the I+S than in the A sector toward higher levels. One may then ask what prevents a dilution of quality and lowering of average compensation in the I+S sector. Are the technological constraints also applicable to the hierarchy of labor above the minimum entrance level in modern technology? There are grounds for giving a positive answer. The manning tables of numerous plants in modern industries show that a few high quality men at the top cannot be replaced by any num-

9. For discussion of this problem, see Richard Eckaus, "The Factor-Proportions Problem in Underdeveloped Areas," *The American Economic Review*, vol. XLIV, no. 3 (September 1955); reprinted in A. N. Agrawala and S. P. Sing, eds., *The Economics of Underdevelopment* (London: Oxford University Press, 1958), pp. 349–380.

ber of lower quality workers. Hence, the hypothesis that connects duality of structure with (I+S)/A differentials in quality of marginal labor and its compensation would also connect it with (I+S)/A differentials in average quality and compensation, even if the two sectors are assumed equal in quality and compensation of marginal labor.

In either version of the hypothesis (and the two are complementary, each accounting in part for the differentials to be explained) labor of high quality that stems from greater investment in human capital (or is evaluated as such, when it reflects natural endowment) may secure a higher relative return than some basic labor in the underdeveloped than in the developed countries. To illustrate: in some real terms of differences in formal education the quality of the I+S labor in less developed countries may be 110, and that in the more developed 125, both relative to some basic quality standard in each group taken as 100. But in the underdeveloped countries the rate of return on investment in formal education may be much higher than in the developed countries; and the return to higher quality labor in the I+S sector in the underdeveloped countries may be 150, compared with 100 for the labor in the A sector, whereas in the developed countries the corresponding index may be only 125 relative to 100. These differences, like those in the rate of return per unit of material capital already discussed, are part of the sectoral price structure, which differs in this direction at least in the relation of A prices to I prices among underdeveloped and developed countries. It is worth noting in the present connection because it sharpens the distinction between the volume of additional inputs in human capital (or its equivalent in natural capacity) and the possible differences in relative prices of the resulting addition (and thus of the implicit rate of return) among the several groups of countries. In other words, it would be unwarranted to associate the higher service income per worker differential between the I+S and A sectors in the less developed countries with quality differentials that would loom equally large in the price structure of the developed countries.

(c) The last explanation to be considered here has already been hinted at in the reference to the "cost of moving." If work in the I+S sector involves changes in conditions of life that impose greater costs than in the A sector, costs other than those associated with different quality requirements, the rate of compensation should be higher in the I+S sector — for labor of the same quality. This would mean higher product per worker; and it may well be that this difference in costs is relatively wider in the less developed than in the more developed countries.

Two comments are relevant. First, if the differences in cost of living reflect differences in resource inputs required to secure the same goods or to assure satisfaction of needs at the same level (in the cities as in the countryside), labor in the cities must still yield a higher real product per worker; and this higher real product, relatively greater in the less developed countries, must still be explained. The reference to differences in living costs and to costs of moving only indicates that *unless* such higher costs are covered by higher productivity, the I+S sector is not likely to emerge in urban conditions, but would have to be developed in the countryside. It does not explain how the higher productivity of labor in the I+S sector is secured; it merely asserts that part of this higher productivity is absorbed in higher living costs, and cannot add to the real income of labor in the I+S sector.

Second, can we assume that cost of living differentials between the A and I+S sectors, on a relative basis, are wider in the less developed than in the developed countries? Insofar as these differentials are connected with inputs into transportation and distribution — the movement, say, of food products from the countryside to the cities — it may well be that the less efficient systems in the less developed countries cause a greater proportional addition to costs. But, on the other hand, both the density of the urban sector and the transformation of living conditions resulting from the migration from the countryside to the cities appear to be greater in the developed countries; and were demonstrated by the crude approximations to the extra cost of urban life in the United States used in Chapter II, which indicate a rise, not a decline, in the relative differentials in the course of growth. The tentative conclusion, and it can be little more than an educated guess, is that the relative difference in living costs associated with employment in the I+S rather than in the A sector is probably not wider in the less developed countries (in which much more of the I+S output is produced in the countryside) than in the developed countries. Thus, while cost differentials suggest that the per worker real product of the I+S sector should be higher than that of the A sector, they contribute little to the explanation of the greater disparity in the less developed countries.

In this brief discussion of the possible explanations of the higher $(I+S)/A$ ratio of product per worker in the less developed countries, no reference was made to "residual" or total factor productivity. If it could be assumed that labor and capital inputs of the same quality are valued at the same rate in all the sectors, residual productivity after their subtraction from the sectoral outputs might be lower in the A than in the $I+S$ sector, and more so in the less developed countries. But such an estimate would have meaning only if the basic assumption could be verified by specific data on the quality of labor and capital and on their compensation; and even then questions would arise as to why, if quality equivalent units of labor and capital yield different outputs and hence earn different returns, movement toward equalization fails to occur. As the discussion shows, no such data are available; and much of the earlier discussion could, indeed, be rephrased in terms of sectoral differences in "residual" productivity. But without the detailed data, differences in sectoral input quality cannot be distinguished from those in "residual" productivity, or from institutional obstacles to mobility and equalization of factor returns.

Whatever the formulation, the discussion tended justifiably to emphasize various aspects of duality of structure in the less developed countries, and suggest that such duality, if present in the developed countries, plays a much less important role. The two apparently isolated markets for capital; the constraints of modern technology in the $I+S$ sector on the use of labor, compared with absence of such constraints in the A sector; the contrast between the minimum living requirements at the higher level of economic performance, associated with the modern sector, and the lower level of service income per worker in the A sector were all claimed to be characteristic of the underdeveloped countries, and much less relevant to the developed. But a variety of other differences in institutional structure is associated with the aspects of dual structure explicitly discussed. Thus, the low return on capital in the A sector in the less developed countries is a combination of extremely low rates of return on the equity of individual farmers with possibly high rates of return on liquid funds provided by individual landlords cum moneylenders or even by nonpersonal banking institutions. There may therefore be a third rate of return, and a third capital market in which the equity of individual farmers is involved, and one that is in the nature of a distress market. Likewise, the labor use by modern components of the I+S sector may require some institutional practices in order to assure stability of the labor force, and these practices may set up long-term barriers to an effective movement of labor into these advanced enclaves — which suggests structural inequalities within the I sector (or within the S sector) that may be as wide as those between the I+S and A sectors. These comments are made to stress the interweaving of structural differences in technology and markets of the several sectors and subdivisions with the institutional conditions of employment and compensation of the different components of the labor force, in generating various intersectoral inequalities in product as well as in service income per worker. Furthermore, a proper analysis would involve far more disaggregation than that attained; and additional data on institutional characteristics of labor and capital markets, and conditions of life and work in the different sectors — especially for the less developed countries that differ so much in all these respects from the more developed economies, and on which study has been only recently begun.

Finally, although much of this discussion has dealt with the (I+S)/A ratio for total product or service income per worker, it is also applicable to other intersectoral ratios. Thus, the higher product per worker ratios of the S sector to the I sector, and particularly of trade to services or to the I sector, in the less developed countries are presumably connected with the higher returns on capital in trade than in the I sector, despite the existence of some modern components in the latter. And the differences in per worker product among the subdivisions of the I sector itself are surely not fortuitous. Indeed, almost any intersectoral ratio of product per worker reflects a fairly complicated bundle of technological requirements and institutional responses. The statistical evidence presented in the tables relates only to the broadest similarities and differences associated with the specific levels of per capita product and hence of overall economic performance; and the speculative discussion of various relevant hypotheses is, in the nature of the case, even more summary.

VI

Sectoral Shares in Labor Force: Long-Term Trends

Changes in Shares: The Three Major Sectors

Table 38 presents a summary of long-term changes in shares of the three sectors in labor force for the developed and a few less developed countries. In addition to shares in total labor force (excluding those not allocated by industry), the table shows, where possible, shares in labor force adjusted by weighting the number of women in the A sector by 0.2, and in the other sectors by 0.6. But this adjustment, which should allow for most of the effect of changing proportions of unpaid family labor and of differing levels of skill and compensation between men and women, has little effect on either the levels of, or trends in, the shares. In one or two cases, notably Japan, the adjustment does change the level markedly, reflecting the large proportion of women in all sectors: an allowance similar to that made in line 55 for 1920 would bring the share of the A sector in 1872 down to less than 75 percent. But by and large, the adjustment does not modify the findings significantly, and we can concentrate on columns 1–3.

(a) The initial share of the A sector in the presently developed countries, before entry into modern economic growth, was fairly high, ranging in most cases (France, Belgium, Germany, Denmark, Norway, Italy, the United States, Canada) from 50 to 65 percent; it was distinctly lower in Great Britain, the Netherlands, and Australia, and higher in Sweden, Finland, and Japan. Since the cross-section in Table 29 shows that the share of the A sector at the lowest benchmark level was as high as 80 percent, and only declined

249

Table 38. Long-term changes in shares of major sectors in labor force.

	Shares in total labor force (%)			% of women in total labor force	Shares in adjusted labor force (%)		
	A (1)	I (2)	S (3)	(4)	A (5)	I (6)	S (7)
Great Britain							
1. 1801/11	34.4	30.0[a]	35.6[a]	—	—	—	—
2. 1851/61	20.2	43.2[a]	36.6[a]	—	—	—	—
3. 1851/61	21.6	56.9	21.5	30.5	23.0	5.89	18.1
4. 1921	9.1	58.8	32.1	29.4	9.8	61.8	28.4
5. 1921	7.2	56.9	35.9	29.5	7.7	59.2	33.1
6. 1961	3.7	55.0	41.3	30.8	3.9	58.8	37.3
7. Change, 1851/61 to 1961	−16.0	0	+16.0	+0.2	−17.0	+2.5	+14.5
France							
8. 1856	51.7	28.5	19.8	31.2	48.2	31.5	20.3
9. 1962	20.0	43.6	36.4	33.4	17.6	47.1	35.3
10. Change, 1856 to 1962	−31.7	+15.1	+16.6	+2.2	−30.6	+15.6	+15.0
Belgium							
11. 1846	50.9	37.1	12.0	36.7	47.5	39.2	13.3
12. 1964	5.9	52.4	41.7	30.8	5.6	55.8	38.6
13. Change, 1846 to 1964	−45.0	+15.3	+29.7	−5.9	−41.9	+16.6	+25.3
Netherlands							
14. 1849	45.4	29.4	25.2	29.5	41.8	33.3	24.9
15. 1960	11.0	50.5	38.5	22.3	11.2	53.3	35.5
16. Change, 1849 to 1960	−34.4	+21.1	+13.3	−7.2	−30.6	+20.0	+10.6
Germany							
17. 1852/55/58	54.1	26.8	19.1	—	—	—	—
18. 1882	48.4	31.7	19.9	—	—	—	—
19. 1882	47.3	38.5	14.2	24.2	42.2	42.7	15.1
20. 1907	37.1	45.0	17.9	30.7	28.8	52.1	19.1
Interwar boundaries							
21. 1925	30.7	46.5	22.8	35.9	23.0	53.7	23.3
22. 1939	26.0	47.7	26.3	37.1	18.3	54.7	27.0
Federal Republic							
23. 1946	29.3	44.5	26.2	36.7	21.7	51.8	26.5
24. 1964	11.3	54.6	34.1	36.4	7.9	59.3	32.8
25. Change, from 1882 over periods shown	−32.9	+17.8	+15.1	+7.4	−31.9	+17.9	+14.0
Switzerland							
26. 1880	42.4	45.5	12.1	32.2	40.4	47.1	12.5
27. 1960	11.2	55.9	32.9	30.1	11.9	58.5	29.6
28. Change, 1880 to 1960	−31.2	+10.4	+20.8	−2.1	−28.5	+11.4	+17.1
Denmark							
29. 1874–75	51.1	48.9		—	—	—	—
30. 1912	39.2	60.8		—	—	—	—

Table 38 — continued

	(1)	(2)	(3)	(4)	(5)	(6)	(7)
31. 1911	43.1	29.4	27.5	31.3	42.5	32.1	25.4
32. 1960	17.8	44.5	37.7	30.9	19.0	47.1	33.9
33. Change, 1911							
to 1960	−25.3	+15.1	+10.2	−0.4	−23.5	+15.0	+8.5
Norway							
34. 1865	63.7	19.9	16.4	—	—	—	—
35. 1890	49.9	29.5	20.6	—	—	—	—
36. 1891	50.1	23.2[a]	26.7[a]	31.6	49.5	24.8[a]	25.7[a]
37. 1920	37.0	37.6	25.4	27.8	37.7	40.4	21.9
		(29.0[a])	(34.0[a])			(30.8[a])	(31.5[a])
38. 1960	19.6	48.6	31.8	22.9	20.8	50.9	28.3
39. Change, 1891							
to 1960	−30.5	+16.8	+13.7	−8.7	−28.7	+16.5	+12.2
Sweden							
40. 1860	64.0	18.8	17.2	24.0	61.7	21.8	16.5
		(16.8[a])	(19.2[a])			(19.4[a])	(18.9[a])
41. 1870	75.7	9.5[a]	14.8[a]	31.9	72.5	11.7[a]	15.8[a]
42. 1910	48.3	32.2	19.5	27.8	45.6	36.1	18.3
43. 1960	13.8	52.7	33.5	30.7	14.7	55.9	29.4
44. Change, 1860							
to 1960	−50.2	+33.9	+16.3	+6.7	−47.0	+34.1	+12.9
Finland							
45. 1880	71.2	13.3	15.5	28.6	68.8	15.4	15.8
46. 1960	35.6	37.8	26.6	39.4	32.2	42.8	25.0
47. Change, 1880							
to 1960	−35.6	+24.5	+11.1	+10.8	−36.6	+27.4	+9.2
Italy							
48. 1861/71	57.5	25.8	16.7	—	—	—	—
49. 1881/1901	56.4	28.1	15.5	—	—	—	—
50. 1881/1901	58.4	28.7	12.9	35.8	54.2	31.5	14.3
51. 1964	25.2	46.4	28.4	28.0	21.7	49.9	28.4
52. Change, 1881/							
1901 to 1964	−33.2	+17.7	+15.5	−7.8	−32.5	+18.4	+14.1
Japan							
53. 1872	85.8	5.6	8.6	—	—	—	—
54. 1900	71.1	15.7	13.2	—	—	—	—
55. 1920	54.6	25.4	20.0	37.6	47.0	30.3	22.7
56. 1964	27.6	37.4	35.0	40.3	20.4	42.7	36.9
57. Change, 1872							
to 1920	−31.2	+19.8	+11.4	—	—	—	—
58. Change, 1920							
to 1964	−27.0	+12.0	+15.0	+2.7	−26.6	+12.4	+14.2
Canada							
59. 1871	52.9	47.1		—	—	—	—
60. 1911	37.2	62.8		—	—	—	—
61. 1911	37.1	37.4	25.5	13.4	38.8	37.9	23.3
62. 1965	9.5	41.1	49.4	29.0	10.1	43.8	46.1
63. Change, 1911							
to 1965	−27.6	+3.7	+23.9	+15.6	−28.7	+5.9	+22.8
United States							
64. 1810	83.7	16.3		—	—	—	—
65. 1840	63.4	36.6		—	—	—	—

Table 38 — continued

	(1)	(2)	(3)	(4)	(5)	(6)	(7)
66. 1839	64.3	16.2	19.5	—	—	—	—
67. 1869/79	50.0	29.0	21.0	—	—	—	—
68. 1869/79	48.6	29.0	22.4	14.9	—	—	—
				(1870/80)			
69. 1929	21.2	38.0	40.8	21.9	—	—	—
				(1930)			
70. 1929	19.9	38.8	41.3	21.9	—	—	—
				(1930)			
71. 1965	5.7	38.0	56.3	32.8	—	—	—
				(1962)			
72. Change, 1839							
to 1965	−55.9	+21.0	+34.9	+17.9	—	—	—
				(1870/80			
				to 1962)			

Australia

73. 1861	29.5	70.5		—	—	—	—
74. 1901	25.1	74.9		—	—	—	—
75. 1901	33.0	33.9	33.1	21.7	34.3	35.3	30.4
76. 1961	11.1	48.9	40.0	25.1	11.5	51.3	37.2
77. Change, 1901							
to 1961	−21.9	+15.0	+6.9	+3.4	−22.8	+16.0	+6.8

New Zealand

78. 1896	37.0	34.5	28.5	18.1	39.1	35.2	25.7
79. 1961	14.5	46.8	38.7	25.1	15.1	49.0	35.9
80. Change, 1896							
to 1961	−22.5	+12.3	+10.2	+7.0	−24.0	+13.8	+10.2

Spain

81. 1877	70.5	15.5	14.0	20.4	69.3	17.0	13.7
82. 1964	34.9	40.1	25.0	23.3	33.5	42.4	24.1
83. Change, 1877							
to 1964	−35.6	+24.6	+11.0	+2.9	−35.8	+25.4	+10.4

Argentina

84. 1895	39.6	28.0	32.4	—	—	—	—
85. 1960	21.4	43.1	35.5	22.6	22.2	44.8	33.0
86. Change, 1895							
to 1960	−18.2	+15.1	+3.1	—	—	—	—

Chile

87. 1920	38.9	35.3	25.8	26.1	40.8	34.8	24.4
88. 1960	29.6	35.4	35.0	22.4	31.7	36.9	31.4
89. Change, 1920							
to 1960	−9.3	+0.1	+9.2	−3.7	−9.1	+2.1	+7.0

Colombia

90. 1925	68.5	16.0	15.5	—	—	—	—
91. 1962	44.6	26.8	28.6	—	—	—	—
92. Change, 1925							
to 1962	−23.9	+10.8	+13.1	—	—	—	—

Mexico

93. 1910	64.7	14.4	20.9	16.9	68.6	13.8	17.6
94. 1960	54.6	22.3	23.1	18.0	55.1	23.5	21.4
95. Change, 1910							
to 1960	−10.1	+7.9	+2.2	+1.1	−13.5	+9.7	+3.8

Table 38 — continued

		(1)	(2)	(3)	(4)	(5)	(6)	(7)
Egypt								
96. 1907		71.2	14.1	14.7	4.8	71.0	14.3	14.7
97. 1960		58.3	15.6	26.1	7.9	58.0	16.1	25.9
98. Change, 1907								
to 1960		−12.9	+1.5	+11.4	+3.1	−13.0	+1.8	+11.2
Philippines								
99. 1939		72.9	13.9	13.2	30.9	70.9	15.4	13.7
100. 1962		61.6	17.2	21.2	36.4	60.9	18.5	20.6
101. Change, 1939								
to 1962		−11.3	+3.3	+8.0	+5.5	−10.0	+3.1	+6.9
India								
102. 1881		74.4	14.6	11.0	30.9	74.4[b]	13.8[b]	11.8[b]
103. 1951		76.1	12.0	11.9	23.4	72.9[b]	13.6[b]	13.5[b]
104. 1951		77.4	9.9	12.7	29.2	72.7[b]	12.2[b]	15.1[b]
105. 1961		73.5	13.1	13.4	31.5	69.1[b]	14.9[b]	16.0[b]
106. Change, 1881								
to 1961		−2.2	+0.6	+1.6	−5.2	−5.1[b]	+2.5[b]	+2.6[b]
Ceylon								
107. 1881		68.2	14.0	17.8	—	—	—	—
108. 1953		56.7	17.2	26.1	24.2	52.6	18.9	28.5
109. Change, 1881								
to 1953		−11.5	+3.2	+8.3	—	—	—	—

—: information not available.

[a] The I sector excludes and the S sector includes transport, storage, and communication.

[b] Male labor force only.

When years in the stubs are connected by a slash (/), data are for the single years indicated; when connected by a dash (–), they are for all the years in the interval.

The adjusted shares in columns 5–7 were derived by weighting the number of women in the A sector by 0.2, and those in other sectors by 0.6 (see notes to Table 4, and text discussion in Chapter V).

Unless otherwise indicated, the underlying data are from P. Bairoch and others, *International Historical Statistics*, vol. 1, *The Working Population and Its Structure* (Brussels: Institut de Sociologie de l'Université Libre de Bruxelles, 1968), based in turn on the censuses of the respective countries and subsidiary sources. Whenever there is significant discontinuity in the available series, the shares for the overlapping years are given (for example, for Great Britain, lines 2–3, and 4–5); and the total change is the sum of changes within the two (or more) intervals. The notes that follow indicate other sources that were used.

Lines 1–2: Phyllis Deane and W. A. Cole, *British Economic Growth, 1688–1959*, 2nd. ed. (Cambridge: Cambridge University Press, 1967), table 30, p. 142.

Lines 17–18: Walther G. Hoffmann, *Das Wachstum der Deutschen Wirtschaft seit der Mitte des 19. Jahrhunderts* (Berlin: Springer Verlag, 1965), table 20, pp. 204–206.

Lines 29–30: Kjeld Bjerke and Niels Ussing, *Studier over Danmarks Nationalprodukt, 1870–1950* (Copenhagen: G. E. C. Gads, 1958), table I, pp. 142–143.

Lines 34–35: Central Bureau of Statistics, *Trends in Norwegian Economy, 1865–1960*, no. 16 of *Samfunnsøkonomiske Studier* (Oslo, 1966), table 21, p. 54.

Lines 48–49: Census data summarized in Associazione per lo Sviluppo dell'Industria nel Mezzogiorno (SVIMEZ), *Statistische sul Mezzogiorno d'Italia, 1861–1953* (Rome, 1954), tables 45–46, pp. 39–41.

Lines 59–60: O. J. Firestone, *Canada's Economic Development, 1867–1953* (London: Bowes and Bowes, 1958), tables 65–66, pp. 184–185. For 1871 we assumed that fishing and trapping and forest operations were in the same proportion to agriculture as in 1881.

Lines 64–65: Paul David, "The Growth of Real Product in the United States Before 1840," *Journal of Economic History*, vol. XXVII, no. 2 (June 1967), table 4, p. 166.

Lines 66–67: Share of the S sector is estimated from Robert E. Gallman and Thomas J. Weiss, "The Service Industries in the Nineteenth Century," in Victor R. Fuchs, ed., *Production and Productivity in the Service Industries*, vol. 34 of *Studies in Income and Wealth* (New York: Columbia University Press for the National Bureau of Economic Research, 1969), tables 6, 9, pp. 299, 303. The remainder, that is, the A and I sectors, was apportioned (by subdivisions) in accordance with the estimates by Stanley Lebergott in "Labor Force and Employment, 1800–1960," in Dorothy Brady, ed., *Output, Employment, and Productivity in the United States after 1800*, vol. 30 of *Studies in Income and Wealth* (New York: Columbia University Press for the National Bureau of Economic Research, 1966), table 1, p. 118.

Lines 68–69: Columns 1–3 are based on John W. Kendrick, *Productivity Trends in the United States* (Princeton: Princeton University Press for the National Bureau of Economic Research, 1961), table A-VII, p. 308. For column 4 here and in lines 70–71, data are from the Bureau of the Census, *Historical Statistics of the United States, Colonial Times to 1957* (Washington, D.C., 1961), and *Historical Statistics, Colonial Times to 1957, Continuation to 1962 and Revisions* (Washington, D.C., 1965), series D 13–25, D 36–45, shares in labor force extrapolated back by shares in gainfully occupied.

Lines 70–71: Department of Commerce, *The National Income and Product Accounts of the United States, 1929–1965: A Supplement to the Survey of Current Business* (Washington, D.C., 1966), table 6.6, pp. 110–113.

Lines 73–74: The sum of estimates for 1861 to 1891 for Victoria, South Australia, New South Wales, and Queensland, from N. G. Butlin, *Investment in Australian Economic Development, 1861–1900* (Cambridge: Cambridge University Press, 1964), table 40, p. 194; carried forward to 1901 by estimates of labor force (excluding women in agriculture) given in Colin Clark, *Conditions of Economic Progress*, 3rd. ed. (London: Macmillan, 1957), table III, pp. 510 ff.

Line 84: United Nations, Economic Commission for Latin America, *Estudio sobre la Mano de Obra en América Latina*, mimeographed copy prepared for the Commission meeting at La Paz, May 1957, table A-VIII-1, p. 236; table A-XI-2, p. 312, and table XII-14, p. 342. The estimates are comparable with those in line 85.

Lines 90–91: The entry for 1925 is from ECLA, *Análisis y Proyecciones del Desarrollo Económico: III. El Desarrollo de Colombia* (Santiago, 1956), table 4, p. 17; for 1962 as reported in International Labour Office, *Yearbook of Labour Statistics, 1965* (Geneva, n.d.).

Lines 102–103: Alice Thorner, "The Secular Trend in the Indian Economy, 1881–1951," *Economic Weekly* (Bombay, June 1962), table 8, p. 1164, and table 9, p. 1165. The 1881 estimate is based on the breakdown (of non-A sectors) for four major states; and general labor is included with the A sector.

Line 107: Donald R. Snodgrass, *Ceylon: An Export Economy in Transition*, Economic Growth Center of Yale University (Homewood, Ill.: Richard Irwin, 1966), table A-26, pp. 322–323. The estimates are comparable with those in line 108.

to about 65 percent at the $150 benchmark level, one may conclude that for most developed countries, the initial share was already somewhat lower than in many less developed countries today, a finding consistent with their generally higher initial per capita product. This is unlike the finding for product, that the shares of the A sector in the presently developed countries on the eve of their industrialization were as high as those of the lower per capita product countries today (see Chapter IV).

The share of the A sector in the labor force in many of the developed countries may have declined well before their entry into modern economic growth. This was presumably true for Great Britain in the eighteenth century and the Netherlands, and is suggested by the conjectural estimates for the United States for 1810–1840. For the older European countries (Great Britain, the Netherlands, Italy, and perhaps France and Germany), the initially moderate share of the A sector in labor force, like their initially higher per capita product, may have been a cumulative result of premodern "industrialization," that is, of a capacity to utilize nonagricultural activities (manufacturing, shipping, or foreign trade) and thereby to increase total product per capita, if not necessarily the shares of the non-A sectors in product.

(b) The share of the A sector in labor force declined in all countries, in most by substantial fractions. The prevalence of minus signs in the appropriate lines indicates that this movement is widespread, reaching even into the less developed countries. One should also note that in Australia, where the share of the A sector in product did not decline until the recent decades, census figures show that the share in labor force began to drop sharply early in the twentieth century.

There are, however, some interesting exceptions. Data in the original source indicate that in Italy the share declined significantly only after 1921; yet the share of the A sector in total product, in constant prices, declined from over 46 percent in 1861–1870 to 42 percent in 1891–1900. More important, in several less developed countries, the share of the A sector in labor force declined, if at all, only in recent years. Thus, the figures for intervening years (not given in the table) indicate that it dropped only slightly in India from 1881 to 1961 and in Ceylon between 1881 and 1921; in Egypt it even increased slightly between 1907 and 1937. This stability of the share in labor force over these long periods is particularly significant since in some less developed countries the share of the A sector in product declined.

(c) In all the developed countries, and in those less developed that show a significant decline in the share of the A sector in labor force, the shares of both the I and S sectors rose. The rise in the share of the I sector in labor force was consistent and quite sizable, both absolutely and relatively. In view of the equally prevalent and sizable rise in the share of the I sector in product, this pattern in the share in labor force should have been expected. Less expected is the limited rise in the share of the I sector in comparison with the decline in the share of the A sector. In Great Britain (back to the mid-nineteenth century), Belgium, Switzerland, Canada, and the United States, the share of the I sector rises much less than the share of the S sector; and in France, Denmark, Norway, and New Zealand, the rises in both are fairly close to each other. Thus, the dominance of the I sector found for the shares in product is not found here: it does not offset most of the decline in the share of the A sector.

(d) The rise in the share of the S sector in the labor force is quite widespread, and in contrast with the absence of a consistent upward trend in its share in product. The rise may seem suspect because of possible understatement of the share at earlier dates. But such understatement would also affect the share in product, so we may accept the finding as fairly valid. The rises are especially striking in several developed countries — France, Belgium, Switzerland, Finland, Italy, the United States, Canada, and New Zealand. Even in some of the less developed countries — Colombia, Egypt, the Philippines, and Ceylon — the share of the S sector rises more than that of the I sector. Apparently, some major factors — possibly the difficulty of substituting capital for labor in the S sector in the developed countries, and the use of the S sector as a refuge for the inadequately employed labor force in the less developed countries — produced these significant shifts in the labor force toward the S sector in many countries in both groups.

Two aspects of the findings in Table 38 merit emphasis. The first relates to the speed with which the structural changes occurred, particularly the decline in the share of the A sector in labor force, and the corresponding rise in the shares of other sectors. With the typical movement over a century to a century and a quarter in the share of the A sector from between 50 and 65 percent to about 10 percent or less, the trend must have been much more conspicuous than it could have been in the preceding centuries. If the maximum share of the A sector in the labor force is set at 80 percent, which is certainly realistic for the older countries of Europe, the decline to 50 to 65 percent on the eve of entry into modern economic growth meant a downward movement of some 15 to 30 percentage points over several centuries — not 40 to 55 percentage points over little more than a century. In this respect — the acceleration of structural change associated with modern economic growth — labor force and product agree.

The second aspect is relevant particularly to sectoral shares in labor force. A decline in the share of the A sector from, say, 60 to 10 percent over a century means that, with the total labor force growing, say, 1 percent per year (about the same as total population), or by a factor of 2.71 in a century, the labor force in the A sector declined from (0.60 × 100), or 60, to (0.10 × 271), or 27.1, while the labor force in the non-A sectors grew from 40 to roughly 244, or more than sextupled. Of course, these differences are similar to those in the growth rates of the *products* of the A and non-A sectors. But labor force, which is a substantial and relatively constant part of total population, has a natural rate of increase, whereas product does not; and this natural rate of increase of the labor force is determined by forces that are not necessarily responsive to the differential opportunities of economic growth. For example, despite smaller demand for rural than for urban labor force, the rate of natural increase of rural population, and hence of the A labor force, is no lower than that of urban population. Since the growth differentials within modern economic growth among industries, occupations, and the like, are so much greater than the disparities in rates of natural increase among sizable population groups, it is obvious that the latter cannot be fully responsive to the former.

In fact, over the decades of modern economic growth, rates of natural increase (the balance of births over deaths) have been consistently higher for the rural than for the urban population — largely because of higher birth rates, and partly (in the earlier periods) because of lower death rates.[1] There was thus a conflict between the natural growth differentials for the population groups associated with the different sectors and the differentials in growth of employment opportunities in these sectors. This conflict was hardly an accident insofar as delay in the decline of birth rates was partly associated with delay in the spread of modern economic growth to the countryside. Its significance for many aspects of economic growth cannot be exaggerated. It brought about vast streams of migration, not only internal, from the countryside to the cities in the developed countries, but also to the developed

---

1. See Simon Kuznets, *Modern Economic Growth: Rate, Structure, and Spread* (New Haven: Yale University Press, 1966), pp. 120–127, for illustrative evidence and a brief discussion of the implications.

countries overseas. It brought about a dissociation between status by family origin and employment opportunities within the economic system. It created incentives for intragenerational changes in industrial and occupational attachment, and even more for intergenerational movements — with all the consequences in the way of generation gaps, economic and social mobility even without spatial mobility, and a cleavage between generations that eventually reduced the authoritarian position of the older generations in modern society. This shift in sectoral structure of the labor force, combined with the demographic trends and differentials in rates of natural increase, had vast consequences for conditions of life, institutions, and the prevailing views of the populations of developed countries that proved to be the dominant factor in changing the consumption structure, the social structure, and even the ideology of society.

The two general comments just made stress the decline in the share of the A sector and the rise of the other sectoral shares in labor force. Obviously, they also apply to the shifts between the I and S sectors, and to movements among subdivisions within each. The conspicuously accelerated rises in the shares of the I and S sectors must also have characterized the shares of at least some of their subdivisions. A more detailed industrial classification would reveal the meteoric rise of some completely new branches of production — and the equally striking decline of some older branches that were rapidly displaced by innovations. Differences in rates of natural increase are found not only between the rural and urban populations, but also among cities of differing size; and indeed among large groups of occupations. These demographic differentials are not closely associated with differentials in growth of employment opportunities generated in the course of modern economic growth, and are not nearly as large. The resulting disparities between demographic and economic growth differentials mean internal migration, and intra- and intergenerational mobility even within the non-A sectors. In observing the shifts among the shares of the subdivisions of the I and S sectors in labor force, we must bear in mind the implications for internal mobility of labor and population (and for the movement of other production factors).

Changes in Shares: Subdivisions of the I and S Sectors

Table 39 sheds some light on the sources of the relatively limited rise in the share of the I sector in labor force. Like its share in

Table 39. Long-term changes in shares of subdivisions of the I sector in labor force, adjusted for women in A and other sectors, developed countries (percentages).

	Mining (1)	Manufacturing (2)	Construction (3)	Transportation and communication, electricity, gas, and water (4)	Total I (5)
Great Britain					
1. 1851/61	5.2	40.6	6.7	6.4	58.9
2. 1921	8.7	35.9	6.2	11.0	61.8
3. 1921	8.4	35.8	4.7	10.3	59.2
4. 1961	3.6	37.3	8.1	9.8	58.8
5. Change, 1851/61 to 1961	−1.3	−3.2	+2.9	+4.1	+2.5
France					
6. 1856	1.6[a]	23.0	5.0	1.9	31.5
7. 1962	3.0[a]	28.4	9.7	6.0	47.1
8. Change, 1856 to 1962	+1.4	+5.4	+4.7	+4.1	+15.6
Belgium					
9. 1846	3.0	32.6[b]	2.6	1.0	39.2
10. 1964	3.2	36.3[b]	8.7	7.6	55.8
11. Change, 1846 to 1964	+0.2	+3.7	+6.1	+6.6	+16.6
Netherlands					
12. 1849	0.2	21.5	5.9	5.7	33.3
13. 1960	1.6	32.5	10.2	9.0	53.3
14. Change, 1849 to 1960	+1.4	+11.0	+4.3	+3.3	+20.0
Germany (changing boundaries)					
15. 1882	4.0	29.4	6.4	2.9	42.7
16. 1907	5.7	32.9	8.8	4.7	52.1
17. 1925	5.0	35.4	6.7	6.6	53.7
18. 1939	2.6	36.9	8.5	6.7	54.7
19. 1946	4.2	31.9	7.6	8.1	51.8
20. 1961	3.4	39.6	9.2	7.3	59.5
21. Change, from 1882 over periods shown	−1.5	+12.7	+5.8	+1.1	+18.1

Table 39 — continued

	(1)	(2)	(3)	(4)	(5)
Norway					
22. 1920	1.7	23.9ᵉ	5.2ᵉ	9.6	40.4
23. 1960	0.7	26.2	10.4	13.6	50.9
24. Change, 1920 to 1960	−1.0	+2.3	+5.2	+4.0	+10.5
Italy					
25. 1936	0.8	22.9	6.5	5.0	35.2
26. 1964	0.8	29.4	12.9	6.8	49.9
27. Change, 1936 to 1964	0	+6.5	+6.4	+1.8	+14.7
Japan					
28. 1920	1.9	19.2	3.6	5.6	30.3
29. 1964	0.8	27.0	7.5	7.4	42.7
30. Change, 1920 to 1964	−1.1	+7.8	+3.9	+1.8	+12.4
United States (unadjusted labor force)					
31. 1839	0.6	8.9	5.2	1.5	16.2
32. 1869/79	1.5	18.2	5.3	4.0	29.0
33. 1869/79	1.6	17.8	4.5	5.1	29.0
34. 1929	2.2	22.2	5.0	8.6	38.0
35. 1929	2.2	22.8	5.0	8.8	38.8
36. 1965	0.9	25.9	5.6	5.6	38.0
37. Change, 1839 to 1965	+0.2	+16.8	+1.2	+2.8	+21.0

ᵃ Electricity, gas, and water included with mining.

ᵇ Electricity, gas, and water included with manufacturing.

ᵉ 1920 apportionment between manufacturing and construction based on that for 1930.

When years in the stubs are connected by a slash (/), data are for the single years indicated; when connected by a dash (–), they are for all the years in the interval.

For sources and procedure, see notes to Table 38.

product, the share of mining in labor force is small and its movement is dependent upon the weight of the subdivision at the early dates. If mining is relatively important to begin with, say 2 percent or more, its share tends to decline; if it is small to begin with, its share may rise. At any rate, mining is too small to have much of an effect on the trend in the share of the I sector as a whole.

The key to the moderate rise in the latter lies mostly in manufacturing and partly in the transport, communication, and public utility subdivision. In five of the nine countries — Great Britain (from 1921 to 1961), France, Belgium, Norway, and Italy — the share of manufacturing accounted for much less than half of the total rise of the I sector. Since manufacturing dominated the I sector at the start, accounting for at least six-tenths, it is obvious that in these countries the relative employment opportunities in manufacturing did not rise much despite its rapid growth. Even in some of those countries (such as the Netherlands and Japan) in which the rise in the share of manufacturing was more impressive, it was not relatively as large as the rise in the share of construction or of transport and public utilities.

The share of the transport, communication, and public utilities subdivision declined in Great Britain from 1921 to 1961 and rose slightly in Germany, Italy, and the United States. Yet in some countries the rise was quite substantial. One might expect that, as in the case of manufacturing, the marked rise in productivity in the transport and public utility subdivision would mean a moderate rise in the share in labor force associated with a substantial rise in the share in product. But there is diversity in the record.

The share of the construction subdivision in labor force shows the most consistent substantial rises. This may be a reflection of the failure of productivity to rise as much as in the other subdivisions. Because of this failure, a substantial rise in the share in product would be accompanied by a large rise in the share in labor force. The only exception in our limited sample is the United States, where, because of the marked retardation in the rate of population growth, the share of construction in labor force rose slightly (and its share in product declined slightly; see Table 22).

Keeping in mind the reason for the moderate rise in the share of manufacturing in labor force, let us glance at the trends in shares of branches of manufacturing (Table 40). Here the estimates of total labor force and of labor force in manufacturing were adjusted for number of women in the A and other sectors for only a few countries. But the broad results are not affected by the adjustment.

The differences among the branches with respect to trends in the share in labor force — the fairly general declines in the shares of textiles and clothing, and of wood and other products, and the fairly general rises in the shares of metals, chemicals, and food products — are to be expected. These contrasts are far more conspicuous than

Table 40. Long-term changes in shares of branches of manufacturing in labor force, unadjusted and adjusted for women in A and other sectors, developed countries (percentages).

	Total manufacturing (1)	Food, beverages, and tobacco (2)	Textiles and clothing (3)	Wood products (4)	Paper and printing (5)	Chemicals and petroleum products (6)	Nonmetal minerals (7)	Metal products (8)	Miscellaneous, leather, and rubber (9)
Great Britain									
Unadjusted labor force									
1. 1851	40.9	4.5	25.0	1.8	0.9	0.5	1.0	6.5	0.7
2. 1921	35.9	2.1	12.3	3.3	1.9	0.8	0.9	14.0	0.6
3. 1921	36.1	3.3	11.5	1.6	2.1	1.1	1.3	13.3	1.9
4. 1961	36.1	3.1	5.8	1.3	2.6	2.1	1.4	18.3	1.5
5. Change, 1851 to 1961	−5.0	−2.6	−18.4	+1.2	+1.5	+1.3	0	+12.5	−0.5
Adjusted labor force									
6. 1851	40.6	5.0	22.9	2.0	0.9	0.6	1.1	7.3	0.8
7. 1921	35.9	2.1	10.4	3.7	1.9	0.8	0.9	15.5	0.6
8. 1921	35.8	3.2	9.9	1.8	2.1	1.2	1.3	15.8	0.5
9. 1961	37.3	3.0	5.1	1.4	2.6	2.2	1.5	21.2	0.3
10. Change, 1851 to 1961	−3.2	−3.1	−17.3	+1.3	+1.5	+1.2	0	+13.6	−0.4
France									
Unadjusted labor force									
11. 1866	23.1	2.0	11.3	3.9	0.4	0.2	—	3.1	2.2
12. 1962	27.3	2.8	4.7	1.2	1.7	2.1	1.0	12.0	1.8
13. Change, 1866 to 1962	+4.2	+0.8	−6.6	−2.7	+1.3	+1.9	—	+8.9	+0.6[a]

Adjusted labor force									
14. 1866	24.4	2.3	10.6	4.5	0.5	0.2	—	3.7	2.6
15. 1962	28.4	2.9	4.1	1.3	1.7	2.2	1.2	13.3	1.7
16. Change, 1866 to 1962	+4.0	+0.6	−6.5	−3.2	+1.2	+2.0	—	+9.6	+0.3[a]
Belgium									
Unadjusted labor force									
17. 1846	31.8	1.8	23.5	2.3	0.3	0.1	0.4	2.9	0.5
18. 1961	36.5 (35.7)	4.1	8.3	1.8	1.8	3.1	2.2	13.6	1.6
19. Change, 1846 to 1961	+4.7	+2.3	−15.2	−0.5	+1.5	+3.0	+1.8	+10.7	+1.1
Adjusted labor force									
20. 1846	32.6	2.3	22.1	2.9	0.4	0.2	0.5	3.6	0.6
21. 1961	37.3	4.2	7.4	2.0	1.9	3.3	2.3	14.6	1.6
22. Change, 1846 to 1961	+4.7	+1.9	−14.7	−0.9	+1.5	+3.1	+1.8	+11.0	+1.0
Netherlands									
Unadjusted labor force									
23. 1849	21.0	1.9	10.5	1.8	0.5	0.2	0.4	3.2	2.5
24. 1947	28.2	4.9	6.5	1.8	1.6	1.1	1.0	9.7	1.6
25. 1953	27.1	5.1	6.1	1.3	1.8	1.5	1.2	9.0	1.1
26. 1963	31.3	5.1	5.6	1.5	2.5	2.3	1.3	11.6	1.4
27. Change, above periods	+11.4	+3.0	−4.5	+0.2	+1.8	+1.7	+0.7	+9.1	−0.6
Adjusted labor force									
28. 1849	22.6	2.3	10.1	2.1	0.6	0.3	0.5	3.7	3.0
29. 1947	29.8	5.3	6.0	2.0	1.7	1.2	1.1	10.8	1.7
30. Change, 1849 to 1947	+7.2	+3.0	−4.1	−0.1	+1.1	+0.9	+0.6	+7.1	−1.3

Table 40 — continued

	(1)	(2)	(3)	(4)	(5)	(6)	(7)	(8)	(9)
Germany (changing boundaries)									
Unadjusted labor force									
31. 1849/52/55	21.5	3.4	11.0	2.5	0.3	0.2	1.1	2.5	0.5
32. 1882	25.3	3.8	11.0	2.7	0.8	0.4	1.9	4.0	0.7
33. 1882	27.2	3.9	11.7	3.0	0.9	0.3	0.4	6.2	0.8
34. 1907	29.4	4.2	9.3	3.0	1.5	0.9	0.7	8.1	1.7
35. 1946	28.3	3.4	6.0	3.0	1.0	1.2	—	9.9	3.8
36. 1961	37.1	4.0	5.7	2.3	1.8	2.5	1.4	15.8	3.6
37. Change, above periods	+14.8	+1.3	−2.7	−0.5	+1.9	+2.1	—	+9.3	+3.4[a]
Denmark									
Unadjusted labor force									
38. 1911	19.7	4.1	7.0	1.8	0.9	0.5	0.9	3.9	0.6
39. 1950	26.4	4.9	5.4	2.2	1.7	0.9	1.3	7.5	2.5
40. 1953	26.4	5.0	5.7	2.2	1.9	1.2	1.3	7.8	1.3
41. 1963	30.6	6.2	4.0	3.0	2.8	1.2	1.5	10.5	1.4
42. Change, above periods	+10.9	+2.0	−3.3	+1.2	+1.7	+0.4	+0.6	+6.3	+2.0
Norway									
Unadjusted labor force									
43. 1900	21.4	1.8	8.4	3.9	1.5	0.3	0.8	3.8	0.9
44. 1930	20.4	2.9	5.1	3.1	2.4	1.0	0.5	5.0	0.4
45. 1930	16.3	2.4	4.3	1.7	2.2	0.8	0.9	3.7	0.3
46. 1960	23.9	3.5	3.5	2.2	3.2	1.6	0.9	8.2	0.8
47. Change, 1900 to 1960	+6.6	+2.2	−4.1	−0.3	+1.9	+1.5	−0.3	+5.7	0

Sweden

Unadjusted labor force

48. 1910	24.0	2.1	4.8	4.1	1.5	0.5	1.9	5.6	3.5
49. 1950	34.3	3.3	5.7	3.3	3.2	1.2	1.7	13.7	2.2
50. 1953	32.4	3.4	6.0	3.1	3.7	1.2	1.5	12.3	1.2
51. 1963	33.0	2.8	3.8	2.7	3.7	1.2	1.3	15.8	1.7
52. Change, above periods	+10.9	+0.6	−1.3	−1.2	+1.7	+0.7	−0.4	+11.6	−0.8

Finland

Unadjusted labor force

53. 1920	12.4	0.8	2.8	3.8	1.7	0.1	0.4	1.6	1.2
54. 1950	21.0	2.4	4.3	3.5	2.9	0.6	1.1	5.3	0.9
55. 1953	21.2	2.4	4.4	3.3	3.0	0.6	1.0	5.6	0.9
56. 1963	21.8	2.7	3.6	3.0	3.3	0.8	1.0	6.5	0.9
57. Change, above periods	+9.2	+1.9	+0.7	−0.6	+1.5	+0.7	+0.7	+4.6	−0.3

Japan

Unadjusted labor force

58. 1920	15.8	1.3	6.5	2.4	0.8	0.5	0.8	3.2	0.2
59. 1960	21.7	2.1	4.1	1.9	1.6	1.6	1.1	7.8	1.4
60. Change, 1920 to 1960	+5.9	+0.8	−2.4	−0.5	+0.8	+1.1	+0.3	+4.6	+1.2

Canada

Unadjusted labor force

61. 1871	13.2	1.1	1.8	3.7	0.4	0.3	0.6	3.2	2.1
62. 1911	20.0	2.9	3.3	4.6	1.3	0.6	0.8	5.1	1.4

Table 40 — continued

	(1)	(2)	(3)	(4)	(5)	(6)	(7)	(8)	(9)
63. 1951	26.4	3.8	4.1	2.7	3.1	1.3	0.7	9.0	1.7
64. 1953	25.6	3.6	4.2	2.6	2.9	1.3	0.6	9.1	1.3
65. 1963	25.7	3.9	3.7	2.2	3.0	1.4	0.8	9.1	1.6
66. Change, above periods	+13.3	+3.0	+1.8	−1.4	+2.8	+1.1	+0.3	+5.8	−0.1
United States									
Unadjusted labor force									
67. 1849	14.7	1.0	4.9	1.7	0.4	0.3	0.5	2.9	3.0
68. 1879	18.8	2.2	5.4	2.3	0.9	0.5	1.0	4.4	2.1
69. 1899	20.0	2.2	4.5	3.1	1.5	0.7	1.1	5.2	1.7
70. 1929	22.2	2.3	4.3	2.2	2.0	1.1	0.9	7.6	1.8
71. 1929	22.8	2.6	4.4	2.3	2.0	1.1	0.9	7.7	1.8
72. 1965	25.9	2.6	3.2	1.6	2.4	1.5	0.9	11.9	1.8
73. Change, above periods	+9.4	+1.3	−0.9	−1.0	+1.4	+1.0	+0.3	+8.1	−0.8
Australia									
Unadjusted labor force									
74. 1911–13	19.6	3.1	5.3	3.4	1.5	0.5	b	5.1	0.7
75. 1953 (F)	28.1	3.6	5.4	3.4	1.6	1.2	b	11.6	1.3
76. 1963 (F)	27.6	3.2	4.4	3.0	1.8	1.2	b	12.8	1.2
77. Change, 1911–13 to 1963 (F)	+8.0	+0.1	−0.9	−0.4	+0.3	+0.7	b	+7.7	+0.5

(F): fiscal year beginning July 1.
—: information not available.

a Includes nonmetallic minerals.

b Included in column 4.

Labor force excludes those unclassified by industry whenever the latter is given. For adjusted labor force, women in agriculture are weighted by 0.2, and women in other sectors by 0.6 (see notes to Table 38).

When years in the stubs are connected by a slash (/), data are for the single years indicated; when connected by a dash (–), they are for all the years in the interval.

Miscellaneous includes leather and rubber, unless otherwise indicated.

Great Britain

Lines 1–4, 6–9: Data are from Bairoch, *International Historical Statistics.* In lines 1–2 and 6–7, rubber is included with chemicals, miscellaneous with metals, and column 9 covers leather only.

France

Lines 11–12, 14–15: Data are from Bairoch. In lines 11 and 14, column 5 is for paper only and column 9 includes footwear. In lines 12 and 15 tobacco is included with chemicals.

Belgium

Lines 17–18, 20–21: Data are from Bairoch. Total manufacturing includes electricity, gas, and water, except for the figure in parentheses in line 18. Chemicals (column 6) includes rubber throughout and electricity, gas, and water in lines 18 and 21. The latter is included with non-metallic minerals (column 7) in lines 17 and 20.

Netherlands

Lines 23–24, 28–29: Data are from the Bos memorandum cited in the notes to Table 1. Miscellaneous includes leather, rubber, diamonds, and applied art.

Lines 25–26: Total manufacturing (column 1) for 1947 is from the *Demographic Yearbook, 1955* (New York, 1955), and for 1960 from the *1964* issue. The ratio of manufacturing to labor force is interpolated and extrapolated along a straight line. Columns 2–9 are based on unpublished United Nations data.

Germany

Lines 31–32: Data are from Hoffmann, *Das Wachstum der Deutschen Wirtschaft,* table 15, pp. 196–199, for manufacturing and from table 20, pp. 204–206, for total labor force.

Lines 33–36: Data are from Bairoch. In line 33 miscellaneous is included with metals, and column 9 covers leather and rubber only. Line 35 excludes nonmetallic minerals, included with mining.

Denmark

Lines 38–39: Data for total manufacturing and subgroups in 1911 and for subgroups in 1950 are from Institut National d'Etudes Demographiques, *Migrations Professionnelles* (Paris: Presses Universitaires de France, 1957), table XII, p. 208, and table XX, p. 214. The share of manufacturing in total labor force in 1911 is based on the INED figure for manufacturing and Bairoch's figure for total labor force; for the share in 1950 both figures are from Bairoch.

Lines 40–41: Column 1 is from the United Nations, *Demographic Yearbook, 1955* for 1950, *1964* for 1960, and the International Labour Office, *Yearbook of Labour Statistics, 1960* for 1955; and interpolated and extrapolated along a straight line. Columns 2–9 are based on unpublished United Nations data.

Norway

Lines 43–44: For column 1, line 43, manufacturing is from INED, *Migrations*, and total labor force is from Bairoch; for line 44 both are from Bairoch. Columns 2–9 are based on INED, *Migrations*, table XIX, p. 214.

Lines 45–46: Data are from Central Bureau of Statistics, *National Accounts, 1865–1960*, no. XII, 163 (Oslo, 1965), table 47, pp. 328–331. In line 45, column 2 excludes beverages and tobacco, column 8 includes miscellaneous, and column 9 covers leather and rubber only.

Sweden

Lines 48–49: Data are from Östen Johansson, *The Gross Domestic Product of Sweden and Its Composition, 1861–1955* (Stockholm: Almqvist and Wiksell, 1967), table 58, pp. 156–157. Total labor force was adjusted to include construction in 1910, on the assumption that its per worker contribution to GDP was 0.7 of that for manufacturing (as suggested by the relation of the two in *ibid*, table 59, pp. 156–157). Manufacturing includes power stations and mining. Columns 2–9 are based on INED, *Migrations*, table XVIII, p. 213.

Lines 50–51: The ratio of manufacturing to total labor force is from the *Demographic Yearbook, 1955* for 1950, *1964* for 1960, and the *Yearbook of Labour Statistics, 1968* for 1965; and interpolated along a straight line. Columns 2–9 are based on unpublished United Nations data. Mining is excluded.

Finland

Lines 53–54: For column 1, line 53, manufacturing is from INED, *Migrations*, table XXI, p. 215, and total labor force is from Bairoch; for line 54 both are from Bairoch. Columns 2–9 are based on the INED data, the 1952 distribution being used for 1950.

Lines 55–56: Column 1 is from the *Demographic Yearbook, 1955* for 1950, *1964* for 1960; and interpolated and extrapolated along a straight line. Columns 2–9 are based on unpublished United Nations data.

Japan

Lines 58–59: Data are from Bairoch. Rubber is included with chemicals.

Canada

Lines 61–63: Column 1 for 1951 is from M. C. Urquhart and K. A. H. Buckley, eds., *Historical Statistics of Canada* (Cambridge: Cambridge University Press, 1965), series C 130–151, extrapolated to 1871 by data in Firestone, *Canada's Economic Development*, table 65, p. 184. Columns 2–9 are based on Urquhart and Buckley, series Q 1–11 and Q 30–137, the distributions being for 1870, 1910, and 1951.

Lines 64–65: Column 1 is from the *Demographic Yearbook, 1955* for 1951, *1964* for 1961, and the *Yearbook of Labour Statistics, 1963* for 1962, and *1964* for 1964; and interpolated along a straight line. Columns 2–9 are based on unpublished United Nations data.

United States

Lines 67–68: For column 1, see notes to Table 38, lines 66–67. Columns 2–9 are based on unpublished Gallman estimates.

Lines 69–70: For column 1, see notes to Table 38, lines 68–69. Columns 2–9 are based on Kendrick, *Productivity Trends*, table D-VII, p. 488, for the absolutes in 1929, and table D-IV, pp. 468–475, for indexes back to 1899.

Lines 71–72: See notes to Table 38, lines 70–71.

Australia

Line 74: Column 1 (for 1911) is from Colin Clark, *Conditions of Economic Progress*, table III, p. 510, and excludes women in agriculture. Columns 2–9 are based on the shares in line 75, extrapolated by indexes given in A. Maizels, "Trends in Production and Labour Productivity in Australian Manufacturing Industries," *Economic Record*, vol. XXXIII, no. 65 (August 1957), table III, p. 168. Leather is included in column 3.

Lines 75–76: Column 1 is based on the *Demographic Yearbook, 1955* for 1947, *1964* for 1961, and the *Yearbook of Labour Statistics, 1959* for 1954 and *1968* for 1966; and interpolated along a straight line. Columns 2–9 are based on unpublished United Nations data.

those for the shares in product in Table 23, but the comparison is complicated by the much smaller sample of countries in that table. Another distinctive aspect of Table 40 is the striking magnitude of the decline in the share of the textiles and clothing subdivision in some older European countries. In Great Britain, even with adjustment for a lower weight of women (dominant in the clothing branch), the decline was 17.3 percentage points (line 10, column 3); in France it was 6.5 percentage points, a major drop since the share of *all* manufacturing at the start was only about 24 percent (line 16, column 3 and line 14, column 1); in Belgium it was 14.7 percentage points (line 22, column 3); in the Netherlands it was 4.1 percentage points, with an initial share of all manufacturing of only 22.6 percent (line 30, column 3, and line 28, column 1); in Norway it was 4.1 percentage points, with an initial share for all manufacturing of 21.4 percent (line 47, column 3, and line 43, column 1); and in Japan, the decline of 2.4 percentage points is quite substantial since the share of all manufacturing at the beginning of the period covered was only 15.8 percent (line 60, column 3 and line 58, column 1). Apparently, in several countries, particularly the older European ones, manufacturing employment in the early period of economic growth was dominated by the textiles and clothing subdivision; and its share even in the total labor force was large (in Great Britain and in Belgium it was over a fifth of the countrywide labor force). Then, with economic growth and the structural shifts within manufacturing, employment in this major branch declined far more than its share in product; and this decline was a major cause of the moderate rise in the share of all manufacturing in labor force. At the same time, the *rises* in the shares of those manufacturing branches that have substantial employment, particularly the metal products groups, are quite sizable, ranging from 5 to 12 or 13 percentage points; but they are not large in comparison with a decline of some 50 to 60 percentage points in the share of the A sector in labor force.

The marked internal shifts in labor force among the branches of manufacturing suggested by Table 40 would be even more revealing with a more detailed classification. Quite possibly, the movement of the share of textiles would differ from that of clothing; and there would be considerable diversity in the movement of the shares of the various branches within the metal products group. In general, further disaggregation is likely to reveal *more* shifting within manufacturing; and this additional shifting is likely to be the greater, the more distinctive the subbranches included under one head. Much is concealed in Table 40 by the combination of simple wood products with furniture, basic metals with highly finished metal products, and beverages and tobacco with food.

In view of the large rise in the share of the S sector in labor force, observed for so many countries in Table 38, and since the sector is so heterogeneous, it would have been helpful to have data on a proper classification. The range of its coverage is from unskilled services to highly professional activity; from services engaged in distribution and finance to those engaged in public defense; from business services to education and recreation. But, perhaps for obvious reasons, the data on this broad group of activities have never been organized for proper analytical use. The only subdivisions that are widely available are commerce and other services (Table 41, panel A). Commerce includes trade, finance, and commercial real estate; and in respect to employment, trade (above all, retail trade) dominates this subdivision. The other services subdivision includes all other activities and, as just suggested, is extremely diversified.

Panel A, for fifteen countries, covers most of the developed group, although for some countries the period is too limited. The most striking finding is that in all these countries not only the share of the S sector in labor force but also the shares of both subdivisions rise. In some countries the share of commerce rises more than that of services; in others the converse is true. But these are questionable details. The significant finding is the prevalence of rises. As already indicated, the estimates may be affected by understatement of the shares in the early periods. But since the upward trend is so consistently observed and for countries with different susceptibility to such biases, although in some cases for periods only within the twentieth century, we can accept the evidence as strongly supporting a generally observed and conspicuous rise in the shares of the S sector and of its commerce and other services subdivisions in labor force (adjusted and unadjusted).

Panel B, although limited to four countries, suggests some significant trends for the subdivisions of other services. As might have been expected, the share of domestic services, which was quite substantial in the early periods (the low share for France may reflect peculiarities of the basic data), dropped sharply, particularly in the recent decades. However, the decline was more than offset by the

Table 41. Long-term changes in shares of subdivisions of the S sector in labor
force, developed countries (percentages).

A. Shares of commerce and other services in total labor force (adjusted for number
of women in A and other sectors)

	Commerce (1)	Other services (2)	Total S (3)
Great Britain			
1. 1921	13.3	19.8	33.1
2. 1961	15.4	21.9	37.3
3. Change, 1921 to 1961	+2.1	+2.1	+4.2
France			
4. 1856	5.6	14.7	20.3
5. 1962	13.3	22.0	35.3
6. Change, 1856 to 1962	+7.7	+7.3	+15.0
Belgium			
7. 1846	3.7	9.6	13.3
8. 1964	14.3	24.3	38.6
9. Change, 1846 to 1964	+10.6	+14.7	+25.3
Netherlands			
10. 1849	7.2	17.7	24.9
11. 1960	15.8	19.7	35.5
12. Change, 1849 to 1960	+8.6	+2.0	+10.6
Germany (changing boundaries)			
13. 1882	5.3	9.8	15.1
14. 1907	7.3	11.8	19.1
15. 1925	10.5	12.8	23.3
16. 1939	10.6	16.4	27.0
17. 1946	8.3	18.2	26.5
18. 1961	13.2	18.0	31.2
19. Change, above periods	+7.0	+5.4	+12.4
Switzerland			
20. 1880	7.4	5.1	12.5
21. 1960	13.0	16.6	29.6
22. Change, 1880 to 1960	+5.6	+11.5	+17.1
Denmark			
23. 1911	11.3	14.1	25.4
24. 1960	14.8	19.1	33.9
25. Change, 1911 to 1960	+3.5	+5.0	+8.5

Table 41 — continued

	(1)	(2)	(3)
Norway			
26. 1920	10.6	11.3	21.9
27. 1960	12.4	15.9	28.3
28. Change, 1920 to 1960	+1.8	+4.6	+6.4
Sweden			
29. 1910	5.9	12.4	18.3
30. 1960	12.5	16.9	29.4
31. Change, 1910 to 1960	+6.6	+4.5	+11.1
Italy			
32. 1881/1901	3.4	10.9	14.3
33. 1964	14.3	14.1	28.4
34. Change, 1881/1901 to 1964	+10.9	+3.2	+14.1
Japan			
35. 1920	12.3	10.4	22.7
36. 1964	20.7	16.2	36.9
37. Change, 1920 to 1964	+8.4	+5.8	+14.2
Canada			
38. 1911	10.4	12.9	23.3
39. 1965	20.7	25.4	46.1
40. Change, 1911 to 1965	+10.3	+12.5	+22.8
United States (unadjusted labor force)			
41. 1839	4.2	15.3	19.5
42. 1869/79	6.6	14.4	21.0
43. 1869/79	8.2	14.2	22.4
44. 1929	20.2	20.6	40.8
45. 1929	20.4	20.9	41.3
46. 1965	22.8	33.5	56.3
47. Change, 1839 to 1965	+16.8	+18.1	+34.9
Australia			
48. 1901	14.3	16.1	30.4
49. 1961	19.2	18.0	37.2
50. Change, 1901 to 1961	+4.9	+1.9	+6.8
New Zealand			
51. 1896	12.1	13.6	25.7
52. 1961	17.6	18.3	35.9
53. Change, 1896 to 1961	+5.5	+4.7	+10.2

Table 41 — continued

B. A more detailed breakdown of S sector, selected countries (shares in total labor force, unadjusted)

	Trade (1)	Banking, insurance (2)	Hotels (3)	Personal service (4)	Domestic service (5)	Professional service (6)	Government (7)	Totals (8)
France								
54. 1906	6.6	1.1	2.8	1.5	4.2	2.1	4.6	22.9
55. 1954	9.4	2.1	2.7	0.9	2.8	3.3	8.0	29.2
Netherlands								
56. 1899	10.9	0.5	1.3	1.1	10.5	3.6	2.6	30.5
57. 1947	13.4	1.8	2.0	1.3	5.0	7.5	4.7	35.7 (36.8)
Norway								
58. 1910	7.7	0.3	1.4	1.1	12.6	3.0	1.6	27.7
59. 1930	9.4	1.4	1.7	0.7	10.4	4.1	1.6	29.3
60. 1930	8.6	1.2	1.6	0.8	8.3	5.1	1.3	26.9
61. 1960	11.4	1.7	1.8	1.1	2.6	8.9	5.6	33.1

	Trade and finance (1)	Domestic service (2)	Other personal and business service (3)	Education (4)	Other professional activities (5)	Government (excluding education) (6)	Totals (7)
United States[a]							
62. 1839	4.2		10.7	0.8	1.3	0.6	17.6
63. 1869	6.2		9.2	1.3	1.5	1.0	19.2
64. 1870	6.5	7.4	2.0	1.5	1.1	0.8	19.3
65. 1930	15.7	4.9	5.2	3.5	3.7	2.2	35.2
66. 1929	20.3	5.1	5.3(1.1)	3.0	3.0	4.5(0.6)	41.2
67. 1965	23.4	2.1	5.9(2.0)	6.0	6.5	12.4(3.8)	56.3

[a] Excludes hand trades in lines 62–65.

Lines 1–53: For sources of data and the adjustment for weights of women, see notes to Table 38.

Lines 54–59: Based on Institut National d'Etudes Demographiques, *Migrations Professionnelles*, table VII, p. 152, table XI, p. 158, table XII, p. 159, and table XIII, p. 160, for France; table X, p. 116, table XXII, p. 128, and table XXV, p. 130, for the Netherlands; table XII, p. 208, table XXVIII, p. 220, table XXX, p. 222, and table XXXI, p. 224, for Norway. Total labor force excludes those unclassified by industry and unemployed. Personal services in column 4 is limited to laundries, cleaning and dyeing establishments, barber and beauty shops, and the like. Figure in parentheses in line 57 includes persons not allocable between column 6 and 7.

Lines 60–61: Based on Central Bureau of Statistics, *National Accounts, 1865–1960,* table 47, pp. 328–337. The estimates refer to "full-time equivalent man-years." Community and business services are classified here under professions.

Lines 62–63: From Robert E. Gallman and Thomas J. Weiss, "The Service Industries in the Nineteenth Century," table 6, p. 299, and table 9, p. 303.

Lines 64–65: From *Historical Statistics of the United States,* series D57–71, p. 74. The entries are shares in total labor force excluding unallocated.

Lines 66–67: Based on *The National Income and Product Accounts of the United States, 1929–1965,* table 6.6, pp. 110–113. The estimates are for full-time employees (partially employed reduced to full-time equivalent) and all self-employed. Automobile services are included with trade. Repairs and hand trades are included (in column 3), but by 1929 they accounted for only 0.6 percent of total labor force; in 1965 for about 0.4 percent. The figures in parentheses in column 3 are for business services, and in column 6 for defense employment, included in the respective totals.

sharp rises in the share of professional services, heavily dominated by the curative professions, and in that of educational services, for the United States both private and public; and by the equally sharp rise in the share of governments, only partly due to the rise in the defense force (for example, for the United States, nondefense government employment rises from 3.9 percent in 1929 to 8.6 percent in 1965). The shares of hotel and restaurant employment, and of personal services (excluding business) tended to be constant, to decline, or to rise slightly — and at any rate were not quantitatively important within the other services group.

The declines in the shares of domestic and personal services and the rises in the shares of educational, professional, and governmental services are generally observed and fairly conspicuous for the four countries in the table. One may reasonably assume that a larger sample of countries for longer periods would confirm not only these trends but also the impression conveyed by the estimates for the United States (and Norway) that they have accelerated since the 1920's.

Time Trends and Cross-Sections

Many of the long-term trends in the sectoral shares in labor force in the developed countries, summarized in Tables 38–41 — declines in the shares of the A sector, rises in the shares of the I and S sectors, the diversity of movement among the shares of subdivisions of the I sector and of the branches of manufacturing — conform roughly with the relations between per capita product differentials and differences in sectoral shares in labor force in the 1958 cross-section in Tables 28–30. But we now ask, as we did for the sectoral shares in product, whether the cross-section is a good indicator of the response of sectoral shares in labor force to increases over time in per capita product. In the tests that follow labor force is used without adjustment for the proportions of women workers.

The first test, relating to long periods going back to the pre-World War I period, is summarized in Table 42. Since there are more long-term records of sectoral shares in labor force than for shares in product in constant prices, and the long periods covered are similar, it is possible to group them, although some ad hoc estimation is required to fill the gaps and piece out the shares in one or two countries (for example, apportion the I+S share in Denmark between the two sectors, for years before the recent decades). Using the available data for eighteen countries, we can establish the cross-section relations in 1910–1911 and 1960–1961, and, on the basis of the averages underlying these cross-sections, estimate the proportional changes in sectoral shares that should have occurred and compare them with the levels and changes in per capita product observed from this sample. The observed and estimated proportional changes were calculated not for each country individually, but for groups of countries, arrayed in increasing order of per capita product in the initial period, and on the basis of the geometric means of per capita product and the arithmetic means of sectoral shares.

Even though the sample is larger than that for sectoral shares in product, Table 42 still covers only the upper ranges of per capita product. For 1910–1911 the lowest per capita product average is more than $150 (in 1958 prices, line 1); and the lowest benchmark value that can be set is $200. Thus, the data give no indication of the movement over time in the sectoral shares for per capita product that rises from below $100 to $200, in 1958 prices. But for the upper ranges, the sample yields results that are quite close to the cross-section in Table 29, where the share of the A sector in 1960 is 31.4 percent for the $500 value and 17.0 percent for the $1,000; the shares in line 12 are 32.8 and 19.0 percent, somewhat higher but with about the same decline. The differences in the shares of the I and S sectors are equally minor.

It is apparent from panel B that the cross-section estimates will fall short of the observed changes in the sectoral shares in labor force. Thus, at the benchmark values found in both cross-sections, from $400 to $1,000, the shares for the A sector are consistently and substantially lower in the 1960–1961 cross-section than in the 1910–1911 cross-section; while the shares of the I and S sectors are con-

Table 42. Observed and estimated changes in shares of major sectors in total labor force, eighteen countries, 1910–1911 to 1960–1961.

A. Shares for groups of countries in increasing order of GDP per capita

	Groups (three countries each)						Average, cols. 1–6
	I (1)	II (2)	III (3)	IV (4)	V (5)	VI (6)	(7)
1910–11							
1. GDP per capita, 1958 $	155	283	446	641	737	1,009	459
Shares (%)							
2. A	55.9	54.1	51.8	35.8	20.1	31.2	41.5
3. I	23.4	27.9	29.0	39.0	51.3	39.4	35.0
4. S	20.7	18.0	19.2	25.2	28.6	29.4	23.5
1960–61							
5. GDP per capita, 1958 $	361	663	1,092	1,231	1,435	1,882	977
Shares (%)							
6. A	42.0	24.2	20.9	13.8	12.3	11.0	20.7
7. I	31.3	43.5	46.8	47.7	50.5	45.6	44.2
8. S	26.7	32.3	32.3	38.5	37.2	43.4	35.1

B. Cross-section shares for benchmark values of GDP per capita

	Benchmark values (1958 $)						
	(1)	(2)	(3)	(4)	(5)	(6)	(7)
1910–11	200	300	400	500	600	800	1,000
Shares (%)							
9. A	55.0	52.5	48.4	42.1	35.7	28.2	30.9
10. I	25.0	28.0	31.1	35.5	39.9	43.7	39.7
11. S	20.0	19.5	20.5	22.4	24.4	28.1	29.4
1960–61	400	500	600	800	1,000	1,200	1,600
Shares (%)							
12. A	39.0	32.8	30.0	23.8	19.0	16.2	11.8
13. I	33.4	37.6	39.8	43.5	46.3	48.0	48.1
14. S	27.6	29.6	30.2	32.7	34.7	35.8	40.1

Table 42 — continued

C. Absolute changes in estimated and observed shares, forward projection from the 1910-11 cross-section (%)

	Benchmark value intervals (1958 $)				Sum of cols. 1–4
	200–400 (1)	300–600 (2)	400–800 (3)	500–1,000 (4)	(5)
Changes in A share					
15. Estimated	−6.6	−16.8	−20.2	−11.2	−54.9
16. Observed	−16.0	−22.5	−24.6	−23.1	−86.3
17. Ratio, line 15 to line 16	0.41	0.75	0.82	0.48	0.64 (0.59)
Changes in I share					
18. Estimated	+6.1	+11.9	+12.6	+4.2	+34.8
19. Observed	+8.4	+11.8	+12.4	+10.8	+43.4
20. Ratio, line 18 to line 19	0.73	1.01	1.02	0.39	0.80 (0.74)
Changes in S share					
21. Estimated	+0.5	+4.9	+7.6	+7.0	+20.1
22. Observed	+7.6	+10.7	+12.2	+12.3	+42.9
23. Ratio, line 21 to line 22	0.07	0.46	0.62	0.57	0.47 (0.33)

D. Absolute changes in estimated and observed shares, backward projection from the 1960-61 cross-section (%)

	Benchmark value intervals (1958 $)				Sum of cols. 1–4
	800–400 (1)	1,000–500 (2)	1,200–600 (3)	1,600–800 (4)	(5)
Changes in A share					
24. Estimated	+15.2	+13.8	+13.8	+12.0	+54.8
25. Observed	+24.6	+23.1	+19.5	+16.4	+83.6
26. Ratio, line 24 to line 25	0.62	0.60	0.71	0.73	0.66 (0.66)

Table 42 — continued

	(1)	(2)	(3)	(4)	(5)
Changes in I share					
27. Estimated	−10.1	−8.7	−8.2	−4.6	−31.6
28. Observed	−12.4	−10.8	−8.1	−4.4	−35.7
29. Ratio, line 27 to line 28	0.81	0.81	1.01	1.05	0.89 (0.91)
Changes in S share					
30. Estimated	−5.1	−5.1	−5.6	−7.4	−23.2
31. Observed	−12.2	−12.3	−11.4	−12.0	−47.9
32. Ratio, line 30 to line 31	0.42	0.41	0.49	0.62	0.48 (0.48)

Entries in parentheses in column 5 are unweighted geometric means of the ratios in columns 1–4.

The eighteen countries included in this table are: Mexico, Japan, Chile, Spain, Italy, Norway, Sweden, the Netherlands, Finland, Belgium, Denmark, France, New Zealand, Switzerland, Great Britain, Canada, Australia, the United States. The labor force data are for 1910 or 1911 (1909 for the Netherlands, and 1920 for Chile) and 1960 or 1961, and are taken from Bairoch, *International Historical Statistics*.

Gross domestic product per capita for 1960–61 in 1958 prices is the geometric mean, based on the estimates for 1958 and 1963 in current prices given in the United Nations, *Yearbook of National Accounts Statistics, 1966* (New York, 1967), table 7B. The 1963 figures were shifted to the 1958 base by means of the price index implicit in GNP for the United States, given in the *Economic Report of the President* (Washington, D.C., February 1969), table B-3. They were then extrapolated to the pre-World War I period closest to 1910–11 (1910–14, 1911–13, or 1911) by indexes of per capita product at constant prices.

For fourteen of the eighteen countries the sources were given in the notes to Table 1 or Table 3. The sources for the other four countries are as follows:

Chile: Based on an index of aggregate output (back to 1908–09) and gross domestic product (back to 1925); with population from the United Nations, *Demographic Yearbook* and Economic Commission for Latin America, *Economic Survey of Latin America, 1949* (New York, 1951), table 2A, pp. 271–272.

The index of aggregate output includes agriculture, mining, manufacturing, gas and electricity, and government, and is based either on volume of output, or value deflated for price changes. It is given annually (to a 1929 base) for 1908–57 in Marto A. Ballesteros and Tom E. Davis, "The Growth of Output and Employment in Basic Sectors of the Chilean Economy, 1908–1957," *Economic Development and Cultural Change*, vol. XI, no. 2, part I (January 1963), table 1, pp. 160–161. Conversion to the 1925–29 base was by simple division. (An alternative presentation is found in the United States, Eighty-seventh Congress, 2nd. Session, Joint Economic Committee Print, *Economic Development in South America* [Washington, D.C., 1962], pp. 97–114.)

Gross domestic product is based on ECLA estimates, as shown in Alexander Ganz, "Problems and Uses of National Wealth Estimates in Latin America," in Raymond Goldsmith and Christopher Saunders, eds., *Income and Wealth, Series VIII* (London: Bowes and Bowes, 1959), table II, p. 225. This series and the CORFO estimate given in Ballesteros-Davis, table 6, pp. 170–171, have similar movements from 1940 to 1954. GDP for later years is from the usual United Nations sources.

Spain: Through 1935 from Consejo de Economía Nacional, *La Renta Nacional de España*, vol. I (Madrid, 1945), pp. 110, 112, 116, for national income in current and in 1929 prices; and p. 220 for population (given annually for 1906–42). For 1939–45 national income in current and 1929 prices is from Consejo de Economía Nacional, *La Renta Nacional de España en 1952* (Madrid, 1953), p. 28; population is from United Nations sources.

For product in the years between 1945 and recent years (covered in United Nations sources) see Instituto Nacionale de Estadística, *Anuario Estadístico de España* (Madrid, respective years), *1960*, p. 567; *1963*, p. 272.

Finland: For 1913 to 1938, both population and product are from Clark, *Conditions of Economic Progress*, table XX, pp. 121–122 (national income including imputations and adjusted for changes in trade). For later years the product index is from United Nations, *Statistical Papers*, Series *H*, no. 9 (New York, 1956), table 2; and from the usual United Nations sources for years after 1950.

New Zealand: Real product and population from 1901 (interpolated along a straight line for per capita product between 1910 and 1925–29) to 1946–49 from Clark, *Conditions of Economic Progress*, pp. 171–172. Beginning with 1946–49 GNP in current prices is from the Census and Statistics Department, *New Zealand Official Yearbook, 1966* (Wellington, 1966), p. 711, adjusted for price changes by the movement of the retail prices of all goods shown in *ibid.*, p. 703. Population is from the usual United Nations sources.

Lines 1, 5: Geometric mean of estimates for the three countries in each of the six groups in the array by increasing per capita product.

Lines 2–4, 6–8: Arithmetic mean of the shares for the three countries included in each group. Averages in column 6 are arithmetic means of the six group averages.

Lines 9–14: Shares corresponding to benchmark values in the cross-section calculated from the group averages by our standard procedure.

Lines 15, 18, 21: Derived from the 1900–11 cross-section (lines 9–11).

Lines 16, 19, 22, 25, 28, 31: Differences between lines 9 and 12, 10 and 13, and 11 and 14, respectively.

Lines 24, 27, 30: Derived from the 1960–61 cross-section (lines 12–14).

sistently and substantially higher. In other words, at identical levels of development, reflected in identical per capita product, there was a marked shift downward in the share of the A sector and upward in the shares of the I and S sectors.

Consequently, the finding in panel C is predetermined. Since the per capita product for most groups doubled over the half-century, the expected changes from the two cross-sections, backward and forward were estimated for a standard rise of 100 percent in per capita product. On the basis of the results of both the forward and backward estimation, the decline of the share of the A sector is underestimated by about four-tenths — an understatement similar in magnitude to that found on the average for the share of the A sector in product, for fewer countries in Table 25. The understatement of the rise in the share of the S sector is even greater relatively, being more than a half. For the share of the I sector, the estimated changes come somewhat closer to the observed, the understatement averaging about a fifth. Generally speaking, the understatements are greatest for the lowest per capita product span (that is, in column 1); but the sample is too small to permit useful distinctions among the different spans in the per capita product range.

The test can be repeated for a sample of forty countries with a much wider range in per capita product, but limited to one decade, from 1950 to 1960 (Table 43, based on population censuses for dates that differ slightly among countries). The results are strikingly different, not only from those observed for the longer period of half a century and primarily for developed countries in Table 42, but also from those in Table 26 for 1953–1965 for the shares of the three sectors in total product.

Two major conclusions are suggested by the cross-sections in Table 43. First, between 1950 and 1960 the share of the A sector, for identical levels of per capita product, tended to rise, rather than decline as it did over the long period in Table 42, and as the A sector share in product did over the short period from 1953 to 1965 (see Table 26, lines 9–14). Correspondingly, the shares of the I and S sectors in labor force tended to be lower in 1960 than in 1950. Second, this rather distinctive shift in the cross-section from 1950 to 1960 was confined to countries with per capita product below the $675 benchmark (in 1953 prices; to convert to 1958 prices the levels should be multiplied by 1.13). For the $900 and $1,200 benchmark values the share of the A sector is distinctly lower in 1960 than in 1950, and those of the I and S sectors, especially the I sector, are distinctly higher.

This shift in the cross-sections yields disparities between observed and estimated changes that are different for the lower and for the higher per capita product groups (panels C–D). For the lower per capita product groups, the observed declines in the share of the A sector and the observed rises in the shares of the I and S sectors *fall short* of the estimated (lines 15–23, columns 1, 3); unlike the case with shares in product, the estimated changes derived from the cross-section show a greater than observed decline in the A sector share and a greater than observed rise in the I and the S sector shares. The shortage in the observed, relative to estimated changes, is particularly conspicuous for the I sector, both in panel C (lines 18–20, columns 1, 3) and in panel D (line 31, column 4). For the upper ranges of per capita product, however, beginning with the $450 benchmark value in panel C and group VI (with an average per capita product of

Table 43. Observed and estimated changes in shares of major sectors in labor force, forty countries, 1950 to 1960.

A. Shares for groups of countries in increasing order of GDP per capita

Groups (five countries each)

	I (1)	II (2)	III (3)	IV (4)	V (5)	VI (6)	VII (7)	VIII (8)
1950								
1. GDP per capita, 1953 $	56.8	118	164	190	296	489	795	1,204
Shares (%)								
2. A	72.9	68.6	62.7	58.2	42.6	31.1	22.4	17.2
3. I	9.7	17.0	19.2	20.3	27.4	38.0	46.7	44.7
4. S	17.4	14.4	18.1	21.5	30.0	30.9	30.9	38.1
1960								
5. GDP per capita, 1953 $	75.4	149	201	277	426	748	1,079	1,469
Shares (%)								
6. A	76.0	65.4	56.1	47.4	39.0	21.8	15.2	11.7
7. I	9.8	16.8	22.0	26.7	31.0	44.4	47.9	47.9
8. S	14.2	17.8	21.9	25.9	30.0	33.8	36.9	40.4

B. Cross-section shares for benchmark values of GDP per capita

Benchmark values (1953 $)

	65 (1)	80 (2)	135 (3)	270 (4)	450 (5)	675 (6)	900 (7)	1,200 (8)
1950								
9. A	71.8	70.1	64.8	47.2	34.0	26.1	21.4	17.2
10. I	11.0	12.9	17.6	26.6	36.0	41.4	43.7	44.7
11. S	17.2	17.0	17.6	26.2	30.0	32.5	34.9	38.1
1960								
12. A	—	74.9	65.2	49.0	35.8	26.2	19.8	14.5
13. I	—	10.5	16.6	25.8	34.2	40.5	44.5	47.2
14. S	—	14.6	18.2	25.2	30.0	33.3	35.7	38.3

C. Absolute changes in observed and estimated shares, derived from the two cross-sections, standard rise of a third in product per capita (%)

	Estimated forward from 1950		Estimated backward from 1960	
	Initial values $80, 135, 270 (1)	Initial values $450, 675, 900 (2)	Terminal values $107, 180, 360 (3)	Terminal values $600, 900, 1,200 (4)
Changes in A share				
15. Observed	−12.06	−18.14	−12.06	−18.14
16. Estimated	−16.08	−14.67	−19.10	−18.48
17. Ratio, line 16 to line 15	1.33	0.81	1.58	1.02

Table 43 — continued

	(1)	(2)	(3)	(4)
Changes in I share				
18. Observed	+7.41	+9.31	+7.41	+9.31
19. Estimated	+10.79	+7.32	+11.76	+11.12
20. Ratio, line 19 to line 18	1.46	0.79	1.59	1.19
Changes in S share				
21. Observed	+4.65	+8.83	+4.65	+8.83
22. Estimated	+5.29	+7.35	+7.34	+7.36
23. Ratio, line 22 to line 21	1.14	0.83	1.58	0.83

D. **Proportional changes in shares for single groups, about 1950 to about 1960, observed compared with estimated from initial cross-section (groups as in lines 1-4)**

	Increase in GDP per capita (%) (1)	A (2)	I+S (3)	I (4)	S (5)
Observed, groups I–V					
24. Group I	60.4	−0.02	+0.06	+0.26	−0.05
25. Group II	6.5	+0.01	−0.02	−0.11	+0.08
26. Group III	28.1	−0.10	+0.17	+0.20	+0.13
27. Group IV	44.9	−0.17	+0.23	+0.22	+0.24
28. Group V	37.2	−0.09	+0.07	+0.07	+0.06
Averages, groups I–V (geometric means)					
29. Observed	34.2	−0.07	+0.10	+0.12	+0.09
30. Estimated (from 1950 cross-section)	34.2	−0.11	+0.15	+0.22	+0.10
31. Ratio, line 30 to line 29		1.5	1.5	1.8	1.1
Observed, groups VI–VIII					
32. Group VI	50.6	−0.31	+0.14	+0.21	+0.05
33. Groups VII	37.9	−0.32	+0.09	+0.06	+0.15
34. Group VIII	20.0	−0.32	+0.07	+0.04	+0.10
Averages, groups VI–VIII (geometric means)					
35. Observed	35.6	−0.32	+0.10	+0.10	+0.10
36. Estimated (from 1950 cross-section)	35.6	−0.20	+0.07	+0.06	+0.08
37. Ratio, line 36 to the 35		0.6	0.7	0.6	0.8

—: information not available.

The sample includes those countries for which the shares in labor force were available both about 1950 and 1960 and for which per capita product in constant prices was available for the initial and terminal years of the period, as well as for 1958. For procedures used to extrapolate GDP per capita in 1958 by indexes of per capita product in constant prices, and the sources of the latter series, see notes to Table 26.

The countries included are, in increasing order of per capita GDP about 1950:

Thailand, India, Pakistan, Philippines, United Arab Republic, Haiti, Paraguay, Turkey, Ecuador, Morocco, Honduras, Dominican Republic, Spain, Portugal, El Salvador, Colombia, Nicaragua, Brazil, Japan, Mexico, Greece, Costa Rica, Chile, Puerto Rico, Ireland, Italy, the Netherlands, Germany (FR), Argentina, Finland, Belgium, France, Norway, Denmark, Switzerland, Australia, Sweden, New Zealand, Canada, and the United States.

For sources of the shares of sectors in labor force in panel A (and the data on GDP per capita) see notes to Tables 28 and 29. For the procedures used to derive the shares in cross-section at benchmark values of GDP per capita (in panel B) see notes to Table 14.

In panel C, for given initial benchmark values (say in 1950, for forward projection) I calculated the shares from the 1950 cross-section, taken as observed; and then estimated the 1960 values, corresponding to the increased value of per capita GDP in 1960, from the 1950 cross-section. These yielded the *estimated* changes, to be compared with the observed changes (the latter are the differences between the calculated shares in 1950 based on the 1950 cross-section and the shares in 1960 based on the 1960 cross-section). The entries in lines 15–16, 18–19, 21–22 are sums of changes in these shares.

In panel D the calculations are made for the individual groups, and for the specific increases in their per capita GDP, rather than for the standard increase of a third used in panel C. Also, the actual shares in 1950 and 1960 (based on the 1950 grouping) are used as observed values, rather than shares calculated for corresponding levels of GDP per capita from the 1950 and the 1960 cross-sections.

$489) in panel D, the estimated changes, if the backward and forward projections in panel C are averaged, do not exceed those observed, and the understatement in the estimate is fairly consistent. In the upper per capita product countries the observed decline in the share of the A sector and the rise in the shares of the I and S sectors, associated with the rise in per capita product, were greater than expected from the cross-section — not appreciably short of them as was the case with the low per capita product countries. The major conclusion — that, despite a sharp decline in the share of the A sector and sharp rises in the shares of the I and S sectors in product, the share of the A sector in labor force in the less developed countries declined far less than expected; and those of the I and S sectors, particularly of the I sector, rose much less than expected — merits further study to see whether the shortfall in the shift of the labor force is a general finding, and whether it is associated with the pressure of population and labor force on an inadequately growing employment market. And the contrast between the lower and the higher per capita product countries makes this finding for the post-World War II decade all the more intriguing. Because of the weaknesses of the basic data and the problem of definitions of the labor force in the less developed countries, this conclusion can only be tentative. Nevertheless, its bearing on the use of cross-sections for estimating time trends remains clear.

The shift in the cross-section over the postwar decade suggested in Table 43 is partly confirmed for a somewhat different period and

Table 44. Observed and estimated changes in shares of major branches of manufacturing in total labor force, 1953 to 1963 (based on 1953 and 1963 cross-sections).

	A. Shares in manufacturing and in total labor force, at benchmark values of GDP per capita					
	Benchmark values (1953$)					
	81 (1)	135 (2)	270 (3)	450 (4)	900 (5)	1,200 (6)
Shares in manufacturing labor force (%)						
1. Food, beverages, and tobacco						
(a) 1953 cross-section	30.2	30.6	29.1	22.2	15.3	—
(b) 1963 cross-section	26.6	28.3	28.0	23.5	15.1	14.0
2. Textiles and clothing						
(a) 1953 cross-section	26.8	29.6	27.1	24.4	20.1	—
(b) 1963 cross-section	29.9	29.8	27.2	24.4	19.1	16.6
3. Wood, paper, printing, and leather						
(a) 1953 cross-section	18.3	13.8	14.0	15.3	16.6	—
(b) 1963 cross-section	13.5	14.0	13.7	14.2	15.9	16.4
4. Rubber, chemicals, and petroleum products						
(a) 1953 cross-section	5.9	5.9	5.4	5.8	5.9	—
(b) 1963 cross-section	4.8	5.3	5.2	5.7	6.3	6.3
5. Industrial raw materials						
(a) 1953 cross-section	7.1	8.6	7.6	8.6	8.6	—
(b) 1963 cross-section	11.1	8.0	6.8	7.8	9.1	8.9
6. Fabricated metal products						
(a) 1953 cross-section	11.7	11.5	16.8	23.7	33.5	—
(b) 1963 cross-section	14.1	14.6	19.1	24.4	34.5	37.8
Shares in total labor force						
7. Total manufacturing						
(a) 1953 cross-section	8.4	10.7	17.2	22.6	28.6	—
(b) 1963 cross-section	8.1	10.4	15.3	21.1	27.6	28.9
8. Food, beverages, and tobacco						
(a) 1953 cross-section	2.6	3.3	5.0	5.0	4.4	—
(b) 1963 cross-section	2.2	3.0	4.3	5.0	4.2	4.0
9. Textiles and clothing						
(a) 1953 cross-section	2.2	3.2	4.7	5.5	5.8	—
(b) 1963 cross-section	2.4	3.1	4.2	5.2	5.3	4.8
10. Wood, paper, printing, and leather						
(a) 1953 cross-section	1.5	1.5	2.4	3.5	4.7	—
(b) 1963 cross-section	1.1	1.5	2.1	3.0	4.4	4.8

Table 44 — continued

	(1)	(2)	(3)	(4)	(5)	(6)
11. Rubber, chemicals, and petroleum products						
(a) 1953 cross-section	0.5	0.6	0.9	1.3	1.7	—
(b) 1963 cross-section	0.4	0.6	0.8	1.2	1.7	1.8
12. Industrial raw materials						
(a) 1953 cross-section	0.6	0.9	1.3	1.9	2.5	—
(b) 1963 cross-section	0.9	0.8	1.0	1.6	2.5	2.6
13. Fabricated metal products						
(a) 1953 cross-section	1.0	1.2	2.9	5.4	9.5	—
(b) 1963 cross-section	1.1	1.5	2.9	5.1	9.5	10.9

B. Observed and estimated changes in shares in total labor force, 1953 to 1963 (percentages, changes for standard rise of a third in GDP per capita)

	Total manufacturing (1)	Food, beverages, and tobacco (2)	Textiles and clothing (3)	Wood, paper, printing, and leather (4)	Rubber, chemicals, and petroleum products (5)	Industrial raw materials (6)	Fabricated metal products (7)
$81 in 1953 to $108 in 1963							
Observed shares and changes							
14. Shares, 1953	8.4	2.6	2.2	1.5	0.5	0.6	1.0
15. Shares, 1963	9.4	2.6	2.8	1.3	0.5	0.9	1.3
16. Changes	+1.0	0	+0.6	−0.2	0	+0.3	+0.3
Estimated changes							
17. Forward	+1.3	+0.4	+0.5	0	+0.1	+0.2	+0.1
18. Backward	+1.3	+0.4	+0.4	+0.2	+0.1	0	+0.2
$135 in 1953 to $180 in 1963							
Observed shares and changes							
19. Shares, 1953	10.7	3.3	3.2	1.5	0.6	0.9	1.2
20. Shares, 1963	12.4	3.5	3.6	1.7	0.6	0.9	2.1
21. Changes	+1.7	+0.2	+0.4	+0.2	0	0	+0.9
Estimated changes							
22. Forward	+2.7	+0.7	+0.6	+0.4	+0.1	+0.2	+0.7
23. Backward	+2.0	+0.5	+0.4	+0.3	+0.1	+0.1	+0.6
$270 in 1953 to $360 in 1963							
Observed shares and changes							
24. Shares, 1953	17.2	5.0	4.7	2.4	0.9	1.3	2.9
25. Shares, 1963	18.5	4.6	4.7	2.6	1.0	1.4	4.2
26. Changes	+1.3	−0.4	0	+0.2	+0.1	+0.1	+1.3

Table 44 — continued

	(1)	(2)	(3)	(4)	(5)	(6)	(7)
Estimated changes							
27. Forward	+3.0	0	+0.5	+0.6	+0.2	+0.3	+1.4
28. Backward	+3.3	+0.4	+0.6	+0.5	+0.2	+0.4	+1.2
$450 in 1953 to $600 in 1963							
Observed shares and changes							
29. Shares, 1953	22.6	5.0	5.5	3.5	1.3	1.9	5.4
30. Shares, 1963	23.8	4.6	5.2	3.6	1.4	2.0	7.0
31. Changes	+1.2	−0.4	−0.3	+0.1	+0.1	+0.1	+1.6
Estimated changes							
32. Forward	+2.5	−0.3	+0.1	+0.5	+0.2	+0.2	+1.8
33. Backward	+2.7	−0.3	0	+0.6	+0.2	+0.4	+1.8
$675 in 1953 to $900 in 1963							
Observed shares and changes							
34. Shares, 1953	26.1	4.6	5.7	4.2	1.5	2.3	7.8
35. Shares, 1963	27.6	4.2	5.3	4.4	1.7	2.5	9.5
36. Changes	+1.5	−0.4	−0.4	+0.2	+0.2	+0.2	+1.7
Estimated changes							
37. Forward	+2.5	−0.3	+0.1	+0.5	+0.2	+0.2	+1.8
38. Backward	+2.7	−0.3	0	+0.6	+0.2	+0.4	+1.8
$900 in 1953 to $1,200 in 1963							
Observed shares and changes							
39. Shares, 1953	28.6	4.4	5.7	4.7	1.7	1.5	9.6
40. Shares, 1963	28.9	4.1	4.8	4.7	1.8	1.6	10.9
41. Changes	+0.3	−0.3	−0.9	0	+0.1	+0.1	+1.3
Estimated changes							
42. Backward	+1.3	−0.1	−0.5	+0.4	+0.1	0	+1.4
Average changes							
Two lower per capita product groups (lines 14–23)							
43. Observed	+1.35	+0.1	+0.5	0	0	+0.15	+0.6
44. Estimated	+1.8	+0.5	+0.5	+0.2	+0.1	+0.1	+0.4
Four higher per capita product groups (lines 24–42)							
45. Observed	+1.1	−0.4	−0.4	+0.1	+0.1	+0.1	+1.5
46. Estimated	+2.4	−0.1	0	+0.5	+0.2	+0.2	+1.6

—: information not available.
Lines 1–13: See the notes to Table 30.
Lines 14–42: See the notes to Table 43 for the procedure.
Lines 44, 46: See the notes to Table 27.

a different sample in Table 44, which covers shares of the manufacturing branches. Lines 7a and 7b indicate that between 1953 and
1963 the share of manufacturing in total labor force at identical
benchmark values declined slightly, and in this respect it agrees
with the decline found for the share of the I sector. But in the case
of manufacturing, this decline persists through the full range of per
capita product.

The special interest of Table 44 attaches, however, to the shares
of the branches. For the share of manufacturing as a whole, the
observed rise falls distinctly short of the rise that should have occurred according to either a forward or backward projection. This
is shown in the summary averages in lines 43–46, column 1; and
the shortage is even greater for the higher than for the lower per
capita product levels. But in some ways the difference is deceptive.
For the lower per capita product levels, that is, for the less developed
countries, the smaller rise in the observed than in the estimated
share of manufacturing results from the smaller observed rises in
several branches, particularly foods, wood, leather, and paper, and
chemicals. For the higher per capita product levels, the observed
rise is also short of the estimated for the wood and paper group, for
chemicals, and for industrial raw materials. But the disparity for
total manufacturing to a large extent results from a greater decline
in the observed shares than in the estimated shares for the food,
and textile and clothing groups; it is significant that at the various
levels of per capita product the observed share of the food products
group, and to a great extent that of the textile and clothing group,
do not rise as much or decline as little as the cross-section suggests.
This is the major reason for the shortfall of observed changes in
all manufacturing. Thus, in lines 43–44, practically all of the disparity in column 1 of 0.45 percentage points comes from the food
products group alone (0.4 percentage points). In lines 45–46, more
than half of the total shortfall of 1.3 percentage points is the result
of the shortfall in the food and textile and clothing groups (0.7
percentage points). Obviously, the cross-sections are unreliable for
projecting changes in shares of three big branches: food products,
textiles and clothing, and wood, leather, paper and printing; and
they are relatively more successful in projecting the share of the
metal products branch. The inference is that, at least during the
postwar period, the relations between per capita product and employment in the large consumer goods branches shifted markedly.

Changes in Sectoral Product Per Worker

Table 45 summarizes the long-term changes in product per worker for the three major sectors, relative to countrywide product per worker, with the product total, when possible, excluding finance and rent. Since all the entries are in terms of relatives, an entry of less than 1.0 means that the sectoral product per worker is lower than the countrywide product per worker; and a rise (or decline) in the relative means that the product per worker in a given sector grows more (or less) than the product per worker for the country as a whole (except for the minor effect of exclusion of finance and rent).

Estimates based on sectoral shares in product in both current and constant prices are included — the former for two reasons. The first and less important is that the trends in sectoral product per worker are roughly the same over long periods for shares in current and constant prices, for the countries in which both sets of shares are available; hence the current price shares are an adequate approximation to long-term trends in relative output per worker in the major sectors, when constant price shares are not available. The second and more important reason is that product per worker in current prices may be a tolerable approximation to relative income per member of labor force attached to the sector; and long-term changes in relative sectoral income per member of the labor force may be interesting even if the approximation is rough. The underlying labor force data in Table 45 are not adjusted for equivalent units, and include unpaid family workers, women workers, and so on, as fully as the underlying census data. They must, therefore, be compared with the cross-section in Table 31.

(a) In practically all the countries and periods, the relative product per worker for the A sector is distinctly below 1.0 (column 1). In this sense long-term records conform with the current cross-section, in which the relative product per worker in the A sector ranges from 0.63 to 0.75 in the relevant per capita product ranges (largely from $150 to $1,000, see Table 31, line 1). Therefore, both the relative product per worker for the I+S sector and the intersectoral (I+S)/A ratio are usually well above 1.0.

Significant exceptions to this finding reveal that the long-term record differs markedly from what the cross-section would lead us to expect concerning relatives for the A and I+S sectors and the

Table 45. Long-term trends in relative product per worker, major sectors.

	Sectoral product per worker relative to adjusted country-wide product per worker				Intersectoral ratios		Weighted measure of ine- quality (7)
	A (1)	I+S (2)	I (3)	S (4)	(I+S)/A (5)	S/I (6)	

Great Britain

Current prices (excluding income from dwellings)

1. 1801/11	1.16	0.93	0.63[a]	1.28[a]	0.80	2.03[a]	27.6
2. 1907 (1901/11)	0.93	1.01	0.81[a]	1.26[a]	1.09	1.56[a]	21.0
3. 1907 (1901/11)	0.96	1.00	0.87	1.27	1.04	1.46	16.6
4. 1963–67 (1961)	0.95	1.00	1.02	0.98	1.05	0.96	2.0

France

1954 prices (excluding income from dwellings)

5. 1896	0.59	1.33	1.51	1.07	2.25	0.71	36.6
6. 1963 (1962)	0.44	1.14	1.22	1.05	2.59	0.86	22.6

Belgium

1963 prices (no exclusions)

7. 1910	0.40	1.18	0.84	1.86	2.95	2.21	44.2
8. 1963–67 (1964)	1.05	1.00	0.95	1.06	0.95	1.12	5.2

Netherlands

Current prices (no exclusions)

9. 1913 (1909)	0.66	1.14	0.92	1.43	1.73	1.55	26.6
10. 1950 (1947)	0.76	1.06	1.07	1.05	1.39	0.98	9.4

Current prices (excluding finance and income from dwellings)

11. 1950 (1947)	0.77	1.06	1.16	0.93	1.38	0.80	14.2
12. 1965 (1960)	0.80	1.02	1.06	0.98	1.28	0.92	6.0

Germany

1913 prices (excluding income from dwellings)

13. 1850–59 (1852/55/58)	0.87	1.15	0.71	2.20	1.32	3.10	33.2
14. 1935–38 (1939)	0.65	1.12	1.24	0.91	1.72	0.73	22.6

Federal Republic, 1954 prices (excluding finance and income from dwellings)

15. 1950 (1946)	0.35	1.27	1.29	1.23	3.63	0.95	38.2
16. 1963–67 (1964)	0.50	1.06	1.21	0.83	2.12	0.69	23.0

Denmark

Current prices (no exclusions)

17. 1870–79 (1870/80)	0.80	1.27	—	—	1.59	—	23.2
18. 1950–51 (1950)	0.77	1.08	—	—	1.40	—	11.4

Current prices (excluding finance and income from dwellings)

19. 1950–51 (1950)	0.86	1.05	1.19	0.88	1.22	0.74	15.2
20. 1963–67 (1960)	0.66	1.07	1.21	0.91	1.62	0.75	18.6

Table 45 — continued

	(1)	(2)	(3)	(4)	(5)	(6)	(7)
1929 prices (no exclusions)							
21. 1870–79 (1870/80)	0.73	1.35	—	—	1.85	—	30.4
22. 1950–51 (1950)	0.74	1.09	—	—	1.47	—	13.2
1955 prices (excluding finance and income from dwellings)							
23. 1950–51 (1950)	0.83	1.06	1.20	0.89	1.28	0.74	16.4
24. 1963–67 (1960)	0.85	1.03	1.21	0.82	1.21	0.68	19.0

Norway

Current prices (excluding income from dwellings)							
25. 1865	0.61	1.66	1.78	1.50	2.72	0.84	48.6
26. 1950	0.55	1.16	1.18	1.12	2.11	0.95	23.2
Current prices (excluding finance and income from dwellings)							
27. 1950	0.60	1.14	1.24	0.97	1.90	0.78	22.6
28. 1963–67 (1960)	0.45	1.13	1.22	1.00	2.51	0.82	21.6
1963 prices (excluding finance and income from dwellings)							
29. 1950	0.62	1.13	1.15	1.10	1.82	0.96	19.8
30. 1963–67 (1960)	0.43	1.14	1.25	0.97	2.65	0.78	24.0

Sweden

Current prices (excluding finance and income from dwellings)							
31. 1861–70 (1860/70)	0.75	1.58	1.48	1.68	2.11	1.14	35.0
32. 1963–67 (1960)	0.52	1.08	1.14	0.98	2.08	0.86	14.6
1959 prices (excluding finance and income from dwellings)							
33. 1861–70 (1860/70)	0.71	1.67	1.28	2.05	2.35	1.60	40.2
34. 1963–67 (1960)	0.44	1.09	1.14	1.01	2.48	0.89	15.4

Italy

Current prices (excluding finance and income from dwellings)							
35. 1861–70 (1861/71)	0.88	1.18	0.81	1.89	1.34	2.33	24.8
36. 1881–1900 (1881/1901)	0.80	1.28	0.83	2.26	1.60	2.72	32.6
37. 1963–67 (1964)	0.58	1.14	1.13	1.17	1.97	1.04	21.4
1963 prices (excluding finance and income from dwellings)							
38. 1861–70 (1861/71)	0.77	1.34	0.68	2.58	1.74	3.79	44.0
39. 1881–1900 (1881/1901)	0.74	1.37	0.77	2.69	1.85	3.49	43.6
40. 1963–67 (1964)	0.60	1.14	1.14	1.13	1.90	0.99	20.2

Japan

Current prices (no exclusions)							
41. 1879–83 (1880)	0.75	2.25	—	—	3.00	—	41.6
42. 1959–61 (1960)	0.42	1.28	—	—	3.05	—	38.0
1934–36 prices (no exclusions)							
43. 1879–83 (1880)	0.79	2.06	—	—	2.61	—	35.4
44. 1959–61 (1960)	0.37	1.31	—	—	3.54	—	41.4

Table 45 — continued

	(1)	(2)	(3)	(4)	(5)	(6)	(7)
Canada							
Current prices (excluding income from dwellings)							
45. 1870 (1871)	0.95	1.06	—	—	1.12	—	5.4
46. 1920 (1921)	0.75	1.13	—	—	1.51	—	17.4
Current prices (excluding finance and income from dwellings)							
47. 1919–23 (1921)	0.64	1.19	1.27	1.10	1.86	0.87	25.0
48. 1963–67 (1965)	0.77	1.02	1.29	0.80	1.32	0.62	24.0
United States							
Current prices (excluding finance and income from dwellings)							
49. 1839	0.75	1.45	1.80	1.16	1.93	0.64	32.4
50. 1899	0.49	1.33	1.45	1.18	2.71	0.81	40.2
51. 1929[b]	0.56	1.11	1.27	0.96	1.98	0.76	21.4
52. 1963–65[b]	0.67	1.02	1.28	0.84	1.52	0.66	22.0
1859 prices (excluding finance and income from dwellings)							
53. 1839	0.78	1.39	1.69	1.14	1.78	0.67	27.8
54. 1899	0.44	1.36	1.77	0.83	3.09	0.47	52.6
1929 prices (excluding finance and income from dwellings)							
55. 1899	0.76	1.12	1.13	1.11	1.47	0.98	15.8
56. 1929	0.55	1.12	1.34	0.92	2.04	0.69	25.8
Australia							
Current prices (excluding finance and income from dwellings)							
57. 1861–70 (1861/71)	0.72	1.18	—	—	1.64	—	22.2
58. 1891–1900 (1891/1901)	0.77	1.12	1.18	1.05	1.45	0.89	15.6
59. 1935–38 (1933)	1.15	0.96	0.87	1.06	0.83	1.22	11.0
60. 1963–66 (1961)	1.17	0.98	1.12	0.81	0.84	0.72	15.2
1910–11 prices (excluding finance and income from dwellings)							
61. 1861–70 (1861/71)	0.61	1.25	—	—	2.05	—	30.8
62. 1891–1900 (1891/1901)	0.81	1.10	1.11	1.08	1.36	0.97	12.8
63. 1935–38 (1933)	1.24	0.93	0.78	1.13	0.75	1.45	19.4

—: information not available.

[a] The I sector excludes and the S sector includes the transport and communications subdivision.

[b] Product (national income) excludes income from the rest of the world. Labor force is the full-time equivalent of persons engaged, excluding those in finance and real estate.

All entries are calculated from the sources of the underlying data cited in the notes to Tables 21 and 38. When more than one series was used, the share for the most recent period was extrapolated back with the earlier series as an index, and the results (for the underlying shares) were adjusted to add to 100.

When years in the stubs are connected by a slash (/), data are for the single years indicated; when connected by a dash (–), they are for all the years in the interval.

Entries in parentheses in the stubs refer to the dates for the labor force when these differ from those for product.

The measure of inequality in column 7 is the sum, signs disregarded, of the differences between shares of the sectors in product and in labor force.

(I+S)/A ratio. In Great Britain in the early nineteenth century, when it was in the early stages of modern economic growth with a per capita product of about $200, relative product per worker in the A sector was more than 1.0, with corresponding results for the relative of the I+S sector and the intersectoral ratio. Other countries can be added if the expected lower limit of relative product per worker in the A sector is set at 0.75 — a warranted decision, since the ratio in the 1958 cross-section for the $150 to $500 range is between 0.63 and 0.65. Among these countries are Germany in 1850–1859, Denmark in 1870–1879, Sweden in 1861–1870, Italy in the nineteenth century, the United States in 1839, Canada in 1870, Australia in 1891–1900, and Japan in 1879–1883. In other words, in nine of the thirteen developed countries covered, the relative product per worker in the A sector in these early periods was significantly *higher* than that suggested by the current cross-section. And, of course, in these cases relative product per worker in the I+S sector and the (I+S)/A ratio were appreciably lower.

(b) In the recent cross-section, relative product per worker in the A sector rises only slightly as we move to high per capita product levels: from 0.63 at the benchmark levels of $150 and $300 to 0.75 at the $1,000 level (see Table 31, line 1). But the relative product per worker in the I+S sector and the (I+S)/A ratio drop sharply over the same range (the former from 1.64 to 1.05, and the latter from 2.60 to 1.40). Since all the developed countries covered in Table 45 enjoyed substantial rises in per capita product in all periods, the cross-section would lead us to expect stability or only a minor rise over time in relative product per worker in the A sector, a marked decline in the relative for the I+S sector, and a sharp drop in the (I+S)/A ratio.

For the developed countries and the long periods — disregarding for the moment the apparent reversal in the long-term trends that occurred in the recent decade or two — the pattern expected from the cross-section is found in only two or three countries. In Belgium the (I+S)/A ratio drops markedly, primarily because of the sharp rise in relative product per worker in the A sector; in the Netherlands it declines from 1913 to 1965; in Denmark it drops from 1870–1879 to 1950–1951; and in Norway it declines from 1865 to 1950. Finally, in Australia, an exception in many other respects, the (I+S)/A ratio, initially above 1.0, drops to well below 1.0, while relative product per worker in the A sector rises to significantly above 1.0. In other developed countries, the (I+S)/A ratio rises appreciably to relatively recent dates: in Great Britain from 1801/11 to 1907 (and possibly later, although we have no estimates for the decades between the mid-1920's and 1950); in France between 1896 and 1963; in Germany between the 1850's and 1935–1938; in Italy between the 1860's and the 1960's; in the United States in the nineteenth century; in Canada from 1870 through the 1920's; and in Japan from the 1880's through the 1950's. Finally, in Sweden, the ratio was slightly higher in the 1960's than in the 1860's, in constant price volumes; and was only slightly lower in current price volumes.

On the basis of the foregoing evidence, the following general conclusion may be suggested. Over the long periods up to the recent decade or two, despite the sustained rise in per capita product, the (I+S)/A ratio did not decline; in other words, the relative products per worker in the two major sectors did not converge, as they did in the recent cross-section; and in many countries they tended to diverge. It was probably only after the 1920's that convergence became evident in several countries. The precise date of this shift in the trend cannot be determined from Table 45, or from the data underlying it; but given the economic depression of the 1930's, the convergence probably emerged during World War II. For any substantive analytical purposes, its concentration in the post-World War II decade or two is significant.

(c) In all seven countries in which the (I+S)/A ratio rose appreciably, the trend was largely the result of a marked decline over time in the relative product per worker in the A sector — a decline from initial levels which were, as noted under (a), higher than the levels in the cross-section at relevant benchmark values of per capita product. Although the underlying estimates are rough approximations, the widespread character of the finding suggests that it is not caused by vagaries of data. Apparently through much of the period of modern economic growth, the percentage rise in product per worker in the A sector could not keep pace with that in product per worker in the I+S sector. This does not mean that per worker product in the A sector did not rise, but rather that it rose at a lower rate than in the rest of the economy. And it is in this crucial respect that the longer-term past fails to conform to the current cross-section. The recent reversal of these older disparities between the A and the I+S sectors in growth rates in product per worker was striking, since the sharp rise in the relative product per worker in the A sector means a high rate of growth of labor productivity in the sector. There is a strong suggestion of changes in the A sector (possibly initiated elsewhere but affecting the A sector) that amounted to a recent agricultural revolution in the developed countries.

(d) While in the majority of developed countries the long-term trend in the $(I+S)/A$ ratio was upward, despite substantial rises in per capita product, it is possible that in several less developed countries the $(I+S)/A$ ratio also rose while per capita (and perhaps per worker) product was stagnant. In Chapter IV it was observed that in three less developed countries — India, Egypt, and Honduras — the share of the A sector in total product apparently declined, and fairly substantially, although per capita product failed to rise. In India and Egypt, for which the relevant data are available, the share of the A sector in labor force was relatively constant over the long period back to the beginning of the century: in India until the recent years, and in Egypt at least until 1937 and perhaps to a later date. This combination of a constant share of the A sector in labor force and a declining share in product, while per capita (and per worker) product was stagnating, implies that the $(I+S)/A$ ratio was rising, and that product per worker in the A sector was actually falling. The underdeveloped countries with a rising $(I+S)/A$ ratio, like the developed, represent nonconformity to the patterns suggested by the recent cross-section. However, the absolute decline in product per worker in the A sector implied for the less developed countries is quite different from the finding for the developed countries.

(e) In observing the movement of the sectoral relatives for the I and S sectors, we are limited to a smaller sample of developed countries. Nevertheless, some general conclusions can be suggested; or at least intriguing questions raised.

Table 31 indicates that at the $150 level the sectoral relatives for the I and S sectors are roughly the same, both between 1.6 and 1.7; then, with movement to the higher per capita product levels, the relatives drift down — that for the I sector to 1.15 and that for the S sector to 0.93 at the $1,000 level. Columns 3 and 4 of Table 45 reveal that in several countries the initial sectoral relative for the I sector is distinctly below 1.0 (Great Britain, through the nineteenth century; Belgium and the Netherlands in 1913; Germany in the 1850's; and Italy even toward the end of the nineteenth century). In all these countries the sectoral relative for the S sector is well above 1.0.

Consequently, in these countries the initial S/I ratio was well above 1.0, and much higher than the level of 0.96 indicated in the cross-section in Table 31. In Great Britain and Belgium the early ratio is over 2; in the Netherlands it is 1.55 in 1913; in Germany it is over 3; in Italy it is 2.72 or 3.49; and even in Sweden, not mentioned as a case of nonconformity so far, it is 1.14 or 1.60. On the other hand, in France, Norway, and the United States the initial relatives for the I sector are well above 1.0; and the S/I ratios are low, and represent no significant deviation from what might have been expected from the cross-section. It may be that in many of the cases in which sectoral relatives for the I sector were low and S/I ratios were high the per worker product in the I sector was kept low by the large weight of textiles, clothing, and wood products. Whatever the explanation, the fact of nonconformity for the majority of countries remains.

(f) In the movements over time, the relative for the S sector tends to decline; and naturally so, since the initial level is unusually high in the majority of the countries. But the relative for the I sector, which, according to the cross-section in Table 31, should also have moved down toward 1.0, does not do so with the rise in per capita product over time. It rose in Great Britain, Belgium, the Netherlands, Germany, and Italy, and tended to remain constant in Canada. These rises and constancy in the relative for the I sector are again failures to conform to the trend expected from the cross-section.

We should also expect that in those countries in which sectoral product per worker in the I sector rose (or failed to decline), the relative for the manufacturing subdivision would show a similar trend. But we cannot test the inference adequately because data for comparable long periods and the same countries for shares of manufacturing in both product and labor force are limited (see, however, Tables 22, 23, 39, and 40).

It follows that the S/I ratio declines in almost all countries — and in most of them the decline is far greater than should have been expected from Table 31. In the latter, as we move from the $300 to the $1,000 benchmark value, the S/I ratio drops from 0.96 to 0.81, a decline of about a seventh with the per capita product more than tripling. The declines in column 6 of Table 45 are much sharper, although the rises in per capita product are narrower. To give one example: for Belgium the ratio declined from 2.21 in 1910 to 1.12 in 1963–1967, a drop of about a half over fifty-odd years, during which per capita product did not quite double.

(g) The two ratios discussed so far, $(I+S)/A$ and S/I, represent *unweighted* measures of sectoral inequality in product per worker. Since neither measure is affected by the size of the sectoral shares in total labor force, the movement in the ratio may be accompanied by a progressive loss of impact. An $(I+S)/A$ ratio of 2.0 has one meaning when both the A and the $I+S$ sectors account for 50 percent of the labor force, and another when the A sector is only 5 percent and the $I+S$ sector is 95 percent of the labor force.

The total measure of inequality in the cross-section (based on the three major sectors) declines from 47 points at $150 to 14 points at $1,000 (see Table 31, line 13). As the earlier discussion of the initial levels of the A sector suggested, column 7 of Table 45 shows that in many developed countries, the weighted measure of inter-sectoral inequality in the *initial* period is appreciably lower than one would have expected from the current cross-section. This is true of Great Britain, the Netherlands, Germany, Denmark, Sweden (for current price volumes), Italy (for current price volumes), Canada, the United States, and Australia — all with inequality measures of 35 points or less. Furthermore, in nine developed countries — Great Britain, France (in which the intersectoral ratio rose), Belgium, the Netherlands, Germany, Denmark, Norway, Sweden, and Italy (after 1881–1900) — the weighted measure of inequality declined over the long period. But in the other four, even the weighted measure of sectoral inequality in product per worker failed to decline — throughout the period, or through most of it until the recent decades.

Because of the intriguing differences between the trends over time in relative product per worker in the several sectors and in the key intersectoral ratios, and those that would have been expected from the current cross-section, the latter were also compared with the changes over the recent decade. This comparison should be revealing because the long-term records suggest that the post-World War II decade witnessed a reversal of the trends, at least for most developed countries.

Table 46 summarizes the results for sectoral product per worker

Table 46. Changes in relative product per worker, major sectors, 1950 to 1960.

A. Twenty countries, five groups of four, arrayed in increasing order of 1950 GDP per capita in 1958 $, based on sectoral shares in product in constant prices

	Product per worker, relative to total (excluding banking, insurance, and real estate, and income from dwellings)				Intersectoral ratios	
	A (1)	I+S (2)	I (3)	S (4)	(I+S)/A (5)	S/I (6)
Group I ($127; 16.8%)						
1. 1950	0.72	2.04	1.98	2.13	2.83	1.08
2. 1960	0.67	1.86	1.93	1.78	2.78	0.92
Group II ($169; 38.1%)						
3. 1950	0.64	1.56	1.41	1.67	2.44	1.18
4. 1960	0.62	1.48	1.46	1.46	2.39	1.00
Group III ($299; 39.4%)						
5. 1950	0.59	1.37	1.13	1.62	2.32	1.43
6. 1960	0.56	1.35	1.27	1.41	2.41	1.11
Group IV ($651; 43.6%)						
7. 1950	0.62	1.15	1.21	1.09	1.85	0.90
8. 1960	0.75	1.07	1.16	0.94	1.43	0.81
Group V ($1,018; 32.0%)						
9. 1950	0.62	1.13	1.25	0.99	1.82	0.79
10. 1960	0.70	1.06	1.25	0.84	1.51	0.67

B. Twenty-four countries, six groups of four, arrayed as in panel A, based on extrapolating shares of A sector in current product (usually for 1960) by FAO indexes of agricultural production

	Product per worker, relative to total (excluding banking, insurance, and real estate, and income from dwellings)					
	A		I+S		(I+S)/A	
	1950 (1)	1960 (2)	1950 (3)	1960 (4)	1950 (5)	1960 (6)
11. Group I ($62; 39.3%)	0.76	0.61	1.63	2.12	2.14	3.48
12. Group II ($173; 35.2%)	0.66	0.63	2.00	1.65	3.03	2.62
13. Group III ($252; 44.4%)	0.64	0.57	1.25	1.28	1.95	2.25
14. Group IV ($487; 60.4%)	0.53	0.68	1.22	1.09	2.30	1.60
15. Group V ($725; 34.6%)	0.56	0.75	1.19	1.08	2.12	1.44
16. Group VI ($1,284; 23.0%)	0.62	0.76	1.09	1.04	1.76	1.37

The twenty countries in panel A were all for which sectoral shares in both labor force and product in constant prices could be calculated — permitting an estimate of relative product per worker (to a total excluding finance and income from dwellings) for each country, in a constant sectoral price structure, at the initial and terminal years of the period. The entries in lines 1–10, columns 1–4, are geometric means of the product per worker relatives. The intersectoral ratios in columns 5 and 6 are calculated from columns 1–4.

The following countries (in increasing order of their GDP per capita in 1958 dollars around 1950) were included: Pakistan, Turkey, Ecuador, Honduras, Dominican Republic, Portugal, El Salvador, Colombia, Nicaragua, Greece, Chile, Italy, Germany (FR), Belgium, Argentina, Finland, France, Norway, Denmark, Canada. For sources of estimates of product per capita in 1958 dollars see the notes to Table 26.

For the countries in panel B the shares of the A sector (in total product, excluding finance and income from dwellings) were established for a recent year (usually 1960) from the usual sources; and extrapolated by the movement of the index of agricultural production of the Food and Agriculture Organization, relative to that of total product. The former indexes are given in the annual issues of the Food and Agriculture Organization of the United Nations, *Yearbook of Agricultural Production.*

The following countries were included (in increasing order of GDP per capita in 1958 dollars around 1950): Thailand, India, Pakistan, United Arab Republic, Turkey, Honduras, Portugal, Spain, Colombia, Japan, Greece, Chile, Ireland, Italy, the Netherlands, Germany (FR), Argentina, Finland, Belgium, France, Norway, Denmark, Canada, the United States.

The entries in parentheses in the stubs indicate the geometric mean product per capita about 1950 and the percentage increase in the group per capita product over the period.

The entries in panel B, columns 1–4 are also geometric means of the sectoral relatives for the countries in each group. The intersectoral ratios in columns 5 and 6 are calculated from columns 1–4.

at two dates, about 1950 and 1960, for two samples of countries, in both of which sectoral shares in product (at constant prices, and excluding finance and rent) and in labor force (unadjusted for conversion to equivalent units) were available for both dates. In one sample the basic data are direct estimates of sectoral shares in product taken from the national accounts; in the other the share of the A sector in product at constant prices was approximated by extrapolation from one current year (usually 1960) by the differential movement of the FAO index of agricultural production and of the aggregate product in constant prices. The second sample, although larger, is subject to wider error than the first; and, of course, does not distinguish between the I and S sectors.

For each sample the countries were grouped in increasing order of per capita GDP in the initial year, and then for each group the geometric mean of the individual country relatives of sectoral product per worker was calculated. The results are quite impressive, and consistent with the findings on the movements over the post-World War II period of sectoral shares in product and labor force in the lower per capita income, less developed countries, as compared with those in the higher per capita product, developed countries.

First, in both samples, the lower per capita product groups show relatively little movement in the $(I+S)/A$ ratio (lines 1–6, column 5; and lines 11–13, columns 5–6). For the sample based on national accounts, the three lower income groups, with per capita product about 1950 ranging from $127 to $299 (in 1958 dollars), show, as expected, much larger $(I+S)/A$ ratios than the higher income groups — about 2.3 to 2.8, compared with 1.4 to 1.9 in the upper product groups (with per capita product in 1950 of $651 to over $1,000). But these intersectoral ratios for the three lower groups are about the same in 1950 and 1960, a stability which one would not expect from the cross-section, since in each of these groups per capita product rose significantly over the period, the increase ranging from 17 to 39 percent. The results for the sample based on the FAO indexes are somewhat more erratic, with the ratio rising in two of the three lowest groups.

By contrast, in both samples the intersectoral inequality as measured by the $(I+S)/A$ ratio decreases markedly for the upper per capita product, developed countries. In panel A, the average $(I+S)/A$ ratio drops from 1.8 to 1.4 for group IV and from 1.8 to 1.5 for group V; in panel B, the $(I+S)/A$ ratios for the three upper product per capita groups also decline sharply. Yet in panel A, the average rise in per capita product was somewhat smaller for group V than for groups II and III; and in panel B, the average rates of growth in per capita product of groups V and VI, with marked reductions in the $(I+S)/A$ ratio, were lower than the average for groups I–III.

The disparity between less developed and developed countries in response of intersectoral inequality, as represented by the $(I+S)/A$ ratio, to a rise in per capita product is confirmed when we consider the results for individual countries, and record the frequency with which the ratio rose or declined over the period. For the sample in panel A we find that in seven of the twelve countries in the three lowest per capita product groups, the $(I+S)/A$ ratio rose between 1950 and 1960, whereas in five it declined; and in seven of the eight countries in the higher per capita groups it declined, rising only in Argentina. The results would be reinforced slightly if we moved Italy, the top per capita product country in group III, to the developed division. With that shift, we would have seven rises and four declines in the eleven low product countries; and eight declines and one rise in the nine upper product countries. In the larger sample in panel B, the results are equally striking. In eight of the twelve countries in the lower three groups, the $(I+S)/A$ ratio rose, and in four it declined; in eleven of the twelve countries in the upper three groups the ratio declined, and in Norway only, it rose slightly. In short, the marked reduction in the disparity in product per worker between the A and I+S sectors in the developed countries and its absence in the less developed countries were a widely observed feature of the post-World War II decade.

Second, the S/I ratio — for the sample in panel A — tended to decline, as we would have expected from the cross-section, and the movement is observed in both the less developed and the developed countries. In every group the S/I ratio was distinctly lower around 1960 than around 1950; and the declines from the initially higher ratios were absolutely, and even proportionately, greater in the less developed than in the developed countries (column 6, lines 1–10). The widespread character of the movement is confirmed by a count of frequencies: in ten of the twelve countries in groups I–III the ratio declined, and it rose in only two; and in seven of the eight countries in groups IV and V it declined, and it rose in only one. I could have considered the magnitude of this decline in the S/I ratio to determine whether it was fully accounted for by the relations between this ratio and differences in per capita product in the recent cross-section, but, in view of the significant and illuminating disparities between the cross-section and the observed changes in the $(I+S)/A$ ratio, it did not seem worthwhile to pursue the question further.

The first broad conclusion is that during the post-World War II decade the basic intersectoral inequality in product per worker, that between the A and the I+S sectors, did not respond to rising per capita (and presumably per worker) product in the less developed countries, but did so in the developed countries. This is consistent with the findings of Tables 26 and 43 that in the case of product, in the less developed countries, the observed declines in the share of the A sector and rises in the share of the I+S sector over the post-World War II period were *greater* than those expected from the cross-section; and in the case of labor force, the observed declines in the share of the A sector, again over the post-World War II period, were *smaller* than those expected from the cross-section. For the developed countries we found no such contrast; in them, the *observed* declines in the share of the A sector over the post-World War II period in *both* product and labor force were greater than expected from the cross-section. One problem with the separate analysis of shares in product and in labor force was that the former related to the period 1953–1965 and the latter to the span between about 1950 and 1960. But the results suggested by a comparison of Tables 26 and 43 are fully confirmed by Table 46, which is based on shares in product and labor force for an identical period and identical sample.

The second broad conclusion relates to the widespread post-World War II decline in the S/I ratio, which characterizes both less and more developed countries (panel A, column 6). The cross-section relations indicate that the S/I ratio is 0.96 at the benchmark levels of $150 and $300, and then declines to 0.85 at $500 and 0.81 at $1,000 (see Table 31, line 11). The S/I ratios for 1950 in Table 46 are well above the cross-section levels for groups I–III, but decline conspicuously and much more than one would expect from the cross-section. The reason lies primarily in the movement of the sectoral relatives of product per worker for the I sector (column 3): whereas in the cross-section this relative, like that for the S sector, declines as we move from the $150 to the $1,000 benchmark value (from 1.67 to 1.15), no such movement appears over the post-World War II decade — there are two rises, two minor declines, and one case of no change from 1950 to 1960 in column 3. Clearly, in the post-World War II decade the rise in the share in product (more marked than in the cross-section) and the much lesser rise in the share in labor force (less marked than in the cross-section) were more conspicuous for the I sector than for the S sector. For this reason the decline in the S/I ratio was much greater than could have been expected from the cross-section.

Both the failure of the (I+S)/A ratio to decline significantly and the sharp decline in S/I ratio during the 1950's in the less developed countries may reflect the difficulties in finding proper employment for their growing labor force. This may be one reason why the share of A in the labor force has not declined sufficiently. Per worker productivity in the S sector may also have been diluted by the higher proportion of low-income employment.

VII

Summary and Interrelations

A Summary of Findings

This review of the long-term records of aggregate growth and of production structure was limited to the developed countries, those in which per capita product and the level of industrialization and modernization were high enough to testify to successful exploitation of the potentials of modern economic growth. The one or two Communist countries that might have qualified on the basis of per capita product were excluded because of their distinctive social structure and a highly variable and rather short growth record. The few less developed countries over the long term were included only for illustrative purposes; and the additional ones in the post-World War II years for a more complete analysis of cross-section associations.

The following summary of findings does not cover all the points raised in this book's detailed discussion. Its purpose is primarily to assemble the major results, in order to facilitate the discussion of the interrelations among the distinctive characteristics of aggregate growth and trends in production structure.

1. For the long period since the entry of the fifteen to eighteen presently developed countries into modern economic growth, that is, since dates ranging from the late eighteenth century for Great Britain to the 1880's for Japan, but concentrated between the 1830's and 1870's, total product grew roughly 3 percent, population about 1 percent, and per capita product about 2 percent per year. These

303

rates — almost a tripling of population, more than a fivefold rise in per capita product, and a rise in total product by a factor of at least fifteen over a century — were far greater than those previously observed in Japan and the older developed countries in Europe. (For the European offshoots overseas such a comparison is irrelevant since they were relatively empty territories in the early days.) The acceleration in growth over the preceding centuries for both per capita and total product was large enough, and has by now lasted long enough to warrant the view that the last one and a half to two centuries represent a *new* economic epoch that reflects the emergence of a new group of factors large enough to dominate growth over a long period.

2. Except for Japan, the presently developed countries are all in Europe, or are European offshoots overseas. At the time of their entry into modern economic growth they were already economically in advance of the rest of the world, with per capita product at least two to three times as high as per capita product today in the populous underdeveloped countries of Asia and Africa. This historical association among modern economic growth, the European affiliation of the developed countries, and their initially high per capita product (all with the conspicuous exception of Japan), makes it extremely important to distinguish, in the analysis of modern economic growth, between elements that can be specifically assigned to this historical connection and those that cannot, and that can therefore be conceived as transferable within non-European institutions and economic contexts.

3. The less developed countries have failed to enter the developed group either because of the low initial levels of their per capita product or because of the low rates of growth in per capita product during the past century to century and a half — or, usually, for both reasons. It follows that the current international difference in per capita product, which is roughly between fifteen and twenty to one (based on the average for the developed countries and that for the populous Asian countries with per capita GDP in the early 1960's of below $100), results partly from differences in growth rates over the nineteenth and twentieth centuries, and partly from disparities in initial per capita product. Furthermore, since most countries that have enjoyed modern economic growth had initially high per capita product, international differences have grown wider

and have continued to do so even through the post-World War II years.

4. Given differences in date of entry and in growth rates of population and total product, even among the developed countries, the generally high growth rates characteristic of modern economic growth suggest rapid shifts in total economic magnitude (and in per capita product) among the developed countries themselves. Adjustments of political relations to these shifts in economic magnitude (and economic power) are, therefore, required at frequent intervals — probably more frequent than if growth rates were lower and the cumulation of international disparities were slower.

5. Acceleration or deceleration in the aggregate growth rates of developed countries has been consistent in only a few cases. In some, particularly the European offshoots overseas, population growth has slowed down because of reduction in the relative contribution of immigration compared with pre-World War I decades; and, since per capita product showed no marked acceleration in these cases, the growth rate of total product also slowed down. This pattern of retardation in population growth is not found among the older developed countries. Perhaps, given the long swings in growth rates (noted under point 6), the period is too short for testing consistent long-term acceleration or deceleration of growth rates in population and per capita product. The stability is significant, since, as the shifts in production structure show, the growth of most segments of total production does drop off after a while, bringing about a decline in their shares in the countrywide aggregate. Thus, the absence of a trend toward retardation of growth, although typical of total or per capita product, is not typical of subdivisions within a country's economy; and implies the sustaining effects of entries of new subdivisions (industries) with higher than average growth rates.

6. For the few countries for which a long and continuous record of growth can be observed for the decades before World War I (the later period is affected too much by major world wars), we find long swings in growth rates (fluctuations over a span of some twenty years), with fairly conspicuous peaks and troughs in the decennial growth rates. The associations among these swings and the plausible connections behind them strongly confirm their existence in a variety of economic aspects of the developed economies. The two

world wars in the twentieth century, of course, put their own stamp on these fluctuations; and the proper interpretation of the rather high rates of growth in the post-World War II decade to decade and a half requires careful consideration of the prewar long-term trends and of the long swings in them.

7. The high rate of growth in product per capita associated with modern economic growth can be credited to a large degree to growth of productivity, that is, of output per unit of input — input measured within the accepted framework of national economic accounting, and limited to manhours of labor and to material capital (nonreproducible and reproducible), the latter measured at original or, preferably, reproduction cost). With this measure of input, the rise in productivity amounts to at least eight-tenths of the rise in per capita product in several countries. With rates of increase in per capita product so much higher in the modern economic growth epoch than in earlier centuries, we may reasonably assume that the rate of increase in productivity was also much higher.

8. Under the conventional definition of inputs, major factors limit the increase in input per capita; consequently, the high growth rate of per capita product *must* be the result of the high growth rate of productivity. Labor input per capita is limited by the proportion of labor force to total population and by the number of working hours. The proportion of labor force to total population has been relatively stable during the long period of modern economic growth, the rise in the proportion of population of working ages (the result of a decline in birth rates and in death rates at the lower ages) having been largely offset by the rise in the age of entry into labor force (with extended education) and the lowering of the age of retirement (with the greater weight of employee-status jobs that limit employment of older workers). The hours per week or year worked by the labor force have declined, especially in the later phases of economic growth, because higher per capita income has permitted the choice of more leisure rather than more income. The rise in material capital input is limited by the fraction that weights its growth, that is, the share of capital returns in total income, which has declined over time from over 40 to about 20 percent. And, more important, the growth rate of capital stock has been slower than the growth rate of product, partly because nonreproducible assets were a large proportion of the initial capital stock and partly because special factors limit the level and upward

trend in the savings and capital formation proportions in total product as the latter grows over time. The rate of growth in the combined input of labor and capital per capita was probably lower in the later periods because of the greater decline in hours and reduced weight of capital. Given stability of the growth rate in per capita product, this would mean an acceleration in the growth of productivity.

9. Since per capita manhours and material capital grew so little, and since the growth of per capita product was largely the result of a high growth rate of productivity, improvements in quality of labor and capital — improvements not caused by any extra input of resources — were responsible for the high rate of growth of per capita product so characteristic of modern economic growth. These "costless" improvements are connected with the tremendous increase in the stock of useful knowledge, much of it traceable to growth of science viewed as a social institution devoted to the production of new tested and hence potentially useful knowledge. This inference is supported by the connection between the rapidly growing segments of modern developed economies in their succession over time and science-oriented-and-linked technological innovations.

10. It may be argued that conventional economic accounting overestimates the growth of productivity because it omits various current and capital costs. Among the omitted current costs are actual outlays, now classified under consumption but properly debited to changes in conditions of life caused by economic growth and the accompanying shifts in production structure (as, for example, greater individual outlays on sanitation, and so on, in urban conditions; or greater outlays by government caused by the complexities of large-scale enterprises requiring regulation, or urban policing and similar needs). Other current costs may not involve actual outlay, but represent diseconomies of scale for which no economically feasible offset has been provided (such as air pollution by automobiles or the pervasive noise of transistor radios in public areas). The major omitted capital costs are those of education, formal or on-the-job training, both viewed as long-term investment in quality of labor as a productive factor.

11. It is far from easy to distinguish between final outlays on food, clothing, and such, that have to do with "the good life," and those required by changed conditions of a job, or between long-

term "investment" in education in preparation for a mode of life and such investment as equipment for a job. It is not surprising that conventional economic accounting avoids the problem by disregarding such questionable costs. But the problem exists; and a rough illustrative calculation of the effects of merely reclassifying several overt outlays, now considered consumption, as either current or capital costs (based largely on data for the United States) indicates a perceptible reduction in the growth rate of net national product per capita from, say, about 1.9 percent per year to 1.7 percent), an even greater reduction in the growth rate of productivity (from about 1.5 percent per year to about 0.9 percent); and a resultant reduction in the ratio of growth of productivity to that of per capita product (from 0.8 to 0.56). Even these reduced rates of growth of product per capita and of productivity are high compared with premodern centuries — if only because of the enormous acceleration shown by the measures derived by conventional economic accounting and the limited scope of the adjustments mentioned. But although in the calculation the additional costs of economic growth reflected in actual outlays reduce only partially the enormous acceleration represented by modern economic growth, the question of hidden costs remains a major problem. A critical scrutiny of all the costs and returns, not only of actual output and input, might yield different results and would be useful, granted that it would involve debatable speculation. Such an approach would be one way of considering the implications of the economic and social past for the future that cannot be revealed in the market-oriented records of conventional national economic accounting.

12. Before we review the trends in production structure, it should be emphasized that the growth rates of product and productivity just discussed, although based on overtly observed and recorded output and input, are completely dependent upon the definitions of goals of economic activity and the related criteria for distinguishing between returns and costs, between output and input. The conventional economic accounting and analysis (and the foregoing discussion) rest upon the basic assumption of the primacy of the final consumers, as individuals or in some collective capacity — so that their consumption determines final output, thereby permitting the distinction of costs, inputs, and intermediate products. On another assumption — such as one in which the growth of political power for the spread of an ideology is considered paramount

— net product would equal the increase in the number of individuals loyal to the ideology and the increase in their "loyalty," however measured; plus the increase in the stock of tools by which such loyalty can be applied for the spread of the ideology. Consumption by individuals would become either a current or capital cost; and the levels and trends of net product and productivity would not be at all like those that we are discussing. This dependence of definitions and measures on broadly accepted goals and criteria of economic and social activity does not make the measures less useful in revealing the quantitative parameters in societies broadly geared to such goals and in those aspiring to them, but it does limit the bearing of the results to these societies and reduces their relevance, at least as explanatory data, to societies otherwise oriented and governed.

13. The three major sectors distinguished in this review of production structure are: A, agriculture, and related industries like fisheries, forestry, and hunting; I, mining, manufacturing, construction, electric power, gas, and water, transportation, storage, and communication; and S, trade, finance, insurance, and real estate, income from dwellings, and a variety of personal, professional, recreational, educational, and governmental services. Trends in the shares of these sectors in gross or net domestic or national product in the course of growth in developed countries are familiar: a marked decline in the share of the A sector, from over 40 percent in the initial decades to less than 10 percent in recent years; a marked rise in the share of the I sector, from between 22 and 25 percent in the initial decades to between 40 and 50 percent in recent years; and a slight but not consistent rise in the share of the S sector (except in a few countries like France, the United States, and possibly Canada which show somewhat more conspicuous rises). These trends are found in the shares in both current and constant price volumes, the latter available for only a few countries. One might have expected that because of the greater effect of modern technology on costs of I than of A sector products, the changes in the shares of the two would be greater for constant than for current price volumes. But no such difference is found, either because the price indexes are not sufficiently sensitive, or because the assumption is not entirely valid.

14. The rise in the share of the I sector is largely contributed to by manufacturing, the share of which rises from between 11 and

15 percent in the initial decades to over 30 percent, accounting for about two-thirds of the rise in the share of the I sector (and of the decline in that of the A sector). Within manufacturing, the shares of the metal fabricating and the chemical-petroleum branches rise conspicuously, whereas those of the textiles and clothing, and wood and leather branches decline. Of the other subdivisions of the I sector, it is the share of transportation and public utilities that rises relatively most rapidly. Among the subdivisions of the S sector, only the share of government services tends to rise in most countries. Long-term changes in the shares of the other subdivisions of the S sector are minor, and show much diversity among countries.

15. The rates of change in the shares of the A sector, the I sector, and the latter's major subdivisions, must have been far higher than in the preceding centuries. Thus, the decline in the share of the A sector, by some 30 percentage points in a century to a century and a half, for the older developed countries of Europe (and Japan), may be compared with what was probably a decline of 20 percentage points over several centuries from a peak that, judging by the least industrialized countries of today, must have been over 60 percent (assignable in Europe roughly to the early Middle Ages).

16. The reduction in the share of the A sector in product, the rise in that of the I sector, and the rather inconsistent and limited rise in that of the S sector, all conform with cross-section associations between per capita product and shares of sectors in total product in recent years. Yet, although per capita product is the dominant factor in the cross-section associations, the changes in shares over time that can be *estimated* from it, fall short of the *observed* trends by a substantial margin. Thus, on the average for several countries, the observed proportional decline in the share of the A sector exceeds the decline estimated from the cross-section (for 1958, but a similar result could be expected from the cross-sections for other years) by a ratio of 1 to 0.6; and the observed proportional rise for the I+S sector is twice that estimated from the cross-section. This means that the share of the A sector declined even when per capita product did not rise (and indeed such cases can be found among the less developed countries also); and that some institutional and technological factors moved the whole regression curve represented by the cross-section downward over time for the share of the A sector and upward over time for the share of the I+S sector. Similar shortages of the estimated changes, based

on the cross-section, in the sectoral shares and even those for branches of manufacturing are found for a shorter post-World War II period (from 1953 to 1965), even though the cross-sections are derived from data for the same period. The size of the shortfalls of the cross-section estimates, and their differences at different levels of per capita product point to the significance of the growth factors that the cross-section fails to reflect — and fails in different ways for countries at different levels of development.

17. The share of the A sector in labor force declined sharply in the course of growth of the developed countries, from initial levels ranging between 50 and 60 percent to levels from below 10 to about 20 percent in the early 1960's (labor force adjusted by weighting the number of women in the A sector by 0.2, and in the other sectors by 0.6 — to allow for unpaid family labor in the A sector and the lower productive capacity of women than of men in other sectors). The share of the I sector rose from initial levels that ranged between 20 and 40 percent to levels that were well above 40 in most countries — but, unlike the changes in the shares in product, the rise of the I sector share was not dominant relative to the decline in the share of the A sector. The rise in the share of the I sector in the labor force of most developed countries was either smaller than or about the same as that of the S sector. The moderate rise of the share of the I sector in labor force is due largely to the moderate rise of the share of manufacturing and contrasts with the dominant role of the rise of manufacturing in product. It follows that the share of the S sector rose markedly, offsetting a large part of the decline in the share of the A sector. While the structure of product was "industrialized" in the narrower meaning of the term associated with the rise of manufacturing, construction, and the I sector in general, the structure of labor force was partly "industrialized," partly "servicized"; indeed, in some developed countries like the United States, the S sector accounted toward the end for more than half of total labor force. Within the S sector the share in labor force of domestic service (and similar services, such as laundries, outside the home) declined, but the shares of other service subdivisions increased generally and substantially — even though the shares in product showed no marked trend.

18. With the share of the A sector in labor force declining between 35 and 50 percentage points in a century or a century and a quarter, the shifts in production structure of labor force, like those

in the structure of product, were far more rapid than those that must have occurred in the older countries in premodern centuries. Even in the older European countries, like Belgium, the Netherlands, France, and Germany, the initial levels, about the middle nineteenth century, of the share of the A sector in labor force were between 50 and 60 percent; and the highest premodern share, again judging by data for the least industrialized countries of today, must have been between 70 and 80 percent. Any industrialization and urbanization of the labor force in earlier centuries that brought the level at the beginning of modern growth in presently developed countries to between 50 and 60 percent must have been at rates much lower than 25 to 40 points per century. This rapid shift is of particular importance in dealing with labor force, that is, with the members of the economic society whose growth we are studying. Population and labor force increase by processes that are not necessarily and closely affected by economic change — and through most of the decades of modern economic growth the rates of natural increase of rural population and agricultural labor force were higher than those of the urban and non-A sector labor force. This conflict between demographic trend differentials and the differentials in economic growth and employment opportunities was the cause of much internal migration, separation between family roots and employment locus, intra- and particularly intergenerational shifts — with all the consequences of such economic and social mobility. The acceleration of these rates of shift, the faster tempo of internal mobility, is a distinctive and crucial characteristic of modern economic growth.

19. The trends in shares of major sectors in labor force conform with cross-section associations between per capita product and shares in labor force for recent years. But again, as in the case of product, the cross-section parameters tend to underestimate the expected trends, and by similarly wide margins. Thus, for eighteen countries for which sectoral shares in labor force can be observed over a half century extending from 1910–1911 to 1960–1961, the cross-section associations for either the initial or terminal year, yield estimates that fall short of the observed changes by four-tenths for the share of the A sector, over a half for the share of the S sector, and about a fifth for the share of the I sector. In a similar test for a post-World War II decade (from 1950 to 1960) the cross-sections overestimate the changes for the lower per capita product countries, and under-

estimate those for the higher per capita product countries — indicating that for the less developed countries the decline of the share of the A sector and the rises of the shares of the I and S sectors were smaller than should have resulted, on the basis of the cross-sections, from the rise in per capita product; whereas for the developed countries, these shifts in sectoral shares in labor force were greater than should have been expected. On the basis of the forward projection (the 1950 cross-section), the observed decline in the A sector share in the lower per capita product countries was one-fourth lower than that estimated; the observed decline in the high per capita product countries was one-fourth higher than that estimated.

20. The relative sectoral product per worker is derived from the shares in product and in labor force — with or without adjustments of product and labor force (to exclude pure property income components like the income from dwellings and the finance, insurance, and real estate subdivision; and to reduce the weight of the female labor force) which do not affect significantly the major levels and trends. In the cross-section comparisons for recent years, the relative product per worker in the A sector is distinctly below 1.0 (that is, lower than the average for all sectors) at low per capita product levels and tends to rise toward 1.0 in the higher per capita product countries, while the opposite is true of the relative product per worker for the I+S sector. By contrast, the initial levels of the relative product per worker in both the A and I+S sectors in many developed countries are much closer to 1.0 — and the major intersectoral disparity, measured by the (I+S)/A ratio, which declines from above 4.0 to 1.8 in the cross-section ranges of per capita product from $70 to $500 (1958 dollars), is far lower than that for most of the presently developed countries in their initial decades. In other words, the duality of structure — a large A sector with rather low per worker product contrasted with a small I+S sector with much higher per worker product — typical not only of the least developed countries but even of countries in the $200 to $500 range in the current cross-section, did not characterize most presently developed countries in the initial phases of their modern growth (when their per capita product fell within the $200 to $500 range).

21. In many developed countries relative product per worker in the A sector tended to decline; and the intersectoral (I+S)/A ratio tended to rise over the long period — at least before World War II.

These trends are not what should have been expected from the cross-section associations, which show a clear convergence of differences in sectoral product per worker, and a marked decline in the $(I+S)/A$ ratio, with the shift from lower to higher per capita product. It is only since World War II that there apparently has been a general, and fairly marked, decline in the intersectoral inequality ratio, generated largely by a more rapid rise in per worker product in the A sector than in the rest of the economy.

22. Analysis of a much larger sample, including both developed and less developed countries, for the post-World War II period (roughly between 1950 and 1960), indicates that in the *lower* per capita product countries, despite substantial rises in per capita product, relative product per worker in the A sector did not rise; and the intersectoral inequality ratio, $(I+S)/A$, did not decline. In the higher per capita countries (well over \$600 in 1958 prices), relative product per worker in the A sector tended to rise and the intersectoral inequality ratio tended to drop. This additional case of differential nonconformity between cross-section estimates and observed time trends suggests an important conclusion: in the post-World War II period, the industrialization growth process in the less developed countries, marked in the shares in product, was limited in the case of labor force, widening the already wide contrast between the A and I+S sectors.

Relation Between Aggregate Growth and Production Structure: An Additional Illustration

Two of the findings just summarized deserve further exploration: the high rate of growth of per capita product and productivity; and the high rate of shift in production structure. I emphasized that for the developed countries both the rate of aggregate growth and the rate of shift in production structure are much higher in the period of modern economic growth than those in their premodern past, and, needless to say, than those in the recent century to century and a half for the less developed countries. The historical association of the high rates of growth of per capita product and productivity with the high rate of shifts in production structure is confirmed positively, by the experience of developed countries, and negatively, by the experience of the less developed countries.

Before exploring factors behind this association, I reemphasize the serious limitations of the data on sectoral structure of both product and labor force, already touched upon, arising from the failure of the classification to reveal the technologically new components. Since the high and accelerated rate of technological change is a major source of the high rates of growth of per capita product and productivity in modern times and is also responsible for striking shifts in production structure, it is frustrating that the available sectoral classifications fail to separate new industries from old, and distinguish those affected by technological innovations. The analysis of modern economic growth would benefit from data on the technologically new and the technologically old components of agriculture and manufacturing, and on the components in professional services and the like. The failure of the easily available data to do so is no accident; they reflect the natural tendency to distinguish components that are important because of their size, because of the institutional conditions required for their production, because of the position of these products on the scale of immediacy and priority of demand, and the like. Technological innovation is only one facet, and one that does not lend itself easily to distinction and measurement. As a result, both the true rate of shift in production structure and its connection with the high rate of aggregate growth are grossly underestimated.

Some illustrative evidence on the effects of technological change on structure of output is provided in Table 47. Here I take advantage of the long-term series for the United States, from 1880 to 1948, on value of product in constant prices for thirty-eight branches of manufacturing (excluding liquors and beverages, because of the effect of Prohibition on the record, and the miscellaneous branch, because of identification problems).

Using two simple and seemingly mechanical criteria — the size of the share in 1880; and the rate of growth (or multiplication) from 1880 to 1914 — I formed four broad groups of these branches. Group A includes branches whose product accounted for 0.6 percent or less of total value product in 1880, and whose output grew by a factor of at least 6 between 1880 and 1914. Group B includes branches whose product accounted for more than 0.6 percent of total product in 1880, and whose product grew by a factor of at least 6 from 1880 to 1914. Group C includes the branches whose output grew during 1880–1914 by a factor of less than 6 but more than 3, regardless of the size of their product (in relation to the

Table 47. Changes in shares of branches of manufacturing in output and capital of total manufacturing grouped by rapidity of growth in initial period, United States, 1880 to 1948.

	I. Shares in value of output in 1929 prices (%)		
	1880 (1)	1914 (2)	1948 (3)
Group A. Share in 1880 of 0.6 percent or less; growth factor, 1880 to 1914, of 6 or more			
1. Canned foods	0.4	1.0	1.6
2. Silk and rayon goods	0.3	0.8	1.6
3. Knit goods	0.3	1.0	1.3
4. Rubber products	0.2	0.5	2.3
5. Fertilizers	0.2	0.5	0.4
6. Chemicals proper, acids, compounds, etc.	0.4	0.8	2.2
7. Petroleum refining	0.3	1.2	10.4
8. Metal building materials and supplies	0.3	2.1	2.1
9. Electrical machinery and equipment, radios, etc.	0.1	1.8	4.9
10. Office equipment (metal)	0.1	0.4	0.5
11. Motor vehicles	0	1.5	6.8
12. Locomotives	0.6	1.4	0.7
13. Airplanes, etc.	0	0	0.8
14. Total, group A	3.2	13.0	35.6
(a) Automobile subgroup (lines 4, 7, 11)	0.5	3.2	19.4
(b) Other	2.7	9.8	16.2
Group B. Share in 1880 of more than 0.6 percent; growth factor, 1880 to 1914, of 6 or more			
15. Bakery and confectionery products	2.1	3.5	2.6
16. Other food products	1.6	4.4	4.6
17. Paper products	1.1	2.3	2.7
18. Printing, publishing, etc.	2.7	5.3	3.1
19. Stone, clay, and glass	2.2	3.5	2.4
20. Iron and steel	4.1	7.5	8.3
21. Other nonferrous metal products	1.5	4.3	2.6
22. Total, group B	15.3	30.8	26.3

Table 47 — continued

	(1)	(2)	(3)
Group C. Growth factor, 1880 to 1914, of less than 6 but more than 3			
23. Sugar refining	1.1	1.2	0.6
24. Tobacco products	2.4	2.2	2.2
25. Cotton goods	5.2	4.2	1.2
26. Clothing	5.8	6.7	4.9
27. Allied chemical products, paints, varnishes, etc.	2.8	3.7	4.9
28. Hardware	1.1	1.1	0.9
29. Precious metal products, jewelry, etc.	0.5	0.6	0.6
30. Agricultural machinery, etc. (metal)	0.6	0.5	1.6
31. Miscellaneous machinery: factory, household, etc.	5.3	5.7	6.0
32. Total, group C	24.8	25.9	22.9
Group D. Lagging industries (all other); growth factor, 1880 to 1914, of less than 3			
33. Mill products (food)	6.0	3.4	2.0
34. Packing house products	12.4	8.4	5.0
35. Woolen and worsted goods	3.5	2.0	0.6
36. Carpets, floor coverings, tapestries, etc.	0.9	0.6	0.4
37. Textiles, n.e.c.	2.5	1.6	2.1
38. Boots and shoes	4.2	2.8	0.9
39. Other leather products	7.9	2.9	0.7
40. Sawmill and planing mill products	11.3	5.7	1.3
41. Other wood products	8.0	2.9	2.2
42. Total, group D	56.7	30.3	15.2

Growth factors	1880 to 1914	1914 to 1948	1880 to 1948
43. Total output	4.33	3.51	15.17
44. Group A	17.59	9.61	168.77
(a) Automobile subgroup	27.71	21.28	588.60
(b) Other	15.72	5.80	91.02
45. Group B	8.72	3.00	26.08
46. Group C	4.52	3.10	14.01
47. Group D	2.29	1.76	4.07

Table 47 — continued

	II. Shares in total capital in 1929 prices (%)		
	1880 (1)	1914 (2)	1948 (3)
48. Group A	6.0	16.2	39.2
(a) Automobile subgroup	1.0	4.2	22.6
(b) Other	5.0	12.0	16.6
49. Group B	21.3	33.0	26.5
50. Group C	29.8	27.7	23.2
51. Group D	42.9	23.1	11.1

Growth factors	1880 to 1914	1914 to 1948	1880 to 1948
52. Total capital stock	8.18	2.16	17.68
53. Group A	22.09	5.23	115.50
(a) Automobile subgroup	34.36	11.62	399.57
(b) Other	19.63	2.99	58.70
54. Group B	12.67	1.73	21.99
55. Group C	7.60	1.81	13.76
56. Group D	4.40	1.04	4.57

The underlying data are from Daniel Creamer, Sergei P. Dobrovolsky, and Israel Borenstein, *Capital in Manufacturing and Mining: Its Formation and Financing* (Princeton: Princeton University Press for the National Bureau of Economic Research, 1960), table A-10, pp. 252–258, for value of output; table A-8, pp. 241–247 for total capital (both in 1929 prices).

Because of changes in Census scope in 1900, two values are given for that year. In calculating the growth factors from 1880 to 1914 for the total and the individual branches, growth was therefore compounded from the two segments, 1880–1900 and 1900–14. But no correction was made in the shares shown in columns 1–2, which are to somewhat incomparable totals. The differences are, however, too slight to matter.

The one exception we made in grouping the industries was to place clothing in Group C rather than Group B, because the break in 1900 (a much lower value in 1900 comparable with later years) exaggerates the growth factor for the total period.

A rough allocation of the total output and capital in 1948 for cotton, silk and rayon, and woolen and worsted goods, was made on the basis of the 1937 breakdown.

Lines 44–47: Derived from line 43 by applying the percentage changes in the shares in total value of output in lines 14, 22, 32, 42.

Lines 48–51: Shares in total capital for the same groups of branches (shown in lines 1–13, 15–21, 23–31, 33–41).

Lines 53–56: Derived from line 52 by applying the percentage changes in the shares in lines 48–51.

total) in 1880. Group D comprises all other branches, that is, those whose output grew by a factor of 3 or less from 1880 to 1914. It should be noted that the growth factor for the total output of the thirty-eight branches over the 1880–1914 period was 4.33.

Several interesting results are revealed by this classification.

(a) The only branches with output not more than 0.6 percent of total manufacturing output in 1880 that failed to grow by a factor of more than 6 over the 1880–1914 period were precious metals, jewelry, and so forth, and agricultural machinery (lines 29–30). By contrast, eleven branches with output in 1880 of less than 0.6 percent of total value product had a growth factor from 1880 to 1914 larger than 6.[1]

To be sure, this result is partly a matter of classification; other branches, which might have had a small output in 1880 but failed to grow significantly, were probably no longer distinguished and were merged into larger groups. But two aspects of the finding are none-theless significant. First, most of the branches in Group A represent loci of quite recent or impending technological changes. This is certainly true of rubber products (increasingly dominated by auto-mobile tires), petroleum (increasingly dominated by the demand for automobile fuel), and motor vehicles — which have been com-bined into an automobile subgroup. But it is also true of most of the other branches in A: canned foods, silk and rayon (because of recent emergence of rayon), chemical fertilizers, chemicals proper, metal building materials, electrical machinery, metal office equip-ment, and locomotives. On the other hand, the large but lagging Group D includes the older food products, textiles, and wood in-dustries, in which any technological innovations made had too limited an effect to induce average growth. The second aspect is that in 1948 well over a third of the value of product of total manu-facturing was in branches that did not exist in 1880, or were so small that they accounted in all for about 3 percent of manufac-turing output.

(b) Group B, which also shows higher than average growth in 1880–1914, comprises industries that contributed a larger fraction of total manufacturing output than those in Group A in 1880 and in which technological innovation was relatively recent — but not as recent or as basic as in the new industries in Group A. New types

1. The underlying data are for value of output, rather than for value added or contribution to gross or net domestic product. Since the older and lagging industries are food products, textiles, wood, and so forth, branches in which the ratio of net output to value of total product is appreciably lower than in the more rapidly growing branches, the shifts in Table 47 exaggerate somewhat the shifts that would be shown by value added or contribution to domestic product. But the general findings would remain unchanged.

of food products, for increasingly urban markets, are in this group; and the other branches are relatively rapidly growing industries like paper, printing, and basic metals. In all the industries in Group B major technological changes were introduced in the nineteenth century, but all these industries were already well established by 1880.

(c) One should note the persistent effect of technological innovations. In nine of the eleven branches in Group A with some output in 1880, the growth rates were well above the average for total manufacturing not only in 1880–1914 but also in 1914–1948. The two exceptions are fertilizers — reflecting, one assumes, the slow growth of agriculture over the 1914–1948 period, and locomotives — reflecting the sharp decline in the growth of railways. By contrast, for four of the eight branches in Group B, also with higher than average growth rates from 1880 to 1914 (bakery and confectionery products; printing and publishing; stone, clay, and glass; and other nonferrous metal products) the growth rate over 1914–1948 is lower than that for total manufacturing.

An even more telling indication is provided by the shares for each group as a whole (lines 14, 22, 32, 42). The share of Group A rises from 3.2 to 13.0 percent over the first period, and then to 35.6 percent over the second period; and it is the only group for which the share rises significantly in *both* subperiods. Both subgroups of A also show the continued rise and the continued excess of growth rates over that for total output. By contrast, the share of Group B rises sharply over the first period, from 15.3 percent in 1880 to 30.8 percent in 1914; but then it declines to 26.3 percent in 1948. The share of Group C rises slightly over the first span, then drops over the second. Finally, the sharp declines in the share of Group D in both periods produce a drop from well over half of total product in 1880 to only a seventh in 1948.

(d) The differences in the growth factors of output over the scant seven decades are striking: that for the output of Group A is 169, whereas that for Group D is only 4, a ratio of more than 40 to 1. The contrast is even sharper for the automobile subgroup of A with a factor of 589. This shift in the structure of manufacturing output is far wider and more rapid than any shown in the tables in Chapter IV — and would be even for the shares of the manufacturing branches in domestic product.

(e) Two aspects of the interplay between the aggregate growth rate — in this case the growth of total value product for manufacturing, and the growth rates of components, in this case of "new" and "old" industries — should be explicitly mentioned. First, the growth rates of output of all the groups and even of total manufacturing show some retardation (compare columns 1–2, lines 43–47). Even the growth factor for the automobile subgroup drops from 27.7 in the first period to 21.3 in the second. But the decline in the growth factor for the total, from 4.33 to 3.51, is more moderate than that for any of the four groups. Since the aggregate growth rate for each period is a mean of the growth rates for the four groups, weighted by their shares at the initial date, retardation in growth for each group could be accompanied by stability (or even acceleration) in the growth rate of the aggregate. For example, if we changed the growth rate for Group B in the second period from 3.00 to 5.7 — which would still be appreciably below the factor of 8.7 for the first period — the aggregate growth factor in line 43, column 2, would become 4.33, identical with that for the first period. We could also demonstrate that the growth rate for the aggregate could accelerate, while those for all four groups slowed down. The important point is that the "new" industries, with small shares at their initial stages but with enormous growth rates, serve to sustain aggregate growth despite retardation in growth of all or most of the older (and newer) component industries.

(f) The second aspect is concerned with the contribution of a "new industry," particularly the timing of its major contribution to the growth of the aggregate. This point is best illustrated by the automobile subgroup. This "new" and eventually very important component of manufacturing and of the economy as a whole, grew at a *more rapid* rate in the first period than in the second. But its contribution to the 333 points that were added in the first period to the initial total of 100 (with a factor of 4.33) was only 13.9 points, or about 4 percent of the total proportional addition. In the second period, although its growth rate was lower, it contributed 68 of the 251 points added to the initial total of 100, or well over a quarter. Thus a "growth" industry will exercise its greatest effect not in the early and turbulent phases of its own growth, but at some later stage — after it has acquired a large enough base for its higher than average growth rate to make a substantial contribution to aggregate growth.

(g) Finally, we observe the differences in growth rates of total

material capital used among new, technological innovation-origi-
nating industries, and the older, less-innovation-affected branches
(panel II). Since the groups are identical with those in panel I —
and the capital values (like value of output) are given in 1929
dollars — the panels are comparable. Group A accounted for a
higher share of capital than of output in 1880, 6 rather than 3 percent; but this disparity diminished over time, and in 1948 its share
of capital was 39.2 percent, while its share of output was 35.6. But
these are details, and the comparison is qualified by the use of value
of output in panel I (rather than of the net contribution to product).
The main point is that the high rates of change in structure of
manufacturing output found when we distinguish the innovation-
originated industries are accompanied by similarly wide and rapid
shifts in the structure of total capital used in manufacturing — and
presumably also in the distribution of the total labor force attached
to this important subdivision of the I sector.

I have dwelled at length on Table 47 in order to illustrate several
quantitative aspects of the rapid structural change connected with
technological innovations — within the major subdivisions distinguished in preceding chapters, supplementing thereby the findings
presented in the earlier chapters and summarized in the first part
of this chapter. Moreover, discussion of the relations between aggregate growth and shifts in production structure, although only
exploratory, is also made easier.

Relation Between Aggregate Growth and Shifts in Production Structure: General Comments

In view of the historical association between high rates of growth
in per capita product and productivity and the high rate of shifts in
production structure, both in modern times, a general exploration
can be centered on two propositions. First, given high rates of
growth of per capita product and productivity, associated with extensive application to problems of production of new knowledge
and of technological innovation (much of it originating in science),
the rate of shift in the structure of production is also likely to be
high. And second, extensive *application* to problems of production
of new knowledge and high rates of growth of per capita product
and productivity, which, according to the first proposition, generate
a high rate of shift in production structure, are, in turn, indispen-

sable for a high rate of growth in the stock of useful knowledge and of science itself (the major permissive factor in modern economic growth), and thus may induce further growth of per capita product and productivity, at high rates. Obviously, such propositions cannot be "proved"; but discussion can suggest the interrelations between aggregate growth and production structure, which, if studied further, should provide the elements for a tested theory.

(a) Three suggestions may indicate why a high rate of growth of per capita product should be associated with a high rate of shift in production structure.

First, given the rising supply of goods per capita, one should consider the effects of the basic structure of consumer wants — with respect both to priority and satiability. Undoubtedly the priority scale, which reflects the hierarchy of needs related to the physiological characteristics of the human species, has been dominant through the ages in shaping the structure of production. The large weight of the agricultural sector in the premodern economies reflected the priority of the need for food under conditions of low productivity. And, given the satiability of the demand for food, much of the major structural shift referred to as industrialization was the result of a limited rise in the demand for products of the A sector with rising output per capita. These remarks apply also to other needs and corresponding products with high priority and limited satiability. If the structure of consumer wants, characterized by these differences in response to a higher supply of goods, is persistent and largely invariant to different institutional conditions under which this increased supply is secured, the higher the rate of increase in per capita product, the greater the shift in the structure of consumer demand; with some allowance for the fact that, as per capita supply rises, the locus of large shifts in the structure of demand itself moves (from the range of "necessities" at lower levels of per capita product, to that of "superior" goods and "luxuries" at upper levels).

But, granted this connection between the high rates of growth of per capita product and productivity and the high rate of shift in the structure of demand due to structure of wants, one may question the weight of its contribution to the high rate of shift in production structure in modern economic growth for reasons mentioned in Chapter III. Within modern economic growth, technological innovations that create "new" goods are prominent; and changes in conditions of life often accompany technological innovations, whether they create new goods or provide new ways of producing the old goods. Both of these effects of new knowledge and technological innovations are superimposed in the course of growth on the pre-existing structure of wants, creating new demand pressures either in adjustment to changed conditions of life or in response to the new goods. Since modern development has pushed per capita supply of goods far above the level at which high priority needs of physiological and similar character are dominant (and hence possibly invariant to social structure and technology), one may doubt that a basic structure of human wants, with a definite and clearly differential response to increased supply of goods, has been a major factor in producing the rapid shifts in production structure that accompanied modern economic growth.

Second, modern economic growth was initiated at different dates in the presently developed countries, and it has reached even today only a minority of the world population. As indicated in Chapter I, the sequential initiation of the rapid growth process among the presently developed countries, and its limited penetration into and contribution to the growth of the less developed countries, meant widening differentials in per capita product as well as in growth rates. International trade and other international flows also produced shifts in the structure of a country's output, since the changing composition of its exports and imports reflected changes in comparative advantage vis-à-vis the rest of the world. The latter changes may in turn have been the result of the higher growth rate in the given country than in the rest of the world — which, associated with a higher rate of technological change, may have shifted the locus of comparative advantage within its own economy; or they may have resulted from the fact that the current flow of technological change reduced the cost of transport and communication, thus extending the range of the international trade network within which the developed country could exploit its comparative advantage. In either case, a high rate of growth in per capita product, reflecting as it usually does a high rate of technological advance, would make for rapid shifts in comparative advantage; and hence would add to the shifts in the *domestic production* structure.

Until suspension by the world wars of the twentieth century (to be resumed after World War II, at a more moderate rate), foreign trade showed a striking expansion, at an appreciably greater rate than output even in the group of developed countries, let alone the world as a whole. Some rough estimates suggest that the proportion of foreign trade to world output may have risen from a few percentage points (perhaps 3) at the start of the nineteenth century, to as high as a third just before World War I.[2] This sharp rise in the proportion of foreign trade to total product characterized the older developed countries, and those underdeveloped countries that were drawn into the network of world trade. In the "young" countries overseas, those which began as small offshoots of Europe and grew extensively over wide territories separated from their European origins (such as the United States), foreign trade proportions did not rise — but only because internal growth was much more rapid and relied extensively on territorial expansion, in itself a source of major structural changes.

The contribution of the foreign trade engagement and of the shifts in comparative advantage is an inverse function of the size of a country's economy, being the greater, the smaller the country. Foreign trade was a key factor particularly in the small developed countries, making it possible for them to attain the high level of per capita productivity of the developed group; the rise in their foreign trade proportions may have been a major factor in the high rate of shift in the structure of domestic production. In the large countries, with foreign trade a small percentage of total output, the contribution of expanding foreign trade to shifts in domestic production structure probably was more limited.

We come now to the third, and perhaps most important, link between the high rates of growth of per capita product and productivity and the high rate of shift in structure of production: the high rate of technological innovation and its diffusion. To the extent that growth of aggregate product and productivity is dependent upon technological innovation, the rate of change in structure of production must be high because technological innovation is selective and its economic impact shifts over time from one branch of production to another (as Table 47 illustrates).

The observation is supported by the identification in the eco-

2. For this and other findings in this section see Simon Kuznets, "Quantitative Aspects of the Economic Growth of Nations: X. Level and Structure of Foreign Trade: Long-Term Trends," *Economic Development and Cultural Change*, vol. 15, no. 2, part II (January 1967), pp. 2–26; and Simon Kuznets, *Modern Economic Growth: Rate, Structure, and Spread* (New Haven: Yale University Press, 1966), chapter 6, pp. 300–334.

nomic history of developed countries of the growth industries, that is, those that at any given time grow much more rapidly than the rest of the economy, usually because they are the locus of current technological innovation. These industries are few in number, and differ from generation to generation. Currently they appear to be connected with electronics, atomic energy, and space exploration; and among the services, those of health, education, and recreation. In the last generation the growth industries were connected with the internal combustion engine, selected chemicals and petroleum, and small electric power household durables. In the generations before the last electric power and communications appeared to lead the procession — and so on back to the few major industries associated with the Industrial Revolution. In contrast to this selectivity and shift of locus over time, one can visualize a model in which technological innovation is evenly distributed among all existing branches of production, and no new ones are created. Even then there would be some structural shift among branches of production in response to the rise in per capita income, reflecting different income elasticities of consumer demand for products of various industries, and differential effects on comparative advantage in international trade. But such structural changes in production would be a small fraction of those that actually occurred with selectivity and shift of locus of technological innovation — if only because the overall rise in per capita product would be much lower, for reasons already indicated. It is therefore important to ask why technological innovation is selective and shifts the locus of its impact.

A major technological innovation is the application of an invention, a new ingenious combination of existing knowledge, to satisfy a large latent demand that could not be satisfied until the invention — the technological breakthrough — had been made; and indeed, until it spread, and in spreading elicited the hundreds of minor inventions and thousands of improvements which by their cumulative impact drastically reduced relative cost (and thus satisfied the demand, which is large only in response to a much reduced relative price). A technological innovation that has a major economic impact is a combination of three components: an invention that provides a framework around which a whole succession of minor inventions and improvements can be built; a supply of material capital and, more particularly, of human capital (such as inventors, engineers, and organizers), whose engagement and concentration on the problems of the major invention will assure its effective improvement and diffusion; and a large potential demand, often revealed by an obvious bottleneck in the production process of a recent growth industry. Each of these components imposes a constraint so that, given the potential demand, there may not be enough human capital to satisfy both this demand and the one already absorbing the current supply of inventors and improvers. Or antecedent basic and applied science may not have advanced sufficiently even though the promise of the major invention is clear. Or the conditions of life and work at the time may indicate only a few cases of latent demand — and in this connection the very difference in income elasticity of consumer demand for various goods would make for selectivity since invention is responsive to potential rewards.

Selectivity means necessarily a shifting industry locus. If an industry, identified by the specific nature of its raw materials, processes, and product, has already been affected by a major technological innovation, and if the spread of the latter succeeded in drastically reducing the cost of the product, and shifted it from the luxury class, with price-sensitive demand, to a low-cost necessity, with demand no longer responsive to price, further technological change, no matter how revolutionary in engineering terms, is not likely to induce further acceleration of growth of output. This tendency, toward exhaustion of cost-reducing opportunities in industries that once benefited from modern technological innovation, serves to shift the attention of inventors to more promising areas. It often leads to technological innovations that set up a *new* industry in competition with the one that benefited in the past, and thus further restrict the latter's growth potential.[3]

The discussion so far has dealt with the direct effects of techno-

3. On the effects of this exhaustion of cost-reducing potentials of technological innovation on the growth patterns of various industries, the retardation in the growth of their output, and the continuing shift in industry-mix in which the emergence of new industries with higher than average growth rates tends to prevent aggregate growth from slackening, see Simon Kuznets, *Secular Movements in Production and Prices* (Boston: Houghton Mifflin, 1930), particularly chapter I; also Arthur F. Burns, *Production Trends in the United States since 1870* (New York: National Bureau of Economic Research, 1934), particularly chapter IV. For an illuminating analysis of the responsiveness of invention to potentials of demand see Jacob Schmookler, *Invention and Economic Growth* (Cambridge, Mass.: Harvard University Press, 1966), particularly chapters I, VI, VII. This recent monograph summarizes the work of a lifetime on quantitative analysis of invention and inventive activity, their effect on productivity, and their responsiveness to the structure of demand.

logical innovations on structure of production. Now we note the indirect consequences of shifts in the structure of production: changes in conditions of life and work, many of which create new, and some potentially large, demands. These new demands, which might never have emerged had it not been for the effects of past innovations and past high rates of growth, may provide a stimulus to further innovations, and thus sustain the high rate of aggregate growth, at least as conventionally measured.

Some of the consequences that lead to new demands are links in a short chain and are easily recognizable. The spread of the motor car, which has led to air pollution in thickly settled cities, has created a demand for some remedy (a pure offset to diseconomies of scale); and the same spread of motor cars has created conditions that make suburban housing and shopping centers feasible, thus creating a demand for the latter. Other chains of consequences may link much broader processes and suggest wider effects, as in the case of urbanization, largely because of increased scale of plant, which has contributed to the spread of the small family, and the greater demand for market supply of recreation services (professional), and for mechanical household equipment to replace the domestic service that is in increasingly limited supply and whose relative prices are continually rising.

These illustrations show the connection between structural changes in production and changes in demand at some later date. There is no need to add to them, for it is obvious that such changes in demand in turn provide a stimulus for further innovation and growth. To be sure, new demands may also emerge as a real factor in the market, if a technological innovation makes it possible to satisfy some long-standing desire or dream, as in the case of air travel, the demand for which can be traced to the Icarus legend. And the emergence of such a demand cannot be interpreted as a result of new conditions of life and work created by directly antecedent changes in the structure of production. But all I argue here is that the latter do provide a large, if partial, contribution to new demands, in various ways and in sufficient magnitude to produce pressure for new innovations and consequently a high rate of overall growth.

(b) The connection between mass application of new knowledge, associated for reasons just suggested with a high rate of shift in production structure, and the further rise in per capita product and productivity can be discussed in two steps: the link between mass application of new knowledge and further growth in the stock of useful knowledge and science; and the connection between a high rate of growth in the stock of useful knowledge and high growth rates in per capita product and productivity.

First, large-scale *application* of new knowledge and of technological innovations is a necessary, if not sufficient, condition for a high rate of growth of the stock of useful knowledge and of science, if only because it generates more product per capita, and thus provides extra resources for investment in the production of new knowledge — not an unimportant matter, if one considers the full range of the infrastructure of education and training on which flourishing science must rely. Granted that such resources are one major prerequisite, a social and ideological framework within which science can prosper is also necessary: over premodern centuries a large investment was made in training priests, theologians, and soothsayers, and, while many of them did contribute to useful knowledge, the rate of accretion was not impressive. But, given a proper framework for science, and the availability of a modern institution with its emphasis on empirically tested knowledge and its premium on originality, that is, on *new* knowledge rather than on the exegesis of some authoritative and venerable doctrine, substantial resources are still necessary for investment in science — a capital good with a long lead time and unknown specific ends. A high rate of rise in per capita product permits an even higher rate of growth in investment in this type of capital, as is evidenced by the enormous growth in the number of scientists in the developed countries and the spectacular increase in the complex material capital required, particularly in the post-World War II years.

But there are other connections between wide-scale uses of existing knowledge, whether or not embodied in a technological innovation, and a high rate of growth in the stock of useful knowledge and of science proper. Much of science relies on an inventory of descriptive knowledge and of empirical measures, hopefully tested for accuracy and reliability — and all such knowledge is potentially useful for problems of economic production. But, unless this knowledge is widely applied, it is not fully tested; and wide application necessarily adds considerable empirical data, even when such existing knowledge is not recombined in the form of an invention. The supply of this ever-increasing stock of empirical data produced by ever-widening application — in mining, in trade, in manufacturing, in agriculture — maintains the progress of science, and the latter leads toward discoveries of some *general* features of nature, and thus provides a basis for technological application and further discovery.

The contribution of wide application to progress of science and to increase in stock of useful knowledge is even greater when existing knowledge is recombined in the form of a useful invention. The extensive application of a major invention, its diffusion in mass production, is bound to add further detail and information about the underlying forces, processes, and materials not contained in the scientific discovery or even in the invention before its spread in mass use. It may also generate new tools, the efficiency of which is assured only as a result of the cumulation of minor improvements that come with extended use. This additional knowledge and these new tools may, in turn, provide a base for new advances in basic science, often in unexpected directions and ways.

The scientific discoverer and pioneer is rarely interested in the specific features of his discovery that are relevant to practical application alone. It is the resulting inventions and the widely applied technological innovations that are, so to speak, the experimental laboratories for continuing exploration of properties of the components of nature. These inventions and innovations that supply the new knowledge of the specific practical features and the new tools for applying them also perforce aid the advance of basic research and its high rate of growth. Illustrations of the connection abound in the history of modern science and technology, ranging from the relation between the development of the steam engine and the emergence in the 1820's of modern thermodynamics, to the unexpected bonuses produced by inventions and application in the field of electro-magnetic short waves, originally indicated in the Maxwellian equations of 1864 and first demonstrated by Hertz in 1887, which have eventuated in radio and radar astronomy — new fields within an old science, made possible by new tools.[4] And the

4. That the work of Sadi Carnot, the foundation of modern thermodynamics, was stimulated by the development of the steam engine, is suggested by its very title, "Réflexions sur la puissance motrice du feu et sur les machines propres à développer cette puissance" (Paris: Bachelier, 1824); and the date confirms the connection. The basic analysis of conversion of energy that resulted in the two laws of thermodynamics is a continuation of the approach by James Watt, which warrants our characterizing his invention (or series of inventions) as the first notable application of modern science to problems of production. On the former connection see R. J. Forbes, "Power to 1850," in Charles Singer, E. J. Holmyard, A. R. Hall, and Trevor I.

space explorations of today, which have become feasible only because of successive *applications* of new scientific discoveries on a wide scale, promise to open new fields of basic science by providing it with new tools; these in turn may lead to more inventions and applications, with the high rate of additions to new knowledge maintained or raised. In short, without the continuous stimulation of the new information and new tools provided by inventions and technological innovations adequately applied and extensively spread, the rate of addition to useful knowledge, increasingly provided by science, would probably have been a small fraction of what it in fact was (difficult as the measurement is).[5]

Another possible link, not noted so far, is that between application and both motivation and criteria in scientific work. Would the empirically testable and empirically oriented character of modern science have emerged and been maintained and strengthened if it had not been conclusively demonstrated that it "works" — not only in the laboratories, but under the much less controlled conditions of life in general? One could assume both generous support (in the way of economic resources) for science (or similar "basic," not-directly-practical intellectual work) and a supply of competent individuals. And yet the failure to apply the results on a sufficiently wide and practical scale might deprive science not only of the stimulus of new tools and new knowledge but also of the pressure to reach results from which a bridge could be built to operational

---

Williams, eds., *A History of Technology,* vol. IV (Oxford: Clarendon Press, 1958), pp. 163–165.

For a fascinating history of the interplay between scientific discovery, invention, innovation, and additions to knowledge in the exploitation of electro-magnetic short waves see W. Rupert MacLaurin, *Invention and Innovation in the Radio Industry* (New York: Macmillan, 1949). Although this monograph is now more than twenty years old and deals with a field that has, since then, undergone great advance and transformation, it remains the most instructive account, based on materials of a single industry, of the connections that are crucial in understanding the pattern of modern economic growth.

5. The discussion does not imply that the contribution to knowledge of the spread of a technological innovation in mass production continues forever, and thus is an undiminished function of volume of output of the innovation-originated product. Beyond a certain point there may remain little to be learned — so that the umpteen-billionth radio or motor car cannot be expected to yield as much knowledge as the first few hundred thousands. But it does suggest that fairly substantial diffusion of a technological innovation is required; and that without it neither the knowledge of additional properties of nature nor the emergence of new tools (often warranted economically only by mass diffusion of an initial innovation) is assured. It would be interesting to try to establish the duration and volume of the diffusion phases of technological innovations in which the yield of additional knowledge and of further inventions remains significant.

reality (the kind of bridge constructed by inventors and innovators who apply the results of science to production problems). The consequence might be a "mandarinization" of science, which would lead work in directions in which its testable and empirically oriented character could be maintained only with difficulty (it might not remain what we now call "science"). It is hard to visualize such an eventuality because, in historical fact, modern science has been inextricably interwoven with wide application and with a social philosophy that has raised science to high rank because of its eventual practical utility. But such a connection can perhaps be glimpsed in societies in which some elements of science were supported and venerated, but without pressure for practical application (for example, in astronomical and natural speculation in Greek philosophy); and in which science was harnessed to functions other than the provision of a basis for practical application.

Second, with a high rate of growth in the stock of tested and potentially useful knowledge, and in basic and applied science, it seems reasonable to assume a high rate of *application* of new knowledge, and of inventions and technological innovation — high at least as compared with premodern times. To be sure, we are taking as given what we should document: the more favorable social climate for new knowledge and innovation; the market mechanism that assures large economic and social rewards and an increasing supply of capital if a rich vein of potential demand is struck; and a rapidly rising supply of inventors, adapters, innovators, and other groups with the education and ability to bridge the gap between the discovery of an item of "pure" knowledge and its mass application, or that of the invention to which it leads. But to demonstrate these favorable conditions for application would take us too far afield. We may reasonably assume that the obstacles to translation of an increased stock of knowledge into greater product and productivity are relatively no greater, and are probably less, than those of premodern times when the rate of growth of tested knowledge was appreciably lower.

This tells us nothing of the time pattern of relations between growth in the stock of useful knowledge and the rate of application — which, in turn, determines further growth in per capita product and productivity. Granted that extensive application of available knowledge makes for further additions to the latter and for a high rate of growth in stock of knowledge and in the further advance of science, a high rate of application, and hence of growth in per capita product and productivity, does not follow automatically. Obstacles to the application of a growing stock of knowledge may also be growing rapidly, tending to offset, or more than offset, the stimulus of the greater production possibilities provided by the growing knowledge and technology.

Important as this link is, it is not germane to the main point here. I am only arguing that extensive application of the available stock of knowledge — which means high rates of growth of per capita product and productivity as well as a high rate of shift in production structure — is a necessary, if not sufficient, condition for further rapid growth of the stock of useful knowledge and further advance of science. I am also arguing that such a high rate of growth in the stock of useful knowledge and further advance of science are a necessary, if not sufficient, condition for further high rates of growth of per capita product and productivity. This means, in short, that, while a high rate of aggregate growth is almost inevitably accompanied by a high rate of shift in production structure, extensive application and a high rate of shift in production structure are, in turn, indispensable for a further high rate of aggregate growth. Hence, rapid structural shifts, not only in economic production but also in other aspects of an economy and society (to be discussed later), must be viewed as requirements, and possibly costs, of a high rate of aggregate growth.

High and Low Growth Components and Limits to Aggregate Growth

With the help of simple algebra, the relations between growth rates for slowly and rapidly growing, "old" and "new" components (like those illustrated in Table 47 and discussed in the preceding section in connection with technological innovations) and the growth rates in per capita product and productivity can be shown. Thus, it is possible to specify somewhat further where the limits of aggregate growth lie — in a skeleton model of modern economic growth, with sharp differences between the rates of growth of "new" and "old" components and hence marked shifts in production structure.

An illustrative exhibit is provided by Table 48. To simplify matters, we assume a constant population (population growth, in

Table 48. Illustrative relations between aggregate growth rate and growth rates of low growth, high growth, and new components.

A. Product in current prices

	Time I			Growth factor, Time I to Time II	Time II		
	Quantity Q (1)	Price P (2)	Value V (3)	(4)	Quantity Q (5)	Price P (6)	Value V (7)
1. Low growth products (M)	95	10	950	3 (G_m)	285	5	1,425
2. High growth products in Time I (H)	5	50	250	15 (G_h)	75	5	375
3. New products (N)	0		0	∞	18.95	25	473.7
4. Total product	100		1,200		378.95		2,273.7
5. High growth products as % of total (Time I)	5		20.833				
6. New products as % of total (Time II)					5		20.833

B. Growth rate of product in constant prices, terminal price weights

	Time I			Time II		
	Q (1)	P (2)	V (3)	Q (4)	P (5)	V (6)
7. M component	95	5	475	285	5	1,425
8. H component	5	5	25	75	5	375
9. N component	0		0	18.95	25	473.7
10. Total product	100		500	378.95		2,273.7

Growth factor,

$$G_{II} = 2273.7:500 = 4.5474$$
$$= [3.0(475:500) + 15.0(25:500)] \cdot [1 + \{(20.833):(100 - 20.833)\}].$$

Letting the m, h, and n subscripts refer to the M, H, and N components — quantity, price, and value — and the t subscript to total product,

$$G_{II} = [G_m(Q_{mI}P_{mII}:Q_{tI}P_{tII})$$
$$+ G_h(Q_{hI}P_{hII}:Q_{tI}P_{tII})] \cdot [1 + \{V_{nII}:(V_{tII} - V_{nII})\}]. \quad (1)$$

In further discussion and equations, the right-hand bracket in equation (1) is referred to as the (1 + N ratio).

Table 48 — continued

C. Growth rate of product in constant prices, initial price weights

	Time I				Time II		
	Q (1)	P (2)	V (3)		Q (4)	P (5)	V (6)
11. M component	95	10	950		285	10	2,850
12. H component	5	50	250		75	50	3,750
13. N component	0		0		18.95	91.7[a]	1,737[b]
14. Total product	100		1,200		378.95		8,337

Growth factor,

$G_I = 8,337:1,200 = 6.9475$

$\qquad = [3.0(950:1,200) + 15.0(250:1,200)] \cdot [1 + (20.833:79.167)]$

$G_I = [G_m(Q_{mI}P_{mI}:V_{tI}) + G_h(Q_{hI}P_{hI}:V_{tI})] \cdot (1 + N \text{ ratio}).$

[a] Derived from columns 4, 6.
[b] 20.833 percent of total product.

any case, is subject to its own regularities, not closely connected with economic growth), and therefore all references in this section to percentage change in total product are in fact also to per capita product. Thus, discussion of limits to growth applies to both total and per capita product; and, in view of our finding in Chapter II that productivity accounted for the major part of the growth in per capita product, it also applies implicitly to limits to growth of productivity.

In Table 48 total product consists of three components: one with a low growth factor (M); a second with a much higher growth factor, the result of a recent innovation or technological change (H); and a third, which comprises entirely new products (N), not existing in Time I but emerging in Time II to provide the H component of Time II. Given the growth factors for components M and H, and some assumptions concerning the relative magnitude of the N component (set here at the resource share of the H component in Time I), all that is necessary to calculate the growth rate of total product, at both initial and terminal prices, is an assumption concerning the trends in prices; and here we assume that the high price of component H declines relatively to the low price of component M.

The growth factor for total product is lower than that for the H component because the latter has a small weight in total value product in Time I — even though the weight is used twice, first for the

venient formulae for the main factors that set upper limits to the growth rate of total product. If we assume that the price of the H component declines relative to that of the M component, we assume realistically a correlation between the ratio of G_h to G_m and the decline in the ratio of P_h to P_m. If, to simplify the algebra, we posit that the two variables change in direct proportion to each other, we can write:

$$G_h : G_m = (P_{hI} : P_{mI}) : (P_{hII} : P_{mII}). \tag{3}$$

If, to simplify further, we assume that the price of H declines by Time II to equality with the price of M, $(P_{hII} : P_{mII})$ becomes 1, and equation (3) can be rewritten:

$$G_h : G_m = P_{hI} : P_{mI};$$
or
$$G_h = G_m(P_{hI} : P_{mI}). \tag{4}$$

On these assumptions, the equation for G_{II}, the growth factor for total product, at terminal price weights — which is more relevant to our purposes than growth of total product at initial price weights — becomes:

$$G_{II} = G_m[1 + \{(P_{hI}:P_{mI}) - 1\} \cdot \{Q_{hI}:Q_{tI}\}] \cdot (1 + N \text{ ratio}). \tag{5}$$

Before interpreting equation (5) we should note that the expression $\{(P_{hI} : P_{mI}) - 1\} \cdot \{Q_{hI} : Q_{tI}\}$ is, for the range of values of most interest to us, close to the share of total resources in Time I (at prices of Time I) devoted to the H component (the precise expression for which would be $[P_{hI}Q_{hI} : P_{tI}Q_{tI}]$.[7] It is therefore per-

7. In the following tabulation we compare the values of the expression in equation (5), designated A for approximation, and the true share of total resources in Time I devoted to the H component, designated S, under different assumptions concerning the $(P_{hI}:P_{mI})$ ratio and the share of Q_{hI} in Q_{tI}:

Share of Q_{hI} in Q_{tI} (%)	$P_{hI}:P_{mI} = 3$		$P_{hI}:P_{mI} = 5$		$P_{hI}:P_{mI} = 8$	
	A	S	A	S	A	S
(1)	(2)	(3)	(4)	(5)	(6)	(7)
1	0.02	0.029	0.04	0.048	0.07	0.075
2	0.04	0.058	0.08	0.093	0.14	0.140
3	0.06	0.085	0.12	0.134	0.21	0.198
4	0.08	0.111	0.16	0.172	0.28	0.250
5	0.10	0.136	0.20	0.208	0.35	0.296
6	0.12	0.161	0.24	0.242	not relevant	
7	0.14	0.184	0.28	0.273	not relevant	
8	0.16	0.207	0.32	0.303	not relevant	
...						
15	0.30	0.346	not relevant		not relevant	

The calculation was carried only to the point where the share of the resources de-

missible to substitute the share of total resources in Time I (at prices of Time I) devoted to the H component, for the expression in equation (5), which then becomes:

$$G_{II} = G_m[1 + (Q_{hI}P_{hI}:Q_{tI}P_{tI})] \cdot (1 + N \text{ ratio}).$$

But by my assumptions, followed in Table 48, the share of the N component is set by the share of resources devoted to the H component in Time I; and for this case, the final equation for the growth factor of total product (terminal price weights) becomes:

$$G_{II} = G_m[1 + (Q_{hI}P_{hI}:Q_{tI}P_{tI})]^2. \tag{6}$$

It follows that the growth rate of total product is a function of two factors: the growth rate for the low growth component; and the share of the total product devoted in Time I to the H component, this share (plus 1) squared (reflecting the contributions of the H and the N components). If there are limits to the growth of total product, they are set by the factors that constrain the rate of growth of the slowly growing M component and the proportion of total product (or of total resources) that the economy devotes to the higher cost, higher priced, more rapidly growing H (and hence N) component. On the assumption that the growth of the M component is governed largely by low income-elastic types of demand, the proportion of resources devoted to the H (and N) component is the dominant factor affecting the aggregate growth rate. But this proportion is *not* identical with the material capital formation proportion, a good part of which may be committed to the M component and which, more important, does not reflect the type of labor and management resource availability that may be crucial for the type of production required by the H (and N) component.

We can now examine the implicit assumptions in Table 48 concerning the distribution of resource inputs and their productivity (Table 49). First, by setting much higher prices per unit for the H than for the M component in Time I, I implied that the former required greater input of resources of equivalent quality. And second, by assuming that the price of the H component would decline so much more than that of the M component, I implied that the productivity of resources put into the H component would rise

voted to the H component in Time I was 30 percent. When this share lies between 20 and 30 percent, and $P_{hI}:P_{mI}$ is substantial, the approximation and the true share are fairly close.

Table 49. Resource inputs and growth of productivity implied in the analysis in Table 48.

| | Resource inputs in comparable units (constant prices) for Time I and Time II and equal among components | | | | | | |
| | Time I | | | Growth factor | Time II | | |
	Q (1)	P (2)	V (3)	(4)	Q (5)	P (6)	V (7)
1. M component	79.167	12	950	1.5	118.75	12	1,425
2. H component	20.833	12	250	1.5	31.25	12	375
3. N component	0		0	∞	39.475	12	473.7
4. Total product	100	12	1,200		189.475	12	2,273.7

Derived from product in current prices, Table 48, lines 1–4, by equating the proportional increase in productivity of resource input to the proportional reduction in current prices from Time I to Time II; and keeping resource prices (for comparable units) constant at the Time I level.

The equation for the growth factor for total resources, G_r (with G_{mr} and G_{hr} the resource growth factors for the M and H components respectively) is then:

$$G_r = [G_{mr}(Q_{mI}P_{mI}:V_{tI}) + G_{hr}(Q_{hI}P_{hI}:V_{tI})] \cdot (1 + N \text{ ratio}). \qquad (7)$$

But $G_{mr} = G_m:G_{me}$, in which G_{me} is the growth factor for efficiency of the resources in the M component; $G_{hr} = G_h:G_{he}$, in which G_{he} is the growth factor for efficiency of the resources in the H component.

Since equation (4) shows that $G_h = G_m(P_{hI}:P_{mI})$, and the derivation of lines 1–4 above shows that $G_{he} = G_{me}(P_{hI}:P_{mI})$, equation (7) can be rewritten as:

$$G_r = (G_m:G_{me})(1 + N \text{ ratio}), \qquad (8)$$

or, in application to the illustration above, $1.89475 = 1.5(1.26317)$.

It follows that the growth factor for productivity, with estimates based on terminal prices, is:

$G_{eII} = G_{II}:G_r$, and from equation (6) for G_{II} and equation (8) for G_r we have:

$$G_{eII} = \frac{G_m[1 + \{(P_{hI}:P_{mI}) - 1\} \cdot (Q_{hI}:Q_{tI})] \cdot (1 + N \text{ ratio})}{(G_m:G_{me})(1 + N \text{ ratio})}$$

$$= G_{me}[1 + \{(P_{hI}:P_{mI}) - 1\} \cdot (Q_{hI}:Q_{tI})] \qquad (9)$$

or, in application to the illustration here, the growth factor in productivity is 2.40, i.e., (2.0)(1.2); or 4.5474 (from Table 48) divided by 1.89475 (from line 4, column 5, divided by 100).

much more than that of resources put into the M component. In the illustration these differences between the H and M components with respect to factor input and productivity were directly proportional to the differences in prices and price trends. Finally, by fixing current prices in Time II at half of those in Time I, even for the M component, we implied that residual productivity even for the M component would be 2.0. Once this is assumed, the change in productivity for the H component and the effect of the N component are given.

Table 49 shows the differential movement in productivity per unit of resource input for the H and M sectors; and equation (8) indicates the factors that, under the assumption used, determine the growth rate of the factor inputs for the economy as a whole; and equation (9) indicates those that determine the growth rate (at terminal price weights) of total productivity in the economy. Equation (8) reveals that factor inputs grow at the rate characteristic of inputs in the M component, raised by the N (new products) ratio, that is, under the assumption here, by the ratio of resources in Time I devoted to the H component. Equation (9) shows that the growth factor for productivity for the economy as a whole equals the rise in productivity for the slowly growing M sector, also raised by the ratio of resources in Time I devoted to the H component. Thus, the growth of productivity is also determined by two factors: the growth rate of productivity in the larger, slowly growing M component; and the share of total resources in Time I devoted to the rapidly growing H (and N) component. If there are limits to growth of productivity (or of product per capita), they lie in the factors that constrain productivity growth in the nondynamic sectors of the economy; and in those that limit the share of total product or of resources that can be devoted to the new, rapidly growing H (and N) component.

The assumptions used to simplify the models detract from the realism of the illustrations. For example, the assumption that the proportion of resources (volume) devoted to the H component to those devoted to the M component is the same in Time II as in Time I is unrealistic (Table 49, line 2, columns 1, 5). Other unrealistic oversimplifications were involved, for example, in equating the share of the N with that of the H component in total resources. But the qualifications resulting from oversimplification seem minor since the procedure has enabled us to identify the possible sources of limitation on growth, viz., the gradual exhaustion of growth opportunities attached to specific innovations, the continuous shifting of the focus of innovation within the economy, and the distinction among components (despite their changing identity) between those that are currently affected by high growth potential innovations and others for which this period is past. The insight provided by these simple models, while yielding no substantive answer regarding the specific limit to growth rates of product per capita and of productivity, is important, since it emphasizes the structural changes in the course of modern economic growth.

It must be stressed that my discussion rests throughout on the nonsubstitutability between components M, H, and N in satisfying wants. The relatively low growth rate of the M component cannot be avoided by substituting the H component for it — in the equivalence suggested by the prices in Time I. Such substitution would mean that a given value of resources put into H satisfies the established wants equally as well as the same resource value put into M; and this is definitely not the case. Input of thousands of manhours and capital into the H component, for example, into passenger cars and television sets, does not substitute for the equivalent or even larger volume used in producing food and clothing. If such equivalence existed and substitution was possible, it would be advantageous to shift *all* production to the H component, and "eat," "wear," or otherwise use passenger cars and television sets, even at a higher resource per unit of satisfaction of hunger, and so on, since a much higher growth rate of product and productivity would thus be assured by limiting the share of the M component. The discussion rests not only on a connection between the upper limit on growth and stability of wants, current or materialized after a new product, an innovation, has had time to grow into an established good, but also on the *specific* nature of this stable structure of final demand and related technology, which prevents easy substitution between the M and H components.

Of course, artificial "substitution" can be induced by a dictatorial government. It can force a shift of resources into the H component by restricting effective demand and supply of the M component, even though in a free market the income elasticity of demand for the latter is positive and may even be high (as in many less developed countries). Any government intervention in order to influence the free market choice between the M and H components, and shift a higher proportion of resources to the latter, affects the "substitution" condition. But I would be digressing too far, if I were to consider such modifications of the illustrative analysis. That analysis was introduced primarily to call attention to the relation between the aggregate rate of growth, with terminal price weights, and the underlying structure of final demand, and to indicate the limited share of high-growth-inducing innovations in the total body of a country's technology. The essential argument is that the specific structure of final demand tends to be stable; and that it limits both the relative proportion of innovations that can be introduced at any given time and the length of time over which an innovation, once introduced, can retain the high relative valuation that it enjoyed in its initial time period. Furthermore, the general corpus of technology, while subject to differing overall rates of improvement depending upon a country's economic and technical development, is usually dominated by well-established practices in which reserves for sizable cost reductions are likely to be limited. It is in this sense that there is a structure which can change but in which there is only limited elasticity of substitution of one part for another.

Structural Changes: Economic and Noneconomic

Changes in structure of production are necessarily followed by changes in other aspects of economic structure. Thus, a shift away from agriculture toward industry also means a shift toward productive processes with much larger minimum, average, or optimal scale of plant. A rapid increase in the size of plant, assisted by the technological revolution in transport and communication, means not only depersonalization of the firm but also changes in conditions of work of the participating labor force. Furthermore, if the shift away from agriculture occurs in one country only, comparative advantage in international trade changes; and the consequent shifts in the structure of exports and imports have repercussions on the structure of domestic production. The rising scale of plant was a major factor in the rapid urbanization that was so typical and striking an accompaniment of modern economic growth in Europe and overseas; although it should be stressed that urban agglomeration reflected not only the movement away from agriculture, but also the changing structure within the nonagricultural sectors. Urbanization and the shifts to employee status within impersonally organized economic firms meant major changes in the pattern of consumer demand — with consequent changes in the composition of final output.

But we are more interested here in the effects of changes in economic structure on other social institutions, not primarily economic in character, and on far-reaching social views that are dominant in a society. These can be illustrated by sequences in which the initial link is a change in economic structure proper, but subsequent links are in wider and noneconomic realms, even though at some further remove there is a doubling back to economic effects.

The first illustrative sequence begins with a marked increase in scale of plant, as measured by fixed capital invested and number of employees engaged. One immediate effect is that the larger plant cannot be run by an individual proprietor, or even several members of a family; and unless the modern corporate form is available, it must be developed as a social innovation (which, in fact, did occur in the first half of the nineteenth century, with refinements made later).[8] Another immediate effect is that a new type of firm must be developed for efficient operation of the plant, with the proper combination of labor, management, and material capital, as well as for the mobilization of the necessary capital resources; and, in particular, labor and management must be selected on the basis of objective criteria rather than family attachment.

The emphasis on filling positions within the enterprise (with consequences for role in society) on the basis of objective tests of performance (formal education, examination, and certification, and the like) rather than on the basis of family origin and status has long and repeatedly been noted as a feature of modern society, whether formulated by Sir Henry Maine as the movement from "status to contract" or by modern sociologists as the shift from "ascriptive norms in a highly particularistic context" to "achievement norms in a wider universalistic context."[9] Two major consequences follow. The first, of course, is the requirement of legal freedom for the individual in the disposition of his own faculties —

8. The reference is to limited liability and anonymity of diffused ownership; the generality of the charter, which permits the modern corporation freedom of operation (that is not otherwise illegal), but prohibits legally monopolistic (exclusive) functions vis-à-vis others; the perpetuity of the charter; and the ease of incorporation. In all these respects the modern corporation differs from the specially chartered, exclusive, unlimited liability, short-term, monopolistic (with respect to countrymen) corporations of the centuries preceding the nineteenth. See A. A. Berle and Gardner Means, *Modern Corporation and Private Property,* rev. ed. (New York: Harcourt, Brace, and World, 1968), book II, chapter 1.

9. See Bert F. Hoselitz, "Social Structure and Economic Growth," *Economia Internazionale,* vol. 6, no. 3 (August 1953), pp. 52–57, reprinted in his *Sociological Aspects of Economic Growth* (Glencoe, Ill.: Free Press, 1960), pp. 23–51; the quotations are from p. 33.

since its absence would limit, if not bar, investment in the training and education required and the full cooperation of the human factor with the other productive factors in the enterprise. It is no accident that slavery was found incompatible with modern economic growth — to a point where a civil war was fought in the United States to clear the way for such growth. The second consequence is that emphasis on an individual's competence, relevant for both parents and children, was a strong inducement to a lower birth rate — to assure the adequate investment in human capital in both generations, especially the younger. It is hardly an accident that, with some delay, the small family, with a few children, emerged in the developed countries — with the birth rate declining to well below the level warranted by the drop in overall and infant mortality.

To be sure, the emphasis on objective performance tests of individuals required by the emergence of the large-scale firm was bolstered by the conflict, mentioned in Chapter VI, between the higher rates of natural increase and the lower rates of growth of employment opportunities in the countryside than in the cities, a conflict which produced internal migration and detachment of migrant labor from its family and home roots, and led to the emergence of an "anonymous" urban labor force that could be judged only by objective criteria of performance. Yet this internal migration resulted in good part from the structural changes in economic production. But even if we disregard this element, we could establish a sequence from the emergence of the large-scale plants, to changes in legal structure (for both enterprise and labor), to shifts in demographic patterns, to changes in social philosophy (since emphasis on objective performance criteria implies status equality of individuals). These legal, demographic, and philosophical changes in turn affect such an economic variable as structure of consumer demand.

A second illustrative sequence begins with the changes in the structure of production, some of which represent the results of major technological innovations and hence, being something "new," call for new types of legal and social framework to accommodate them (illustrated above by the large-scale plant and the modern corporation). Since these "social" innovations must be approved, and often supported, by the sovereign organs of society, the function of the state as a clearing house for the legal and institutional innovations called for by economic and technological innovations is important. It is particularly important because such shifts in economic structure do not have the same effect on the several groups in society attached to various positions within the system: while some groups stand to gain a great deal, others stand to lose, if only relatively. Conflicts may thus be generated by the impact of economic growth, since structural shifts mean different rates of growth for different parts of the economy, and hence for the different groups associated with them; and proposals for resolving the conflicts may only generate more conflicts. The history of developed countries is replete with examples of continuous struggle among various interest groups within economic society over structural changes — whether the specific issue be corn laws, or factory legislation, or regulation of corporations, or administration of the public domain, or slavery and freedom of labor, or centralized versus decentralized banking. And it is the function of the sovereign state, primarily concerned with longer-term interests of the community at large, to resolve these conflicts with the minimum of strain, and preserve the viability of the economy as an organized unit capable of making the decisions needed to accommodate the continuous changes in economic structure that accompany modern economic growth. Finally, since much of modern economic growth requires an elaborate infrastructure in which the difficulty of capturing the returns may discourage adequate private investment, the state, representing the community, must either itself construct the transport, communication, and power utilities and accept responsibility for the educational infrastructure, or at least assist private entrepreneurship.

In these three respects — as a clearing house for necessary institutional innovations; as an agency for resolution of conflicts among group interests; and as a major entrepreneur for the socially required infrastructure — the sovereign state assumes key importance in channeling the explosive impacts of continuous structural changes, in providing a proper framework in which these structural changes, proceeding at revolutionary speed, are contained and prevented from exploding into a civil war (as they sometimes may, and have). Thus, the high rate of change in economic structure is linked to the importance of the sovereign state as an organizing unit. It is not accidental that, in measuring and analyzing economic growth, we talk of the economic growth of *nations* and use *national* economic accounts. In doing so, we imply that the sovereign state is an important factor in modern economic growth; that, given the transnational, worldwide character of the supply of useful knowledge and science, the major permissive factor of modern economic growth, the state unit, in adjusting economic and social institutions to facilitate and maximize application, plays a crucial supplementary role.

Since modern economic growth, with its continuous technological and social innovations and its rapid rate of structural change, needs a state framework to serve as umpire, channel change peacefully, and accept direct responsibility for requisite infrastructure, a variety of further consequences follow — but these are in a direction which an economist hesitates to follow, since they lead to realms of which he is ignorant. Let me put them into the form of questions. A sovereign nation-state, with such demanding functions, presumably should have the support of the population and not have to rely on a policeman's nightstick, or worse, on an army's tanks and machine guns. Underlying such support is a feeling of community of kind, an acceptance of the idea that the good of the nation is more important than the interests of subgroups and individuals — what might be called modern nationalism. Were the various movements toward unification and separation in the nineteenth and twentieth centuries efforts to shape the nation-state into a base for common decisions, decisions acceptable despite their unequal impact on regions, industries, and occupations? And were the delays in attaining the required minimum organizational readiness responsible for the delay of some presently developed countries in entering the modern economic growth process? The sequence is long from the beginnings of modern economic growth in Great Britain, the pioneer country in the late eighteenth century, to the most recent major entry, either Japan (where growth began only in the 1880's) or Russia (with its first spurt in the 1890's and the second in the 1920's). Is there some connection between the intensification of nationalism associated with modern economic growth, the disparate sequence of entry into modernization (which meant that the follower countries fell more and more behind while they were lagging), and the rather aggressive attitude of the modern nation-state upon its entry and after some success in modern economic growth — particularly if it is so large that its absolute economic weight can upset the rough balance that existed before its growth? And to what extent does this aggressive policy of a recently developed nation-state serve both as a positive element — in spreading modern economic growth elsewhere through increased foreign trade, possible capital investment, and in general, a vigorous penetration into the less developed regions — and as a negative element — in generating tension among the developed countries and imposing obstacles in the less developed regions to the emergence of a strong, native nation-state that could mobilize the existing community of feeling for growth-oriented policies acceptable to the population?

Such questions could easily be multiplied, but their importance and the difficulty of testing the validity of the connection assumed between the consequences suggested and the original linkage of an effective nation-state to the demands of modern economic growth are sufficiently illustrated.

Given the pervasive character of structural changes, in which shifts in economic structure necessarily lead to changes in demographic patterns (of birth and death rates, of family structure, of location of population, and so on), in legal and political institutions, and in some elements of social ideology, two conclusions are suggested. First, high rates of growth of per capita product and productivity are closely associated with, and indeed require, changes in economic structure; the latter are closely connected with, and indeed require, shifts in population structure, in legal and political institutions, and in social ideology. Thus, there is a connection between the high rate of growth associated with modern economic development and a variety of structural changes, not only economic but also social; not only in institutions but also in ideology. This does not mean that all the historically associated shifts in economic and social structure and ideology are *requirements,* and that none of them could be avoided or substituted for.[10] It does mean that *some* structural changes, not only in economic but also in social institutions and beliefs, are required, without which modern economic growth would be impossible.

The second conclusion relates to the higher rate of change in some aspects of social structure than in the premodern past — similar to the patterns of economic structural change. This conclusion seems valid for some of the easily measurable, noneconomic

10. In this connection, see Alexander Gerschenkron, "Reflections on the Concept of 'Prerequisites' of Modern Industrialization," *Economic Backwardness in Historical Perspective* (Cambridge, Mass.: Harvard University Press, 1962), pp. 31–51.

magnitudes; for example, the rate of change of demographic variables such as birth rates, death rates, and urbanization rates in the
developed countries in the last two centuries compared with the
much longer past in say Western Europe. By contrast, it is difficult
to test this inference for political or ideological processes which do
not lend themselves to measurement. And it may well be that the
difficulties, not so much of measurement but of rapid change in
reality, are characteristic of these noneconomic, nondemographic
social institutions and beliefs, that they are in fact the source of
some major problems generated by modern economic growth in the
developed countries — as well as of the slow spread of such growth
throughout the world.

The Sequences of Structural Change and Growth

The foregoing discussion has repeatedly suggested long chains of
sequence within the pattern of modern economic growth: one being
from additions to the stock of useful knowledge and science to
technological innovation, to growth in productivity, to changes in
structure of production, to changes in other aspects of economic
structure, to changes in political and social structure and beliefs,
and back again to changed conditions of life and work, with their
effects on demand; another being from science to technology, to
innovation, to more learning, to more science, and so on — all
qualified by economic and social conditions that determine how
widely the innovation will be applied, and hence how much new
knowledge will be acquired and what new tools will be created
for further advance of knowledge, science, and technology. It may
be of interest, in conclusion, to suggest some peculiar features of
these long sequences of change in economic and social structure
and growth that characterize modern economic development.

The first feature of interest is that sequences do not always run
directly from one economic change, for example, in the structure
of production, to an economic result, such as the demand for labor
of higher skills. The two are often linked via the effect of an economic change on conditions of life, which produces a demographic
response (birth rates and family size), which creates a demand for
some new good. Thus, even if we were to concentrate on the first
economic impulse and on the final economic result (final for our
purposes), the attempt to connect the two would involve us in

demographic patterns and other factors and processes mostly non-economic in character. Such sequences from economic impulse to economic effect that contain demographic, political, and ideological links can easily be multiplied, and are clearly basic in the mechanism of economic growth in recent centuries (as they were earlier). In general, the structural changes in the economic growth process set up transformations throughout the social matrix, not merely in economic activities and institutions. It is from this pervasive transformation of the social matrix that new economic effects emerge. It follows that economic measures relate to economic changes and their economic results, possibly separated by a number of non-economic links, and that economic analysis attains completeness largely by means of restrictive assumptions regarding these intervening variables. If the measures and quantitative work yield some consistent parameters that reveal limited variability over long periods and among a number of countries, the results may be caused by some persistent constraints imposed by our very system of measurement (particularly when we deal with the broad aggregates) and by such major economic variables as govern our allocation of resources between the present and the future; even so, one could not rely too much on their relative invariance in time and among countries. And if our economic models, based on restrictive assumptions, seem plausible, it may be because we tend to concentrate on those stretches of reality in which economic changes and economic links dominate economic growth; and rule out others, explicitly or implicitly, as not "normal." But the limits within which pure economic analysis and theory of economic growth can move are uncomfortably narrow; and the feasibility of measuring and analyzing the noneconomic links within an analytical framework common to them and to the economic variables is a matter of key importance.

Second, sequences of the type illustrated are spread over a fairly long period; entail a number of links, any one of which allows for some slippage; and the eventual effect, eventual only in the sense that we choose to end the sequence at that link, is therefore a cumulative result of a complicated set of variable linkages over a period, during which other sequences, also affecting economic and social life, and therefore influencing our specific sequence, may have occurred. Forecasting such a sequence with any assurance is almost impossible, and history is replete with what in retrospect seem ludicrously erroneous predictions of the effects of a given innovation. Since we are dealing with changes largely originating in technological innovations, that is, with events that have strong elements of the completely new, and since the sequences of changes set into play by them cross many levels of social institutions and beliefs over a long period, a reliable prediction of the major effects at further remove can hardly be expected. Thus, to have forecast the eventual effects of the spread of the motor car, even as late as the 1920's in the United States — when it was just beginning to shift from its role as a capital good used primarily by farmers to a mass production consumer good — would have meant the ability to draw out long, cumulative sequences of social change for which nobody's knowledge was adequate at the time, and probably is not even today.

The difficulty of forecasting long-term effects of a major innovation is paralleled by similar problems with the long sequence from a scientific discovery to the technological innovations to which it might give rise — at a future time, with a long and variable distance. To repeat an example already used, it would have been almost impossible for any forecaster in 1887, when Hertz made his discoveries, or even in the beginning of the twentieth century when Marconi was applying Hertz's discovery to wireless telegraphy, to predict that the first *economically major* technological innovation would be its application in the home entertainment industry in the late 1920's, half a century after Hertz and a quarter of a century after Marconi. To be sure, any addition to tested knowledge that science provides, no matter how remote it may seem from practical application, is potentially useful, that is, usable for technological innovation; for technology is a modification of the processes of nature for the benefit (or at any rate purposes) of man, and anything that we know about the former may turn out to be relevant to the latter.[11] But the distance between discovery and application may be long; and it will be covered only when the combination of complementary conditions is favorable — and "favorability" depends not only upon the many components that are involved on the supply and demand side, but also upon the many side-effects of further scientific discovery and of other technological innovations.

11. For several cases of uncertain and surprising relations between "pure" scientific discovery and eventual major *practical* application see I. Bernard Cohen, *Science, Servant of Man* (Boston: Little, Brown, 1948).

Third, the near impossibility of making a *complete* and relatively *reliable* prediction of the long-term consequences of a given major technological innovation means failure to foresee not only the favorable or neutral, but also the adverse consequences. Documenting such failures of foresight in past history requires an exhaustive investigation of the record to prove the absence of a clearly indicated prediction sufficiently ahead of time to change the course of events. Proving such negatives is difficult in any circumstances, and not possible here. I shall illustrate the point in terms of tentative questions. Was it foreseen, or at the time predictable, that the spread of the motor car, by inducing migration of the middle and high income groups from the cities to the dormitory suburbs, would result in a breakdown of the urban tax base and lead to a near-collapse of effective municipal government — with all the ensuing problems with which major cities in the United States are presently struggling? Was it foreseen that the restriction of immigration to the United States in the 1920's would result in stabilization of the country's labor force, cessation of outflow of recent immigrants back to their home countries in depressed years (thus exporting the country's unemployed), and necessitate the provision of some adequate unemployment insurance or similar offset to unemployment of the resident labor force? Were diseconomies of scale — such as the congestion and pollution produced by multiplying motor cars, and congestion and noise produced by multiplying air traffic — predicted in the early stages of the technological innovations that introduced them? Were the consequences of urbanization of the Negro labor force in the United States, and of the shift of large proportions of the Negro population from the rural South to the urban parts of the North, West, and Midwest, with their attendant problems of adjustment of the migrant population — not light under any circumstances but particularly heavy in the case of a minority long subject to adverse discrimination — adequately anticipated? Granted that some of these questions suggest connections that may not be fully defensible, they do serve to illustrate the sequences in which structural changes originating in the process of economic growth often yield unexpected consequences that are socially undesirable and require some effective policy action. Yet the failure to predict them means that awareness of a problem emerges only *after* the problem has reached substantial dimensions, and has become so pressing as to win recognition and hearing among a welter of problems competing for attention and policy treatment. The number and magnitude of such sequences leading to major "problems" could easily be extended, particularly if some validity is assigned to the linkage between the technological innovations and structural changes in economic growth, and the changing climate and pressures in international relations.

Fourth, even if some negative consequences are foreseen, prompt action to forestall them is inhibited by two factors: the uncertainties of the forecast, which call for a large reduction of the weight to be attached to its substance, positive or negative; and the high valuation which contemporaries of the early phases of a technological innovation (and the associated structural change) put on the new product. If a prediction had suggested the problem to be created in two or three decades by traffic congestion in the cities, the impulse to an immediate counteracting policy would have been weakened by the argument that "there's plenty of time and conditions may change." Also, any policy measure conceived in response to this problem that impeded the spread of the motor car would have been blocked by the high value attached *at the time* to the motor car and its potential uses. In view of the limited capacity of society to deal with the many "problems" needing solution, the lag in the attempt to avoid or inhibit the long-term undesirable consequences of technological innovation and of the associated structural change is almost inevitable. The broad conclusion follows that modern economic growth, with its rapid pace of aggregate growth and high rate of structural shifts (which are interdependent and reinforce each other), is also productive of a cumulation of problems that cannot be foreseen in time, and whose magnitude and novelty are to some extent functions of the magnitude of the aggregate growth rate and of the rate of structural shift underlying it.[12]

12. This combination of positive achievements with unforeseen and long unresolved problems is not an exclusive feature of modern economic growth, but is true of any growth process that is based on the new and hence on the partly unknown. Thus, the premodern urbanization process in Europe, surely an important contributor to economic growth, carried with it higher mortality of the more densely settled urban population — and it would be difficult to argue that this result was expected. The "problem" was perceived later, but the means of proper response did not come until the nineteenth century. The argument could be repeated with reference to the outward expansion of Europe, which brought with it not only more trade and booty but also new types of disease. And the differential impact of this expansion on religious conformity created "problems" for both the orthodox and the nonconformists that led to extensive bloodshed and are similar to some of the thorny (and bloodshed-producing) quasi-religious disputes of today.

We have thus returned full circle to the range of questions involved in nonconventional costs of economic growth, touched upon in Chapter II. Here, however, the problems related to these costs are seen perhaps more clearly as consequences — unforeseen or disregarded — of rapid shifts in production structure and hence in the economic and social structures at large; and the lines of connection between the latter and the high rate of aggregate growth have perhaps also become more apparent.

Index

Index

The letter "t" following a page number indicates reference is to a table.

A sector: capital, 239, 241; coverage, 106, 109; female workers, 53–54t, 57, 218–220t; and foreign trade, 131t; and government expenditures, 87, 128; labor force, 60t, 199, 200t, 202, 203t, 204, 205, 217, 218–220t, 221, 222, 224t, 226, 231–233t, 233, 234, 235t, 236, 237, 239, 242, 249, 250–253t, 255, 257, 258, 275, 276, 277–279t, 281, 282–284t, 295, 301, 311; labor income, 241, 243, 247; male workers, 218–220t; manhours, 60t; premodern, 153, 256, 310, 323; prices, 137t; and private profits, 128; product, 104t, 106, 107, 108t, 110, 111t, 121t, 122, 128, 130, 131t, 144–148t, 152, 153, 158, 174, 182, 184–185t, 186, 188–190t, 191, 192, 199, 204, 205, 231–233t, 236, 249, 281, 295, 301, 310; product per worker, 156, 209–210t, 211, 213, 227–228t, 229, 231–233t, 235t, 236, 289, 290–292t, 293, 298t, 301; productivity, 295; products, 128, 130, 131t, 132, 141; response to product growth, 108t, 109, 110, 111t; unpaid family workers, 57, 218–220t

Abramovitz, Moses, 44n

Agriculture, 101, 132, 133, 135, 343. *See also* A sector

Bairoch, P., 54n, 253n, 267n, 268n, 269n, 279n

Ballesteros, Marto A., 279n

Banking, insurance, and real estate. *See* Finance

Benchmark values, 110

Berle, A. A., 344n

Birth rates: and labor force, 55, 56, 306; and population, 41; premodern, 349; and product, 50, 345; rural vs. urban, 257

Bjerke, Kjeld, 17n, 149n, 253n

Borenstein, Israel, 134n, 169n, 318n

Bos, H. C., 16n, 54n, 267n

Buckley, K. A. H., 18n, 75n, 135n, 150n, 169n, 269n

Burns, Arthur F., 327n

Butlin, N. G., 19n, 151n, 169n, 254n

Capital consumption, 64, 77, 87, 90, 239, 240

Capital formation: in construction, 89, 162; classified as consumption, 9; educational outlays, 76, 77; health outlays, 77; labor input in, 89; material, 88; net vs. gross, 63, 68; nonconventional, 88; premodern, 67; proportion, 61, 64, 65, 68, 69, 73, 75, 88, 307, 339; in research and development, 76; sectoral destination, 201

Capital input: concept, 66; growth, 52, 61, 74t, 92, 93t; limit to, 306; measurability, 102; in nonreproducible capital, 65; and productivity, 247; and utilization, 70; weight, 52, 70, 92

Capital-product ratio, 61, 64, 66–68, 71–73

Capital stock: in A sector, 239; at constant prices, 61; definition, 52; educational, 90, 92, 245; growth, 62–63t, 63,

357

low growth sectors, 339; limiting factors, 306; in new and old industries, 334–335t, 340t; nonconventional, 76, 94–95; and product, 51, 73; sectoral, 99, 102; shifts in, 241; and technology, 99; and urbanization, 80; weights, 52, 72, 75. *See also* Capital input; Labor input

Family expenditures. *See* Household consumption

Farm families, consumption, 81, 82–84t, 86

Female workers: in A sector, 53–54t; factors affecting, 56–57; and intersectoral ratios, 229; male equivalents, 57, 216, 249, 311; in manufacturing, 214; and population, 52, 53–54t, 55; and product, 225; proportion of paid labor force, 217; sectoral, 218–220t, 221, 250–253t; in trade, 230

Final products: consumption, 308; conventional, 75; and education, 51; at final price, 132–134, 138; specification, 7; structure, 179; value, 127

Finance: income from assets, 71, 72, 208, 239, 240, 306; labor force, 205, 274t; product, 104t, 107, 108t, 109, 111t, 121t, 123, 171–173t; and product per worker, 208; response to product growth, 108t, 109, 111–112t

Firestone, O. J., 18n, 254n, 269n

Flow of goods to consumers. *See* Household consumption

Forbes, R. J., 330n

Foreign trade: in A sector products, 130, 131t, 157; comparative advantage, 324, 343; growth, 324–325; in I sector products, 130, 131t; and long swings, 49; and nation's size, 325; and product, 118; and sectoral shares, 130, 141; structure, 100

Fuà, Giorgio, 17n, 150n, 173n

Gainful workers. *See* Labor force

Gallman, Robert E., 4, 18n, 150n, 169n, 254n, 269n, 275n

Ganz, Alexander, 31n, 151n, 279n

Garland, J. M., 67n

Gerschenkron, Alexander, 42n, 348n

Giannone, Antonio, 67n

Gilbert, Milton, 137n

Gini, Corrado, 67n

Ginsburgh, V., 16n

Goldsmith, Raymond W., 67n, 92n, 239n

Government: activities, 102; expenditures, 7, 76, 78, 87, 307; functions, 345–347; income, 128; labor force, 60t,

61, 274t, 275; prices, 139; product, 104t, 108t, 111t, 121t, 127, 170, 171–173t, 174, 310; response to product growth, 108t, 111–112t

Gross domestic product, 20; and personal disposable income, 128, 141; sectoral shares, 131t. *See also* Product, total

Haig, Bryan D., 19n, 151n, 169n

Health, outlays on, 76, 77, 87

Hertz, Heinrich, 330, 351

Hoffmann, Walther G., 16n, 149n, 168n, 253n, 267n

Hooley, Richard W., 32n, 151n

Hoselitz, Bert F., 344n

Household consumption: of A sector products, 101, 130, 131t; and consumer demand, 128; and economic costs, 308; growth, 94; of I sector products, 130, 131t; and intermediate products, 76–78; share in product, 86; structure, 258, 323

I sector: coverage, 106, 309; and demand structure, 132, 141; and domestic consumption, 128, 130, 131t; female workers, 218–220t; and foreign trade, 130, 131t; and government expenditures, 128; labor force, 60t, 200t, 203t, 204, 205, 218–220t, 221, 224t, 226, 231–233t, 236, 250–253t, 255, 259–260t, 275, 276, 277–279t, 280, 281, 282–284t, 302, 311; male workers, 218–220t; premodern, 158, 310; prices, 137t; and private profits, 128; product, 104t, 106, 108t, 109, 111t, 113, 121t, 122, 128, 131t, 144–148t, 158, 160–162t, 174, 188–190t, 191, 192, 204, 205, 231–233t, 255, 302; product per worker, 209–210t, 211, 227–228t, 229, 231–233t, 290–292t, 295–296, 298t, 302; response to product growth, 108t, 111–112t; unpaid family workers, 218–220t

Ideology, 76, 258, 328

Imports. *See* Foreign trade

Income from assets, 71, 72, 208, 239, 240, 306

Inequality, sectoral: and capital stock, 238; elimination of, 234–236; and labor force, 229, 242–243; in labor income per worker, 238, 241; and living costs, 245–246; measure, 209–210t, 211, 227–228t, 290–292t, 297; and product per capita, 237, 238, 301; and productivity, 247; and return on capital, 238–241; and return on labor, 243–245

Innovations, 258, 326, 331, 336–337

worker, 209–210t, 211, 231–233t, 233, 237; response to product growth, 108t, 109, 111–112t

Transportation and communication: labor force, 200t, 203t, 205, 259–260t, 261; product, 104t, 108t, 111t, 121t, 122, 160–162t, 163, 261; product per worker, 209–210t; productivity, 261; response to product growth, 108t, 111–112t, 112; and technology, 100, 343

Umemura, Mataji, 150n

Underdeveloped countries: A sector, 129–130, 152, 153, 174, 250, 281, 295; capital markets, 247; duality of structure, 157, 241, 245, 247, 313; employment problems, 302; foreign trade, 130, 131t; growth, 2, 28–29, 30–33t, 175, 304; institutional structure, 248; intersectoral ratios, 295; labor force, 234, 245, 281, 312–313; non-A output, 234; population, 27, 30–33t; price structure, 152; product, 192; product per capita, 181, 192; product per worker, 301; production structure 154–155, 175, 192; productivity, 214; technology, 349

Urbanization: and capital stock, 88; and consumer demand, 85–86, 162, 205, 328, 343; and costs, 78, 86, 87, 95, 97, 132, 135, 307; growth, 76; and household expenditures, 81, 82–85t, 85, 86; and housing, 162; and labor force, 56, 222–223, 352; premodern, 312, 349; and product, 87; and technology, 79–80, 135

Urlanis, B. Ts., 68n

Urquhart, M. C., 18n, 75n, 135n, 150n, 169n, 269n

Ussing, Niels, 17n, 149n, 253n

Valuation problems, 135–139

War and economic growth, 20, 37, 42–43, 96–97

Watt, James, 330

Weber, Adna F., 21n

Weiss, Thomas J., 150n, 169n, 254n, 275n

Yamada, Saburo, 17n

Zwingli, U., 16n